The Wicked Ways of
MALCOLM
McLAREN

The Wicked Ways of
MALCOLM McLAREN

by Craig Bromberg

1817

HARPER & ROW, PUBLISHERS, New York
Grand Rapids, Philadelphia, St. Louis, San Francisco
London, Singapore, Sydney, Tokyo, Toronto

FIRST EDITION

Library of Congress Cataloging-in-Publication Data

Bromberg, Craig.
  The wicked ways of Malcolm McLaren.

  Includes index.
  1. McLaren, Malcolm, 1945– . 2. Impresarios—
England—Biography.   3. Rock music—History and
criticism.   I. Title.
ML429.M36B7   1989   784.5'4'00924 [B]   88-45926
ISBN 0-06-096204-6

89 90 91 92 93 CC/RRD 10 9 8 7 6 5 4 3 2 1

To my parents and brother
with gratitude and love

In memory of Vladimo Bromberg

CONTENTS

ACKNOWLEDGMENTS

My gratitude goes out to all who gave so much of their time, patiently explaining stories they often knew only half of before we began—but several deserve special thanks.

Vivienne Westwood sat through nearly a week of interviews, generously helping me to understand her former partner in minute detail. Peter York opened doors for me in London where I didn't know doors existed. Rene Daalder gave me crucial assistance in reaching into the Hollywood community. Fred Vermorel graciously provided his detailed knowledge of McLaren's formative years in art school and with Bow Wow Wow.

A particular note of thanks goes to Rory Johnston, who served as McLaren's American assistant for many years and later took over the management of Bow Wow Wow when McLaren got bored. A master of detail, Rory was particularly instrumental in guiding me through the tortuous route McLaren's career took as it wended its way from Bow Wow Wow through Soweto to Hollywood. I am deeply indebted to him for his help.

From the start, Miles Chapman has been my guru on matters great and small. His expert knowledge of London's style culture and of British life in general was an invaluable guide to this American. I can only say that I was, and am, honored by his contribution to my work. Thank you.

Others were helpful on a daily level. In London, Brer Ruthven did his best to help me amass the clippings where much of the story can already be found, with McLaren's lies intact. In New York, Mali Austin McNeil and Cyndi Lee helped me turn some two hundred hours of microcassettes into over one thousand pages of transcripts. And thanks to the generous support of the Djerassi Foundation for the Arts in Woodside, California, I was able to complete a large portion of the manuscript during autumn 1987.

A project of this nature cannot be accomplished without the support of one's friends, and so I would also like to thank those who provided various combinations of friendship, support, and inspiration. My personal debts are many, and to Jack Bankowsky, Jim and Alice Bercovitz, Susan Braham, Leslie Fratkin, Steven Henry Madoff, Phyllis Meshover, John and Debbie Orenstein, Jude Ray, Annie Sanders, James Stein, David and Clare Thomas, and Avraham Weiss I offer deep gratitude.

Robert Cornfield, my agent, guided a nervous novice through the hazards of writing an unauthorized biography. His support and encouragement made it possible for me to sustain this project over the four years it took to research and write. Craig Nelson, my editor at Harper & Row, put me on the trail of a tightly turned manuscript. I am indebted to them both.

The final note of thanks, however, belongs to my parents and my brother, without whom this book would not have been written.

AUTHOR'S NOTE

Wicked? No one knows what wicked is anymore. Today, wicked is a moral anachronism: black knights and late-night swashbucklers. Compared with the banal malevolence of those whom we recognize as the true embodiment of twentieth-century evil—Hitler, Stalin, and all their murderous bureaucrats—the wicked are gentlemen schemers whose only crime is that they take a perverse delight in their own misconduct. But perhaps it's time to restore the word to our lexicon to describe those who instinctively seek out and take advantage of legal loopholes, create computer viruses, run renegade operations in Latin America, and steal millions in insider stock swaps—those who litter the public realm with supposedly victimless crimes, committed, all too often, in the name of some misplaced ideal. Mostly, these wicked remain undiscovered—at least until they are led away in handcuffs on the evening news. But occasionally, they flaunt their misdeeds *before* getting caught, telling us how they have swindled their way to the top in a confused orgy of selfishness and ideology. Ladies and gentlemen, introducing *The Wicked Ways of Malcolm McLaren*. . . .

Prologue:
1 DECEMBER 1976

———

Fame requires every kind of excess. I mean true fame, a devouring neon, not the somber renown of waning statesmen or chinless kings. I mean long journeys across gray space. I mean danger, the edge of every void, the circumstance of one man imparting an erotic terror to the dreams of the republic. . . .

Fame, this special kind, feeds itself on outrage, on what the counselors of lesser men would consider bad publicity—hysteria in limousines, knife fights in the audience, bizarre litigation, treachery, pandemonium and drugs. . . .

(Is it clear I was a hero of rock 'n' roll?)
　　　　　　　　　　　　　　—*Don DeLillo,* Great Jones Street

Begin, not with a sound but with an image.
Because that's how it always begins: with a picture, a look, the televisual moment. With a dollop of fame and a dose of excess. Nobody *really* listens to the music anymore, you say. That's just a joke, maybe the biggest joke of them all. Because at the end of the day, they just tune out the noise, turn off the radio, fold back the covers, and *go to sleep.* The music is just an excuse for selling something else—selling records, selling clothes, politics, style.

But if it's the image you begin with, you still *must* have that sound. For noise is power, and any noise that will make people forget the past, that will make them believe in themselves and in their futures, above all, any noise that will silence *them*—all the Thems—is a noise that will be born of disorder, of chaos, of anarchy.

That's your noise: the rumble of a revolution. A sound that exterminates the pygmy giants of the record industry, instills fear in the hearts of chief executive officers, and topples evil governments. A sound you call the Sex Pistols.

The name is ingenious, an amalgam of sexual outrageousness and outright commercialism. A plug for SEX, the boutique you own with your common-law wife, Vivienne Westwood, and a nod to one of your art school heroes, André Breton: "The simplest surrealist act consists of going out into the street revolver in hand and firing at random into the crowd as often as possible."

The Sex Pistols: not a six-shooter or a revolver, but a hot rod, primed to ejaculate its noxious effluvia over the airwaves and under the noses of the old, the bourgeois, the ruling classes. The Sex Pistols: a noise to make people forget, make people believe, a noise to drown out all other noises. The Sex Pistols: a monologue, *your* monologue, the monologue of Malcolm McLaren, masquerading as the sound of music.

And so you start, with four boys—none over twenty-one—gathered out of the style-ridden streets near your shop on the lower reaches of the King's Road.

On guitar, Steve Jones, a hot-blooded, hot-wiring, professional thief with the literacy of an eight-year-old and the leering sexual appetite of an overgrown teenager. The drummer, Paul Cook, Jones's best friend since the age of ten, is a solidly built boy who recently left his job at a local brewery. As long as he keeps his mouth shut and his hands on the skins, he'll do just fine. Glen Matlock, the bass player, is the only one who can actually play his instrument well enough to write songs. A poxy art school graduate with a penchant for Paul McCartney, Matlock's worked in the shop since he was sixteen. By now he's a fixture, but not much more. He means well. And then there's the singer, a screamer, a ranter, a last-minute epiphany with a poetic gift—that snarling front man with the cruelest diction and the unkindest teeth, Mr. Johnny Rotten.

Talent? Well, it's not a question of talent; it's a question of *style*. The way Rotten sneers. The way Jones smiles. The way you tell some interviewer how "sick and fed up" people are of "this country telling them what to do"—and then start snickering with the boys once the tape has stopped rolling.

Call it the Style of Fuckyouism: *Fuck you, fuck off, "don't waste my time"* (Rotten's favorite expression). Not some precious, aesthetic response to the world, but something they have to feel: *Fuck you, fuck off,* *"don't waste my time."*

Without it, these Sex Pistols would merely be one more musical fad, four ridiculous rock 'n' roll malcontents with dumb manners and a smart manager.

But with it—with Rotten writhing and ranting onstage, panting to keep up, throwing himself at the audience, exploding cans of warm lager on their sodden heads, telling them to get lost, piss off (Don't they get it? FUCK OFF!)—these boys are the very face of noise as ritual sacrifice, as the provocation of anxiety and the threat of chaos and destruction. Fuck-youism, wearing an errant, gloating smile.

In fact, the sound itself is not all that unusual. The most basic 4/4 beat under a strafing guitar and surprisingly melodic bass riffs. No embellishment: no synthesizers, no double drum kits, no acoustic guitars. No Boring-Old-Fart rock 'n' rollers preaching to the kids about love. ("I don't need a Rolls Royce, I don't need a house in the country, I don't need to live in the south of France. Oim 'appy as I yam," Rotten tells journalist Janet Street-Porter.) It's all propulsion and emotion, veins bulging, teenage excess blown up to adult proportions and then some. Straight rock 'n' roll.

But then, music per se was never anything more to you than an alibi allowing you to drift away from the present and all its responsibilities to a legend-filled past or a fantasy-filled future. For Malcolm McLaren, rock 'n' roll is merely the sign of something else: an excuse for selling records, clothes, politics, or style.

Still, attitudes don't sell on their own, and now that the Sex Pistols' first single is finally out—"Anarchy in the U.K.," three minutes and thirty seconds of unbridled fury—and the plans for the Anarchy Tour have been laid—nineteen dates in twenty-three days, the group's first fully national tour with support from the Damned, Johnny Thunders & the Heartbreakers, and the Clash—the moment of truth—from the Scene to the Supermarket—would finally seem to be at hand.

For over the past year and a half, not one of your schemes—not the big, big contract with EMI Records (home of the Beatles and the Rolling Stones), not the heavy advance buildup in the music press, not even the bannings from venue after venue, the petty controversies masterfully leaked to the gossip pages—has turned these Sex Pistols into a household word.

And *that's* the name of the game. For what is sound without vision? And what is vision if it is not seen? Without the swoon of the audience, the alchemical sophistry of fame—*the hit record*—this rock 'n' roll thing is just *music.* "What most people don't realize," you say much later, "is that the whole thing is about getting as much money as possible in as short a time as possible with as much style as possible."

So begin with the image.

That's how it always begins: with TV. Because when no one has money to buy records, when clothes are just a tool of image making, when scandal and attitude are mere instruments of noise, it's the flickering image on the screen that becomes the final arbiter of fame.

Lately, it's an obsession. Three, four, five times a day, you call the EMI promotions manager, Eric Hall, a fast-talking Jewish boy from the East End, to ask where things stand. "Any word about *Top of the Pops?*" you ask. "I'm trying, Malcolm," says Hall. "How many plays on Radio One?" you bark. "Only four today, Malcolm." "Who do we have doing interviews from *Melody Maker?*" "Are you sure the ads have been placed in *NME?*" "What kind of radio are we getting up north?" "Have you heard anything about Sunday's *London Weekend* show?" On and on.

This latest buildup began the last Friday in November, November 26, the day "Anarchy in the U.K." was finally released with one spin on John Peel's late-night show on BBC Radio One, the traditional place for over-the-top pop.

By Sunday the 28th, the Sex Pistols had finally made it onto the telly. London Weekend Television (LWTV) broadcast interviews with outraged music journalists, snips of a live gig at the Notre Dame Hall near Trafalgar Square the week before, and even a short interview with Malcolm McLaren speaking "on behalf of" his group.

And then, two days before the start of the tour, Wednesday, December 1, 1976, early afternoon, there's a phone call from Eric Hall.

"Malcolm, listen, it's Eric—great news. I just spoke with someone from the *Today* show and they've got some problem with a Queen interview that was supposed to air tonight, some clearance problem or whatever. So I said, 'How about the Sex Pistols?' and they took a look at the promo and I was surprised 'cause they said they want them live—but you have to be there with the boys by 5:00."

Hall is not quite prepared for such a vehement response. "No way, man, no way," you scream into the phone. "My boys are not going on any local TV show. No one's gonna rob their image for some Bill Grundy. Over my dead body."

"But Malcolm, what else have you got? The tour starts in a few days. Listen, you gotta take what you can get."

"Eric, I told you before, unless you get those boys a shot on *Top of the Pops* or *Old Grey Whistle Test,* they're just not doing any TV."

"Malcolm, listen to me, listen, you fucking schmuck. I'm grafting my bollocks off here trying to get your group away. It's a nice plug, it ain't a great plug, but Malcolm, do me a favor. Trust me. Let's do this show tonight and it'll be a great plug, a great promotion."

But who expected Hall to jump in his little blue Granada and zoom up to Harlesden? And who could have expected that Hall would make an appeal from "one Yiddisher boy to another"? No, you resisted, you fought. "No way are you going to rob my boys of their image. I've got this whole thing running so fast, so well, getting all national coverage. And then you come up here with a local TV show? Forget it, man. We don't need that."

But the Sex Pistols do need it, and Eric Hall knows it and even convinces you of it. Except for one slight caveat: "Eric, you gotta get the boys a limousine."

"Malcolm, a limousine? You want a limousine for the Sex Pistols? What about their image?"

Image, shmimage. "My boys have got to travel *in style*—no limo, no show." Besides, the limo can pick up the arriving Johnny Thunders at the airport after the show. Kill two birds with one stone.

Half an hour later—just enough time to round up some of the band's friends (Siouxsie Sue and Sue Catwoman, Debbie and Tracie from the shop, and a few others from that claque called the Bromley Contingent)—a Princess Daimler from the stables of the Berryhurst Car Hire Service arrives at the Roxy Cinema, at 8 Craven Park Road in Harlesden.

"Fuckin' hell, Malcolm, where we goin' now?" Sex Pistols on the go: drinking and spilling cans of lager, bumming fags from one another, having a jolly old time. Climb in boys: You're going to be on TV. . . .

Within twenty minutes the five of you arrive at Thames Television studios in Euston Square and are led to an ugly little greenroom, the so-called hospitality suite of the *Today* show starring Bill Grundy.

Now the boys hardly know who this Grundy character is, but what you do see of this portly, pompous Mancunian rushing around the studio in the hour or so before the show is just enough to set them off—"Hey, what's happened to his chin?" Slumped down in his chair with his hand cradling his jowls and his head bobbing over his shoulders, Grundy epitomizes the corporate fogy who's had one too many glasses of wine (or, more probably, whiskey) over lunch. And in fact, this is not such a mistaken impression: Grundy has only returned within the last few hours from his weekly *"Punch* Lunch"—an interview visit to a favorite restaurant in preparation for the column he writes for the faded humor magazine.

As Grundy runs through the other segments on the show—"I think I interviewed the prime minister that day," he later recalls—the Sex Pistols and friends run through several bottles of wine and numerous cans of lager. There is scarcely any time at all to coach the boys except to tell them to make sure they plug the record and tour. People are coming in and out of the greenroom every second. (An incredulous technician: "No one here wants makeup?")

And then, just after the boys have finally been ushered over to a row of seats on the tiny set, tripping over themselves in that wonderful rush of adolescent nervousness that strikes with the first glance into the brilliant arc of the TV lights, Bill Grundy starts his intro:

". . . And that's just it fellas, yeah, isn't it? Yeah. They are punk rockers: the new craze, they tell me. They are heroes, not the nice clean Rolling Stones." *Hhunh?* "You see, they are as drunk as I am; they are clean by comparison. They are a group called the Sex Pistols. And I'm surrounded now by *all* of them." *And how, you stupid fool.*

On the monitor off to the side, a segment of Sunday's *London Weekend* show of the band playing at the Notre Dame Hall is being shown. Grundy is squinting at some papers clutched in his hand. Forty-four seconds later, he launches into his first question.

"I'm told that *that* group"—Grundy hits his leg with the sheaf of papers—"have received £40,000 from a record company. Doesn't that seem, uh, to be slightly opposed to their"—(deep breath here)—"anti-materialistic view of life?"

Someone moans. And Matlock, two seats away from Grundy, answers: "No, the more the merrier." *Charming:* spot-on.

"Really?"

"Oh, yeah," says Matlock, all mock innocence, nudge-nudge, wink-wink.

"Well, tell me more then," says Grundy.

Jones, wearing a brand-new SEX-shop T-shirt—a pair of succulent woman's tits emblazoned across his chest—fields this one, sneering, "We've fuckin' spent it, ain't we?" and Cook laughs.

Grundy: "I don't know. Have you?"

Matlock: "Yeah, it's all gone."

"Really?"

"Down the boozer." A giggle here. A camera pans to the side to get a better view.

"Reeaally?" Grundy's voice climbs half an octave. "Good *Lord!* Now, I want to know *one* thing. . . ."

A pause and a giggle: "What?"

"Are you serious or are you just making, trying to make me laugh?"

"No, it's gone, gone."

"Really?"

"Yeah."

"No, but I mean about what you're doing?"

"Oh yeah."

Bit of a letdown this.

"You are serious?"

Matlock just mumbles: "mmmm."

"Beethoven"—Grundy launches into a list—"Mozart"—*he can't be serious*—"Bach and Brahms"—*you can't believe this*—"have all died. . . ."

Rotten cuts in: "They're all heroes of ours, aren't they?" More of a threat than a question.

"Really? With wha-? What're you saying, sir?" Grundy's attention is now drawn to Rotten, over at the far side of the set, grinning into his hand.

Rotten pushes his upper lip into a smile, looks bored, stretches each syllable to the breaking point: "Ohhh, they're *wonn-der-ful* people."

"Are they?"

"Ohhh yaaasss. They reee-al-ly turn us onnn."

Someone else, probably Glen, typically taking Grundy at his word, starts to answer: "Well, they're dead . . ."

But Bill Grundy has a riposte to Rotten: "Well, suppose they turn other people on?"

The camera turns to Rotten, his fluffy mohair sweater color-TV perfect, and John whispers under his breath: "That's just their tough shit."

Grundy, astonished: "It's what?"

Rotten refuses the bait: "Noth-ing. A rude word. Next question?"

But Grundy won't let it go. "No, no. What was the rude word?"

"Shit." *That's it, boy.*

"Was it really?" *Oh God, oh no, please don't let this happen. Come on, boys! do us a favor!*

"Good heavens!" says Grundy, now treading on Rotten's turf, playacting with sarcasm: "You frighten me to death."

Rotten seems to have heard this conversation a thousand times before. "Oh, all right, Siegfried. . . ." The girls standing behind the band giggle, diverting Grundy's attention.

"What about you girls behind?" (Matlock interrupts: "He's like your dad in' 'e, this geezer?" Long pause: "Or your granddad?")

The girls giggle; the camera zooms in on a pair of bright blue lips.

Grundy addresses the first girl he sees: "Are you, er, are you worried or are you just enjoying yourself?"

Siouxsie, resplendent in tuxedo shirt and dotted bow tie and braces, answers Grundy straight, perhaps shyly: "Enjoying myself."

"Are you?"

"Yeah."

"Ahhhh. That's what I thought you were doing." Someone exhales deeply, in pretend disgust.

"I've always wanted to meet you," she meows.

Grundy, stupidly, pursues: "Did you really?"

"Yeah," she says with a big smile.

And then, for whatever unknown reason, Grundy tries to come back with his own brand of sarcasm: "We'll meet afterwards, shall we?"

Someone sighs and a giggle is heard, but superstud Jones hears the sexual innuendo and flips the tables completely: "You dirty sod," he says accusingly. Noise from all. "You dirty old man." Everyone laughs; Grundy is momentarily nonplussed.

"Well, keep going, chief," he says, "keep going."

And then, a heart's beat pause after the final hiccup of a gulped-down laugh, the announcer abjectly surrenders to the shambles his show is becoming.

"Go on, you've got another five seconds."

"You dir-"

"Say something outrageous." A tired challenge.

Now he's gonna get it: Jones could say anything.

"You *dir*-ty bastard."

"Go on, *again.*" Almost a command.

"You *dir*-ty fucker."

"Whaaat a cle-ver boy." High-pitched giggling.

"What a fuckin' rotter," Jones continues, but by now, the show is a total mess, and Grundy's staff is motioning for him to stop, stop it before it goes any farther. Besides, they're running out of time. At the edges of the set, everything is jumping into chaos.

"Well, that's it for tonight," says Grundy, wrapping-up almost as if nothing unusual had happened. "The other rocker, Eamonn"—a waiting guest—"I'm saying nothing else about him." And then two half turns, one

toward the camera—"We'll be back tomorrow, I'll be seeing you soon"—
and then one final glance back toward the band: "I hope I'm not seeing
you again.

"From me though, goodnight."

But from here on in, it's anything but a good night. In fact, it's all
something of a blur: Someone screaming in the control room, Grundy
walking away disgusted, the boys hoofing it back to the limo on the double
in a fit of giggles. *What a laugh. What a fucking idiot that bloke was. Did
we handle it well, Malcolm?*

Everyone goes back to the dilapidated rehearsal room at the Roxy
Cinema in Harlesden, and, almost immediately, you slink off with Bernard
Rhodes, the Clash's manager and an old pal, to continue plotting the tour,
until your secretary, Sophie Richmond, drags you back to the limo to pick
up Thunders and his crew at Heathrow. By the time you arrive back in
London, Grundy seems a million miles away—someone to smirk at, to
despise. All that matters now is the tour.

Or so you think.

In fact, Thames Television's switchboard was lit up before the *Today*
show even ended, and the first call from EMI came within the hour—
whoever it was, says Sophie, "spluttering, angry, telling us we've had it!"
The next day, there's to be a meeting with Leslie Hill, managing director
of EMI Records, and you are nervous already. Indeed, face-to-face with
the angry editorials of nearly every daily newspaper in the nation, the
immediate denunciations from members of Parliament, and worst of all,
the constant threats of tour cancellations—one venue in Southend, Essex,
has already canceled its gig next Saturday—your reaction slowly turns
from glee to panic. Suddenly, the absurd page-one banners—"THE FILTH
AND THE FURY" *(Daily Mirror);* "THE NIGHT OF THE NASTIES: FOUR-
LETTER PUNK GROUP IN TV STORM" *(Daily Mail);* "WHY I DID IT—BY
GRUNDY" *(The Sun);* "PUNK FILTH" *(Daily Express)*—no longer seem so
absurd. Thames Television has even issued an on-the-air apology (and
started an investigation) over what is now being referred to as "the incident." "Because the program was live," a faceless announcer intones, "it
was impossible to foresee the language that would be used."

You smoke cigarette after cigarette, brush the ashes off your black
leather jeans, twist your silver Aleister Crowley ring until your knuckle
turns white, and call every friend you can think of. *My god, man, they're*

threatening to drop us from the label! Nearly two years of work down the drain! An M-shaped vein on your forehead, normally invisible under your milky English skin, swells and glows. The phone rings for the thousandth time: "EMI, Malcolm." There must, you think, be some way out of this mess.

The next day, Hill is angry but reasonable. "We're not firing the Sex Pistols just yet," he says, "but we are very, very angry. So angry that the EMI corporate board is already putting pressure on our record division to do just that. I'm still holding firm," says Hill, "but unless the Sex Pistols are kept in line and out of trouble, they'll definitely get the sack. (Another EMI official differs. "After this row," he tells the *Evening Standard,* "it's anyone's guess how big they could be.")

You speak quietly and slowly, somewhat out of character. Try to show some bottle. "It's Grundy's fault. Grundy goaded them. *He* was ill-prepared. Not them. And you can't blame *me*. All I've tried to do is build some momentum for a band that would be at number one if only EMI promoted them right."

Hill says that for the band to stay with EMI there must be drastic changes, but something about being lectured to like this unnerves you, reminds you of some other scolding somewhere in your past.

Then you remember. Not the sound, but the Image. Not Malcolm McLaren, media manipulator, but Malcolm Edwards—the name you grew up with—the boy who always got away with murder, the boy who played truant and got away with it, the boy whose mum didn't care what happened to her son, and whose grandma raised him instead.

Because every time Malcolm comes late to school—every day, that is—Malcolm's grandma writes the headmaster a little note that always ends apologetically (both to the headmaster and to Malcolm) with the same old line.

"Boys will be boys," she writes.

Exactly what you tell Leslie Hill and the so-called gentlemen of the press, throwing the ball back into the hypocrite's court. And the color creeps back into your cheeks.

"Boys will be boys."

Because boys break the rules and get away with it.

Because boys don't care.

Because some boys have their wicked, wicked ways.

PART ONE

Who wickedly is wise, or madly brave,
Is but the more a fool, the more a knave.
—Alexander Pope, Essay on Man

1
MYTHS OF A
LEGENDARY CHILDHOOD

His mother is dead. His mother isn't dead. Even if he knows, he's not telling. Maybe he doesn't know. He certainly doesn't seem to care. Who can you believe, then? Have a look in the death register? (But under what name: McLaren, Edwards, Corrie, Levi, the real and adopted names of all his stepparents?) Ask Vivienne, his former "companion" of nearly eighteen years: "I'm absolutely sure Malcolm told me his mother died four or five years ago," she says. Search out other relatives? There are only two: a brother, Stuart, a London taxi driver invisible in the ranks, and a half-brother named Colin. No one knows anything about him at all. Friends? All dead or disappeared. Are you really sure, Vivienne? "I can only tell you what I remember, but you'll have to ask Malcolm."

McLaren is in Los Angeles, cackles at me across the ocean. "My mother, man? My mother? Why do you want to talk to her? I don't know *where* my mother is. Haven't seen her in years. The last time I saw her was about sixteen years ago. I got on the same tube as her and we sat across from each other the whole ride, from King's Cross to Whitechapel, without saying a single, solitary word." But is she *alive?* "Well," he laughs, "she *may* be alive. But even if she is, she won't talk to *you*. Last I heard, she was living someplace near Brighton—you know Brighton? But that was years ago. Someplace like Hove or Seaford."

After a visit to Brighton, to the death registry, long sessions calling all the McLarens, Corries, Edwardses, and Levis in London and Brighton, wandering around Whitechapel and the East End looking for his mother's old dress factory, some very expensive calls to McLaren in L.A.—"I tell you, I just don't know where she is or if she's even alive, man"—the week before I return to New York, he finally gives me the addresses of the houses he grew up in. (He refuses to tell me where to find his brothers.) One of these houses, the house he lived in from around the age of eleven until he left home at sixteen, is in Hendon, a predominately Jewish suburb in North London.

From the Hendon Central tube, I turn at the corner and walk up the long tree-lined hill that is Cheyne Walk. The houses are big, clean, and stucco-ugly, with semiattached garages and lots of expensive cars: Jaguars, BMWs, Volvos, a Rolls or two. There's even a synagogue a few streets away. Finally, number 31: a large two-story brick house with a well-tended paved garden and rosebushes, a large bay window, and a dappled glass door. Comfortable.

No one's home. I tiptoe around the side. Most of the neighbors seem reluctant to speak with me or are too new to the neighborhood to have heard of either Malcolm McLaren or the Edwardses, the adopted name of Malcolm's stepfather.

Finally, one says that, yes, that *is* the Edwardses' house. "You mean Stuart Edwards?" I ask. "The taxi driver?" No, the neighbor says. "It's rather an older couple. The woman's name is Eve or Emmy, and the man, Martin, well now, he's a rather gruff sort. Quiet. Real working class. 'Corblimey' types. Had a dress factory till recently. But very private; never even been in their house. In fact," she says, "I think they're moving this week. To Brighton."

The very next day then, a bright, cold November Sunday, I wake up early, put on my suit, buy a bouquet of flowers and go to Hendon, up the long hill to 31 Cheyne Walk. A blue moving van sits in front of the house; a white Volvo is parked in the drive. What luck, I think. I'm just in the nick of time to catch them before they disappear.

At first no one comes to the door. An eternity passes. Finally a short, plumpish woman in her late sixties wearing a reddish floral-patterned dress peeks out through a sliver of open door. Dyed ginger hair. Lots of makeup. Tiny fifties-style specs. Big breasts and bushy eyebrows. Little legs. I explain my mission.

"You want to talk to me about who? About my *son?* About my son, *Malcolm?*" The door begins to swing shut. "Go away, just *go away.* I have nothing to say about 'im."

"But Mrs. Edwards," I say. Slam.

I knock on the door again. No answer. The streets are deserted. I wonder how long it will be before a police car cruises the neighborhood.

"Mrs. Edwards," I shout. "Mrs. Edwards, please open the door. I just want to say hello, give you these flowers. I've come all the way from

America just to give you these flowers." I lie: "They're from Vivienne Westwood—you know, Malcolm's wife."

No response. From the second-floor window I see a lace curtain move to the side and then fall back. I knock again, harder this time, try the doorbell, sit down on the front step and wait. Start to write a note.

Finally, the bay window swings open. Martin Edwards, a short, stout man with a thick mustache, spectacles, and a heavy working-class accent leans his head out the window. "Mr. Edwards, just give me ten seconds to explain. . . ."

"Look you: I'm going to give you ten seconds—ten seconds to get off my prop'ty before I come out there and *punch you in the nose.*"

I splutter. "Look, Mr. Edwards, you don't have to be so offensive. I just came by to say . . ."

But he just looks at me and smiles. "Now, I've told you: *Get lost!*" He closes the curtain and walks away, thinks again and opens the window. His voice booms out at me: "And as for those flowers: lemme tell you, you can stuff 'em!"

On the 8th of May, 1945, the Second World War came to its untidy close, and for over a week, Britain expressed its sense of victory, its exhaustion, and its hopes for a speedy recovery with massive celebrations. Imagine: Piccadilly fully lit for the first time in years; throngs of people, some climbing lampposts; strangers kissing strangers; the young princesses, Elizabeth and Margaret, sweeping along anonymously in the exhilarated crowd; sudden trysts between reunited lovers.

The war had taken its toll, but VE-Day and all its celebrations were sure signs that postwar Britain was now going to have its own "coming of age." For the first time in six years of ration and restriction, hardship and sacrifice, a new, modern Britain was being forged. The nation came of age with a sharp baby boom: By 1947, the British birthrate had reached a peak of 20.5 per thousand. And that's where the story of Malcolm McLaren begins.

Nine months and two weeks after VE-Day, Malcolm Robert Andrew McLaren—his real name—was born on the 22nd of January, 1946, at the pair of attached row houses inhabited by his parents and maternal grandparents at 47–49 Carysfort Road, Stoke Newington, London, a quiet, solidly middle-class Jewish neighborhood a short walk from the lush green playing fields of Clissold Park.

Malcolm was born into a family already lacerated with tensions and divisions. His parents—a Scottish layabout and a Jewish lady—were poorly suited to each other. But no matter what differences in family, class, or religious backgrounds might have divided Malcolm's parents—and they do seem to have been considerable—they were forced by Britain's post-war austerity to live with her parents. (Indeed, under the brave new Socialist government elected in 1945 as a reaction to Churchill's aristocratic conservatism, rationing of many basic consumer items continued in Britain until 1953.)

Little is known about Malcolm's father, and I suspect that Malcolm doesn't know all that much about him either. After all, Peter James Philip McLaren left home when Malcolm was two. Pete had been a "sapper" (a mine layer) in a Royal Engineers regiment, and later worked as a motor-engine fitter. By some accounts, he was something less than a stellar dad. Some stories portray Pete as a bright but lazy man who would rather stay home and read with his eldest son, Stuart, than drive the taxi Malcolm's maternal grandmother had bought him. Malcolm, of course, tells people that his father was a cat burglar, but the only evidence of any criminal tendencies is that Pete once bought the boys a bicycle cheap off the back of a lorry.

Malcolm's mother, Emily Isaacs, was the daughter of a rather well-to-do family of Jewish diamond cutters, although her father, Mick Isaacs, was a tailor and her mother, Rose Corrie Isaacs, a would-be actress. Somehow, Emmy did not fit in. Maybe it was marrying Pete—who was not exactly a nice Jewish boy. Maybe she just wasn't thought terribly bright. She certainly wasn't interested in raising her children—especially not Malcolm, who was considered his grandma's pet. Instead, Emmy, single again, went to work as a kind of traveling saleswoman, regularly leaving home for trips up north.

Each day, Malcolm would come home from school to his grandmother's house where Mary, the Isaacs's maid, would fix him tea and jam sandwiches. Then after supper, at six o'clock or so, when it was time for Malcolm to go "home"—back to where he slept and kept his things—he would climb over the little cement wall separating the two houses. When he woke in the morning, his mother had already left for work, and it was back over the wall to Grandma Rose's for breakfast.

Before long, Malcolm was no longer being raised by his mother—who might be off taking tea at the Dorchester with her friends—but by his grandmother, who even made sure that he went to a nursery school where they washed his curly red hair. Emmy, who had married Pete when she was quite young, was now terrified of being "left on the shelf"—despite the fact that Malcolm thought she was a beautiful woman. Perhaps her beauty was yet another reason for her to keep her distance from her boys, for during this time Emmy was supposedly totally "man-mad," seeking husbands left and right, apparently at one time even dating Sir Charles Clore, the retail millionaire owner of Selfridge's department stores.

Everyone who met Malcolm's Grandma Rose thought she was someone special, a marvelous raconteuse and a soulful, streetwise lady. It was Rose's parents who had been the diamond dealers, Sephardic Jews who did surprisingly well for themselves in the tight community of London's largely Ashkenazic diamond trade. Descended from Portuguese aristocracy, Malcolm will tell you.

Rose Corrie Isaacs was a natural story-spinner. She grew up pawning bad diamonds for her father and was supposedly so good at selling them for more than their worth that her father's business boomed. When young, she had wanted more than anything else to be an actress.

Acting was not considered a kosher trade for a girl from a well-to-do Victorian family, but Rose still managed to get closer to the theater than her family liked, for while she was still young, she became pregnant apparently, and was made to have an abortion. Soon afterward, she met and married a tailor named Mick Isaacs—an Ashkenazic Jew whom she, and Malcolm, never grew to respect or even like. Her theater career over before it even started, she began to give private elocution lessons.

"My grandmother lived her life a little bit through my eyes," McLaren says now. "She didn't care about her husband that much and she didn't care about her daughter, didn't care about any of those people very much. For her, the world shut down when she had to marry and she was constantly looking for ways to recompense that. One way, I think, was to live her life through me a little bit."

"I'll tell you the honest truth," says Vivienne Westwood. "And this totally describes Malcolm.

"When he was a little boy of about six years old, he encouraged all the other children to play truant from school and he built a little camp in a wasteground quite near to the school. There were about six of them, and they would each bring biscuits from home every day. And he managed to do this for four or five days and nobody discovered them.

"Then, one day, Malcolm saw his school teacher marching across the grounds. She'd discovered them, knew they were there, and was coming to get them. He said to me that he'd never, in his whole life, *never* hated anybody as much as that woman. If he could have killed her in any possible way, he would have. He had to spend about six months in a class with younger students, but it never really bothered him.

"You see, that really is his attitude. . . . That's the secret. . . . He wants to get people to fuck up, band together, and fight the world. The problem he has is all those people who really believe in him, really believe something's happening. But when the problems come, they always get left behind."

One thing is sure: Malcolm always hated school.

"I think it has to do with the fact that his mother rejected Malcolm and he was brought up by his grandma," says Vivienne. "He had some kind of hate for establishment because he reacted against love. Therefore, patronage of any kind, he has a terrific resistance against."

"I was like a wild animal," says Malcolm, "and I enjoyed being so. You have to understand that my grandma never considered school very clever. She would always put it down."

Besides, no schooling could ever compare to Grandma Rose. "At the age of six, she forced me to read my first book, *Jane Eyre,* with the dictionary on one knee and the fucking book on the other. It took me six months or more to read it, ten pages a day. But within the space of about two years, I was already beginning to rebel. I was desperately trying not to read and by the age of ten or eleven I actually stopped reading."

Obstreperous and untamed, encouraged by his grandmother to loathe school, the boy with unruly red hair pleaded with his mother not to send him to the local William Paton Primary School in Stoke Newington High Street, and for a while, perhaps as long as two years, Grandma Rose taught him at home instead.

But there was something else brewing in Malcolm's life: Emmy had started dating a new man she had met in Brighton, and just before Malcolm's sixth birthday, she and Martin Levi were married. Respect was now the order of the day: respect for a new father, respect for mother, and suddenly, respect for school. Mother and father would brook no more of Malcolm's (or Rose's) nonsense. The Levis were determined that Malcolm get a proper education, and, following his long sabbatical at home, he and his older brother, Stuart, were sent to, of all things, a nearby Jewish parochial school, The Avigdor School in Lordship Road.

Suddenly, Malcolm's entire world was set askew. Where before there was only a man-mad mother and an absentee father, now there was a real father, disciplined, demanding, and Jewish to boot. Levi may not have seemed all that smart to young Malcolm (or to old Rose)—according to Malcolm, Martin could barely read or write when he first became involved with his mother—but he was certainly hardworking, a dress manufacturer with a factory in the East End.

Within a year of their marriage Martin and Emmy purchased a new factory near Whitechapel Road, and changed their names. Henceforward, the McLarens and Levis were to be known as the Edwardses, and Emmy was to be called Eve; Eve Edwards London Limited was the official name of their business. Malcolm McLaren became Malcolm Edwards, a different proposition altogether.

More important than the name change, however, was Malcolm's difficulty passing the 11-plus exam required, in those days, to determine what kind of school (secondary or grammar) he would next attend. A private tutor was hired, but the ten-year-old Malcolm just didn't care. Finally, in 1957, he was admitted to the Whitechapel Foundation, a secondary school he still remembers as "a very, very tough place in the East End."

It turned out to be a lucky break: During his one year at Whitechapel, Malcolm Edwards discovered rock 'n' roll.

It was during morning assembly at school, sometime around Christmas. Malcolm's math teacher, a young man who moonlighted as a jazz pianist—the kind of teacher who would walk into class and start his lesson by telling an anecdote about "Marilyn Monroe and the two cannonballs"—grabbed the stage and played Jerry Lee Lewis's "Great Balls of Fire." Malcolm was knocked out. "I'd never seen anything like it. I thought my head was gonna come off." Soon after, his brother Stuart, an avid Eddie Cochran fan whose ear seemed permanently glued to the "American Top Ten" on Radio Luxembourg, took him to see Buddy Holly at the Finsbury Park Astoria (now the Rainbow).

What started as childhood fancy soon escalated into a frenzy for the latest records, clubs, and clothes.

Especially clothes. Malcolm loved to dress up from the first time he heard rock music in 1957, just one year after Elvis Presley first hit the British charts with "Heartbreak Hotel"—and one year before his induction into the U.S. Army, an event that has gnawed at McLaren ever since. Besides, when Malcolm needed money for the latest disc or a new shirt, his grandma was always there to oblige. Once, he begged his grandfather to make him some clothes. They went up to Mick's workroom and Malcolm wound up with a suit made from some beautiful turquoise fabric that had been used for the boxer Primo Carnera. Sometimes he would wear it for days on end.

If he was a little too young to participate fully in the great social revolution now thought of as the Golden Age of the Teenager—that very first generation of postwar British youth to have spending money jingling in their pockets for records, clothes, cinemas, and clubs, all the detritus of what is now known as youth culture—Malcolm was clever enough to pick up on the little things that would bring him into the kingdom of cool. Like the right way to comb your hair. One week he would part it to the left, the next week to the right, then, backcombed into a "Continental." So long as he reached there before his friends, nothing else really seemed to matter much.

His home life was still chaotic. The adolescent Malcolm wasn't getting along with anyone and was beginning to misbehave seriously, on one occasion even setting off a pack of firecrackers in his parents' living room. Finally, Martin Edwards decided to move his family farther out into the suburbs, and Rose and Mick were persuaded to sell Carysfort Road and buy another house in Cheyne Walk, Hendon. It seemed the perfect location for the Edwardses, and the schools were better in North London.

Malcolm was now sent to Orange Hill Secondary School in nearby Edgware. He hated every minute of it. Each day he would arrive late and each day he was given detention. No playtime for Malcolm. Instead, he was assigned to dig up stones in the garden next to the men's staff room where the teachers could keep an eye on him.

"It was putting up the desk lids and always making sure you could sit in the very back hoping the teacher wouldn't notice you," he says. "You didn't want to know anything about King Harold in 1066 or the economic poverty of India or algebraic equations or some woman asking you to draw a pot of flowers. You just didn't want to know, and from the minute you got there until you got out at 4:30 the only subject for discussion in my opinion was whether you knew what number 25 was in the charts or who was number 19, what you were going to buy on Friday to go out on Saturday night."

Living in Hendon seemed to divide Malcolm farther from the Edwardses. Rose, Mick, and Malcolm lived on the top floor of the house; Martin, Emmy, and Stuart lived below. (A third child, Colin, was born soon after.) The split seemed irrevocable and Malcolm grew to despise the

Edwardses' lack of soul, his stepfather's working-class origins and stupid veneration of hard work. As far as Malcolm was concerned, no love was ever lost here. Indeed, the merest display of parental affection seemed to upset him.

Like the very first time he went out to a club.

He was thirteen and a friend who lived around the corner was going to come along with him. Malcolm was all dolled up; the friend seemed sartorially lost. A bit of an embarrassment, but it didn't seem to matter much just then. The important thing was that they were going out. On their own. But just as they were leaving, at the door of his friend's house, Malcolm's friend wheeled around and kissed his mother good-bye. As soon as they were past the gate, Malcolm turned round and scratched the boy across the face: "What a prick! What a nancy! How pathetic! Kiss your mother? God, ugh, revolting!"

By the time he was sixteen (1962), Malcolm already knew most of London's teenage hangouts. The Shtip, a pinball arcade in North London. La Poubelle. Les Enfants Terribles. La Bastille Coffee Bar. Studio 51. La Discothèque in Wardour Street. The Scene. The Saint Germain des Près (owned by the same mysterious Madame Louise who later ran Louise's, the late-night lesbian club the Sex Pistols often frequented).

In those days, French names may have dominated Soho's seedy array of porn shops, night spots, and coffee bars, but the prevailing youth subcultures that coexisted there—the Hipsters, the Beats, the early Mods—were all based in large degree on whatever trickles of information young Britons could glean about American blacks. (Liverpool, the birthplace of the Merseybeat, was a base for many passing American sailors.) It didn't matter that most of the people who populated the scene were white. If anything, that was better, safer. Disguised as a *Continental* phenomenon—an Italian jacket or a haircut that had somehow wafted across the Channel—it was easier to keep at bay the moral and sexual panic whites (particularly white *parents*) felt about black culture, especially in the wake of the Notting Hill race riots against blacks, mostly West Indian immigrant workers, in the summer of 1958.

The coffee bars (specifically catering to the under-21s) attracted a strange mix of visiting au pairs, vacationing students, and British oddballs. It didn't matter that the first Golden Age of the Teenager had already faded: In the momentary twilight before the Beatles, the trend economy that had surfaced with the first flush of enthusiasm for rock 'n' roll continued to live off Britain's now flourishing economy, especially for the *jeunesse dorée* of London, the golden boys and girls whose wages rose twice as fast as that of their parents between 1945 and 1960.

Indeed, in 1957 the Tory prime minister Harold Macmillan told Britons that "some of our people have never had it so good," and although this was later used against him by Labour's Harold Wilson in the 1959 electoral campaign, Macmillan was basically right. This was the period of *I'm All Right Jack* (the title of a popular Peter Sellers comedy), a time of virtually unrestrained spending on newfangled washing machines, refrigerators, televisions, and vacuum cleaners.

It was in this rising tide of complacent consumerism that Britain's first homegrown youth subculture, the Mods, came about. The Mods started from the same images of progress everyone else did, but then overlaid these symbols with a quietly subversive, self-conscious code of coolness. Being a Mod was all about the way you stood ("you sort of slouched, you put your leg against the wall"), the music you listened to (not only Mod bands like the Who, but also hot R&B, especially Tamla/Motown and anything by the Isleys and the Miracles), the pills you swallowed (up, up, up), the scooters you rode (Vespas or Lambrettas) and the clothes you wore (the *right* parka, the *coolest* tie, and the all-important length of a side vent). Intangible details to some, but to Mods, these were crucial signs of belonging.

Malcolm Edwards would never, ever have associated with Mods. He was *better* than them, if only because he didn't need to be a part of a mob. Or so he says: "They were the suburban version of what was happening in the West End and I was there before them," he brags. "The West End was smaller, more 'beat,' because there was a hangover from the fifties, a snobbery about going to see Modern Jazz. You didn't have any idea of what the hell anybody was playing and you couldn't get hooked on it and you couldn't dance to it, but you went there because it felt good. So you professed to have something to do with the West End, and you professed to be a Beat, and you were very *au fait* with all the clubs which had French names." You means Malcolm.

Amid all Britain's tribal youth cultures, the Teds and the Rockers, the Beats, Hipsters, and Mods—"we" cultures, every last one—Malcolm Edwards chose to dally with all and belong to none, subscribing instead to a culture of one. That, of course, was the culture of none other than Malcolm Edwards himself.

In 1962, as soon as he could, Malcolm left Orange Hill Secondary with a meager two O-level examination passes. Continuing in school was out of the question. A visit with his mother to an ordinary careers office produced a job at Sandeman's Port & Sherry in Orange Street, but as soon as he realized it meant going to Jerez, Spain, Malcolm quit Sandeman's to take a shop clerk's job in a West End haberdashery in the Burlington Arcade.

While clothes were undoubtedly more fun than fortified wines, Malcolm soon began wandering around looking for ways of getting out of work. One route passed through Carnaby Street, then with just five or six shops catering to Mods and other fashion-conscious clients (his favorite was Vince's Man Shop); another took him down Charing Cross Road, past St. Martin's School of Art. Attracted by the long hair and brightly colored cut-off coats of some of the students entering the building, he wandered in. That was the first time Malcolm had ever known there were such things as art schools. He enrolled as a part-time student. One night a week, at 7:30, he would go to St. Martin's and learn to draw the nude.

Now there were other firsts: the first time he had ever seen a naked body other than his own; the first time he had ever really drawn; the first time he had ever felt "a focus to the things I believed in."

"The fact was that I joined the art school so that when I did go to these clubs, I wasn't someone who was just walking around, having bought a black polo-neck sweater and being a poseur on the scene. I was now going to get into this initiation. It meant I was more bona fide. Now, I was a member of the club."

A week after he started classes at St. Martin's, Eve Edwards caught wind of Malcolm's studies. Her son was not going to draw pictures of naked bodies. Malcolm fought, but the very next day his mother phoned the school and had him dropped from the class. It was pathetic. Embarrassing. But since he wasn't yet seventeen there was nothing he could do about it.

If he was underage, Malcolm was also sneaky and persistent: The following week he registered for a class in three-dimensional design, and this time, he was able to stay.

Learning about shapes and colors wasn't as enjoyable as drawing naked bodies, but something began to click, and before he knew what he was getting into, Malcolm found himself staying after class, peppering the instructor with questions. The teacher was Ian Tyson, a painter, and when he saw Malcolm's excitement and realized how desperately this young student wanted (in Malcolm's words) "to be part of the scene," Tyson asked Malcolm why he didn't just come to art school as a full-time student. Malcolm was incredulous. "Is that even possible?" he asked. "If you want," said Tyson, "I'll get you an interview."

"Right around the same time, my local ex–school buddies came rushing into the class one night and asked me to come with them to the Whiskey A Go-Go. 'The Whiskey A Go-Go'? I said. 'I'm kind of beyond that now. I'm into the real club here. I don't need that crap, trying to chat up French au pairs and pretending to speak pidgin French.' It was too dull, so I decided I wouldn't. I refused, and suddenly, the die was being cast."

That spring of 1963, Malcolm went for an interview but was told that he lived in the wrong borough of London. You should try somewhere else, he was told. Harrow Art College, perhaps. That's closer to Hendon.

Malcolm would have preferred to attend the venerable Royal Academy of Dramatic Arts, but apparently he made a mess of his audition there, and finally went to Harrow with his tail between his legs, praying that he would get in.

At Harrow, an imposing, labyrinthine, white-stone edifice, Malcolm was given a stiff interview. First he lied to the interviewer and convinced him that he had passed the entry exams—"I'm very good at lying," he says. But then the interviewer began pawing through what there was of Malcolm's portfolio. "This is terrible, this is terrible, that is terrible, *everything* is terrible," he recalls being told. " 'You realize,' the interviewer said to me, 'that you're going to have to work very hard, that you'll be bottom of the class?' I thought, my God, please, I'm completely hopeless. If I don't get in, my life is ruined." But he did get in, under one condition: Since he came from such a well-to-do family, he had to pay the full tuition fees.

The Edwardses were outraged. Full-time art school? You must think we're made of gold! But once again, Malcolm pitched a fit and threatened to leave home if his parents refused to pay. And once again, Grandma Rose saved the day, persuading her daughter of his good intentions and helping to pay for his tuition.

This time, Malcolm was determined to succeed. Each day, he would practice his drawing. Each week he would go to the Victoria & Albert Museum to study the paintings. Never had he cared about anything as much as art school. No matter that the students seemed ridiculously straight. Malcolm soon found new friends: Fred Vermorel, son of a French chemist cum Resistance leader who became a dry cleaner after the war, a well-read intellectual with a talent for political intrigue; Patrick Casey, a swaggering Hipster with a fondness for dark Teddy Boy clothes from the mid-fifties; and Gordon Swire, a slightly older art student with a quiet demeanor and a pretty older sister named Vivienne.

Most students enrolled in Harrow's Foundation course found that the rapid pace of learning the basics left little time for critical scrutiny; Malcolm, Patrick, and Fred seemed to have time for little else. "Really, I should say he seemed a bit bored with the basics," says the man who became Malcolm's mentor at Harrow, Theodore Ramos, then a suave, thirty-five-year-old visiting lecturer on loan from his regular teaching appointment at the Royal Academy. "His paintings were purer than those of his classmates. If he wasn't a natural painter, he more than half understood the basic ingredients, but immediately rejected them to embrace a very real expressionism."

All seemed to be going well, but with Malcolm's natural propensity for trouble, even he knew it was only a matter of time before he would once again have to face his family's straitlaced ideas of working life. This time, it took until the second term, but the break was irrevocable, as simple as staying out at an all-night party. When he returned home the next morning, unshaven and with tousled hair, his tartan scarf—a constant sign of identification with his biological father—wrapped snugly around his neck, his mother was furious.

" 'I'm not allowing this,' she said. 'I'm phoning the principal. I'm not having you ending up like a beatnik. I'm going to see him tomorrow.'

" 'You do that,' I said. 'Go ahead. You do that. But I'm leaving home.' I ran out of the house and I ran to some friends I knew in Harrow and I stayed there all night. The next night, my friends called me and they said, 'Your mother's been at the school, she was talking with the principal and now he wants to see you.'

"And then I did the thing that nobody thought I would do. I didn't go and see the principal. I didn't ask for his help. I didn't settle things with my mother. I just left. I wanted more than joining the club now. Now, I wanted to join the world."

Of all the stories Malcolm told me about his teenage years, my favorite is the one about the day he ran away from home at the tender age of eighteen. How he grabbed his little haversack and a few clothes, said a hurried good-bye to his Grandma Rose, and took the tube and train out to the very farthest reaches of London, right out in the suburbs of Sidcup, Kent.

Now where, he wondered, and as he looked around the only thing he could see for miles and miles was the broad band of motorway that cut a gray swath through the English countryside. Suddenly, he was terrified of the motorway. Every car seemed to threaten instant death. Sexual molesters—his perpetual childhood worry—lurked behind every bush.

Soon, Malcolm met up with a big, old black man named Charlie who kept everything he owned with him at all times. Curiously, Malcolm wasn't the slightest bit afraid of this hobo. Charlie knew a thing or two about motorways and it wasn't long before the two of them—Malcolm with his haversack and a little blanket fastened around his shoulders by a big pin, Charlie with his enormous satchel of odds and ends—found a lorry to take them on their way.

They ended up in the seaside resort of Eastbourne, and they decided to spend the night there. Nearby was a wood and they went to its edge and laid out their things. The stars came out and Malcolm got scared. He'd never been out in the country before, even though his parents had once taken him on holiday to the south of France. The more he thought about where he was, the scarier it got. He became terrified that a snake was going to bite him.

Don't worry, said Charlie. Here's what we're gonna do. I've got some magic here. And Charlie produced a couple of polyethylene bags and a ball of twine. Now come here, son: Charlie wrapped the bags around Malcolm's feet and tied them up with the twine. Now, you sleep tight.

The next morning, Malcolm and Charlie went down to the pebble beach and collected whatever change they could find to buy breakfast. The sun was shining. It was a wonderful day for travel. They went back to the motorway and hitched to another town.

Here, there was a monastery, where Charlie and Malcolm stayed for seven days. They did a bit of sweeping up, pounded clay, this, that, and the other, and then the two of them split up. Charlie continued on his journey and Malcolm went on with his, hiking down to St. Ives in Cornwall, where, he had heard, the sculptor Barbara Hepworth always needed young people to help out. Malcolm stayed there for a few months and then, one day, it was time to return to London.

But by this time, Malcolm wasn't scared anymore. He had really done it now: For the first time in his life, he was really out on his own. Good-bye, Mum; good-bye, Dad. You can almost hear him saying it: From now on, I'm an artist, an artist, do you hear? An artist! And Malcolm Corrie is my name now, like Rose Corrie. Malcolm *Corrie,* and don't you forget it.

The adventure had begun.

2
DON'T SPOIL
YOUR ROTTENNESS

A Sane Revolution

If you make a revolution, make it for fun,
don't make it in ghastly seriousness,
don't do it in deadly earnest,
do it for fun.

Don't do it because you hate people,
do it just to spit in their eye.

Don't do it for money,
do it and be damned to the money.

Don't do it for equality,
do it because we've got too much equality
and it would be fun to upset the apple-cart
and see which way the apples would go a-rolling.

Don't do it for the working-classes.
Do it so that we can be little aristocracies on our own
and kick our heels like jolly escaped asses.

Don't do it anyhow, for international Labour.
Labour is the one thing a man has had too much of.

Let's abolish labour, let's have done with labouring!
Work can be fun, and men can enjoy it; then it's not labour.
Let's have it so! Let's make a revolution for fun!

—*D. H. Lawrence*

That chick [Christine Keeler] is one of the greatest anarchists of all time. She brought down a government with just one little pussy; I can't do it with 2,000 students.
                    —*Jean-Jacques Lebel, underground journalist*

By 1963, with the Tory government collapsing from the Vassall and Profumo sex-politics scandals, it had become all too easy to sneer at Britain's moral hypocrisy. Her inept finagling with sexual scandals, her lack of fiscal resolve, her hollow pretentions to democratize English life—all these spoke of a country in eclipse. The era of consensus lasting from the postwar years now gave way to more modern cultural tropes of irony and social upheaval. It was a time that gave birth to the satire era, *Private Eye* and *That Was The Week That Was*, and to the anarchic plays of Joe Orton. "You're at liberty to answer your own doorbell, miss," says Detective Truscott in a typical moment from Orton's *Loot* (1967). "That is how we tell whether or not we live in a free country."

Of course, "one little pussy"—Christine Keeler—couldn't quite bring down Harold Macmillan's government all on her own: Inflation, sterling crises, and de Gaulle's crushing veto of Britain's application to the European Community all did their job. But the summertime scandal that unfurled around the stunning twenty-two-year-old "model" and Macmillan's secretary of war, Jack Profumo, was enough to shake the growing complacency that Labour leader Harold Wilson now started to characterize as "thirteen years of Tory misrule."

That October, a greatly weakened Macmillan resigned his office due to "ill-health," but by then, the damage to the Tories and to Britain herself had been done. Macmillan's boasting talk of the rise of "the affluent society" now began to seem like mockery.

Five days after the Profumo affair came to a head, another scandal rose to preoccupy the British public.

This time it was a robbery, the holdup of a mail train loaded with over £2.5 million. It didn't seem to matter that the driver of the train had been coshed over the head and left to die; the public reacted by lionizing the robbers, turning their villainy into a celebration of instant cash and instant success.

The Great Train Robbery represented the consummation of the overnight success story, a process already begun with the transformation of working-class boys—actors Michael Caine and Tom Courtenay, hair stylist Vidal Sassoon, artists and photographers David Bailey, Terence Donovan, and David Hockney—into a New Aristocracy of photographers, actors, artists, fashion and television people, a nobility based on celebrity instead of old school ties. Some sarcastically dubbed them Instant Icaruses, but most of these "young meteors" flew fast and high, and they captured the nation's fickle attentions in what seemed to be a single swoop.

Unmatched among them were four young lads from Liverpool who called themselves the Beatles.

Talk about overnight success: "Love Me Do," the first Beatles' single, was released in October 1962; by the first week of December it had climbed into the Top 20. The next single, "Please Please Me," was released in January and reached number one by March. "She Loves You," released in the summer of 1963, went straight to number one on advance orders. Until recently, there had been only scandal on the front pages; now there was golden Beatlemania. By August, each Briton already knew the message announced on the *Mirror*'s banner: "FOUR FRENZIED LITTLE LORD FAUNTLEROYS WHO ARE EARNING £5,000 A WEEK." Robbing trains seemed like hard work in comparison.

Like the Great Train Robbery, the Beatles' success was no mere accident but the result of shrewd planning and careful insight into the mechanisms of British consumer desires. It wasn't only that the Fab Four's manager, Brian Epstein, cleaned up their act, dressing them in Cardin suits and prohibiting them from swearing and smoking onstage; Epstein also saw that for rock 'n' roll to achieve the kinds of profits demanded by major record companies it had to climb out of the youth market and into the hearts, minds, and pockets of the general public. No longer would rock 'n' roll be thought of as greasy kid stuff dug out of some Merseyside cavern; from now on, it was to be a genuinely popular phenomenon, produced, sold, and advertised like soap powder.

If it seemed that Britain was now being overrun by a foreign and disposable (read: American-influenced) culture of fast cars and instant stars, celebrity, newness, and hype—which *Time* magazine belatedly christened "Swinging London" in early 1966—that did not mean that the traditional British antipathy to modernization, commerce, and good manners was also being overtaken (yet). If anything, all this was only the most visible aspect of a widening schism between Britain's foundering manufacturing industries and its newly expanding service sector: marketing and advertising, betting and entertainment, leisure goods and all the services that supported them.

In June 1964, Harold Wilson was elected prime minister under a banner that promised to bring Britain "the white heat of technology." Many had high hopes for the new regime, but for Malcolm Edwards, there was another message sheathed in this farce of social change with all its glorified bullies, call girls, and overnight success stories. No matter how much he may have hated school, there was no denying that almost anyone who was anyone had passed through this particular back door in the British educational system. Three of the four Beatles had done it; so had many of the "young meteors": All, at one time or another, had attended art colleges.

And so, even though Malcolm had come back to London "to join the world," it must have seemed obvious that he now had little choice other than to return to what he'd left: art school. That was where you found the bright boys, the boys who really counted, the boys in the know.

And return he did. For the next seven years, Malcolm Edwards was to be a "professional" student of art.

In the summer of 1965, Malcolm Edwards came back to London from his mythical voyages in the countryside. Predictably, no one remembers his ever having left London, much less having gone to St. Ives.

Leaving home was undoubtedly a traumatic experience. For a few days, Malcolm disappeared, finally turning up at Fred Vermorel's in a daze, insisting he was only in search of some quiet. Fred had nowhere to let him stay, so Malcolm kipped on the cold gravestones of Harrow-on-the-Hill cemetery. A search party of concerned teachers from Harrow was sent to look for him, but the elusive Edwards, warned by Fred, gave them the slip. He would never go back to Harrow, he told Fred, because his teachers would only send him home eventually, and that he could not do. Fred, loyal to the end, put Malcolm back in touch with Gordon Swire, their old crony from Harrow Art College, now living above the post office cum grocery his parents owned in Station Road, Harrow.

Gordon greeted Malcolm warmly and invited him to stay on his floor for a while, but it soon transpired that Gordon's parents were not particularly fond of having Malcolm as a houseguest. Can't he live with his own parents? the Swires wondered. Malcolm had nowhere to go. Finally, Gordon came up with a temporary solution. "Why not sleep in the backseat of my car," he said, pointing to a black Morris Cowley parked outside. "It's a lot more comfortable than going back to some old gravestone."

The backseat of Gordon's car would have to do until Malcolm worked up the nerve to ask Grandma Rose for some help, which she provided with typical generosity. Within days Malcolm was installed in a bed-sit owned by a Mrs. Gold near Hendon Central. That too was fated to end poorly: When Mrs. Gold peeked into Malcolm's room while he was out buying

Nescafé, she was shocked to find that her lodgings had been turned into a paint-splattered artist's studio. Instant eviction.

For the next few months, Malcolm led a vigorously peripatetic existence, taking more art history classes at South East Essex Polytechnic (from which he was expelled) and moving from one flat to another, first kipping on the floor of Theodore Ramos's studio, then apprenticing himself to a scenic designer with a spare room, then moving in short order to a brothel (which he left when told that some of the forks had been used in a recent abortion) and, with Fred, to a cold-water flat owned by a Greek shoemaker in Soho's Berwick Street. For the first time in his life, Malcolm found out what it was like to be down on his luck. Cut off from home and from Harrow (specifically from Ramos, the one adult who had been willing to be his mentor), he was penniless and adrift. Even his attempts to peddle his paintings around Swinging London's tiny gallery scene proved unsuccessful.

Slowly, Gordon came to displace Fred as Malcolm's best friend. The baby-faced boy with the sandy hair, slurred Northern accent, and retiring, sarcastic manner might not have been as cool as the coyly intellectual Vermorel or the silent, tough, well-dressed prince of darkness, Patrick Casey, but Gordon was a year or two older than Malcolm or Fred, and undeniably clever. He already knew the ropes, knew the routes from art college to polytechnic and back again.

The Swires were from Hollingworth, a tiny Derbyshire mill town in the Tinwhistle Snake Pass, surrounded by the Yorkshire dales on one side and the hills of the Pennines on the other—more prosaically known as a rural suburb of Manchester. Gordon's father came from a long line of cobblers and built planes during the war; his mother was a loom operator at a local cotton mill. Once Gordon's two older sisters, Vivienne (nearly five years his senior) and Olga (just two years ahead of him), reached the end of their school years, the Swires moved down to London, opening the first of their post office cum groceries in Harrow. The Swire children soon went off in different directions: Gordon to the London School of Film Technique (LSFT), Olga to do a university course in sociology, and, in 1962, Vivienne to marry a friendly Hoover factory toolshop apprentice named Derek Westwood.

Derek's dream was to become a pilot, and to finance his training he quit Hoover's and started off on a string of odd jobs: working in hotels, running bingo nights, being an airline steward, and most important (at least to Gordon and Malcolm), working for a small dance hall management firm called Commercial Entertainments, among whose acts was a new band called the Detours—soon to be renamed the High Numbers and then a bit later, the Who.

Thanks to Derek's music connections, Gordon, Fred ("a bit of a band-wagoner, an oddball, a strange guy, a literary sort of man, kept reading C. P. Snow, I never knew why," says Malcolm), and now Malcolm too, were able to lig their way onto the growing rhythm and blues circuit, to gigs at the Railway Hotel in Wealdstone, tiny North London clubs, occasional West End dates at the Marquee Club. Derek managed the hall and Vivienne ran the coat check; Gordon, Malcolm, and Fred would come along for the ride.

R&B was the perfect antidote to the clean-cut harmonies of the Beatles. You wouldn't expect Alexis Korner, the Yardbirds, Cyril Davies, or the Rolling Stones to beg for love in any song starting with the word "please." These were the bad boys of rock, fashionable outlaws following in the footsteps of the pre-Army Elvis Presley, the tradition of hard-drinking, hard-living rock 'n' rollers. That was the whole point of it: There was *history* in these black man's blues, a whole tradition of suffering and soul waiting to be discovered.

By the autumn of 1966, Malcolm and Gordon had become so close—one old schoolmate remembers seeing them dance together so often she thought they were lovers—that a few months after Gordon moved down to North Clapham from his parents' new place in Ruislip, he invited Malcolm to move in as well. By now, Malcolm had been to three more art schools—Reigate, Walthamstow, and in autumn 1966, half a year at Chiswick Poly, to study music, mime, and theater—and Gordon was well advanced in his film career. The dingy Victorian row house at 31 King's Avenue, just south of the North Clapham tube, wasn't very big, but it was comfortable and cheap: best of all, most of the rent was being paid by two American friends of Gordon's, also studying at the LSFT, John Broderick and Chuck Coryn.

Broderick and Coryn weren't the usual sort of Yankee kids freeloading off their parents. Broderick (who has since become a Hollywood production manager and director) had come to London after a four-year stint with the radical San Francisco Mime Troupe; Coryn dropped out of the LSFT after a few months and became a drug smuggler. "Chuck made three trips from Lebanon, and he came into the same airport each time," recalls Gordon. "The third time, they searched him and his suitcase was just full of it. He got jailed and his girlfriend was deported."

Chuck Coryn's arrest left two rooms free at 31 King's Avenue: one, of course, was taken by Malcolm Edwards; the other was taken about a month later by a newly separated Vivienne Isabelle (Swire) Westwood and her three-year-old son Ben.

Some people desire and follow the paths of their desires as directly as they can; satisfied or frustrated, they never seem to lose their way. For others, the path of desire is murkier, more nomadic, leading into culs-de-sac and labyrinths, to procrastination, postponement, hidden collusion, and conspiracy. By almost any account, Vivienne Westwood is one of the latter.

When Vivienne first came to London, she wanted to be a painter, but for her to accomplish almost anything four steps had to be taken where one would normally suffice. Thus, in 1962, Vivienne got married and went to Harrow Art College for one term to learn silversmithing, but then—because "I was very working class and I worried terribly about how I was going to earn my living"—she dropped out, had her baby, and took a job in a factory. "That's how thick I was," she says. "Because all I had to do was go to the headmaster and say I want to transfer to a secretarial college. I didn't *know* there was any other way to be a secretary."

Once she got to the factory, however, Vivienne came to the conclusion that neither office nor factory work was going to make her very happy, and she now decided to go to a teacher training college in Oxfordshire. "I thought if I can't find a way to make a living at painting, at least I can be a teacher and teach someone else to paint."

Vivienne is deliberately imprecise as to whether relocating herself to Oxfordshire was a means of advancing her career or of separating herself from Derek—there were, after all, plenty of teacher training-colleges in London—but she must have known even then that she somehow wasn't suited to being a pilot's wife: "I didn't care about the same things that Derek cared for and I wasn't learning from staying with him. When I met Derek he was very lively and ever such a good dancer. When I married him I didn't want to marry him actually but he was such a sweet guy I couldn't give it up."

But give it up she did, and in 1965, she left Derek, taking Ben with her to live at her parents' home down the road in Harrow.

It was during this period that Vivienne and Malcolm first got to know each other. For his part, Malcolm had already started to admire the buck-toothed, dark-haired Swire sister from afar for quite some time and Vivienne seemed to know it, felt his charm pulling at her, even if she didn't dare acknowledge it. Gordon too seemed to sense that Malcolm fancied his sister even while she was still married to Derek. "He thought she was funny. I can remember her telling Derek to kiss off and Malcolm standing on the other side of the room, laughing at what she said."

Once Derek was out of the picture, however, Malcolm's visits to the Swires became more frequent. Occasionally, he would spend time helping Vivienne make the tiny mosaic earrings—"sort of Aztec-looking square wooden beads"—she sold on Saturdays down the Portobello Road. It was their first collaboration.

"Malcolm would glue white squares of wood together with maybe one red bead and one green bead somewhere off this square, and then he made a black one to go with it. His were more like exercises, more balanced in the way modern art was, instead of what I was doing, which was purple and orange and red all sort of bunged together. His was more artistic, mine more crafts.

"I always thought his ideas were ever so much better than mine."

In the beginning, Vivienne says she never thought of Malcolm as anything more than a friend and a flatmate. Fred Vermorel may remember her playfully pursuing the young Malcolm Edwards, but Vivienne claims she wasn't attracted to him, and for good reason: Malcolm was now affecting the look of a downtrodden art student. "He almost looked like one of those Jewish guys that were led out of the ghetto by the Nazis during World War II," remembers Broderick. "Very tiny, very emaciated, very close-cropped reddish hair, a long overcoat and longish kind of face with a reddish complexion. I had the feeling that he was a persecuted fellow, that he was from a lower-middle-class family that he had been forced out of or left, but in any event, was kind of estranged from. But I figured he was the kind of fellow who would have been estranged anyway."

What looked like the palpable air of estrangement to John Broderick soon seemed to Vivienne nothing less than a wan, bohemian beauty, both precious and unpredictable.

"The most amazing thing about Malcolm was that he seemed quite spectacular at the time really. He had a very, very pale face—I have the feeling that he used a bit of talcum powder or something which is how he got the nickname Talcy Malcy later on—but it looked extremely white and he had very slight hair on his skin and very, very close-cropped hair.

"But once I remember I said something to him—I don't remember what—and he just suddenly exploded in front of me. He didn't have control of his voice like he has now. His lips got very red in the context of his pale face and I remember his mouth—he's got a very well-formed, well-shaped mouth, quite pointed, it is—well, it just opened up, and I could see all the gums inside. I'd never seen anything quite like it. I respected this kind of intensity."

Every evening, the occupants of the house would gather for what seemed to be the same dinner—beans on toast and endless cups of tea. Hours and hours went by sitting before the small electric fire, smoking Woodbines, chatting on till early morning. Broderick remembers feeling as though they were living through a Harold Pinter play. A weird intimacy began to develop out of the very lack of available alternatives; boredom became the handmaiden of romance.

No one was very surprised when Malcolm developed a crush on Gordon's older sister.

Naturally, Vivienne was the last one to see it coming, but that didn't stop Malcolm from devising a scheme, appealing to her motherly instincts, feigning a severe stomachache that she wouldn't be able to ignore. Gulled into action by Malcolm's moaning, Vivienne responded the only way she knew how.

"You see," she says, "I thought Malcolm was somebody very special and somebody that I felt, not quite sorry for, but had to be cared for because they were all sensitive and you had to be careful.

"But he used to get this sick stomach sometimes and he just slept on a mattress on the floor, and one day he was very ill and I told him to come and get into my bed, and I went out to get him some medicine. I just looked after him and he must have really enjoyed it because he wouldn't get out of my bed. And when it was time for me to go to bed, I just had no other recourse but to get into the bed with him."

By Vivienne's calculation, it took over three months for her to fall in love with Malcolm; but by then, of course, there was no doubting that she was already pregnant by him—but only from one of those first two nights, she insists. After that, they stopped having sex for quite some time.

Malcolm now swung back and forth between adulatory love and rageful jealousy. Vivienne had an Italian boyfriend she was determined to see; Malcolm pitched a fit, demanding that it end. (It did.) Vivienne went to teach school; when she returned, she found Malcolm had rearranged all her furniture as a gift to her. Vivienne invited a male friend over to the house for tea—"just a friend"; Malcolm became so incensed, she feared he would kill himself. The next day, Malcolm had shaved his head until it was nicked and scratched and bloodied—"like he'd done it for me or something," says Westwood.

"I really thought he was unhinged. I thought he was going to commit suicide or something. I didn't go to school for three days. Instead, I sat and talked to him. Three nights: exhausting. I didn't dare leave him. By this time, I had no intention of getting involved with Malcolm but I didn't want to hurt his feelings. He was ever so precious and important, I felt a bit crude about it.

"All I knew was that I had done some sort of damage and that I had to be careful, that I couldn't cut this man loose. I thought that *he* thought that I'd committed myself and that therefore I *had* committed myself, but only because he'd been so confiding to me. He thought I'd just thrown him over and not realized the seriousness of the situation. *He'd never had a girlfriend before me.*

"And so I started to—I hesitate to use the right word—not fucking and not making love, because I wasn't in love with him. I guess you could say I started *sleeping* with him."

Once, John Broderick poked his head into Malcolm's room, a tiny maid's room Malcolm had furnished with a single item of furniture, a mattress that would either be placed upright to serve as a sofa or flat on the floor as a bed. It was cold outside but the windows were wide open and Malcolm was peeling the quaint flowered wallpaper off the wall.

"And what do you think you're doing?" Broderick asked with exasperation, wondering who would pay for such home improvements if the dread landlord, Mr. Khana, came by.

"I don't think I have the right to impose meself on me environment, me space," replied Malcolm in the Cockney accent he then affected. "The environment is pure."

"Well, if you don't want to impose yourself on the environment," teased Broderick, "why don't you take a few pieces of lumber, stick them out the window, and hang yourself outside in a hammock. Then you wouldn't even have to be in the room."

Broderick couldn't quite understand what his flatmate was up to, but Malcolm was merely being a good art student.

After all, that was what they taught in English art schools, that was the procedure: First you learn to draw, then you learn to see. And for Malcolm, as for so many British artists of the mid-sixties who were working under the dual influences of Marcel Duchamp's "readymades" and the early British pop art of Richard Hamilton and the International Group, seeing was *doing,* an unknowing gloss on Karl Marx's materialist dictum that philosophers had only *interpreted* the world, but that the point was to *change* it: Change the world and you change yourself. Hence, Malcolm's slogan of this time, "Change *me!*"

Change, transformation, revolution: These were the credos of the art student's world, and people like Malcolm and Fred—who now dressed like a junior mafioso and talked a blue streak about Surrealism—lived this life twenty-four hours a day, eating, sleeping, and drinking art.

The first challenge of art school was simply learning the history. That was the foundation of seeing. One day Malcolm would discover Egyptology, next it was the Renaissance, then the Fauves and the Surrealists, and then back again to the German Expressionists and forward to the Russian Constructivists. Wherever Malcolm's eyes were limited, Fred acted as guide, filling the gaps in his friend's knowledge with odd theories and examples, letting Malcolm in on the subterranean links between the history of art and the history of the world.

Indeed, Malcolm seemed to be fascinated by all things subterranean. Many of his early paintings were simple black monochromes. Never white, light, translucent: Clarity was something Malcolm couldn't seem to grasp. Black was the night, solid and mysterious, the sign of all things turned inside out. Black was about falling in love and getting lost, about the saturnine influence of French existentialism, of melancholy artists such as Baudelaire, van Gogh, Schiele, Artaud—a roll call of tortured souls one could trace straight through to the Rolling Stones.

Was Malcolm really that tortured? Or was all this play about Black just a pun on the covert, mystical underside of the avant-garde, a fashionably extreme existentialism combined with a teenage snob's first attempts to *épater le bourgeois?*

Like most of his peers, Malcolm had fallen under the sway of a critique of painting that aimed to turn paint and canvas into ideas instead of commodities, objects worth money. He was fascinated with Duchamp's readymades, swept away by the Americans Robert Rauschenberg and Jasper Johns, bewitched by Andy Warhol's cool detachment. Nothing grabbed him like Warhol's notion of the artist as reproducing machine, as a mere tool of commodity culture. For no matter what else Warhol's work was about, for Malcolm it could always be boiled down to one idea: "Being good in business," declared Andy Warhol, "is the most fascinating kind of art."

That kind of bald, ballsy, and deliberately banal notion of art making had just the right ring to Malcolm. It enabled a young art student to make the leap from creating work *about* his environment to working *directly* on the environment itself. Instead of painting big black pictures or stripping the wallpaper from his room, Malcolm now began constructing bizarrely bloated "happenings" where several artistic mediums (painting, sculpture, performance) were lashed together. And Malcolm just hoped for the best.

Like that time at the Kingly Street Art Gallery behind Carnaby Street, when Malcolm decorated the gallery with dozens of six-foot-high rolls of corrugated cardboard while "fragments of a noisy Audie Murphy war movie" were projected into the street. A happy enough spectacle until, writes Fred Vermorel, "a drunken soldier crashed screaming through a false [cardboard] floor" and the police paid a visit to the gallery.

Or that time at the Chelsea College of Art when Malcolm was taking evening classes and one of his teachers locked him into his studio, threatening not to let him out "until you paint me a fucking picture." At the end of the evening, Malcolm emerged from the studio dressed as the room.

By the spring of 1967 for Malcolm, for Fred, and for many other art students of the time, these heady student steps toward what would soon be formalized as Conceptual Art undermined the point of going to art school. The time had come for art to serve the cause of revolution.

Of course, there was no revolution, neither in Britain nor in any other industrialized Western nation, but to those who were convinced that change was needed—those who felt that Labour had turned into the party of Tory Socialism—that was precisely the problem. By the spring of 1966 time was running out for Harold Wilson's white-hot technological revolution, and youth was deserting the Labour party in droves—not for the Communist party, but for the mushrooming factions of the New Left.

Suddenly, politics was everything and everywhere, and there were new issues to be found wherever one looked: in Harold Wilson's covert support of the American war effort in Vietnam; in the insularity and elitism of Britain's hidebound class structure; in the bedroom and the artist's studio; in the racial polarization of British society; even, some said, in the very structures of the unconscious mind.

The New Left was also new because it was younger, because this was to be a revolutionary movement led not by the historically alienated class of the boring old fart proletariat Old Left or by their comrades in the

Communist party (most of whom had deserted following the Soviet invasion of Hungary in 1956), but by *students,* twenty-year-olds with the very
best of good intentions.

To some students, the struggle for democratization and equality of
condition expressed itself as a desire to participate in university decision
making. For example, the students' strike at the prestigious London
School of Economics, Mick Jagger's old alma mater, was set in motion
when David Adelstein, the head of the LSE Students's Union, wrote a
letter to *The Times* protesting the appointment of a new school director
(Sir Walter Adams) whose political background included having been the
principal of University College Rhodesia, South Africa's white supremacist
neighbor. For *that* heinous act, Adelstein was suspended; the sit-in protesting his suspension—ironically, victorious—was simply the last scene in
a six-month drama on behalf of what is now recognized to be a basic
student right.

However, students' political motives had now become as varied as the
students themselves. Many just didn't care: 1967 was the year of the
hippie. Operating under influences as diverse as the Amsterdam Provos
and the release of the Beatles' *Sgt. Pepper* album, they thought the Revolution was served just as well by turning-on, tuning-in, and dropping-out
as by fighting the Establishment through some weird political process.

But others did care, and a variety of student organizations catered to
their political whims. The mainstream National Union of Students worked
for basic students' rights and an end to grants cutting and overcrowding.
The alternative Radical Students Alliance (RSA) worked to expand these
aims and organize students as a front line of protest against the "genocide"
in Vietnam. The most radical students created the Revolutionary Socialist
Student Federation (RSSF), hoping for nothing less than a full-blown revolutionary movement that would begin with students leading Britain to
all-out communism; following Chairman Mao's Cultural Revolution, they
would turn the universities into liberated areas, so-called red bases.

Malcolm never belonged to *any* of these organizations, least of all to
the RSA or RSSF; that would have been too serious, too glum and book-
read for his tastes. As Vivienne Westwood says, "everyone knows that
Malcolm just pretends to read, but really he just reads the first and last
pages and skims the rest." However, under the powerful spell of an eloquent Trotskyite activist named Stan who insisted that his young friends
"take a stance," Malcolm began telling people he was a revolutionary. The
true extent of his radicalism, however, seems to have been attending the
massive marches in Trafalgar Square organized by the Campaign for Nu-
clear Disarmament and occasional anti-Vietnam protests outside the U.S.

Embassy in Grosvenor Square during one of which Malcolm was arrested along with Henry Adler, a wealthy Notting Hill intellectual with old Arts Lab connections, for attempting to burn an American flag.

Nor was Malcolm in Paris to witness the dramatic *événements* of May 1968, so widely thought to be part of McLaren's political education that many have actually put him on the scene. For months Malcolm had wanted to visit the Parisian art museums with Fred Vermorel, now studying at the Sorbonne, but all summer long he was stymied by the numerous strikes that had shut down the Channel ferries. That August, Malcolm finally made it, but by the time he got there, the students had long since finished with their strikes and gone on vacation. "I took him on a car tour of the Latin Quarter battlefields," Vermorel writes in his and Judy Vermorel's seminal book, *Sex Pistols: The Inside Story.* "To show off, I insulted a group of some 30 CRS riot police. They suddenly rushed at the car screaming and waving their truncheons. We did an extremely fast U-turn and shot south up the Boulevard St. Michel with Malcolm shitting bricks in the backseat, screaming 'Get the fuck out of here!' "

But for six days in the beginning of June, at the Croydon College of Art where Malcolm Edwards was enrolled along with his new studiomates Robin Scott and Jamie MacGregor-Reid, star painter of the class ahead of Malcolm, nearly three hundred students "occupied" the Croydon annex in one of several copycat student uprisings around the country. They issued statements, held teach-ins, rifled through papers in the principal's office, stole into the college canteen, and at one point supposedly even burned a desk.

"Malcolm came by the studio one day and told me that Hornsey's come out," recalls Scott, the songwriter whose career has shadowed McLaren's ever since the sixties. " 'What do you mean, Hornsey's come out?' I said. 'Well, they're sitting-in. Let's go.'

"Nobody was very happy with the way things were, but they didn't really know what the problem was, so we set up one or two small meetings getting everyone to kind of come out of themselves and admit they were bored. 'Let's break the walls down, where should we start?' The idea was, Yes, let's change the system, but we've got to do something *now* because *this* business of holding meetings is going nowhere. I thought the best thing was to listen in and appear cooperative, but the other students were all going back and informing the head of the department."

Faced with insurrection from within their own ranks, the Croydon radicals panicked and redoubled their demands. What had started as a localized protest for students' rights, an end to examinations, and a loosening of the requirements for admission to art school, now turned into a full-blown student strike with the most radical factions demanding everything from total abolition of the students' union to amnesty for the strikers.

And then, the activists were duped (or so they claimed): Lured to the main college building in Selhurst Road for a six-hour student-staff meeting to discuss the sit-in, they came back to the art annex only to find that they had been locked out. "We have been tricked," Scott, now named Robin the Fair-Haired, told *The Times* that day. "We were given no warning about this. It was all done behind our backs. The authorities have created a situation which could become ugly and violent."

However, according to the school principal, Mr. L. Marchbanks Salmon, no lock-out was intended. "It's news to me," he said. "The most likely explanation is that the caretaker found it empty and decided to lock up for the night."

A group of six students, including Robin Scott, were now deputized to negotiate with the college administration; infuriated by the farcical turn of events, Malcolm suddenly refused to take part, uncharacteristically choosing to take a lower profile.

Scott was baffled by "Malcolm the Rose" pulling out from the negotiating team: "Ultimately, I suppose he didn't want to commit himself; maybe he just lost interest." But Vivienne Westwood remembers another reason for Malcolm's cop-out: He was simply afraid of dying from lack of sleep. "Malcolm had been up straight for three nights and had heard somewhere that if you don't sleep for something like eighty-four hours, you die." Vivienne thought that that was silly, but Malcolm wasn't one to be easily convinced he was wrong.

Malcolm's timing couldn't have been better, for even before the sit-in petered out and discussions with the college got under way, the Croydon disciplinary machinery was being cranked up to deal with the strikers. Robin left to start writing music for TV, and Malcolm went off to join Fred at the Sorbonne, and then to the south of France. Ironically, Jamie Reid, the only radical with a background in politics—his father was political editor of the *Daily Sketch*—was the only one to be punished for his role in the strike. "I was promised a place at St. Martin's to do a postgraduate course," he says, "but because of the sit-in I lost all that and the next year I ended up playing semipro football." Jon Savage in *The Face*, however, writes that Reid narrowly missed "being sent to a mental hospital for his role in the sit-in."

"Everyone was very deflated after the whole thing stopped," says Vivienne Westwood. "They wanted to go back to school, but things were even more regimented than they'd ever been before. And Malcolm was very surprised and shocked and hurt, because all the students said to him,

'Malcolm, what are we going to do?' They wanted to carry on—it was a purity kind of attitude. But Malcolm couldn't tell them to do anything. And they said, 'Well, that's all right for you. You're all right. You'll *always* be all right. You're not like us. You'll always find something to do. But *we're* stuck.' "

They were right, of course, because Malcolm's escape route had long been prepared. He had already applied to Goldsmiths' College, a teachers-training unit of the University of London with a small art annex, located in south London. Fortunately for him, this time he passed his A-level history exam.

Arriving at Goldsmiths', Malcolm was stirred. Paris, he later said, was "a terrific breath of fresh air because it was so visual. I'll never forget—the entire École des Beaux Arts was covered with these giant posters. An incredible sight! And incredible slogans: *Under the paving stones lies the beach!* [sic]" As usual, Fred played Henry Higgins to Malcolm's Eliza Doolittle, explaining the historical significance of such slogans. They were from the Situationists, he told Malcolm. And Malcolm, fascinated by all aspects of revolutionary culture, wanted to know more.

How is it that so many journalists have swallowed whole the canard that Malcolm and Jamie were in Paris during the general strike, getting "mixed up in the *Mouvement du 22 Mars,*" with Jamie supposedly even making posters for the students? Certainly, McLaren himself has encouraged this aura of radical credibility, once even telling Paul Rambali of *The Face* that the Situationists' very lack of a manifesto was what really attracted him to them: "They were just in it for the destruction! It was a way of making great comment, and it inspired me a lot."

Often called intellectual terrorists, it would be more precise to call the Situationists terrorist intellectuals. Frustrated artists who preferred to think of themselves as antiartists, the Situationists followed in the wake of famous café radicals such as Isidore Isou, the self-declared demigod of the semimystical Lettrist movement, Boris Vian, the surrealist poet-trumpeter, and Jacques Vachet, an early friend of Breton's (and a hero of Malcolm's) whose annihilation of art by "sardonic indifference" eventually led him to commit suicide by an overdose of opium in 1919. Like the later generation of Marxist intellectuals who became known as the New Left, the Lettrists recognized that the two avant-gardes of contemporary life—in politics and in art—had to be brought back together for any true revolution to occur. Short of using weapons or art, they said they were willing to try anything at all to accomplish that aim.

The Situationists arrived on the scene in 1957. To the Lettrist love of *détournements*—zany antics such as kidnapping a priest, stealing his clothes, and saying a Mass that ended with a homily on the death of God before the arrival of *les flics*—they added their own notions taken from an assortment of Communist theoreticians who had rebelled from the party line. Disdainful of every aspect of daily consumer life, their byword, if one can sum up such prolix rhetoric in a single phrase, was that contemporary life was a bore.

"A new form of mental illness has swept the planet: banalization," declared Situationist Raoul Vaneigem in *The Revolution of Everyday Life* (1965). "Everyone is hypnotized by work and by comfort: by the garbage disposal unit, by the lift, by the bathroom, by the washing machine. . . . Young people everywhere have been allowed to choose between love and a garbage disposal unit. Everywhere they have chosen the garbage disposal unit."

The Situationist's solution to this hackneyed existence was the "construction of situations"—a polyphony of art forms spontaneously coalescing around the principle of subversion—nothing less than a revolution of farceurs against those who still put their faith in history.

From 1966, at the University of Strasbourg, to the student rebellions at Nanterre in March 1967, to the "occupation" of the Sorbonne and the General Strike that gripped Paris in May and June 1968, the Situationists (and their occasional allies, the Enragés) used the French student population as intellectual guinea pigs in their experiments with the great game of social revolution. Though they tried their best to deny it—and enforced their politics with regular expulsions from the *Internationale Situationniste* (IS)—the Situationists were the Pied Pipers of the student revolution, reduced to plastering the walls with catchy slogans and witty comic strips instructing the workers to "Live without the time of death."

And of course, *Sous des pavés, la plage* ("Under the paving stones, the beach").

In England, the Situationist movement was limited to a handful of people. One of them, Christopher Grey, later the editor and publisher (with Jamie Reid's help) of a Situationist anthology titled *Leaving the 20th Century*, was expelled from the *IS* after a surprise visit from Situationist philosopher and filmmaker Guy Debord. Fred Vermorel writes that on a boast from Grey he had over sixty guerrillas ready for action, "Debord rushed across the Channel to inspect the troops. He was directed by an embarrassed Chris to the home of one Dave Wise and, bursting in, discovered Dave watching *Match of the Day* with a can of McEwan's Special Export. Such idle truck with the state's one-way communication system (i.e., Dave's antiquated six-inch telly) annoyed Debord, who became furious when Dave informed him that the guerrilla combat unit was him and his brother Stuart."

And so it was to Dave and Stuart Wise and their club of sixty ex-Situationist sympathizers, called King Mob after a celebrated group of seventeenth-century English rioters, that Malcolm, and Jamie, now turned for inspiration. Like "smashing Wimpy bars." Or dressing as Father Christmas and handing out toys in Selfridge's department store.

Or taking over Goldsmiths' College for a Free Festival of Situationist-inspired activities.

Compared to the Croydon sit-in, the Free Festival Malcolm organized at Goldsmiths' was big-time.

From the day Malcolm arrived there, he was treated as an outcast by most of the students, scorned by both the radicals of the far left and by the leaders of the center-left students' union—in particular, its president, a young black sociology student named Russell Profitt, now Labour district manager for Brent Council.

Profitt remembers Malcolm Edwards as something of a hippie, albeit a hippie with radical, anarchist tendencies—and that made him dangerous. Malcolm's relations with the student union were tense, even violent, from the start. At one general meeting, Profitt recalls Malcolm sitting in the back row of the auditorium, red hair standing straight in the air, chucking rotten tomatoes at the Student Executive Committee as it worked its way through its regular parliamentary paces. Other students thought Edwards something of a coward. Malcolm Poynter, an artist much more likely than Malcolm Edwards to prove his politics with his fists, once nearly decked Edwards for falsely accusing him of embezzling funds from the union.

Malcolm may have been weak on theory, but with his dress, his behavior, and even his art—ugly brown canvases with strawberries stuck into gesso—he laid claim to being the big revolutionary on campus. Even one of his closest friends at the time, Helen Miniver (later, Wellington-Lloyd) a young South African dwarf with bottle-blonde hair and an impish manner to match her size, remembers that on the day they met—waiting on line for their admissions interview the previous spring—Malcolm had told her that if he didn't get in, he'd just have to find another way to cause a revolution. For her part, Helen had decided that if she didn't get in she would go to Haight-Ashbury and become a hippie. ("We regarded the hippies like the Communist party," Jamie Reid later told *The Face*. "Sort of *over there*. . . .")

Until the idea of the Free Festival, most of Malcolm's radical activities at Goldsmiths' consisted of participating in the inevitable student protests at various campuses across London, including those at the LSE (over the school's support for Labour appeasement of U.S. policy in Vietnam) and various stunts with King Mob, including one at the University of London Union where Malcolm hungrily broke into the student canteen only to be tremendously disappointed that most of the food had already been stolen.

To Malcolm, a real revolutionary act was heisting paints from the Goldsmiths' students' supply store. Helen would drag a red burlap bag through the shop while Malcolm tossed in whatever supplies they needed. Since the store's counter was so high, Helen could pass by unnoticed and she and Malcolm could walk away scot-free.

Malcolm's painting may not have been very distinguished—he seemed much better at drafting and drawing than at painting his ideas— but according to his Goldsmiths' tutor, Peter Cresswell, as a revolutionary he was without peer in picking apart the contradictions in everyone else's lives. "He would identify quite quickly, quite shrewdly what you were about, what you were really looking for, what you were trying to get him to do, what you were offering. If you were saying something banal like 'this painting could be improved by adding a little more red,' he could be very cruel in terms of exposing how irrelevant and how trivial that statement was.

"It sounds as if I'm making this up," Cresswell continues, "but it stuck in my mind because I was very shocked by it at the time. He once said to me, in the context of a tutorial, that the only significant political act was to blast somebody off at the kneecaps. In the context of those days, when politics did have a nonviolent side to it, that was a very violent statement to make."

Yet in 1969, amid a general burgeoning of free concerts in London— the most famous being the massive Rolling Stones gig in Hyde Park that July—Malcolm didn't seem to be in the mood for knee-capping. Instead, he came up with the idea of holding a massive Free Festival in the amphitheater that sits in a natural bowl behind the Goldsmiths' art annex.

With the help of Liz Martin (an early feminist) and Nile Martin (an unrelated Edwards crony), plus the street credibility of a few friends from King Mob, Malcolm came up with an impressive collection of radical stars he claimed to have spoken with. Rock bands (the Pretty Things, Robin Scott, and the newly formed King Crimson), theater (the Lindsey Kemp mime troupe), a lecture by William Burroughs, and a discussion (on "the Revolution, Anti-public relations, formation of resistance groups, etc.") with writer Burroughs, artist Jim Dine, porn novelist–junkie Alexander Trocchi, and cult psychologist R. D. Laing: Malcolm took special delight in billing those he knew would never show—all but the rockers and Trocchi, whom he had met only once before in the most fleeting circumstances.

The big list of names was just what he needed to convince the students' union that *he* had things under control, didn't need anyone else's help thank-you-very-much, especially not the school authorities who, by this time, had all but conceded the students' right to hold the festival.

"The authorities in all honesty couldn't scrub lectures, but they had decided they would allow the thing to go on," says Profitt. "And what a go it was! We were all shocked. The only person who knew what was going on was Malcolm, and maybe Helen. All we knew was that Malcolm had probably got the loudest bands in London.

"The place was absolutely packed. Word had got 'round on the London network that the best bands of the year were going to be at Goldsmiths' and people weren't really sure what they were coming for. The place could just about take 2,000 people but on the first day there must have been something like 20,000! You couldn't walk down the corridor. You couldn't get anywhere. It was absolute and total bedlam."

By now, the college warden, Russ Chesteman, was regularly ringing the students' union to discuss the festival. Noise complaints were pouring in from as far away as Lewisham; the Goldsmiths' switchboard was so tied up that normal school business had become impossible. Over by the amphitheater behind the main building, fights were breaking out when the advertised bands Malcolm had promised failed to show. Prophet was instructed to get hold of the fellow who had organized the thing. After numerous efforts to find him, Malcolm finally phoned in to the union, promising to meet with Prophet to discuss the festival's fate.

Meanwhile, the festival continued, with unbooked bands coming and going under their own steam, college property disappearing, and revolutionary debris steadily filling the amphitheater.

"Some students wanted Malcolm's head on a plate," says Russell Prophet. "And others wanted him to be glorified as a saint for bringing life to Goldsmiths'.

"But in all of this, Malcolm was nowhere to be seen."

When Malcolm did return to Goldsmiths' the next October, he no longer seemed very interested in being a student. Perhaps the Free Festival had convinced him that he really did have some talents that might be useful in the straight world. Or perhaps he felt guilty about how he had treated Vivienne and their son Joseph, now nearly three.

Malcolm hadn't wanted Vivienne to have the baby in the first place. And Vivienne had gone along with whatever Malcolm said. It wasn't until they were nearly to the door of a fancy Harley Street abortion doctor—Malcolm's grandmother supplied the abortion money he later told Vivienne that he had raised by "selling his body"—that Vivienne finally realized she had wanted to have Malcolm's baby all along.

"There was some connection between not loving Malcolm and wanting to have an abortion," she says. "I suddenly realized that I had this wonderful treasure in front of me. It was like my life had been the front of a coin and I had suddenly flipped it and could see the other side. There it was: But I hadn't seen it until then—I must have been so stupid—and I suddenly realized that I could get up and go with this thing."

Instead of an abortion, Malcolm bought Vivienne a blue cashmere suit and they went out to raise a glass to the birth of their child. The celebration was short-lived; Malcolm now pulled back from Vivienne as violently as he had once been drawn to her, and until the day their baby was born, Vivienne lived at her mother's home near Northampton.

"Suddenly, this treasure, on being appreciated decided to run a mile," she whispers. "As soon as I decided that I wanted the baby, he backed off, and he went further and further away the rest of our relationship. 'Hang on,' he said. 'You're having a child or whatever, that's your responsibility, *I'm* not taking part in it. *I'm going to art school.*' He'd got tired of battling me. I don't know, decided I had feet of clay."

By November 30, 1967, the day Joseph Corrie was born—this child was *not* going to be an Edwards—Malcolm had come to accept the idea that he was going to be a father. Caught unawares by her labor pains, Vivienne didn't even have time to tell Malcolm she was giving birth. When Malcolm turned up at the hospital, Vivienne, long-despondent that their relationship wouldn't last through the birth of her child, was overjoyed to see him.

"I remember thinking how lovely he looked with all this snow on his hair and on his big tweed coat. But Malcolm looked at Joseph and he said,

'He's not mine. He doesn't even look like me. He's not my baby. He's got a different father.' "

For the next three years, Vivienne and Malcolm, Ben and Joseph, lived on and off at Aigburgh Mansions, not far from their old home in King's Avenue. Vivienne continued teaching and selling her mirrored earrings to shops on Carnaby Street in her spare time, but sometime in 1969, Joseph became so ill—"I neglected him *so* badly," she says—that she left Malcolm to live with her parents yet again. The summer of the Gold-smiths' Free Festival, Malcolm packed off Vivienne and the two children to stay in a camping caravan somewhere in Wales.

After the festival Malcolm could hardly seem to care less about school, Vivienne, or his kid. During the Christmas holiday of 1969 he had a one-night stand with Helen Miniver, his dwarf friend, and then sometime that spring he married a young Turkish Jewish woman named Jocelyn Hakim to raise some money for a film he had often bragged about having already started.

His subject, the Gordon Riots, an antipapist revolt instigated by Lord George Gordon in 1778, was the perfect Situationist project—the redis-covery of an arcane, seemingly spontaneous, moment in English history that had culminated in the development of Oxford Street as a last bastion against the mob storming the gates of the City. Presented with a brief synopsis, Peter Cresswell thought it was a reasonable thing for Malcolm to try—"he seemed much more suited to film than to painting"—and he arranged for Malcolm to borrow Goldsmiths' sole Bolex camera. However, like other films in Malcolm's future, this one was never to be completed. After shooting several rolls of film with Jamie and Helen, with Fred Ver-morel running sound—standing amid the hustle and bustle of the noonday shopping spree on Oxford Street—this quartet of virgin filmmakers some-how lost the camera on the tube. (Another story goes that Malcolm sold the camera to raise money to open his shop, Let It Rock.)

"In Britain," says Peter Cresswell, "any successful artist must be a harmless radical. Serious radicals we put in jail or execute. It happened to Shaw: He was an uncompromising sort of bloke but he didn't change anything. Shaw's lack of compromise was within the structure of society; Malcolm's is the same. Malcolm's success is based upon society *not* chang-ing, on allowing people an *outlet* for expression without actually changing anything. He can leave everything safely as it is.

"I only wish he'd give us back some money for our camera now. We could set up a decent film department with that money."

London, Paris, New York, Berkeley: The student protests of 1968 undoubtedly fomented certain long-needed reforms in Western life—legal affirmation of the rights of women, minorities, and homosexuals; educational reforms; liberalization of birth control, abortion, and divorce; and, crucially, a gradual whittling away of the war in Vietnam. But just as certainly, some of this movement's most delicate moral purposes and creative energies were siphoned off by those who were willing to shoot the revolutionary wad for the sake of their own egos, those for whom irresponsibility and cynicism (whether about "the System" or their own ideals) were a way of life.

The student movement may have begun, as political philosopher Hannah Arendt wrote in 1970, "not simply carrying on propaganda, but acting, *and, moreover, acting almost exclusively from moral motives.*" But after the dust had cleared, it was clear that different individual *gauchistes* had interpreted "acting" any way they chose. Some had taken to the streets, but many, many others had acted symbolically—as if revolutions were symbolic activities—laying claim to any aspect of the culture that signified rebellion, from rock 'n' roll to macrobiotic restaurants.

"As the sixties sizzled to a close," writes Richard Neville in his seminal *Play Power,* " 'revolution' was on everybody's lips, which in many cases was where it remained. Banks advertised vacancies for bearded accountants . . . Omar Sharif played Che Guevara in a 20th Century Fox wide screen quickie . . . and the Beatles, Rolling Stones and even Elvis Presley pressed the switch marked 'Social Conscience' on their electric Moog synthesisers."

A generation that had concluded that a life of cars and washing machines and televisions was nasty, brutish, and short now was going on to live that very same life, but with the music, clothes, hairstyles, and drugs of its own choosing. By 1970 the Situationists' *crie d'imagination, "sous des pavés, la plage,"* had become a cry of desperation: *"Ne gachez pas votre pourriture"* ("Don't spoil your rottenness").

After six years of Harold Wilson, Labour went down to defeat. A revolution had been lost, but ironically the revolutionaries themselves emerged victorious. In many cases, they now went on to inhabit the very institutions that were the butts of their derision in the sixties. For while some continued the revolution, studying *Das Kapital* in North London basements, freaking out on LSD, or lying dead in some Third World country, there were others, many others, who "sold out." You might have found them selling records, clothes, politics, style. You name it, they sold it.

And that's where you'd have found Malcolm Edwards.

In 1971, Malcolm Edwards went to the passport office birth certificate in hand and filled out an application. "Let's see now," he said, looking at the blank boxes on the form, touching the pen to his pale tongue in a moment of hesitation. Then he began to write. Under "surname," this nice Jewish revolutionary from Stoke Newington wrote in wide, almost exaggerated print: M-c-L-A-R-E-N. And then, in the spaces under "given name": M-A-L-C-O-L-M.

MALCOLM McLAREN. Malcolm McLaren. Malcolm *McLaren.*

Looks good.

Hmm, he thought. *Now,* we're in business.

3
430

The dirty stripper who left her UNDIES on the railings to go hitch-hiking said, you don't THINK I have stripped off all these years just for MONEY do you?

—*Let It Rock* label, 1972

Past the crook in the far end of the King's Road, the part they call World's End, the part the tourists don't usually get to, farthest away from Sloane Square and past the trendy Take 6s, Top Gears, and Jean Machines, the shoe shops and antique marts, lies 430 King's Road: mausoleum of high style, tomb of trendiness, pyramid of pretense. Behind a plate glass window, a black T-shirt decorated with chain and chicken bone lettering spells out the name of the shop: Let It Rock.

The year is 1972, but inside it's supposed to be 1956. Some Billy Fury disk is bleating from the juke, all echo and strings, Malcolm's idea of a blast from the past, but no one listens. These Teddy Boys here—just as much an anachronism as that old radio with the twist-knob or the reddish Anglepoise lamp with the fifties shade near the till—want to know whether there's any beer in the garish pink 'n' black fridge at the back of the shop. No one listens to them either. Everyone nods in dim tribute to the photographs of James Dean and Brigitte Bardot glaring at the world from their frames of glued-up looking-glass shards (some of McLaren's handiwork from the Portobello Road days).

Next to the pinned-up fake leopard skin, the advert for Vince's Man Shop of Carnaby Street (now defunct), the torn-out photographs from *Men's Only* and *Light & Sound,* the display case with the fifties rayon ties, the metal studs, and the neon green striped socks, one of the Teds is looking over a nearly barren rack of lovingly copied drape jackets—bright turquoise (or black or green or pink) lurex with high lapels and fake leopard skin (or velveteen or sequined) collars. Pegged trousers in equally lurid colors. Weird apricot jeans covered in frilly black lace. Boxes upon boxes of mint 78's and new 45's. "Teddy Boys For Ever!" reads the shop flier. "Viva le Rock!"

Search for an explanation of how McLaren and Westwood inherited this troubled parcel of real estate, how they stumbled upon the idea of catering to Teddy Boys when Teds were the walking dinosaurs of street style, and in the end, you'll find yourself balancing McLaren's retrospective alibis—political motives construed in the vocabulary of style—against the sheer fortuity of his situation. For, like most of his big breaks in music, fashion, and film, acquiring 430 King's Road wasn't part of any master plan so much as it was the result of this lucky entrepreneur's strange instinct for finding the golden egg in markets everyone else had always assumed to be saturated.

Teddy Boys got their name and some elements of their style from King Edward VII (1901–10), a famously flamboyant dresser who spent sixty years waiting for his mother, Queen Victoria, to die or call him to the throne. What had started as London's response to the zoot look, sparked apparently by postwar dandies from the Brigade of Guards parading through Mayfair in long drape jackets, narrow trousers, and little stringties had become, by the mid-fifties, an outfit for working-class wide-boys angry with the soft underbelly of postwar capitalism: fingertip-length jackets with velvet collars, contrasting pocket trim, and Van Dyke cuffs; squiggly bootlace string-ties; tight pegged jeans and inch-high crepe-soled brothel creepers. All topped off with a quiff and d.a. (duck's arse) slathered in pungent Brylcreem.

By 1972, the few remaining Teds were either kids dressed by their stuck-in-the-groove fathers, or proles so provincial they were rural, or evolutionary neanderthals long irrelevant to the internecine rivalries of Britain's style subcultures—Rockers, Mods, Rude Boys, Skinheads, Suedeheads. Seeing one or more, usually two, was almost like seeing someone in eighteenth-century costume. They were museum pieces, so behind the times of flower power and cannabis sativa that the forefront of fashion had come to find them interesting again, while all around a new range of shops and styles came to take their place: Granny Takes a Trip, a glamorous fantasy boutique of high-wedged boots and bizarrely appliquéd velveteen jackets; Biba, the nostalgic emporium of neosepia Victoriana; (I Was) Lord Kitchener's Valet; Alkasura; Great Gear Trading Company; and Verne Lambert's retro first floor at the Chelsea Antique Market—always popular at teatime. And, of course, Trevor Myles's Paradise Garage at 430 King's Road.

Year after year London's self-proclaimed tastemakers had kept an eye on the far end of King's Road as the shops at 430 changed owners and styles. By the time McLaren and Westwood came along, the sometime greengrocers had been a restaurant, an unnamed clothes shop owned by ex–naval officer Bill Fuller and his girlfriend Carol Derry—"the cheapest clothes in London this side of Biba"—and, in the Summer of Love, hip haberdasher Michael Rainey moved his menswear boutique, Hung on You, from Chelsea's Cale Street to 430 King's Road.

Sparsely furnished in Day-Glo everything, with scarcely any clothes on display (save the frilly shirts and pastel-colored double-breasted suits popularized by the model agency English Boy), Hung on You has been called a "dipsomaniac's nightmare" *(Evening Standard),* "a hippie boutique for upper-class bucks" *(Over 21)*—not the best strategy at a time when the King's Road was getting increasingly cheesy. Within a year, it closed and Rainey disappeared, later surfacing in Wales.

Then a buffoonish East End entrepreneur named Tommy Roberts stepped forward, with his gift of the gab, his twenty-two-year-old partner Trevor Myles, and their wildly successful boutique Mr Freedom.

Until Mr Freedom opened in 1969, Tommy Roberts was just another overweight Cockney, a former antiques salesman who had owned a Carnaby Street boutique called Kleptomania. As Carnaby Street began to look more and more like a tourist circus, Roberts bought out Rainey's lease on the King's Road shop and, at the suggestion of Trevor Myles, who had recently seen filmmaker-photographer William Klein's underground political cartoon *Mister Freedom,* reopened 430 as Mr Freedom.

To great fanfare, with eight-foot blue stuffed gorillas, giant-sized television counters, and (so wrote journalist Miles Chapman in a magazine history of the place in 1981) "leopard print hot-pants, star-spangled kipper ties, unisex butcher boy caps, T-shirts with clashing satin appliqués of sundaes and rockets and Mickey and Minnie and Donald and Goofy and catch-phrases of the period like 'Slip It To Me' and 'Pow,'" Mr Freedom opened and Tommy Roberts became an overnight media star, Mr Freedom himself.

But being a small-time success wasn't quite enough for big Tommy and within a year he closed the King's Road shop to move Mr Freedom to the more mainstream location of Kensington Church Street where, like Biba, the tiny boutique grew into a mini–department store selling red, white, and blue bedroom sets, dungarees, and ice-cream sundaes.

Six months into the new Mr Freedom, Trevor Myles decided he'd had enough—"it became an ego-orientated business instead of a financially orientated business," he says—and quit. Myles and his American roommate Marty Frommer (soon to become Myles's buyer for Paradise Garage, and much later, back in the States, one of McLaren's cohorts in his attempt to manage the New York Dolls) smuggled large quantities of metal biker studs through Heathrow Airport, selling them to different stores under the name Mr Stud'em, a moniker deliberately intended to get Tommy Roberts's goat. With the money made from Mr Stud'em and £5000 lent by two silent partners, Myles reopened the dormant 430 King's Road as Paradise Garage.

With its petrol-pump cum Bali Hai design, its flocked, tiger-striped '66 Mustang halfback parked outside, and bamboo-caged lovebirds hanging above crowded racks of classic used American jeans, bowling jackets, and Hawaiian shirts, Paradise Garage epitomized Brit fantasies of American youth culture—the whole look put one in mind of what James Dean might have worn on a tropical holiday—and it too was an instant hit.

But Trevor Myles couldn't leave well enough alone, couldn't resist the potent lure of celebrity, and early in 1971 he began to mess around with the formula of Paradise, painting the place shiny disco black, installing an old jukebox, and selling the blackest clothes he could find. "It was much cooler and in some ways indicated what King's Road was going through as a whole," Myles says today. "But of course, what I should have done was to keep it the way it was—I'd be a rich man by now."

Instead, Myles let the store deteriorate, becoming increasingly caught up in a short-lived marriage to a young Danish woman named Lisa whose maiden name he can't remember.

"Trevor was totally off the wall," remembers Bradley Mendelson, his American shop assistant (now a commercial real estate broker in Manhattan). "I was supposed to be working for him but maybe a partner—roles were never really defined, everyone assumed the position they wanted to be. At the end of the day we were taking money out of the till to pay for the girls who were doing the seamstress work and pay for the night's entertainment and then on to the next day."

With Paradise Garage going steadily broke and Trevor Myles preoccupied with his new bride, Malcolm McLaren, stumbling down King's Road with his old Harrow Art College pal Patrick Casey and looking for a shop willing to subdivide its space, dropped in to talk with Myles about selling the old radios and pictures he and Vivienne were peddling along with Viv's earrings down the Portobello Road Saturday afternoons. Myles had never met Malcolm before but McLaren was such a fast talker—"and honestly," says Myles, "I just couldn't be bothered at the time"—that when Marty Frommer suddenly came up with some tickets for Trevor and Lisa to take a three-week honeymoon to Jamaica—the result of a deal with a friendly black pimp who was willing to trade the use of some stolen credit cards for an introduction to a new Scandinavian girl-about-town—Myles simply left word with Bradley Mendelson that McLaren could use the rear part of the shop to sell his own merchandise. Rent was to be £40 a week, but no one remembers McLaren ever coughing up so much as tuppence.

"Nobody was very bothered about it because the store had really lost its aim at that point in time," says Mendelson. "It had became very uncomfortable to be there, very unpleasant. People weren't getting paid, tempers were getting short, and there was no money at that point. Trevor had been really positive about how he wanted to go with the store and was making T-shirts and stuff, so when he got crazy the direction really waned. And that's why, when Malcolm came in, no one really knew what he was doing and no one really cared. The shop had become kind of junky."

During the three weeks that Trevor Myles vacationed in Jamaica, McLaren consolidated his grip on 430 King's Road, steadily moving his merchandise from the back of the shop to the front. Mendelson remembers trying to find Trevor Myles but Myles was not to be found.

"I didn't disappear, exactly," says Myles. "But what happened was that because I had no money, I told my wife that if she had money and she wanted to go out and party with her girlfriend, she should go and do it. And every night, she got in later and later, until finally I asked this friend of mine who was a Teddy Boy, a hairdryer repairman who'd do anything I asked him, to follow my wife. And he tracked her down at Tramps [a London disco]. She had fallen for some Baron von Something-or-other. So I found her out, went completely bananas and off she went—leaving me high and dry."

Malcolm McLaren was the least of Myles's worries.

"I was so caught up with my own situation, going around in my '55 T-bird, looking for the wife I had lost, that I really didn't take any notice. And so I didn't even ask him for any money because *I* had no money at the time, and I could see no real way of getting any out of Malcolm. I was devastated and I couldn't see any way out of it."

Within a matter of months (some say weeks), Paradise was no more, and McLaren and Westwood had acquired 430 King's Road in all but legal deed. With a small chalkboard advertising sign set on the pavement outside the shop, these two neophytes of commerce signaled their intentions to change the entire history of fashion and music: Let It Rock, said the message scrawled on the signboard. Let It Rock. No one could ever have guessed how loudly that cry would soon be heard.

At first, business was terribly slow. There wasn't really any gimmick yet: no Teds, no Rockers, certainly no punks—just a heap of old second-hand clothes, torn-up posters, radios, and records. The detritus of rock 'n' roll nostalgia.

But soon McLaren and Westwood learned that to sell clothes they had to be clean and in generally good repair. Collars had to be replaced, buttons sewn, flares turned into straight-legged trousers. Malcolm would give Vivienne instructions to brighten the fabrics or change a collar and Vivienne would run home to her dye pot and sewing machine. (Until they actually acquired the shop, Vivienne was still teaching school; at one point, she even took—and failed—the entrance exams to the LSE.)

Having stumbled on the second wave of an old cult, they had to capitalize on these Teddy Boy dreams. Even if McLaren didn't actually *like* them all that much—they were customers, not friends—he was shrewd enough to know that the Teds had to be courted if business was to bloom, and who better to do that than Vivienne? Once the shop was shut and the kids fed, it was down on the tube to the Teds' Liverpool Street hangouts where Westwood would beat Let It Rock's drum while McLaren watched from the corner of a smoky pub, nursing a gin and tonic, carefully avoiding being beaten up.

Vivienne's charm worked so well that within a short time small groups of Teds were waiting for the shop to open on Saturday mornings, banging on the doors to be let in, clamoring for a look at the drape suits she had cannibalized from the second-hand rags McLaren dug up on his market days with Patrick Casey. Once open, however, it wasn't just a few odd Teddy Boys who passed through that door. Now began the parade of self-conscious trendies, tastemakers, and rebellious teenagers that still haunt 430 King's Road to this day. Rock 'n' roll clothing had always been a big draw in London's style-ridden street culture, but usually the public had been pulled into the shops by sheer star power. Let It Rock's genius was McLaren's fervent, direct appeal to the *kids,* and the kids alone, to swathe themselves in clothes that signified rock's rebellion. Once the kids turned their backs on the bloated commerce of the bubble-gum pop industry, once they started *believing* in the subversive energy set in motion by these seemingly nostalgic clothes (which Vivienne was now making from scratch), the kids would become the real stars.

McLaren had finally arrived at the gutter aesthetic he has hewed close to ever since: clothing for the well-dressed mob, a politically motivated style pitched as self-consciously as possible to rock 'n' roll's lumpenkids.

Let It Rock's business now began to boom. "Teddy Boys for Ever! The Rock Era Is Our Business!" yelled the store's advertising brochure. McLaren became increasingly accomplished at finding mint records, rock artifacts, and Teddy Boy clothes for growing numbers of connoisseurs and art directors, and Let It Rock was soon designing costumes for films (Ken Russell's *Mahler* and *That'll Be the Day,* starring David Essex and Ringo Starr) and television dance shows. There was publicity—McLaren modeled for a glossy men's magazine—and stars: David Bowie, Iggy Pop, Bryan Ferry, and in early November 1972, the New York Dolls, passing through London on their way to the provinces where they were booked as an opening act for Lou Reed and Rod Stewart.

But the euphoria was not destined to last. For quite some time, Rose and Mick Isaacs had been living down the road from Vivienne and Malcolm in South Clapham, and within the limited degree of communication Malcolm had with his parents, there was an unspoken agreement that he and Viv would look after the frail old couple. It was not a task either of them relished. Mick was apparently something less than a gem. Fred Vermorel remembers that he used to sit "virtually comatose in a chair, with his eyes open and then bellow 'WHERE'S MY FUCKING TEA?' without any warning whatsoever." In spring 1972, he suddenly took ill and died, and Rose plunged into depression. "She wouldn't take help from Malcolm's mother because she was being loyal to Malcolm," says Vermorel, "but she wouldn't take care of herself either. It fell to Malcolm to care for her, but he had less and less time."

On December 12, 1972, after several weeks when Malcolm had put off taking the five-minute walk to Rose's flat, he finally decided to bestow her with a visit. According to Vermorel, once inside, Malcolm was shocked to find his beloved grandmother, "naked and bolt upright in bed . . . dead from starvation." Malcolm was apparently so ashamed of himself and so angry at his parents he didn't even attend Rose's funeral. It's not hard to see why his parents still don't talk with him.

Over the next six months, Malcolm and Vivienne's enthusiasm for Let It Rock seemed to dwindle. Even before they left for a three-week trip to New York's annual National Boutique Show, traveling with Gerry Goldstein, a North London boy who presented himself at the shop one day telling Malcolm how many childhood friends they shared, Malcolm had already begun to despair of the Teds ever living up to his fantasy of inspired rebelliousness. Hidebound in their political conservatism, sexists and racists to a man, the Teds totally missed McLaren's point about the subversive energy of their beer-swilling life-style and retro clothes. Before he left, he even went so far as to change the shop's name—if not yet the shop itself—to Too Fast To Live, Too Young To Die, but mostly because the local council was complaining about the old iron bars hanging over the shop front.

New York was a revelation, the first time McLaren came face-to-face with a culture that took it for granted that young people were an important market simply because of their age. Hanging out at Nobody's (the current downtown nightspot), watching the stars come and go, mixing freely with the kids, McLaren must have realized for the first time the enormity and immense potential of the youth market. In England, being young was virtually a crime; in America, it was a ticket to success.

Gerry Goldstein remembers the Boutique Show, held on several floors of New York's McAlpin Hotel, as a "mad, mad scene, with lots of drugs," a big boost to Malcolm's ego, a place to get orders for what he still called Let It Rock, and grab a chance to meet (or at least see) everyone from Patti Smith to Eric Emerson and Andy Warhol. (When he returned to London, Malcolm bragged that Vivienne was going to be in a film to be made by someone in Warhol's circle.)

But it was also at the Boutique Show, amid all the long-haired entrepreneurs selling (according to *Women's Wear Daily*) pearl-handled roach clips and strawberry rolling papers, bell-bottomed blue jeans and tie-dyed leathers, that Malcolm McLaren first came in direct contact with the New York Dolls. For years, guitarists Sylvain Sylvain (né Steve Mizrahi) and Johnny Thunders had been coming to the shows to sell a line of multicolor handknit sweaters they produced under the Truth & Soul label; this time, they had come just to buy, and they were surprised to see among the shops represented there Let It Rock. The last thing these two expected was that the Let It Rock they had visited in London would be the same Let It Rock upstairs in a sleazy New York hotel room, but there, in a tiny chamber blasting with Bill Haley and plastered with pics of Little Richard, Jerry Lee Lewis, and old nudie pinups, was the strange sparrow-headed fashion maverick whose shop they had visited in London. At long last, Let It Rock seemed to be on the way to actually rocking. But by then it was time to go home.

Returning to the gloom and doom of London—now mired in a wave of increasingly unmanageable strikes, power cuts, and three-day workweeks—could only be depressing by comparison. Life was all work and no play, and McLaren began to resent nearly every aspect of a shopowner's existence, a complaint he now began to spout loudly at Vivienne whenever she was around—which turned out to be less and less as he stayed out later and later with one of his shop assistants, a young American girl named Addie.

"Malcolm was terribly, terribly intense about that shop," says Westwood, "but then he got fed up with it, disillusioned with the Teddy Boys, number one, because although they were some expression of revolt against society, all they really wanted was free clothes and giveaways from the record companies. But number two, they were a cult, and cults want rules and all they ever wanted to know was that they were doing everything right. And he wasn't interested in that, so the shop got into something else."

That something else was biker wear, the rough-and-ready leather jeans and jackets the Rockers had ripped straight off the back of the *Wild Ones*–era Marlon Brando, a definition of American cool. Unlike the Teddy Boys, bikers were something McLaren thought every lad could relate to—even the Americans could get it. Once again, Vivienne was left with the responsibility of producing the clothes and seducing yet another scorned subculture to the shop while Malcolm racked his brains for a way to elevate these démodé Rockers, who'd virtually disappeared since their pitched battles with the Mods in the early sixties, to the status of revolutionary heroes.

Unbeknownst to Vivienne, though, Malcolm was already pining away for something else. Perhaps he already knew that he wanted to manage a band; perhaps it was Addie, who had gone back to America; perhaps he was realizing that the bikers were even worse than the Teds, not only lazy but violent too.

More likely, Malcolm was suffused with nostalgia for New York and for the New York Dolls. The Dolls were quickly becoming an obsession for Malcolm McLaren, his fantasy rock 'n' roll band: a group of virtual teenagers (all between the ages of eighteen and twenty-two) literally teetering off its own rancorous energy, forthrightly declaring itself of, by, and for "the kids." It didn't matter that the Dolls weren't great musicians. That wasn't the point. The Dolls didn't give a shit about anything—except perhaps their clothes—and they let the world know it every chance they got. That first U.K. tour was a shining example of how the Dolls could live up to their bad-boy reputation in mythic proportions: On the heels of a triumphant performance supporting Rod Stewart at the Empire Pool,

Wembley, their drummer, Billy Murcia, died in a bathtub, overdosed on a drug cocktail of methaqualone, morphine, and alcohol.

Malcolm McLaren never even laid eyes on the Dolls during that first tour—the band was whisked away to New York early the next morning before the tabloids and Scotland Yard could get them—and he never had the chance to meet them in person until his brief encounter with Sylvain and Thunders at the Boutique Show, but from the very moment he left New York to the moment the Dolls arrived back in London later that year, he avidly followed their every move through the rock grapevine.

Formed from the shards of several rival bands in February 1972, the original New York Dolls—Sylvain Sylvain (guitar), Arthur Kane (bass), Billy Murcia (drums), Johnny Thunders (guitar), and David Johansen (lead vocals)—played their first real gig in late May at the Palm Room of the Diplomat Hotel on West Forty-third Street. Typically, the Dolls got "bomb reviews," but two weeks later they scored a standing ovation opening for Eric Emerson's Magic Tramps at the Mercer Arts Center. That was the kind of band the New York Dolls were: one night they might be branded hopeless incompetents, the next they were the future of rock 'n' roll.

Onstage, the Dolls were a laugh-a-minute, five sub-urban rejects who deliberately toyed with their audiences' expectations of what a rock 'n' roll band should be. Were they straight or gay? Junkies or aristocrats? Postmodern parodists or mere incompetents? Half the fun was to keep the audience (as well as themselves) guessing. As critic Robert Christgau wrote in an incisive essay on the band, "To be a Doll was to appear twenty-four hours a day in an improvised psychodrama, half showbiz and half acting out, that merely got wilder in front of the microphones."

With their cock-clutching jeans, lipstick smiles, blue eyeliner stares, and weird thrift-shop threads—pink tights, high heels, gold lamé jackets, strapped-on dolls, sleeveless tuxedo shirts, and black sequined top hats—the Dolls looked like a twisted teenage vision of showbiz hell, postapocalyptic kissing cousins of Marlene Dietrich, Bette Davis, and Andy Warhol, five characters in search of a story. Each Doll played his role to the hilt: Syl and Billy were the clownish rock stars with Harpo Marx hairdos; David, the rubber-faced mug with a shoulder-length pageboy, took the role of benevolent ringleader and champion sex symbol; Johnny was the J.D. with a rat's nest of black hair, noise-bombing his way to within a step of disaster;

and Arthur was, well, Arthur, a long-haired creep with heavily kohled eyes hiding backstage with his bass and a bottle.

The Dolls had certainly cobbled together a carousing sound—a cross between the full-tilt R&B of the Rolling Stones, the power-chord hard rock of the MC5, Bob Seger, and the Stooges, and the doo-wop soul of the Shangri-Las and Archie Bell & the Drells, whom they often covered—but it was hardly what one would call dance music. Nor could one say that the rest of America was quite ready to hear Johansen's cross-dressed fantasies of "Frankenstein" ("now I'm asking you as a person/ is it a crime for you to fall in love with Frankenstein"), the media-sick protagonist of "Personality Crisis" ("flashin' on the friend of a friend"), or just plain-old "Trash" ("Trash you gotta pick it up/ take them lights away/ Trash gotta pick it up/ gotta put that knife away"). At the end of the day, the Dolls seemed destined to be a minority taste, despite the growing fascination for glam brought on by David Bowie's gaming transvestitism.

Still, by that June, the Dolls had developed an audience top-heavy with rock luminaries—John Cale, Lou Reed, Bette Midler, Todd Rundgren, and even Bowie himself. Holding forth on Tuesday nights in the mirrored milk-bar ambience of the Oscar Wilde Room (capacity 100) and at Max's Kansas City, the Dolls paraded through a brief Saran-Wrap period and did their best to find a record contract. Various labels expressed interest in the group but none seemed to take them very seriously, if only because their shows often began at least two hours late. To the A&R personnel of the major record companies (most of whom had never even contemplated the idea of a cult band, much less one that played in seedy bars and artsy theaters dressed in drag), the Dolls were just another bunch of plug-ugly glitter rockers with ridiculous rooster-top hairdos. And possibly that's what they would have been without the efforts of an ex–record plugger and A&R man (for Paramount Records) named Marty Thau.

On the very day that Thau left his job at Paramount, he and his wife were walking through the Village, looking for somewhere to celebrate. They picked the Mercer—where the Dolls were having one of their good nights.

"I was walking out thinking to myself, they're either the greatest band I've ever seen or the worst thing I've ever seen," Thau says with a grave face. "I couldn't make up my mind. And when I got to the door, I grabbed my wife and we went backstage and approached them and told them that I was really intrigued. About three weeks later, I met them at Max's Kansas City and we spoke a little bit further and it seemed to me that they were more than just someone to do singles with, so I presented them with the idea of managing them and they said, yes, let's do it."

Thau was so sure of the Dolls' potential that he immediately sought the help of Steve Leber and David Krebs, two business acquaintances who had also recently left jobs, as big-time booking agents at the William Morris Agency, to start their own management firm, Leber Krebs. All three now became partners with the Dolls in Dollhouse Productions and Lipstick Killer Publishing. Leber Krebs was to handle the accounting, booking, legal counsel, and tours; Thau would deal with the group itself— its music, image, press, promotions, and recording; the Dolls would just try to be themselves.

Thau (and Leber Krebs) spent much time and money on the Dolls, buying them clothes, helping them to hone their rough-edged sound, trying (unsuccessfully) to get them to recognize the crucial importance of rehearsal and of arriving at gigs on time, but the Dolls still couldn't get a record contract. Buddah thought the *band* was great but was scared by Johansen; MCA loved *Johansen* but hated the band. Atlantic said they were too crude; Columbia, too loud; Capitol, too weird. RCA and Polydor were interested but never followed through. That left Warner Brothers and the Chicago-based Mercury: not enough companies to stimulate the kind of bidding war Thau wanted, despite a fierce campaign waged on the band's behalf by Paul Nelson, a former *Rolling Stone* music writer who had become Mercury's New York A&R man.

By the end of July, a rave write-up by Roy Hollingworth in London's *Melody Maker* made a British tour the obvious next step. That October, the Dolls did their first U.K. tour, playing before capacity houses in the provinces as a warm-up act for Rod Stewart and Lou Reed. The Dolls made the covers of *New Musical Express* and *Melody Maker* and offers immediately began pouring in. The Rolling Stones opened negotiations to get the Dolls on their private label; Phonogram was hot on Thau's tail; Ahmet Ertegun of Atlantic Records sent a telegram saying he would sign the Dolls sight unseen for $50,000. But Thau held out—he wanted five times as much. The night of November 6, 1972, Thau, Leber, and Krebs were talking with Kit Lambert and Danny Secunda to sign the Dolls to Track Records when word arrived that Billy Murcia had died. The next morning, all deals were off, and the Dolls were shoved onto a 7:00 A.M. flight back to New York.

The Dolls were shaken by Billy's death, but by December they had regrouped with a new drummer, Jerry Nolan, considered by some to be something of a hard nut, and began gigging again, at the Mercer, Kenny's Castaways, and Max's. Little seemed to have changed, until Paul Nelson convinced Mercury's head of publicity to fly into New York to see the band play in late January. Four other Mercury executives had already turned down the Dolls, but this time Nelson was successful and on March 20, 1973, they signed to Mercury—although for far less than Thau had originally planned.

The Dolls rushed into the studio (Mercury gave them only a week to record and mix) with Todd Rundgren at the controls—a last-minute choice after they had been turned down by Phil Spector and Leber & Stoller—and by nearly all accounts they came away with a product that did little justice to the cacophonous din they were capable of creating onstage. Most critics crowed about the album *New York Dolls,* inevitably citing comparisons to the Stones, the Velvet Underground, and Bowie's Ziggy Stardust character, but even today, the record seems unevenly mixed, bluesy where it should have highlighted Thunders's distorted, spill-over guitar style, noisy when Johansen is waxing lyrical. From its black-and-white cover photo of the Dolls looking bored under a lipstick autograph of their logo to its one cover song of Bo Diddley's "Pills," *New York Dolls* had style aplenty, but it never managed to transcend the band's cultish origins and sold 100,000 copies in the United States.

Nearly everyone thought the Dolls could do better, including the Dolls themselves: The only disagreement was about finding the right recipe for success. Long tours through the summer of 1973—sell-out shows at the Whiskey in Los Angeles and support gigs at Madison Square Garden for Mott the Hoople—helped spread the band's cult following nationwide, but it was still only a cult, and by this time, Mercury was becoming increasingly impatient with a band that seemed determined to service the fantasies of its fans with high living and big budgets. According to Paul Nelson, the label had come to the decision that the Dolls "understood nothing of the music business and recording, seemed naive or unable to learn about either, and were rarely encouraged to exhibit any kind of self-control regarding the bankbook or the clock. To say that their record company thought them a mere critics' hype, did not understand them, and eventually grew to hate them would be an understatement."

With the split between the Dolls and Mercury becoming more acrimonious each day and new fights developing between Thau and Leber Krebs over the band's steadily escalating bills, the Dolls decided to return to Europe to finish off the job they had begun a year ago. Once again, it was a shrewd move on Thau's part: The first tour had proven that in England, unlike in America, good critical reception still had commercial impact. Had it not been for Billy Doll's death the first time around, the Dolls would have had a first-class record contract. This time, Thau reasoned, the Dolls would ride a wave of publicity—both positive and negative—straight up the charts.

In London, Malcolm McLaren was ready and waiting, primed by transatlantic phone calls from other Dolls groupies like Frankie Pizzaia, one of the few New York shopkeepers to import Let It Rock's merchandise to America.

Two weeks before the New York Dolls arrived in London, McLaren ferried himself over to Paris to call on a new acquaintance, fashion designer Jean-Charles de Castelbajac. McLaren had never actually met Castelbajac, but sometime in 1972 the young designer had visited London and passed by 430 King's Road, where he was stunned to see some armless T-shirts decorated with bicycle chains, inner tubes, and even the chicken bones that spelled out *Let It Rock* hanging in the shop window. Until that moment, Castelbajac had thought *he* was the only fashion designer working with what he calls "bondage material, everything from things to wash the floor with to clothes and blankets. Everything not done for fashion, I love," he declares in heavily accented English. Unfortunately, McLaren was out at the time, so Castelbajac left him a little message: "I love the thing you do," he remembers writing. "I think we have some common *pensives,* and I would love to meet you."

Castelbajac was certain he would never hear from McLaren, but late one October night, a man in a leather blazer with strange pants and curly red hair knocked on his door. "I noticed that he had a red magnum of Johnny Walker and that his hair was the same color as the bottle," says Castelbajac. "He said, 'Hallo, I'm Malcolm McLaren,' and I didn't remember who he was. But I invited him in anyway and we ended up talking until early the next morning. He stayed for a day and a half at my place and he started calling me 'Charlie,' which nobody else does. And on the last day he told me, 'Charlie, I'm going to come back to see you in two weeks—with the New York Dolls.' "

Mission accomplished, McLaren came back to London to wait for the Dolls' arrival, and from the moment they arrived, he and Vivienne were inseparable from the boys in the band, partying with them at Blake's Hotel, hanging out backstage after their triumphant concert at Biba's Rainbow Room in Kensington High Street, and selling them clothes at a good discount. And when it came time for the Dolls to go to Paris, McLaren escorted everyone to his friend Charlie's, where Castelbajac laid on a small feast, even making a new costume for David Doll—a tuxedo that turned into a Marlene Dietrich outfit. McLaren reciprocated by arranging a big birthday dinner for Castelbajac at La Coupole; Mercury wound up footing the bill.

Some have looked rather cynically on McLaren's early relationship with the Dolls, but at the time, almost everyone was impressed by his enthusiasm for and generosity toward the boys. McLaren and the Dolls had really hit it off. They were kids, *his* kids, and he loved them, loved it when Johansen sang "Looking for a Kiss" ("I didn't come here looking for no f-f-fix/ 'cause I've been poundin' the streets/ all night in the rain/ looking for a k-k-kiss"), loved the Dolls' love of excess.

"Malcolm was like a father to them," says Castelbajac with obvious emotion. "A very positive father. In fact, I first start to love Malcolm in the sense that I always see him attached to the band he was with—like being attached to the family he never had." But Sylvain Sylvain puts this another way: "There never was a bigger Dolls groupie than Malcolm McLaren."

McLaren and Westwood stayed with the Dolls until the band returned to the States, but once back in London, Malcolm started talking with Vivienne about Let It Rock's future. It had been a long if relatively quick journey from the bumbling entrepreneurialism of Let It Rock to the search for rock 'n' roll's sartorial subversions at Too Fast To Live, Too Young To Die, and now in the wake of the Dolls, it all seemed so suddenly passé. There had to be *more*—to the scenemakers of British rock it was as if the Dolls had pinpointed some essential deficiency in the British imagination—and McLaren began to cast around for the people and places in his own universe that could equal the Dolls' dystopian fantasies.

During the spring of 1974, McLaren decided to close Too Fast To Live, Too Young To Die and rethink the entire shop. Shutting down was a financial gamble, especially considering the poor state of the shop's accounting and Britain's ever rising rate of inflation, but McLaren insisted that there was no going back to mere Teddy Boy mischief. The Dolls had left his sartorial historicism in the dust, and he was damned if a bunch of New York punks were going to show him up. A catalogue for "Scandalous Lingerie and Glamour Wear" from the Estelle lingerie shop in Walthamstow clicked a switch in McLaren's brain. If sex itself had become the raison d'être of the revolution, the Dolls' revolution, Let It Rock would now have to *become* SEX, for that was to be 430's new name.

When the shop reopened late that summer, it was almost unrecognizable. From the giant fluorescent pink padded plastic Claes Oldenberg–

style letters that hung over the shop door to the black sponge foam and children's monkey bars that covered the walls, SEX was intended as a sexual romper room for liberated teens, an ultranasty emporium of polymorphous perversity, replete with parallel bars for trouser racks, a big rubber-covered sofa, and a flying trapeze. SEX still sold drape suits, biker clothes, and brothel creepers, but there were also new additions: outlandishly coloured zoot suits; leather shirts and pants with oddly placed zips and studs; kinky French underwear; black latex S&M clothes, rubber masks, whips, chains, and handcuffs; and, most important, a line of T-shirts McLaren had silk-screened by Glen Matlock, a bright seventeen-year-old who had started working for Let It Rock as a Saturday-boy and who was now attending St. Martin's College of Art. (Matlock was also helped by McLaren's friend Bernard Rhodes, a well-read former blues buff and Granny's shop clerk who had dropped out of the pop life to open a Renault repair shop.)

These T-shirts were lewd: Some were printed with scraps of pornographic writing by Alexander Trocchi, one of the few Britons accepted by both the literary establishment and the Situationists; later, others were printed with an image of two half-naked cowboys standing dick to dick, or of Snow White getting it on with the Seven Dwarfs. Later still, others bore slogans commending the joys of mother-fucking. "Pornography," McLaren was fond of saying, "is the laughter of the bathroom of your mind."

"It was Malcolm beginning to feel that he could make, had *always* wanted to make a political statement," says Vivienne. "The idea was that it was 'Rubberwear for the Office,' that to walk down the street in this stuff was subversive. I mean, when you do a jersey with some fist-fucking drawing on it, it's bound to be controversial. You're saying that people have autonomy to do whatever they like and that you don't believe in censorship. Malcolm's idea was that we've all got our little secrets."

If ever there were a perfect moment to pick a fight with the British establishment, McLaren had it now. Deeply polarized by runaway inflation and the energy crisis ensuing from the Arab oil embargo of 1973, Britain now turned out Edward Heath's Conservative government after the second miners' strike in two years. In these shrill times, SEX was bound to hit a sore spot, and on more than one occasion, the shop was visited by the Metropolitan Police porn squad, seeking to bust (or at least fine) the proprietors for violating the obscenity laws.

Like *A Clockwork Orange* gone Fredericks of Hollywood crazy, SEX was the kind of succès de scandale McLaren had always dreamed of— everyone from well-dressed businessmen on covert pornshop crawls to fashion victims and curious kids trooped through the shop—but he still felt dissatisfied, unfulfilled by the pinprick stabs of this new attempt to *épater le bourgeois.* Having taken the risk of closing down for two months—and having been taken for a ride by a greedy contractor—the shop now staggered under the weight of its bills. What had all the risk-taking been for if there were still all these responsibilities to be taken care of? What had happened to the adventure? Running the shop was a bit easier now that he and Viv were able to hire new part-timers like Chrissie Hynde (later lead singer of the Pretenders) and a full-time manager—an ex-thief and drug-dealer named Michael Collins—but it was still only running a shop.

Instead of becoming more dangerous, more rock 'n' roll, SEX began to draw an increasingly arty crowd, artists and designers like Duggie Fields, Andrew Logan, Michael Kostif and his wife Gerlinda von Regensburg and their friends—a clique dressed so oddly that style journalist Peter York later christened them "Thems" because "if you were to see them on the street you'd say something like 'funny red hair,' and someone else would say, 'Oh, yes it's *Them.'*" Thems were a world unto themselves, excessively literate in the language of style, but to McLaren, Thems were only as interesting or important as their looks. He even found their substantial connections to the world of fashion "distant" and "cold," "too English" for his taste. Indeed, so troubled was he by these fine-feathered friends that one night he came back to the shop and daubed his frustration on the wall in bright silver spray paint: "Does Passion End In Fashion?" At the moment, his answer appeared to be that it did not.

As usual, the people who really captured McLaren's attention were the kids, in particular two seventeen-year-old toughs named Steve Jones and Paul Cook who had been stopping into the shop ever since the early days of Let It Rock in the hopes of nicking a new pair of baggy trousers or sueded creepers.

Jones and Cook had met at the age of ten when both had attended the Christopher Wren School in Shepherd's Bush. Now they were as thick as thieves, which was just as well since that was how Jones actually made his living. McLaren was fascinated by this teenager's tales of the outlaw life—Jones started stealing from a local Woolworth's by the age of eight, later graduated to robbing music stores and stealing cars, and was busted thirteen times by 1974—and Jones loved hanging out with McLaren.

"The first time I remember talking to 'im," Jones says in a thick

Shepherd's Bush accent, "was about where he got those baggy clothes from the fifties. I'd go in there [Let It Rock] every day and put records on the jukebox: Flaming Groovies, Alice Cooper, some Presley and early Stones, 'Great Balls of Fire' by Jerry Lee Lewis, and this one song called 'Valerie'—that was real important to 'im. It was like a hangout to me. It was cool, this place. But one of the main reasons I liked hanging out with him was because he used to go down to this club called the Speakeasy on Friday nights and you'd see a lot of rock stars down there. I was just fascinated by all of it and I wanted to be in it and I didn't know how, so I thought stealing the equipment would kind of get me in there somehow."

Eventually, McLaren and Jones began talking music and Jones confessed that he had been playing drums and singing in a little band with Cook's brother-in-law, Del Noone, on bass, and another boy named Wally Nightingale, a friend from the Christopher Wren days, on guitar. According to Jones, Wally was "a real wanker, with glasses"—"one look at him and you could see he weren't one of the lads"—but Wally's parents were middle class and had a big flat in East Acton, where rehearsals inevitably took place. Paul Cook also showed up on occasion, but at this stage he professed to be more interested in his electrician's apprenticeship at Watney's Brewery in Mortlake or in sunbathing in Wally's backyard than in being in a band. There were problems: Del could barely play his bass, and Jones had stolen the equipment before anyone had actually learned to play. Did Malcolm know anyone else? As it happened, he did, and he directed Jones to Glen Matlock, who had a vague memory of having played with Cook in some childhood football game long ago.

Throughout the spring of 1974, Jones, Matlock, and Wally Nightingale rehearsed over at Wally's place and at the Shesuma, a grungy Chelsea rehearsal studio near the Thames, until Wally's dad, a lighting contractor for Lee Electrics, then rewiring the BBC's old radio soundstages at Riverside Studios near Hammersmith tube, offered to let them practice there. By now, the stolid Paul Cook had been persuaded to take up the drums, and Jones—a weedy illiterate who then had a curl of bleached blond hair hanging over his forehead—was trying to be the lead singer. "I was terrified of being a singer," says Jones. "I didn't want to be one, but Wally was playing guitar and Paul was my best friend, so obviously he had to be in the band and he was drums. But for ages he drove me nuts because he could never pick it up. He was so slow at it, he didn't have any soul in him. I thought, he's never going to be a drummer."

Jones sang, Cook persevered, and as the newly named Swankers (after a dance they used to do when they were kids) began to stage regular rehearsals, Jones began asking McLaren to come down to Riverside Studios and have a listen. Months later, McLaren finally acquiesced, bringing Westwood with him, but what he heard was enough to send him off to hide behind the kegs of beer Cook had stolen from Watney's. Once Wally went home, however, McLaren began to make a few "casual" suggestions. "Listen man," he told Jones, "you're not going to make it without another singer. Get another singer, get rid of that guitarist. *You* play the guitar."

McLaren also gave them lessons about what it meant to be a group as opposed to a garage band. "We was playing all these old numbers, you know, Beatles," Cook told one interviewer. "He just said stop playing this shit and write your own stuff or get something together so you definitely know what you're doing. You know, we didn't know what we were doing, we just used to pick random numbers." (Among them: Bad Company's "Can't Get Enough," the Small Faces' "Whatcha Gonna Do About It?," "Alright Now" by Free, Billy Fury's "Do You Really Love Me Too?," "As Tears Go By" by the Stones, the Who's "Substitute," and even "Build Me Up Buttercup" by the Foundations.)

There was one other suggestion: Malcolm said the Swankers had to have a better name—*Kutie Jones* and the Swankers was more like it. "That's when his manipulating started, I guess," says Jones. "Kutie was meant to be 'cutie,' but I hated it because I didn't consider myself cute."

Rehearsals continued and Jones and Matlock kept begging McLaren to manage the band—"we thought he was loaded," says Matlock, "at least enough to make it happen"—but McLaren wasn't interested, especially as long as the Swankers retained the services of the legendarily ugly, bespectacled Wally. At one point, McLaren and Bernard Rhodes even talked *New Musical Express* rock writer Nick Kent into coming to Hammersmith to check out the Swankers, hoping that Kent's reed-thin rock 'n' roll presence might inspire 'the boys' to clean up their act.

"Kent just come down to see us play and after playing about twenty minutes, we was just sitting around and McLaren said to Kent to get Wally out of the way and go play the guitar," Jones remembers. "It was kind of good, kind of refreshing because it was like rock 'n' roll and Kent looked rock 'n' roll, and it was totally opposite from Wally. And we got off on that. That made us realize that Wally was a fucking joke and a nerd. He was just safe, Wally was, because he could play pretty good and his dad had the place."

(Nick Kent: "I actually tried to take over the group, and Malcolm got Glen to come round and tell me to leave. . . . Meanwhile, Malcolm was getting all these gay guys down who couldn't sing, living out this Larry Parnes myth." [Parnes was the classic fifties manager who cleverly named each of his singers after their onstage personas: Johnny Gentle, Vince Eager, Duffy Power, Billy Fury. . . .])

If Nick Kent couldn't convince the ferociously loyal Jones to kick Wally out of the Swankers, nothing could, so McLaren and Rhodes turned their attentions elsewhere, concocting a variety of harebrained schemes designed to move them to the centerstage of the pop world. One idea included a plot to get pop psychologist R. D. Laing to design a men's suit for SEX. Another focused on managing Robin Scott, now struggling for his own foothold in the music business. ("It was evident Malcolm knew nothing about music," says Scott. "Incredibly naive, dear Malcolm, just didn't know what the fuck was going on. I was playing with some other bloke, though, and they didn't like him and I wouldn't get rid of him.") In fact, the only plans McLaren and Rhodes carried out were those that related directly to SEX: the manufacture of a T-shirt emblazoned with the ominous typewritten slogan, "One Day You're Going To Wake Up and Realize Which Side Of the Bed You're On," followed by a long list of names divided into "hates" (including Jagger, Ferry, Fellini, and "all those fucking saints") and "loves" (Eddie Cochran, Durutti, Orton, Kutie Jones and his Sex Pistols, imagination). When they ran out of fashion ideas, the two would-be music moguls spray-painted the interior of SEX with slogans appropriated from the *S.C.U.M. Manifesto* of Andy Warhol's would-be assassin Valerie Solanis.

"I thought she was fantastic, actually," said McLaren. "I thought she wrote one of the most intense manifestos I've ever read, and I was inspired by her and I was inspired by voyeuristic novel writing and the whole incestuous nature of English culture, which ultimately rests upon the image of the closet case and therefore the idea of clothes being treated in a purely sexual manner. Because ultimately, that's really all that anybody wants to do, y'know, they design clothes to make people pretty. So if you can take that and show it for what it is, in its most rogueish and upfront manner, it can be a lot more intriguing. The idea of selling a rubber skirt to a girl who would then go walking into her office amused me, OK?"

It also amused Vivienne, who had, by now, absorbed Malcolm's ideas so well that she was already starting to create her own designs. "After he had picked a few of these [slogans], Malcolm asked me to make a T-shirt for them, and I suspect that this was a slight breakthrough in my designing, really," she says. "Because after about three days, I was exhausted and almost giving up and then I did the most basic T-shirt imaginable. Just two cotton squares with no seams, just sewn down the side and a bit on the shoulders."

The T-shirt was a breakthrough—even now it stands out as one of the most radical designs of seventies fashion—and Vivienne was growing more and more confident of her ability to be a designer: all good for SEX, but not nearly enough to stop Malcolm from going out on his own to explore the rock 'n' roll netherworld with kids like Jones and Cook, and old friends like Helen Wellington-Lloyd, Gerry Goldstein, Robin Scott, and Bernard Rhodes. Viv's professional competence simply did not rank with Malcolm's own emotional life.

Besides, Malcolm was really in love with Addie.

The mysterious Addie Isman. No one seems to remember her very well, and Addie herself is no longer around: According to her father, she died of an accidental barbiturate overdose sometime toward the end of the seventies. The daughter of a wealthy New Jersey family—her father owned a franchise of the Two Guys retail chain—Addie was a pretty, gentle girl with a strong interest in fashion. One thing is sure: McLaren finally told Vivienne he was in love with Addie and declared his determination to follow her to America, perhaps to take up painting again.

And why not? By now, McLaren had plenty of friends in New York: The Dolls were there, Marty Frommer (Trevor Myles's old shop assistant) was there, and there was a chance that he could sell some SEX clothes to Bloomingdale's, of all places. Who knew: Maybe he would even end up managing the New York Dolls?

Toward the end of 1974, McLaren flew to New York to seek his destiny, telling Bernard Rhodes to keep an eye on the Swankers until he returned—and telling Vivienne he might never return.

Back in America, the Dolls were disintegrating under the strain of trying to become a commercial band. A second album, the ironically titled *In: Too Much Too Soon,* dedicated to Diana Barrymore, star of the movie *Too Much Too Soon,* had been recorded with Shadow Morton (of Shangri-Las fame) producing, but of the disc's ten songs, four were clever covers of the kind of cheap B-movie scenarios the Dolls were at home in and the rest was typical Dolls speed trash—novelty smashes guaranteed to make adult listeners turn off their radios. Predictably, *Too Much Too Soon* shipped fewer units than the first album (about 58,000 copies). The backlash had begun.

As musicians, the Dolls had shown much improvement since their first disc; Nolan is often given credit for pulling the band together musically, and Shadow Morton had brought them alive on record despite the spasmodic lack of cooperation—Thunders: "First we had an acidhead [Rundgren], then a drunk [Morton]." But the Dolls were also increasingly prone to the kind of sordid situations that had resulted in Billy Murcia's death. Thunders and Nolan were playing games with speed and heroin; Arthur Kane was so incapacitated by alcohol that he woke up every morning with the DT's and bassist Peter Jordan had to stand in for him at most gigs; and Johansen and Sylvain, while relatively sober, were getting into regular fights over the band's direction. Jagger-style nightlife was Johansen's domain, and according to Sylvain, he even began talking with Steve Paul (then owner of a club called the Scene and later Johansen's manager for his reincarnation as Buster Poindexter) about a solo career. For his part, Sylvain hunkered down with his guitar at home, telling numerous journalists that he wanted to get into reggae.

Through the fall of 1974, the Dolls started losing their live audience. "The first album, only the crazies accepted us and straight America said, what the fuck is this?" Sylvain ruefully comments. "By this time, *they* accepted us and we lost the crazies. So more and more, as '74 passed, we started going back, playing in the same dinky little halls in the sticks we started out in, in places like Passaic and Jersey City."

More damaging than the band's drinking and drugging, and the steady erosion of their cult, was the widening split between Marty Thau and Leber Krebs. Where Leber (the main partner dealing with the Dolls) tended to read the backlash against the Dolls literally, interpreting it as evidence of the group's failure, Thau tried to read it manipulatively, instinctively searching for a silver lining in the dusky clouds. Thau knew that the music press regularly needed bad boys for good copy, and he was eager to exploit every instance of the Dolls' misbehavior as further proof of their rock 'n' roll street credibility. Leber, who had booked the Rolling Stones' American tours while at William Morris, thought Thau was a mere Pollyanna. Thau fired back that Leber had eyes only for the bankbook and was too uptight and bourgeois to take the risks needed to break the band. Tempers flared after a disastrous road trip to Los Angeles to tape a TV show.

"While we were out there, on very short notice, we booked four midnight shows at the Roxy," says Thau. "After the first show, which was a total sellout, I got a phone call from Lou Adler, who was one of the partners in the Roxy, saying the other three shows were canceled. He had *The Rocky Horror Show* and he didn't like the Dolls and was worried about what would happen to his club. It spread total confusion along Record Row on Sunset Strip.

"When we came back to New York, Steve Leber greeted me with,

'Well we're dead in L.A., now.' And I said, 'No, we're not dead in L.A. at all. It just adds to the legend. It depends how you want to look at it, whether you want to parlay it or be saddled with it. As a matter of fact,' I said, 'there was a big promoter, Sepp Donahauer, sitting at a front-row table in L.A., and he loved the show. Not only can we go back to L.A. at any time we want, but this guy will probably even book the Dolls into a bigger place.' " Leber challenged Thau, and Thau called Donahauer in L.A., and promptly booked the Dolls into the Palladium. It was the beginning of the end for Dollhouse Productions.

Over the next few months the rift between Thau and Leber Krebs grew. Leber Krebs offered the Dolls a tour to Japan and a new record contract if they would drop Thau. Thau was furious. "I said to them, 'You better get Leber straight. You're selling out for a $200-a-week paycheck. This thing begins with *us.*' "

From Steve Leber's point of view, Thau and the band were in cahoots. "We kept the Dolls on salary from the very beginning, out of our own pockets," says Leber. "But when I found out the band was using the hard-earned money we were giving them for dentists and doctors on drugs—and remember, Marty was always the one that came to us for the money—that was the end. My end of the deal was to back the band as far as I could, up to a million dollars if necessary, but that means that the band has to live up to its side of the deal. But Marty felt that building the band's bad-boy image without any concern for the business of it all would get the band to cross over."

The Dolls were torn, unwilling either to alienate Leber Krebs or to fire Marty Thau. With Thunders, Nolan, and Kane nodding out, Johansen and Sylvain decided to make the decision themselves. Paul Nelson was telling them to take the deal; unless they recouped Mercury's advance for the making of their first two albums, there was no way they would be allowed to make a third. (According to Nelson, a group of quasi-Dolls—Robeson, Jordan, and Sylvain—dragged themselves into a studio to work on practice demos for the third LP.) The Dolls refused to betray Thau and vetoed the deal, but they also refused to call it quits with Leber Krebs or Mercury. Suspended by Mercury and ignored by their management, it seemed that the Dolls were dead at last.

That is, until Malcolm McLaren showed up.

His arrival in New York was inauspicious. First he stayed with Marty Frommer, then he moved with Addie to an apartment Frommer found on Twentieth Street off Eighth Avenue. Addie was the focus, but according to Westwood, their relationship unraveled very quickly. "He'd gone to meet her father and he liked her family, but suddenly he panicked and thought he'd got in too deep. He ditched the whole thing," she says. "I don't know what was on his mind." Others say that McLaren arrived sometime near Thanksgiving and went to Addie's New Jersey manse to meet her parents. According to this story, Addie had had plastic surgery on her face, and when McLaren first saw her, he failed to recognize her.

The Dolls were apparently as surprised as Addie to see McLaren in New York. "I can honestly say that no one had offered him anything, no one was even in touch with him," the ringlet-haired Sylvain says in classic New Yorkese. "Nobody: Leber Krebs wasn't gonna hire him. Marty Thau certainly wasn't gonna hire him. And we didn't have the power to do anything anyways. *We* didn't have no money. One day, he just shows up, in clubs, in restaurants, at Max's. We were just hanging around and I think he was selling some clothes."

Surprised or not, McLaren and the Dolls set to work immediately. A stormy meeting was held in Frommer's Eighth Avenue antique shop. "Malcolm just stood back and said, 'Let it out! If you have something to say, say it now, because the kids are back'—I had just written a song called 'The Kids Are Back,'" says Sylvain. "And he finally told Johnny and Arthur and Jerry and David—and me—'What the fuck? Is it your fucking egos that are destroying this whole thing? Either let's keep it together or forget it!'"

The Dolls were not unanimously in favor of working with McLaren but they had come too far to be hung out to dry by moneymen, managers, and Mercury Records. Besides, McLaren didn't seem to want anything in return for his services—no contracts, no money, not even the promise of future negotiations. He just wanted to help, and once he was given what seemed to him the band's official go-ahead, he set to work as quickly as he could. Through Frommer, he found a rehearsal loft on Twenty-third Street, enrolled Johnny and Jerry in a methadone clinic, and checked Arthur into the Billy Rose detox center uptown. "It was simple," says Syl. "Here was this beautiful guy who really wanted to help out, and I said, 'Hey, look, let's do it.'"

McLaren didn't bother checking in with either Leber Krebs or Marty Thau to see if his presence as de facto manager was desired—he knew he would only be told to return to London—but the Dolls had set up one last good-faith attempt to make peace with Thau: at Reno Sweeney's, with McLaren in attendance.

"It wasn't presented like 'Here's our new manager' or 'We want him to be our new manager,'" says Thau. "I just assumed that if they wanted him there, it was cool. There were lots of people like that who were helpful." Still, as the meeting dragged on to its uneventful conclusion,

Thau found himself becoming so irritated by McLaren's presence that when the red-haired Londoner went to the bathroom, Thau turned to Sylvain and pointedly asked, "Who the fuck is this guy?" "Just a friend," Thau was told, and that's all McLaren was. For the moment.

With the assistance of Marty Frommer, McLaren now began to plot the Dolls' comeback. "I remember him planning the whole thing," says Frommer, now owner of FLIP, a chain of rock clothing stores with outlets in New York and London. "He was just beginning to work out all the kinks in the idea of the rock band as outlaws. I remember all these late nights staying up talking with him, and he would tell me these incredible plans for something he called the new wave of rock 'n' roll. Instead of toning the Dolls down like their manager wanted, he wanted to make it more outrageous, put them in drag, not just this second-hand thrift shop stuff. I say he *planned* it, the whole thing."

The first step was to give the Dolls a new gimmick, something that would dramatize their difference from the old Dolls and prove, once and for all, their continuing relevance to the music scene. A new Dolls song written by Johansen and Thunders called "Red Patent Leather" (no one seems to remember the lyric) made McLaren's eyes light up with images of a red patent leather cell of Communist Dolls. To McLaren, an invasion of red Dolls across America made perfect sense, evoking a neat symmetry to Richard Nixon's famous entente cordiale with the People's Republic of China. Just as fake fetishism had been the perfect way to get up the nose of the Brits, so fake communism would now be the way to provoke the Americans.

"I tried to turn them from being a bunch of idiotic, sissy nonsense that was definitely loved by the middle class in America, especially the rock critics, and turn them into something that would be a little more danger-ous," McLaren later explained. "The Vietnam War was just about to end. I said to them that red was the color, let's use that, let's use Chairman Mao, let's use the hammer and sickle, let's use all the things that America right now is arrogant about, and let's make it an event."

Johansen claims that the Red Patent Leather Dolls idea was *his:* "It was my idea to do a Communist party," he says with a toothy grin. "But not a Communist party, y'know, but a Communist *party,* with red balloons and party favors." In any event, politics couldn't have been of much importance to the Dolls' decision-making process, for by now, Thunders and Nolan were so far gone that Chris Robeson and Peter Jordan were practically considered bandmembers. If the other Dolls went along with McLaren's (or Johansen's) red roguishness, it was mostly for the *clothes:* "It started with me saying, 'I want a pair of red pants,'" says Sylvain. "Then someone else said, 'OK man, well, I'll get red shoes. Then, OK, let's *all* get red pants.'"

McLaren was only too willing to help. He personally measured the Dolls and rang up Vivienne with an order for their new crimson duds. By the end of February, he had them fitted out in bright red vinyl wet-look jeans and side-zip T-shirts, all at his own expense. (Later, McLaren would claim he had designed these costumes himself.) And he bought a massive red flag emblazoned with the Dolls lipstick logo to hang outside the venue. The stage backdrop, a giant Communist flag with a gold star and hammer and sickle, was made by Johansen's first wife, Cyrinda Fox. The band was flabbergasted by McLaren's "generosity." It turned out to be just the beginning.

As soon as the costumes were ready, McLaren booked a gig at as unlikely a New York venue as possible. This was to be the Dolls' grand reinauguration, the shining send-off to a national tour, and the press release McLaren wrote—his fans call it a "manifesto"—illustrates his neo-Nixonian fantasies:

FOR IMMEDIATE RELEASE
FROM THE PEOPLE WHO BROUGHT YOU
"TOO MUCH TOO SOON"

What Are the Politics of Boredom? Better Red Than Dead.

Contrary to the vicious lies from the offices of Leber, Krebs and Thau, our former "paper tiger" management, the New York Dolls have not disbanded, and after having completed the first Red, 3-D Rock N' Roll movie entitled "Trash" have, in fact, assumed the role of the "People's Information Collective" in direct assocation with the Red Guard.

This incarnation entitled "Red Patent Leather" will commence on Friday, February 28 at 10 P.M. continuing on Saturday at 9 and 11 P.M. followed by a Sunday matinee at 5 P.M. for our high school friends at the Little Hippodrome—227 E. 56 St. between 2nd and 3rd.

This show is in coordination with The Dolls' very special "entente cordiale" with the Peoples Republic of China.

Trash, which had nothing to do with the Warhol-Morrissey-Dallesandro junk opera, was actually a fancy promo shot by some visiting Canadian filmmakers with an experimental camera.

With the Hippodrome date set, McLaren now began looking for additional local gigs. For weeks, he had been bugging every concert promoter around town for a gig, and suddenly one came through: of all people, Howard Stein, who had hated the Dolls ever since he'd promoted their Halloween gig at the Waldorf Astoria Hotel in 1973. (As usual, the Dolls had gone on more than two hours late, broke some large plate glass windows before the show, and then finally played an abbreviated set—Stein, outraged, swore that the New York Dolls would never play one of his theaters again.) But somehow McLaren convinced him that the Dolls were on their way back, had given up their bad habits, and were ready to storm the world with their red patent madness. Grandma Rose's gift of the gab worked again, and Howard Stein booked the Dolls into the Academy of Music on Fourteenth Street for what was projected to be the finale of their summer tour.

Now McLaren felt confident enough to set up a real tour. He started by booking the band into some small Florida clubs, hoping the sunny climate would put some distance between the Dolls and their bad New York habits. McLaren scanned the country from a giant map of the United States tacked up on his living room wall. Each time he booked another gig, another red pushpin was stuck into the map until Florida began to look like the beachhead of a red invasion. VE-Day, the date of the Academy of Music gigs, was set for May 3–5, 1975.

"It was amazing," says Sylvain. "The guy was really into it. He was like a kid doing his baby marketing, but man, it really *worked.*"

Meanwhile, McLaren spent his nights scouring the burgeoning New York music scene with Marty Frommer. The Mercer had literally crumbled to the ground in late 1973, and Max's Kansas City and CBGB's, a Hell's Angels and winos' hangout on the Bowery, were now presenting the bands that would eventually become the leading edge of punk rock.

Punk itself was nothing new. Indeed, the term *punk rock* had been around for ages: The Dolls had worn the moniker of a punk band from the very start of their career in 1972, and from as far back as the early sixties, there had been a slew of punk bands—Mouse & the Traps, ? and the Mysterions, the Shadows of Knight, the 13th Floor Elevators, the Chocolate Watchband, Count V, the Standells, some include the Stooges—littering the record bins with such songs as "Wooly Bully," "96 Tears," "Pushin' Too Hard," "Psychotic Reaction." However, unlike the New York punks of the mid-seventies, most of whom had come to the big city to discover their bohemian roots, these early "garage bands" were based in places like Milwaukee, Detroit, and Minneapolis, and they liked it there. Had it not been for the latter-day punks' self-conscious search for musical roots, they might never have been heard from again.

Like the Dolls, a band many of them admired, these new punks who hung out at CBGB's were third-generation rockers, largely unaware of the originals (such as Bill Haley or Elvis) and disgusted with the insipid disco fodder then making up the bulk of second-generation MOR radio (early Stones, late Bowie, and T-Rex were the important exceptions). These new punks were angry, not just disaffected. They railed against the greed of the established record companies and the bloated indifference of stadium rock stars even as they prayed for the success of their own careers.

At their center were two teenage runaways who had escaped respectively from suburban Kentucky and Delaware within a year of each other in 1967–68. First Richard Hell (né Meyers), a struggling boho writer and would-be publisher with a penchant for the mysteries of the Symbolist poets; next Tom Verlaine (né Miller), a bony guitar ace with a penchant for all things hallucinogenic. Together with another Delaware high school fugitive, drummer Billy Ficca, they formed a seminal, short-lived (maybe six months in 1973) prepunk outfit: the Neon Boys, a whining, chaotic, wheeze of a band that featured the wily Hell vocalizing about how his "Love Comes in Spurts" while Verlaine served up long, sinuous lashes of guitar heroics.

At year's end, Hell, Verlaine, and Ficca had joined forces with guitarist Richard Lloyd, and formed Television, a band whose odd clash of spiraling guitar leads, sheer rhythmic thrust, and druggily poetic lyrics still remains dear to its many nostalgic aficionados. The scene at CBGB's began with Television, when Verlaine talked Lloyd into approaching owner Hilly Kristal with the idea of starting a regular Sunday-night residency for the band in what had been, until then, a bombed-out, neon-lit tavern littered with broken bottles.

"Like the Dolls at the Mercer Arts Center," Hell wrote in the *East Village Eye* in 1980, "we figured that was the best strategy for acquiring a following. It worked, and the Ramones soon formed (we knew Dee Dee) and started playing there. Patti Smith, who was still reading poetry with ten-minute interludes of electric guitar accompaniment from Lenny Kaye, wrote about us in *Hit Parader* and soon was playing there as her band expanded." Blondie (with Debbie Harry) and Talking Heads were next in line.

When McLaren stumbled upon CBGB's—certain it was *his* discovery—it wasn't the winos and bikers that caught his eye; it was Richard Hell, that self-educated suburban refugee with the chaotic hairdo (short sides and a slept-on top) and clothes that seemed to have been found up the street in a Salvation Army trashbin.

To McLaren, Hell was more than just another rock 'n' roller, he was a prophet of city life, as important to one's understanding of postmodern urban malaise as the twin towers of the World Trade Center. McLaren was fascinated when Hell sang his audience anthems like "I Don't Care," told them "You Gotta Lose" ("I hope I'm not being immodest when I tell you/ My mother was a pinhead and my father was a fly"), summed it up by announcing that "(I Belong to the) Blank Generation" ("and I can take it or leave it each day"). Hell wasn't afraid of his audience, wasn't *working* for them, and let them know it with unrestrained drunken callousness. McLaren was knocked out by the raw subversive energy of his act.

Beyond Hell's poetic lyrics and punkish odor, however, McLaren was fascinated with his *look,* his otherworldly version of amphetaminized beefcake and the hacked-up Bowery Boy clothes he attired himself in. To McLaren, Hell was yet another example of the kind of fresh revisioning of Elvis Presley the rock world was so badly in need of. Ever since those early days, journalists have bugged Hell about his visual influence on McLaren, but in his *Eye* piece (titled "Slum Journal" and written "to have some public access without having to speak to journalists"), Hell finally made a modest claim to be the father of the punk ethos: "I originated virtually all the visuals—haircut, torn [via Patti] and safety-pinned clothes, fifties suits with loosened ties, leather jackets [which the Ramones soon improved on] and shirts with scattered geometrical shapes [initiated by Verlaine] and personal messages drawn on them [the first being "please kill me," which Richard Lloyd was talked into wearing at Max's one night]."

"He was a ghostly thing," McLaren proclaims in his best showman's voice. "Doom-gloom, that kind of thing. Typically nineteenth century. That Thomas Chatterton look. With a pastel or a paintbrush he could paint something on his chest and it would be great. It was his own do-it-yourself look, the poetry of that that influenced me. I suppose it was that he didn't have the typical look of a commercial rock star. It was very artistic, and I use that word advisedly."

"I wanted to look the way I felt," Hell says today. "These things were an expression of my personality. But the constant was this definite attitude behind it of do-it-yourself, advocating that for the people who were our audience. It was the same way we went about making our music."

Malcolm McLaren filed it all away for later use.

The Dolls' gig at the Little Hippodrome was chaotic. Jerry Nolan thought the show was "the greatest. People that never liked the Dolls admitted that the Dolls had become a professional band and they really enjoyed us for the first time. I felt, OK, we're gonna do it." But Paul Nelson, faithful to the band despite its managerial rigmarole, remembers that they were barely in tune and had trouble remembering, much less playing, their new repertoire.

Either way, the Little Hippodrome gig showed that the kids *were* back. Someone even stole the banner McLaren had made. Regardless of internal dissension about the band's direction, the evidence was that the Dolls still had an audience and should keep on going. Thunders and Nolan were less than excited about the idea of going to Florida—"Jerry and Johnny said, 'What's the matter with this fucking guy, he's a schmuck, he's not gonna do anything for us,' " reports Syl—but the tour went on as scheduled.

McLaren and the Dolls flew down to Florida—St. Petersburg, Fort Lauderdale, Tampa, some other small Florida clubs—with Roger Mansour (a former member of the original Vagrants) as their roadie. Mansour found a used station wagon for the band and as the Dolls drove through the Southern heat, they slowly discarded their New York clothes for faded Army fatigues. Even the Dolls could see that their Commie clothes would never fly down South.

"Let's face it," says Sylvain, "in America you could be gay, commit incest, do *anything,* but you cannot be a Communist. It was a goof. Even in New York, that whole thing would have been much bigger without the flag. They would have killed us down South with that flag. It was a shock just seeing us with red pants and tight jeans with a hole in your ass. Or an earring. No one knew. All these things had implications that the lowest common denominator didn't know. They didn't understand that shit.

"So"—he takes a big breath—"we were bumming it, in our fatigues, staying in funky places. We didn't make good money, but we ate OK, and we were actually doing what we were supposed to do, getting our shit together after so many years of abuse."

Still, the griping went on. Nolan and Thunders insisted on playing the new Dolls repertoire in the old Dolls style of fast, expensive, drug-filled living, while Johansen, Sylvain, and McLaren wanted to break the band in using the old songs and a relatively sober style. By the time the Dolls reached Tampa, Nolan and Thunders had had enough. They were freaking out, and not about music, clothes, or hotels either: Florida was simply too far from their drug connections.

"It was a week, maybe four, five days, they didn't have their junk, and we were staying at Jerry Nolan's mother's house in Tampa. They couldn't find it in Florida, they weren't about to tell Malcolm, 'Hey, Malcolm, we're gonna go back home to shoot up.' What they *were* saying was, 'This Malcolm guy's a wimp, he's just a jerk.' David was going, 'No, he's OK, he's doing it.' At least he could make some sense out of it."

Not Thunders and Nolan. They kept up their bitching and moaning until communication between the two camps was virtually impossible. Finally Thunders and Nolan called a meeting to state what had already become obvious. They were through. They wanted out. Forever.

"I drove them to the airport with Roger," says Sylvain, "and I remember Jerry taking his bags out of the car, and me turning to him and saying, 'So what about the Dolls?' And he said, 'Fuck the Dolls.' And that's all I had to hear. At that point, I gave up too."

The remnants of the Dolls—Syl, David, a barely functioning Arthur, and a stand-in drummer named Blackie—completed the remainder of the gigs McLaren had set up in Florida; then each went his own way. Johansen flew to New York and Kane stayed with his friend Blackie in Florida. That left McLaren and Sylvain with the old green station wagon, a couple of hundred dollars, and some rock 'n' roll dreams.

They decided that New Orleans was to be their destination, but since neither one knew how to drive, two women hitchhikers were picked off the highway and offered a lift if they'd act as chauffeurs. The girls were dumped as soon as they hit New Orleans, and McLaren booked a room in the heart of the Latin Quarter at the Cornstock Fence Hotel. New Orleans never looked so sad or so beautiful, full of tired old bluesmen in starched white shirts and glassy-eyed whores with nowhere to go. Daytimes were spent wandering in search of vintage blues material. Syl bought a guitar; Malcolm befriended a Cajun midget. At night, an old bluesman named Pres (short for President) introduced them to the joys of Cajun martinis at a bar called the Dungeon, and when the Louisiana night turned to day and they were juiced enough to think about it, these intrepid travelers would stumble back to the Cornstock Fence, wondering how they'd ever get back to New York with neither a driving license nor cash. Finally Syl had to take a driving test; Malcolm (a perpetual nondriver) coached him on the Louisiana law.

McLaren and Sylvain got back in the beat-up green station wagon and headed back to New York City. Syl drove at breakneck speed; McLaren got nauseous in the backseat after eating a bucket of fried chicken he insisted on buying in a Tennessee truckstop. "Malcolm's heart was broken," says Syl. "But all the way up from Florida, he kept saying to me, 'Don't you worry. There are these kids hanging around my shop and they're really good. You can come to England. You can do it.'"

Outside McLaren's house on Twentieth Street, they ran into a Dolls fanatic with the band's lipstick logo tattooed on his arm. Elwood was his name and he was ecstatic to see Sylvain. Syl told him the news. "You fucking guys broke up?" he asked incredulously. "You assholes!" Syl could only nod.

Down by the puffed pink plastic letters that shout out SEX at 430 King's Road, Malcolm McLaren is prancing down the street, gladhanding old friends at the Roebuck pub as if he's been away for years. Effusive, charming, full of bravado, the conquering hero spins a skein of tales about his adventures in America managing the New York Dolls. The Dolls debacle is already behind him, each tale of disaster already turning into a saga of good deeds, near misses, and narrow wins that gets better with each retelling. Everyone's in stitches—oh, great, Malcolm, amazing how you pulled it off: Old Motormouth never lets them down. That Johnny Thunders, he says, incredible, I tell you, you wouldn't believe how stupid he is. Or (more confidentially): I'm not bragging, now, but when those Dolls got onstage dressed in their red patent leather clothes, Johansen with his little red book, you wouldn't believe it—well, the audience was filled up to the rafters, why they were a huge success, why they could have been Giant. Or: wild-animal rock 'n' roll stories: Arthur Kane walking into walls; Thunders so flipped out on speed he imagined every taxi as a narc's roost; Johansen's brilliance, but what an ego. . . . Or, finally, the credo of political credibility: "The only problem with the Dolls was that they got scared of my ideas," he says. "Ultimately groups do. Johansen was asked about me and he said, 'This communism thing is only a laugh, a lark.' After that, it was all downhill. I packed my bags and came back." McLaren as old hand: Oh, well, that's rock 'n' roll for you.

In New York, of course, it's a different story. As soon as he returns to

London, McLaren shoots off missives to Sylvain, to Johansen, and to Richard Hell, pleading with each to come to London, to the red hot SEX scene, so fresh and full of energy.

No one listens.

Hell coldly turns down McLaren's offer to be lead singer of the Sex Pistols, instead joining the Heartbreakers with ex-Doll Johnny Thunders. "He wrote and told me I had to be very serious and not be doing drugs," he says. "It was like a coach. And that was enough to put me off, not only because of the drug business, but because I didn't want to get involved with somebody who was gonna tell me what to do. I hate that."

Sylvain waits for the money McLaren promised him from selling his Vox organ and guitar back in England (the only way McLaren could convince Vivienne to send enough money to fly him back). He and Johansen are still wondering what went wrong, how they got into this mess and what they can do now that the Dolls are over. Leber Krebs wants them to go to Japan as a reformed New York Dolls. (Eventually they will go, but under their own steam.)

Marty Thau, the *real* manager of the New York Dolls, is still furious with his English usurper: How did this red-haired stranger come to take his place in music history as the manager of the New York Dolls? "All's fair in love and war," Thau gravely intones, "and it's a pretty vicious, competitive world we live in. I'm shocked, however, when I read 'Malcolm McLaren, manager of the New York Dolls.' He was not the manager. He had no contracts, he had nothing to do with instituting the Dolls and putting them in a place to be a world entry. It was all after the fact. Either he was inept in a business sense and/or deluding himself to think that those legalities were stupid. If he thought he could just take this thing over by just moving in, he was very naive."

David Johansen, now Buster Poindexter, agrees: "Malcolm McLaren, our manager?" he asks incredulously. "You must be joking. I never thought he was our manager. He was just some nutty English pal-o'-mine. We went to the beach together once. Rockaways. But, hey, if he has to make it into being our manager, that's OK by me. Because you know what I always say: Whenever I'm in England, I always visit my favorite haberdasher, Mr. Malcolm McLaren."

PART TWO

___

Nemo repente fuit turpissimus.
(Nobody reaches the peak of vice in a single stride.)
                                    —Juvenal

4
CHAOS, INDEED

While he was in America, McLaren seemed to be counting on the Swankers being there for him upon his eventual return to London. Yet, once back, the last thing he seemed willing to do was to involve himself with the Swankers. Steve Jones and Glen Matlock say that McLaren quite literally had to be begged before he agreed to look after their fledgling group. For, as long as the legendarily ugly Wally was in the band, McLaren never thought the Swankers had much of a chance. Wally was a wanker, not a Swanker. McLaren called him "the Joker."

But something had happened to the Swankers while McLaren was away. By June 1975, through their own sheer willfullness—"what can a young boy do . . ."—the Swankers had become a tight little band. Nothing fancy, nothing flash, just an ordinary rock combo with a fairly wide range of cover songs, but they had something different. Not the music, which McLaren dismissed as a load of old Faces bollocks. It was the glint in Steve Jones's eyes, a glint of wildness and ambition with a hint of insecurity, radiating a potential for raw sexual energy and the mischief-making excess of rock 'n' roll, that finally convinced him. Besides, Jones kept pestering McLaren about his time with the Dolls. Wanted to know every last detail about Johnny Thunders. That was a good sign.

If necessary, the rest of the band could be replaced.

McLaren now began to visit the Swankers' rehearsals in Hammersmith every weekend. There were no commitments, no contracts or agreements, and McLaren didn't yet provide the boys with the cash or clothes he knew they would eventually need, but the more he looked at these kids, balancing each one's personality and style against his own rebellious desires, the more he came to realize that they were "his boys."

The band of musical juvenile delinquents he had been searching for had been right in front of his nose all along.

Of course, if you asked Steve Jones who the Swankers were, he'd tell you straight out that they were *his* band. After all, it was he who had stolen their equipment, he who was their lead singer, his best mate who was playing the drums. And for the most part it was Jones who gave the Swankers their swank. Jones may have tried to pass himself off as a happy-go-lucky kind of bloke who just wanted his fair share of the kicks, but at the end of the day, he insisted on playing King Spiv, the no-good troublemaker and thief who always got his way. Nothing more or less than a yob, he would say: "scum of the earth, absolutely." If McLaren was going to mess with his mates, his band, he'd better come up with some proof that he knew what he was doing.

With McLaren back in town and pressing them to clean up their act, Jones, Matlock, and Cook finally agreed by mid-July that Wally had to go—despite the fact that he had come up with the guitar riff on "Did You No Wrong," the one Swankers number strong enough to make it eventually into the Sex Pistols' repertoire. (Matlock was chosen to give Wally the bad news.) Jones now picked up the guitar—McLaren gave him Sylvain's gorgeous white Gibson Les Paul as an added incentive—and the Swankers lurched one step closer to being a rock 'n' roll band.

Although McLaren hadn't yet actually committed himself to managing the Swankers—or as he sometimes suggested they should be called, Kid Gladlove, the Strand (after Roxy Music's "Do The Strand"), or even the Damned (soon to be the name of another punk group)—his friendship with Steve Jones kept bringing him closer to a business relationship with the band. When Jones nicked an amp or a guitar—smashed a window in a Shaftesbury Avenue music shop or sneaked past a sleeping roadie guarding some band's equipment before a gig—McLaren would try to fence the stuff on road trips up north with Bernard Rhodes (McLaren didn't learn to drive for another ten years). On one trip to the border of Scotland, he and Rhodes asked a punkish petrol station attendant point-blank if he'd like to join a great new London rock band. The story goes that when Slik guitarist Midge Ure—who later became yet another member of Matlock's Rich Kids and then went on to synth-wiz fame in Magazine, Visage, and Ultravox!—declined the offer, McLaren nudged Rhodes to sell him the amp. Ure supposedly thought that was a better deal.

With Wally gone and the lineup getting stronger each day, McLaren and Rhodes went back to hatching new schemes for the Swankers. McLaren wanted to turn them into a vaguely politicized version of the Bay City Rollers, the tartaned milk-drinking Scottish teeny-bopper group whose meteoric rise was predicated on their image as bad boys putting on a good-boy act. The Rollers' rise to fame had been engineered by former orchestra leader Tam Paton, who kept rotating the band members until he finally came up with a winning combination. It didn't matter that the press called them the Scottish Monkees; when the Rollers rode onto *Top of the Pops,* tartan sales boomed and Tam Paton got rich. If only Steve Jones could be taught the mechanics of being a sex symbol, and the band could come up with some good songs, McLaren was sure his SEX apparel would give the tartan industry (not to mention the long-haired gits of the music industry) a run for their money.

But Bernard Rhodes had a different idea. Rhodes wanted rock 'n' roll that would be militantly working class, a definitive counterculture statement of the teenager's alienation from big-money rock, and he figured that he would supply the revolutionary rigor while McLaren played mischief-maker, merchandiser, and costumier to rock's proletariat. In time, the two discussed a formal partnership, but in the classic tradition of generations of anarchists and Marxists, they couldn't come close to an agreement. "I don't think Malcolm's aims and mine were ever the same," Rhodes later told the Vermorels. "Malcolm would never give anyone half share. He'd always want to be in control."

While Rhodes went off to work with London S.S., one of the precursor bands to the Clash, McLaren and the Swankers were looking for a second guitarist and a new lead singer. McLaren put out the word that anyone who even remotely *looked* like he might be a Swanker should "come down the SEX shop" and have an audition. No one came. Then Glen Matlock spotted John Lydon goofing off at the Roebuck pub, a block up the street. Matlock had told McLaren about this guy when McLaren first arrived back from New York, but McLaren had been uninterested. McLaren never paid any heed to Matlock: He was just the dopey shop attendant, an art-schooler from a good "booge-wah" family (in fact, not all that different from McLaren himself). But this time, Matlock got his boss's attention. I don't know this geezer, he told McLaren, but he's been in and out of the shop with his mates on Saturdays, and he looks good. Just the kind of thing you want. Like the Hunchback of Notre Dame with peroxide-green hair. Everything he says is *fuck you, fuck that, that's just your tough shit.* One long hyperventilated howl of hate against any target he can get his tongue around: pop music, people over thirty, politicians, priests—he even hates himself. Like that friend of yours, Richard Hell, but British.

The next time John Lydon showed up with his mates at the Roebuck pub, Glen Matlock asked him if he'd be interested in joining a band and arranged for Lydon to meet Jones back at the pub. "He was like really piss-taking, you know, and we was piss-taking back," Jones told Judy Vermorel about that meeting, claiming that he, not Matlock, had first discovered Lydon. (Jones later told me that he often lied to journalists, including me.) "We thought he was a bit of a boozer, you know, and like he was really flash." A formal audition was scheduled for the next night, but after another round of drinks it was decided that Lydon should come to SEX and meet McLaren straightaway.

John Lydon didn't need much convincing. He'd do pretty much anything on a dare. When he wasn't boozing it up at the Roebuck, his days were spent cruising up and down the King's Road gobbing at the "weeds" who wouldn't defend themselves against his icy taunts. Besides, Malcolm McLaren was a pretty well-known figure, and Lydon was already well acquainted with SEX. "I thought it was good gear," he told Judy Vermorel. "It says something good about someone who'll wear that kind of gear like and fucking fight back if someone laughs at them." At the very least, maybe Lydon thought he'd even get a free T-shirt out of it.

(Westwood claims she noticed Lydon and his friends John Grey and John Beverley—everyone called him Sid to keep the three separate—long before Matlock brought Lydon to McLaren's attention. "He asked me who was interesting that came into the shop," says Westwood, "and I said Sid, because Sid just overshadowed John on initial contact. But Sid had gone off, doing something with speed, and he just wasn't around.")

When Lydon showed up at SEX, McLaren wasn't exactly sure what to make of this green-haired eighteen-year-old in a ripped-up Pink Floyd T-shirt with the words I HATE scribbled in biro above the band's logo, safety-pinned baggy trousers, and open-toed plastic sandals. Compared with McLaren, clad in his neat, middle-class version of SEX camp, a button-down shirt, patent leather jeans, and high-heeled shoes, Lydon seemed like a street urchin, straight out of Dickensian London. Not quite the sex symbol McLaren was looking for, but interesting.

"John felt a bit on the spot because we'd dragged him back to the shop," says Matlock. "He'd been shooting his mouth off saying he could sing, when of course he couldn't." If Lydon was uncomfortable, it certainly didn't show in his behavior, because when McLaren asked what it was he did anyway—sing? play guitar? bass? what then? ("Yeah," chimed in Jones. "What *can* you do?")—Lydon replied in a confident snarl: "Course I can't sing, but I *can* play a violin out of tune," and everyone cracked up.

Now came the "audition." Jones leaned into the neon glow of the jukebox, selected Alice Cooper's "Eighteen," and asked Lydon to have a go at it. Suddenly, John Lydon was all over the place, jumping and jiving and giggling and thrusting his way through the song, chomping out whatever words he could remember into an old shower head and charmfully gibberishing his way through the rest. By the time he was finished, everyone was doubled over in laughter.

"He was 'orrible," remembers Jones. "Absolutely 'orrible. But he was the best we had had. And when he said, 'I can only sing out of tune' or whatever, we thought that was pretty cool, McLaren thought it was pretty cool. I thought he was a bit of an arsehole because he had an attitude, which was a cool attitude really, but I didn't dig it at the time. I just wanted to be in a band and play rock and this guy was kind of threatening that with his attitude. He weren't, OK let's go and do it. It was like, Uhhhhh."

"I went all the way down to Rotherhithe where they were meant to be rehearsing, but they didn't turn up," Lydon told *Melody Maker* writer Caroline Coon. "I thought they were a bunch of lazy cunts and I said they'd never get anywhere, but Malcolm kept ringing me up."

One week of telephone tag later, a second rehearsal was finally arranged at the Crunchie Frog in Rotherhithe and John Lydon—soon to be dubbed Johnny Rotten because of the state of his mung-covered teeth—was anointed lead singer of the Swankers ("Don't worry, we're changing that," said Matlock of the name). The first rehearsals with Lydon were painful: Jones scratching out some basic chords on guitar, Cook struggling to keep a steady beat, Rotten furious and frustrated trying to sing the Who's "Substitute," Matlock left to hold it all together, everyone threatening to quit. But to McLaren, it was clear that here, at long last, he had finally found his very own rock 'n' roll band. Suddenly they were all *there:* the Sex Pistols, the name of a New York street gang he'd been toying with privately for some time. Steve, Paul, Glen, and John. Fucking hell. The Sex Pistols.

Where would Malcolm McLaren be without them?

McLaren had been back from America for only a few weeks when Michael Collins, the SEX shop manager, told him about an unusual visit from the Metropolitan police. While the boss was away, there had been a series of rapes across the fens near Cambridge, and although the suspected rapist had supposedly worn a leather mask that covered most of his face, it was thought that the Cambridge Rapist had taken refuge somewhere in London.

"I was sure that one of our customers, this guy from Yorkshire, was the Cambridge Rapist," says Collins, "so I phoned up Scotland Yard and they came to interview me and I wound up in all these newspapers holding this mask, smiling at it. It caused so much publicity that we were inundated by people coming to buy more of them. But Vivienne really hauled me off and told me it was *bad* publicity."

"My reaction was the normal, I'd say, stupid reaction, because it had no fantasy to it, I imagine," says Westwood. "I wouldn't have anything to do with the press."

McLaren raged when he found out that Westwood hadn't used the publicity to build up the business. *"Any* publicity is good publicity," he screamed at her. "We have to play up things like this and pretend we really do know the rapist and that we will protect him at all costs."

"I thought, Hmmmm, that's wonderful," McLaren gleefully exclaimed a couple of years later. "I've really got to protect this man, so I thought why don't I associate him with Brian Epstein and the Beatles. So I took this mask that he wore and put it on a T-shirt and put 'Cambridge Rapist' over it in popstar letters. And at the bottom I put a small picture of Brian Epstein and then wrote a few words about him and how the man had not committed suicide but how he died of S&M through loneliness, just to provoke. . . .

"So suddenly Cambridge Rapist T-shirts were being bought by all these fifteen-year-old kids saying, *'This* is a smart T-shirt.' I thought it was fucking great, all these kids buying the shirts and going down to their local disco wearing 'em. . . . Those ideas really invigorated those kids. They saw them as slightly shocking and that's all that was important: to be shocking, to annoy a few people, because they felt so lethargic."

Neither concept nor product, the Sex Pistols were much less successful at the beginning. McLaren could imagine Steve Jones as a SEX symbol, but Johnny Rotten was another story. Unkempt to the point of putrescence (Lydon's last job was janitorial work and he still didn't bathe much) and deformed by a childhood bout with spinal meningitis, the sickly looking Rotten was the last person one would pick to challenge the Scottish soccer lout sexiness of the Bay City Rollers. McLaren's fantasy of the Sex Pistols so far outstripped their reality that instead of basking in the triumph of having put together his own band, he was now thrown into a deep funk, unsure of which way to turn these four ragamuffins.

Help arrived as usual from SEX, where Westwood's increasingly punky designs were beginning to go somewhere. McLaren may have needled his companion about having been born in the Tinwhistle Snake Pass—"You'd be nothing but a factory worker if it wasn't for me," he often scowled at her—but through the years Westwood had transformed herself from an ugly Northern duckling into a style princess whose birdy cheekbones, spiked platinum hair, and two-colored lips set the King's Road on fire. Westwood's clothes were beginning to take on their own look and Westwood herself was being talked of as the new Queen of the King's Road. She was greatly helped by the input of McLaren, who knew how to coax and cajole Westwood's latent talent, and a new SEX shopgirl named Jordan, a bright, plump young woman whose flair for self-promotion soon proved invaluable in creating the first real public awareness of what SEX style was all about.

Jordan had been wearing rips in her shirts and stockings for quite some time before she even heard of Let It Rock. Walking down the street one day in her hometown, Brighton, a stranger stopped to ask her where she had bought her clothes, and when Jordan (née Pamela Rooke) recited her list of second-hand clothes shops, the stranger replied that she had just seen the same sort of stuff at a boutique in London—Let It Rock, she thought it was called. Not long after, Jordan began going out with Frankie Pizzaia, McLaren's friend from New York. One thing led to another, and while McLaren was away in America, Michael Collins hired Jordan to work at SEX.

Just as there had been earlier starlet shopgirls through the mod and hippie years at the Mary Quant boutique and at Biba, so Jordan now became shopgirl-of-the-moment at SEX. The names on the lease may have read McLaren and Westwood, but as often as not, the picture in the paper was Jordan's, wearing "blue leotard and tights, ripped to shit, enormous holes all over them." "I remember the first article," she says. "It was great, a picture of me in a rubber skirt and a T-shirt, and it just said, 'The SEX shop in King's Road was great, but the girl that worked in the shop, Jordan, was even better.' "

Clad in black rubber, with her shredded stockings and brilliant multicolored, masklike makeup, Jordan was like a homegrown female version of Richard Hell, but better: sexier and voluptuous and bossily aggressive all at once. And although that sense of do-it-yourself sexiness was what McLaren had been after at the start—some say Jordan was what McLaren had originally wanted Rotten to be—he now realized that the fantasy of challenging the Bay City Rollers with a SEX idol had thrown him off his true course. If he could just let Rotten be Rotten, the Dickensian urchin he already was, the Sex Pistols would have their own unique style. *Rotten didn't need coaching.*

If anything, it was McLaren and Westwood who now became the avid students, voyeuristically absorbing John and Jordan's tuned-in sense of street style, coopting their ideas into their own better educated and more cynically self-conscious outlook. When Jordan came to work wearing an ordinary oxford-cloth shirt with painted stripes on the sleeves, Westwood dyed the sleeves of a similar shirt in different colors, printed one set of stripes in bleach and another in paint, sewed on a silk photo portrait of Karl Marx—finally adding the stenciled slogan "Dangerously Close To Love"—and then stowed it away where McLaren wouldn't find it. "It was all to give it some sort of guerrilla look, like it came from a South American revolution," she confesses. "I thought, Oh, my God, I'm going to get a whole lecture about what I'm doing, so I hid it." But then McLaren found the shirt tucked away in her closet. "He said, 'That's it! That's exactly what we need.' "

Westwood soon designed a whole range of what she called "punk rock clothes": T-shirts with little plastic-covered holes behind which the wearer could put a photo of his or her favorite revolutionary or rock star; more striped shirts with slogans like "Only Anarchists Are Pretty" and "Modernity Kills Every Night"; black mock turtlenecks with a small zip over one nipple; muslin T-shirts, now printed with giant swastikas and upside-down crucifixes hovering under the word DESTROY; black shirts with adjustable straps crossing the chest for that pseudofascist look; fluffy multicolored mohair sweaters with one sleeve much longer than the other; armbands printed with the words CHAOS and DESTROY; and, of course, the famous "bondage pants," multizipped trousers with a chain of cloth bizarrely connecting each leg of the trousers, and a terry-cloth diaper hanging down over the backside.

Chaos, indeed: Whether McLaren recognized it or not, the Sex Pistols' success was already out of his control. The only thing to do now was to encourage the boys as much as possible to follow the increasingly ferocious slogans that were appearing on the SEX shop's T-shirts. "Cash from Chaos," the shirts would declare. "Anarchy Is the Melody, Do-It-Yourself Is the Key." "Be Reasonable: Demand the Impossible." McLaren's contemporaries may have taken these slogans wryly, but that couldn't be said of the Sex Pistols or the slowly swelling legions of kids trekking down the King's Road to SEX on Saturday afternoons to buy their own bondage pants.

McLaren's first "official" act as the Sex Pistols' manager—there was still no legal agreement between him and the band—was more a matter of convenience than commitment. As soon as it became obvious that lugging the band's equipment to different rented rehearsal rooms each day was tearing into everyone's lives, as well as gouging deep holes in McLaren's pockets, he promised to help the boys find somewhere to call home. According to Westwood, however, he had another reason for wanting to find the band a permanent rehearsal space: After what he had been through with the Dolls, he thought that if all four Sex Pistols lived in the same place—he said he wanted some cross between a gay bathhouse and a college dorm—it would be much easier to get them to rehearse. The boys vetoed that idea, and for a while, it seemed like the Sex Pistols might have ejaculated prematurely, but then Matlock spotted an ad in *Melody Maker* advertising "Tin Pan Alley Studio, To take over, Sacrifice," and showed it to his boss.

"Phone him up and offer him £1,000 without seeing it," said McLaren.

"Are you sure?" Matlock asked incredulously.

McLaren just stared at him; Matlock dialed.

"I think my mate's a bit mad," he told the gentleman at the other end of the line, "but he's offering you £1,000 for your studio without even seeing it."

"Well, I think we can talk business," the voice said, as if by magic. "Why don't you come over."

The voice belonged to Bill Collins, former manager of Badfinger, and when McLaren, Matlock, and Jones visited the studio—a small, run-down, blackened flat in the mezzanine behind a faded Greek bookshop at 6 Denmark Street—Collins gave it to them for next to nothing. "He was getting on a bit," says Matlock, "and he could see our enthusiasm, so he let Malcolm pay him £200 or something like that."

With Denmark Street in their possession, the Sex Pistols began to feel like a real rock 'n' roll band and suddenly grew cocky, but McLaren kept reminding them that there was still plenty more work to be done. No way were they going to be big with the same old junk from the Who ("Substitute"), the Faces ("Whatcha Gonna Do About It"), and (ironically) the Monkees' "I'm Not Your Stepping Stone." ("Did You No Wrong," the song Wally had started, was finally finished, but it wasn't really anything more than a half-baked version of an old Faces number.) Confronted with the inveterate laziness of these deliberate yobs, McLaren put more and more pressure on the boys to rehearse and write songs. To Paul Cook, at least, this kind of pressure was unwarranted, especially considering that McLaren wasn't even paying them yet, and again he threatened to leave. "Cook was getting pissed off, because he said it was just a fuckin' noise," says Jones. "We thought it was rock, just not very good, but John liked it just because it wasn't, because it was noise."

A few songs were written in typically desultory manner by the start of October, with most of the music set down by Matlock with Jones's input, and most of the lyrics by Rotten. (Their records would credit almost all Sex Pistols songs to Rotten-Jones-Matlock-Cook.) First came the pounding "Seventeen" with music by Jones and lyrics by Rotten, except the chorus, whose defiantly yobbish four-word refrain—"I'm a lazy sod"—had Jones's name written all over it. Next were "Kill Me Today," "Concrete Youth," (both of which are lost), and a jeering, leering number called "Submission," inspired, says Matlock, when McLaren, looking for a SEX shop plug, asked him and Rotten to write a song about submission and bondage. "We said, ha, that's a bit naff, innit? So as a joke John and me said, 'I'm on a sub-marine mission for you, baby.' And that's a good measure of the action, because it was a kind of tongue-in-cheek message to Malcolm."

It often seemed that the *only* way McLaren and the Sex Pistols could communicate was by keeping their tongues securely in their cheeks. McLaren believed he was being patient with the band. He kept imagining a one-to-one correspondence between the Dolls and the Sex Pistols: Rotten for Thunders, Matlock for Sylvain, Jones for Johansen, Cook for Nolan—but he always came back to the same point, kept reminding them that without a contract (which would become necessary only when they had enough songs for a record), he was free to walk.

Of course, he didn't walk: The Sex Pistols were too attractive to him for that. And the more he thought about their goofy surliness, the more he realized that the Sex Pistols were *better* than the Dolls. The Dolls had finally been too independent and too bogged down in drugs and petty music-biz politics to provide the vicarious thrills McLaren needed to stay involved; the Sex Pistols were young, stupid, and, so he thought, malleable. Jones may have been Johansen's nearest rival in the sex symbol stakes, but he was ultimately what he said he was, a yob and a thief. Rotten was as sarcastic and uncontrollable as Thunders, but his negativity was just part of his personality, not a drug-induced liability: He couldn't care less about being a star. Cook and Matlock could take care of themselves. The Dolls wouldn't and couldn't go along with McLaren's political provocations; the Sex Pistols might. They could assert their independence all they wished, but they would never escape the tenacious grasp of his personality. Jones and Rotten were like wild animals set loose in the street, but McLaren had the power of a caged lion. So The Sex Pistols may have had grudging, growing respect for him, but the awareness that they were his willing, vicarious subjects was always present. "McLaren is a total fuckin' closet case," Jones says today. "Always has been, always will be."

By mid-October 1975, the Sex Pistols had a full repertoire of songs and were pleading with McLaren to get them gigs. McLaren had other things on his mind: Vivienne was angry, exhausted, and threatening to leave him. McLaren couldn't understand Westwood's fury, but while he was out hunting for publicity at gigs and nightclubs (the Sombrero and the Speakeasy were two of his favorites), Viv was running the shop, making the clothes, and taking care of their kid (Ben, Westwood's child from her first marriage, was away at his first boarding school, but Joseph, Westwood's son by McLaren, was still living at home). It's not fair, Westwood would say. You're damned right, it's not fair, McLaren would respond. "I'm a gentleman and a gentleman shouldn't have to come home to this mess, this slum." Disaster seemed imminent until Helen Wellington-Lloyd, his South African dwarf friend from Goldsmiths', phoned from Johannesburg.

Helen had gotten married and returned to South Africa almost immediately after college, but she had since separated from her South African husband and now, in 1975, was returning to London by herself to find McLaren in crisis. "I called Malcolm and told him I needed a flat," she says, "and he said he would move in with me, but that we had to find something right away. I wanted to buy one, not hire one, so I told him I couldn't do it right away. He said, 'It has to be *now* and it has to be someplace central. Just make sure it has a telephone.'"

Barely big enough to swing a cat in, the sunny, two-bedroom flat Helen found on Bell Street was quickly converted into the first Sex Pistols office. "Malcolm spent quite a lot of time there," snorts Westwood. "He even lived with Helen for a while. Temporarily, he was staying out to get away from me."

Meanwhile, the Sex Pistols had tired of waiting for McLaren to get his act together and they began taking an active role in creating their destiny. Numerous journalists have written that they gate-crashed several gigs, climbing onstage after another band had left its instruments in place, but Jones says it was only "three or four gigs where we would just show up and kind of worm our way in, nothing like the bullshit hype you hear from the press."

On November 6, the band played their first proper gig as support band for rock 'n' roll revivalists Bazooka Joe (one of whose members was Adam Ant) at St. Martin's College of Art, Glen Matlock's school. "I had been going there, so I just spoke to the social secretary," says Matlock. "We did about half a dozen numbers and they [Bazooka Joe] pulled the plug on us and there was kind of a tussle—'You can't use our gear'—real kids kind of stuff."

The sound was spotty and the band was rough—Jones's guitar dissonant and out of tune, Cook barely on the beat, a confused Johnny Rotten screaming away with scant regard for the lyrics, Matlock as usual gluing it all into music—but it was fun (McLaren called it "chaos") and the Sex Pistols were finally onstage. The next night, in a gig arranged by Sebastian Conran, they played at the Central School of Art and Design supporting Roogalator (featuring Julian Scott, the younger brother of McLaren's old Croydon schoolmate Robin Scott), and this time, they were surprisingly able to finish their entire thirty-minute set. In one twenty-four-hour period, everything had changed. On November 6, the Sex Pistols were just another rock 'n' roll band; on November 7, they had come to realize (even if no one else had) that they were operating in an entirely different universe from that of most rock 'n' roll bands. An entire generational schism—Us versus Them; Sex Pistols versus the rest of rock 'n' roll—had opened up overnight.

By the time of their fourth gig, at the Ravensbourne College of Art in Chislehurst, a pleasant suburb close to Bromley, in early December, word had started to spread and a small number of fans who had actually attended some gigs attached themselves to the band. One group in particular, the ultrastylish Bromley Contingent, began showing up at each and every show: Siouxsie Sue (later of the Banshees), William Broad (later, Billy Idol), Steve Bailey (later, Steve Havoc and then Severin), Sue (Lucas) Catwoman, Debbie (Wilson) Juvenile and Tracie O'Keefe (both of them soon to work at SEX), Nils Stevenson (whom McLaren was soon to promise a job as Sex Pistols comanager), and several others. They represented the utmost extreme of the SEX look: all black latex and patent leather, exaggerated kohl makeup, and striped and spangled lurex clothes, futuristically polished to a sexy sheen. Like a horror movie come to life. Or a walking SEX shop. With the Bromleys, the Sex Pistols' own friends, and McLaren's arty companions and old-time pals like Gerry Goldstein and Helen Wellington-Lloyd, the band had accumulated their own following.

Now it was up to McLaren to decide what to do with it.

For months, McLaren had masked his own indecision by taking a wait-and-see attitude to the Sex Pistols' progress. But now that the group had cobbled together a few decent songs and were starting to recognize the importance of being well rehearsed, he began playing the manager's role with more conviction, taxiing over to Denmark Street each morning to make sure Jones and Matlock (the musical center of the band) got out of bed and went to work. After all, there was destiny to consider—destiny and recording contracts.

"I'm going to change the face of the music scene!" McLaren told Nils Stevenson's older brother, Ray, a rock photographer who had once been David Bowie's factotum and who now began documenting the Sex Pistols' career. "All the music at the moment is by and for thirty-year-old hippies. Boring. [The Sex Pistols] are kids playing music for kids. . . . We've got to make it big before everyone else jumps on the bandwagon and we get left behind."

Still, even Malcolm McLaren couldn't sell the Sex Pistols on their musical merits at this stage in their career. If there was going to be a record, there had to be scandal, attitude, and political intrigue.

"None of them came together on the basis of musical taste," he told one interviewer in 1981. "The group wasn't formed because all the group *liked* this type of music—they didn't know *what* music to play. No one knew. No one had a clue. At that time [1976], you didn't have that whole background of the Rolling Stones, listening to black Rhythm & Blues, the kind of music we had when I was growing up. You were literally filled with little bits of David Bowie, Roxy Music, and the Faces, a second generation of rock 'n' roll that had watered it down and polished the edges, turned it into a far more introverted and *alienated* culture. . . . Groups became like an aristocracy; it was something you worshipped, something you paid a lot of money for, to see a group no bigger than a sixpence on the stage.

"*That* wasn't rock 'n' roll. In my opinion, rock 'n' roll was getting up there, stepping out and creating the greatest possible imperfection. The music wasn't important. It was just a declaration of intent and an attitude. If you got that, that's what it was all about."

If McLaren didn't have much to sell by way of music, he still had his enemies clearly in his sights, and so long before the Sex Pistols were ready to play their first gigs, he began looking for a symbolic target to demonstrate their firing power. What he needed was someone tolerant enough to host a giant launch party for the boys, who wouldn't complain when it all went wrong. After a flip through his little black book, the perfect patsy sprang to mind: Andrew Logan, the sculptor and jeweler *extraordinaire* who had, since 1971, sponsored a series of irregularly held evenings called The Alternative Miss World contests.

In the decadent days of 1930s Berlin, Logan's Alternative Miss World contests might not have raised a single eyebrow, but in the atmosphere of mid-1970s London, where celebrity and eccentricity were linked in a peculiar cycle of mutual reinforcement, these beauty contests cum drag shows were well covered by the media, and the full pantheon of British style stars—from David Hockney to Zandra Rhodes, everyone who Peter York later christened Thems—made a point of being seen there. Anyone could be a contestant so long as he (or she) wasn't afraid of being pilloried by the press, but to McLaren, the contests were a hotbed of style elitism. In March 1975, for example, while McLaren was still in America, the contest was "judged" by Hockney, Rhodes, Justin de Villeneuve (Twiggy's ex), and Amanda Lear, among others. To McLaren, Logan's gentle eccentricity—on the night of his contests, he always dresses the right side of his body in kingly splendor and the left side in queenly curvaceousness—epitomized all that was wrong with British style, just as Bryan Ferry, the most popular rock star of Logan's set, epitomized, to him, the sad state of rock 'n' roll.

"I was living by Butler's Wharf at the time, in a studio next to Tower Bridge," Logan recalls, "when Malcolm phoned up and asked if I knew of anywhere down by the river, because he said he had these boys—he called them 'the boys'—he wanted to launch somewhere and he wanted to launch them somewhere interesting. And an Andrew Logan party *was* interesting. It was the thing to do then. I said, Fine, come along, then, and they finally played at my Valentine's Day party. They weren't the *main* attraction, they were just a group that played, just as Adam & the Ants played later on. Same thing. If something is happening in a city and you're doing something by which you can help, you do, don't you?"

To McLaren, St. Valentine's Day was the perfect date for the Sex Pistols to deliver their first body blow to the style Establishment: It would be SEX versus love, and McLaren hoped his boys would be able to steal the limelight and create the first pop scandal of 1976.

When St. Valentine's Day arrived, the Sex Pistols assembled at Logan's loft to discover themselves vastly outnumbered and outclassed by the Thems—socialites, stylists, and Bryan Ferry look-alikes. McLaren's boys immediately went to work, stalking the party like ferocious animals let loose in a city, gobbling up canapes and guzzling down booze, leering and plucking at the pretty girls surrounding them, and when the boys struck up the band to play what would be the first of three nearly identical sets—on a stage that was the set from the court scene in Derek Jarman's *Sebastien*—Andrew Logan's tin-roof ceiling rattled and shook and the audience took cover. "The whole ceiling just sang," remembers Logan. "It went brrr, and *we* scurried into the corner."

"The Sex Pistols started up, and they didn't know what hit them," remembers Jordan. "Andrew was freaking out, actually, because it was like anarchy had been transported into his little paradise and he hadn't realized what was going on there.

"Someone from *New Musical Express* arrived—it might have been Nick Kent—and Malcolm came rushing up to me and said, 'Jords'—that was his nickname for me because that was what they had called that bassist for the New York Dolls, Peter Jordan—'Jords, the enemy is here! They've actually turned up! We've got to do something that will create a scuffle, a story.' And I said, 'Well, what?' and he said, 'Why don't you go up there and take your clothes off.' I said, 'Oh, come on, Malcolm,' and he said, 'No, I'm serious. Now I want you to go up there and take your clothes off, 'cause they're going to take pictures of it. It'll be brilliant, it'll put the band on the map.'

"He was so excited, really excited, desperate to get some scam going, but I was determined, and I told him no, I wouldn't do it. And he bugged me again, so I finally told him that if John pulls me up onstage, if John *takes* my clothes off, I'll do it, but I'm not going to get up there and act like an idiot. He's going to have to have the bollocks to do it.

"But John wasn't very, uh, brave. John liked things to be set up for him, wasn't great at instigatin' it, so Malcolm had a word with him—hand signals and stuff—and in the middle of Iggy Pop's "No Fun," John broke all the zips on my leotard, which was a real piss-off. I was so fed up about that, I just took the back of it and went zoom."

Even if it didn't actually make the *NME*, Jordan's famous striptease struck the long-desired symbolic blow against the Tired Trendies and Boring Old Farts of the fashion and music industries that McLaren had so often dreamed of delivering himself. It was, however, difficult to imagine how the Sex Pistols would perform when and if McLaren ever got them some real gigs. As luck would have it, the week after Logan's party, the Sex Pistols "crashed" the High Wycombe College of Art Valentine's Dance where Screaming Lord Sutch was scheduled to play and caught the eye of Ron Watts, manager of Oxford Street's famed 100 Club.

"They weren't booked or invited, they just arrived and said they were the support band, set up their gear and played," Watts told *Rock Family Tree* scribe Pete Frame. "I thought they were great, so I found out who their manager was and he came down the 100 Club to see me the following week. The outcome was that I began to book them consistently whereas other promoters and venues wouldn't have anything to do with them."

Once they got to the 100 Club, however, the Sex Pistols showed they weren't ready for the big time. Rotten's icy dismissiveness was well suited to McLaren's symbolic maneuvering, but his stroppiness wasn't a put-on and he was difficult to handle in anything more than short doses. Nor was the situation helped by Rotten's pal John Beverley, later known as Sid Vicious; at one of these early 100 Club gigs, Vicious became so infuriated when *NME*'s Nick Kent blocked his view of the band that he took out a length of chain and whacked Kent over the head.

The night of their first official 100 Club gig, March 30, Rotten stayed in the bar with his mates, ignoring McLaren and the band. By the time he teetered before the fifty or so stragglers in the audience, he was falling "arse over tit" and Matlock was furious.

"God damn you, Rotten," he screamed. "Sing in time or don't sing at all, yer fucking up the set."

"What'd you say, Matlock?" Rotten retorted to the glee of the crowd, most of whom were oblivious to the fact that this wasn't a planned part of the band's set.

"Sing in time!" yelled Matlock over Jones's roaring guitar. "And sing in tune too. You sound bloody awful!"

"I'll *kill* you! I'll *kill* you," ranted Rotten, clinging to the mike-stand. "Just step outside and I'll kill you."

With Cook and Jones continuing to play, Rotten grabbed Cook's cymbals, flinging them over the side of the stage, slamming over his mike-stand in the process. Jones, mock furious, kicked Rotten hard in the backside, and Skinny John tumbled off the front of the stage.

"Get back on that stage or I'm telling you now, it's all over," McLaren bellowed at his singer, casually chatting with his mates in the audience amid all the chaos. "That's it, you bloody sod! I'm through with the whole thing unless you *get back on that stage* and finish the bloody concert. You won't even get taxi money!"

Rotten sheepishly moved toward the side of the stage, but by this time, Jones was deliberately busting his guitar strings, proceeding backstage in full tantrum to wreck the club dressing room. Rotten had calmed down enough to clamber back to the footlights, but by now the gig was over, its energy dissipated into the 100 Club's regular booziness. Rotten swanked off with his friends and wasn't seen for the rest of the week.

Ron Watts obviously thought the Sex Pistols and their stylish fans were great—after this debacle, he booked them for a running Tuesday-night residency—but London's other club promoters weren't so impressed with the Sex Pistols' violent histrionics. When the band opened for Eddie and the Hot Rods at the Marquee in mid-March, Rotten once again flew into a rage when he couldn't hear himself over the Hot Rods' P.A. and he tossed a couple of chairs into the monitors, an act that earned the Sex Pistols the honor of being banned forevermore from the venerated club, thrown off the Hot Rods' upcoming tour, and their very first live review in the *NME.*

"Don't look over your shoulder, but the Sex Pistols are coming," read the title of Neil Spencer's short, cynical rave—deliberately omitting all mention of headliners Eddie and the Hot Rods. The Sex Pistols, wrote Spencer, were a "musical experience with the emphasis on Experience": "Springsteen Bruce [*sic*] and the rest of 'em would get shredded if they went up against these boys." As if that weren't enough, the review ended with an anecdote that caused great glee in the Sex Pistols' camp. After the show, Spencer had waded through the debris of broken chairs and beer bottles to ask one of the bandmembers about his musical influences. Steve Jones had gladly taken a moment to set him straight.

"Actually, we're not into music," Jones said.

"Wot then?" asked Spencer.

"We're into chaos."

If you believed the Sex Pistols' reputation in the music press, the word was that McLaren's boys were a joke, the joke consisting essentially of the punch line that in an age of high-tech musicianship, the Sex Pistols were getting famous by being incapable of playing their instruments. (*Melody Maker:* "They do as much for music as World War Two did for the cause of peace.") *This* wasn't music, went the word in the music press, this was *hype,* the cleverly managed triumph of London's latest indigenous rock 'n' roll rejects (in 1976 most hit records came from the other side of the Atlantic). In fact, the Sex Pistols could play quite well by this time—Steve Jones had spent the winter speeding out of his mind playing to Iggy Pop's *Raw Power*—but without the aid of a guitar hero who was convinced that the rumors about the band's musicianship were mere jealousy, the Sex Pistols might well have broken up after their 100 Club bust-up.

"In 1976, things just gravitated toward me, although I definitely was not a punk," says Chris Spedding, the ace session guitarist best known for his work with John Cale, Robert Gordon, Roxy Music, and many others. "I just happened to be one of the only established musicians at the time who looked halfway interesting to them because I had recently had a Top 10 single that made *Top of the Pops,* and in those days I had sort of a Let It Rock look when everyone else had flared trousers, sequined jackets, and long hair."

It was Chrissie Hynde, the former Let It Rock shopgirl, who first turned Spedding on to the Sex Pistols when the two ran into each other in Paris. "Chrissie was the first punk I ever saw," he says, "and when she got back to London, she took me to the 100 Club the night they almost broke up. That was quite an experience: Johnny Rotten was either pushed or jumped off the stage in disgust and McLaren screamed at him that he wouldn't get his taxi fare home if he didn't get back onstage, so at the end of the gig, I took Rotten under my wing and we went out with Chrissie, Chris Ritter [later, Rat Scabies], and my girlfriend at the time, Nora Foster, who is now married to John Lydon. Anyway, Rotten was very upset and said he wanted to leave the group. I told him not to because I believed there was really something there."

Spedding was infuriated by the music media's allegations that the Sex Pistols could not play. "I said, this is interesting, because these people are supposedly knowledgeable about music and they can't see beyond the band's anarchistic attitude. The fact was that these guys could really play. I'd never heard Steve Jones play out of tune *once* in my whole life. And that drummer friend of his could really keep time quite well. It only sounded all over the place because it *looked* all over the place. In fact by any measurable standards—(a) if they play reasonably in time, and (b) if they play reasonably in tune—they passed the test, regardless of whether you liked them or not.

"It was an important opportunity to say, wait a minute: I've been playing twenty years, I'm a respected musician, maybe I can do something here. I don't know if McLaren believed me, but he decided I could be a pawn in his game and that he could use me, and I was pleased to be used 'cause I was so fascinated by the whole situation. I *let* him manipulate me, but I never trusted him because he always had this big cheesy grin on whenever he saw me."

Over a couple of meetings at the Roebuck and at the crêperie up the road from SEX, Spedding offered McLaren his help. "First, I told him I knew quite a few journalists, and that I could try and get one of them to come to a Sex Pistols gig," he says. "That's when his eyes lit up. But then I told him I wanted to produce a demo tape for the band—free of charge, gratis—so he would then have something to prove to people who wouldn't come to a Sex Pistols gig that they really could play, and then he got very cool."

Although Spedding would eventually do that demo for the Sex Pistols, it wasn't until years later that he finally figured out why McLaren had become so icy: Malcolm McLaren didn't want the world to think that the Sex Pistols could play. To McLaren, the Sex Pistols were chaos or they were nothing at all.

Just as McLaren was often a mean and indifferent parent in real life—couldn't be bothered with his son, Joseph, and often made deliberate attempts to embarrass or just plain hurt Vivienne's older son, Ben—so was he often a careless parent to the Sex Pistols; if anything, his cruelty to his own kids outdid his show of indifference to the band. When McLaren deliberately trod on Ben's toe in public, the boy knew he was being tested and refused to cry out, to succumb to his stepfather's sadism. The Sex Pistols, on the other hand, could and did return McLaren's fire, making his life difficult by missing rehearsals or showing up to gigs at the last minute.

McLaren's best weapon with the Sex Pistols was to hold tight to his purse strings, and to use them to his best advantage, he maintained a stern hands-off attitude to the group until the last minute of their perpetual financial crises. Then, and only then, would he very suddenly and majestically swoop down to the filthy Denmark Street studio to save the day, bailing out his surrogate sons with a gig, a flat, some money, or food.

While the Sex Pistols preferred McLaren's handouts to the alternative (getting a job), they never came to feel beholden to him. Quite the contrary. Regardless of his feelings about it, McLaren's just deserts were usually delivered in the form of the chaos and bedlam he himself had encouraged, the same stream of obscenity Rotten slung at everyone else: *Fuck you, fuck off, "don't waste my time."* Irked though McLaren may have been by this insolence, this gloating Fuckyouism, gradually he also came to enjoy it and become proud of it. What more could he expect when he was sending others out to do the bidding he claimed he would do himself: If only he weren't so old (twenty-eight); if only he weren't a tired shopkeeper; if only he didn't have a "wife" and a kid—he always used the singular—to worry about.

"Really, he'd like to be in the band," said Johnny Rotten, explaining why he considered McLaren the "fifth member of the band," "but he couldn't. He could never do it himself. So we do it for him."

Scorned by the promoters and banned by most London venues, McLaren was forced to create gigs by starting his own club, all the while declaiming the growing pub rock scene he suspected of impeding his group's progress. (It's often said that Rotten picked up his best moves from watching Ian Dury, a childhood polio victim, performing with Kilburn & the High Roads at the Hope & Anchor.) The pubs, said McLaren, were hypocrites' dens, full of self-serving musicians "playing what a crowd wants rather than what *they* want because they can make a reasonable living from it. If you want to change things," he declared, "you can't play pubs."

But the Sex Pistols could play a strip joint and so he hired the El Paradise, a Soho skin parlor allegedly owned by Maltese mafiosi, for a string of Sunday nights. On Sunday April 4, the date of the only Paradise gig ever to come off, the Sex Pistols climbed out of the audience onto the club's postage-stamp-sized stage and ripped through their set, but the crowd of newly loyal fans—most of whom were stoned blind with the speed Michael Collins had dumped in the punch—stood blankly in the airless room, rife with the odors of cigarette smoke, stale sweat, and dried cum. Such apathy only made Rotten angrier than he already was about the wretched P.A. McLaren had hired and he screamed at the audience to *get moving*—"Clap, you fuckers, 'cause I'm wasting my time not hearing myself"—but the crowd couldn't have cared less, barely distinguishing between songs, much less between what was "real" and what was merely part of the band's act. It was only when the club's regularly scheduled stripper arrived, insisting on her right to perform for tips, that apathy turned to anarchy: The second set was a gleefully absentminded melee.

For any other rock band, such chaos would have counted as a failure of the highest order, but two weeks later, after a gig at the Nashville, a huge West Kensington country & western pub gone seedy with live music, the Sex Pistols found themselves on the receiving end of a two-page feature interview by "Jonh" Ingham in *Sounds*. "I hate hippies and what they stand for," Rotten told Ingham. "I hate long 'air . . . I'm against people who just complain about *Top of the Pops* and don't do anything. I want people to go out and start something, to see us and start something, or else I'm just wasting my time."

It had been only four months since they had first played in public, but the Sex Pistols were already being bruited about with the kind of fervor usually reserved for long-established cult legends.

With their three gigs at the Nashville, the Sex Pistols confirmed the critics' first impressions and continued to distinguish themselves from the rest of rock *simply by being themselves.* Any chance they got, they insisted that their only motive was to speed up the demolition of pop music, and not to make the Top 10. ("You have to destroy in order to create," McLaren chirped at every opportunity.) With the addition of a decent P.A. hired for Nashville headliners the 101ers, the band's sound suddenly catapulted into a sharp crescendo of white noise and rootsy rock 'n' roll and Rotten's taunting could now be heard as something more than the rants of a spoiled child.

Spedding was right: It *was* music after all, music that made you blink back at the fury of the moment, made you wonder who you really were, made you feel that *you* had the power, that *you* could do it too. To adult ears it was noise, but to those who understood its savage juvenile splendor, the Sex Pistols represented nothing less than a total liberation from Top 10 tedium.

In the classic cliché of adolescents everywhere, once you had experienced it, there was no going back. Soon even the staunchest devotees of other bands were sent into paroxysms of self-worry after seeing the Sex Pistols. After sharing the Nashville stage with Rotten and friends, Joe Strummer, lead singer of the 101ers, vowed never to play again in a rhythm and blues band; that very night, Strummer met up with Mick Jones and quit the 101ers. The Clash came together over the summer.

With that second Nashville gig in the last week of April, the Sex Pistols acquired a large, fanatical claque; seats had become so scarce that when Vivienne Westwood returned from the toilet to find a stubborn punter in her place, Sid Vicious beat the daylights out of the interloper with a hefty length of bike chain and the fracas tumbled onto the stage and back to the audience.

Real blood covered the stage and the Sex Pistols were banned from yet another London venue (a ban they were to break within the week), but Malcolm McLaren had learned to stop worrying and love the revolution. What else could he do? Now that the Sex Pistols had gone this far, the threat of violence—*real* violence, not just the simulated bloodletting of heavy metal—had become as much a part of the Sex Pistols' experience as their music. Thrilling as it was, the music was already beside the point: To those who counted themselves part of the SEX vanguard, it was the very reality of the violence, of seeing fresh blood flow, that gave the Sex Pistols their kick. Any idiot who showed up without the requisite safety-pin earring or SEX gear was simply asking for trouble.

But in this case—in all cases?—the vanguard went about their grisly tasks with the kinds of smiles that somehow belied their best "revolutionary" intentions: smiles only true connoisseurs of violence could appreciate. One need only look at the photo published by *NME* the week after the Nashville fight to see how ruthless this new subculture could be: for there in the frozen instant of some lucky photographer's flash, was a blood-spattered Johnny Rotten, caught in midtumble and wearing the grin of someone who looked for all the world like he was getting away with murder.

5
THE MAIN EVENT

Of course, history was being made, but the Sex Pistols were the least of it. Depending on how you looked at it, the Sex Pistols were either a freak show or a warning signal, but certainly not the main event. From late winter through the spring of 1976, the main event was Britain herself: the virtual collapse of her economy, the wearying dissolution of her postwar affluence, the widening breach between her classes—her decline.

Nothing worked, nothing went right. In just a few months, the price of sterling slipped penny by penny, nearly 40 cents on the dollar; inflation rose a staggering 24 percent (over 150 percent from 1963 to 1975); luxury items (cigarettes and booze, mostly) were taxed 25 percent over retail prices; many wages were compulsorily frozen; unemployment edged toward a million, never as high since 1940; consumer spending tumbled for the first time in 20 years; and £3 *billion* more cuts in health, education, and related state services were on the way.

And all this under a Labour government.

Put simply, as the nation grew poorer, the very basis of its political life began to unravel: Britain had become ungovernable. Labour had fallen hostage to the trade unions that make up its rank and file and the unions had reached the end of their rope waiting for the so-called natural party of the working class to come to their defense. Class conflict, harsh and nasty, was now the rule of the day, the perpetual theme of each confrontation between the government and its alleged supporters. Heavily indebted to the International Monetary Fund and stretched to its limits by the recessionary effects of the Arab oil embargo of 1973, Garden England, it was said, was now in danger of becoming the first industrialized nation to join the Third World.

However, if you were young and had grown up with the (swollen) promises of an affluent welfare state, all this nonsense of a Labour government struggling to come to grips with the unions seemed a mockery of the very values you had been raised to respect. Prime ministers and their policies might change—that March, Harold Wilson dramatically resigned the week after his sixtieth birthday, giving the nod to his deceptively emollient foreign secretary, James Callaghan—but over and over one heard the pundits declare that there was no way out, that the crisis was the inevitable result of economic and political choices Britons had made since the end of the Second World War—accelerated, of course, by the energy crunch of the early seventies.

No way out: nothing beyond the teeming comprehensive schools that deposited you for work at the same factory, office, or dole queue your parents had wasted their time in; nothing beyond the decrepit terraces of futuristic council flats, dreamed up by some hard-nosed ivory-towered professor. No way out: even if you could escape the grip of the classic cradle-to-grave welfare state, even if you had the unlikely desire to go out and *do* something, there were no jobs for you to go to, no money for you to play with, nothing to do even if you had some.

In the oppressively sweltering summer of 1976, a young Briton's choices were limited, perhaps, to two: You could mope along with the rest of Britain—take imaginary refuge from the winter's gloom-doom headlines and get a good tan—or you could turn your back on the glamorous fantasy of England as Tropical Consumer Paradise and put on the disjunct gladrags of the punks parading up and down the King's Road Saturday afternoons. For as summer drew on and the media's portrayal of the unrelenting heat changed from "miracle" to "freak disorder" and Hyde Park's gentle greens turned into dustbowls of burnt sienna—the government even appointed a minister for drought—the punks seemed to be the only ones who hadn't forgotten last winter's crisis.

For the punks tramping down the King's Road, the hot summer of 1976 was apocalypse *now*, the catalytic moment when all the impotent political squabbling about England's decline boiled over into a situation that demanded an unremittingly loud and taunting *no* to everything and everyone in sight: a moment of refusal. You cut wild holes in your T-shirts, put safety pins through your nose or ear or cheek, dyed your hair lurid shades of lime and Vaselined it into submission, ripped your trousers into shreds and safety-pinned them back together, put a dog collar around your neck and called it jewelry: Anything worked so long as it had the right attitude of negation—powered by the nasty, jaw-clenching, amphetamine rush of cheap powdered sulfate. But the general plan was to shock for shock's sake, deliberately mismatching articles of clothing across gender and history with a vicious sense of irony, so that it all became a blur out of time and out of place, an apocalyptic present contrived from a speeding, schizoid jumble of the past.

And if anyone was ever bold enough to ask why—Why this parade of incivility, this insolent rejection of modern life?—the response (if it ever got that far) was that why was not the point. The point was to be able to say *fuck you* and mean it, to leave no place for curiosity-seekers, Carnaby Street tourists or well-meaning sociologists with nothing better to do than to dream up new case studies in alienation, anomie, and the emptiness of the human spirit. The point was to have a laugh while you still could, to cock a snook at the world before it all closed in, before the bombs went off. Not politics, but *anti*politics, chaos, antagonism, and anarchy. Not sound, but fury and strident aggression. Not music, but noise—loud, fast, and speeding. Not love, but SEX: 430 King's Road, home of the Sex Pistols, public face of the punk explosion.

It was impossible not to identify the punks inhabiting the King's Road with the SEX shop and Sex Pistols. Punk was now exploding into the national limelight, and the band's running residency at the 100 Club (every Tuesday night through May and June) spread their gospel from the music papers to the garages of young people throughout Britain. New punk bands sprouted daily: the Clash, the Damned, the Stranglers, Subway Sect, Slaughter and the Dogs, Poly Styrene and the X-Ray Specs, Eddie and the Hot Rods, the Buzzcocks—a host of teen talents with little patience for rock's dues-paying drudgery. For the first time since its infancy, rock 'n' roll was once again becoming something *anyone* could do: a misfit's occupation.

After months of rejections, including one time when he was thrown down a staircase by the promoter of the Roundhouse, Malcolm McLaren was now finding it easy to wangle the Sex Pistols gigs, even at such major venues as Manchester's capacious Free Trade Hall and London's Lyceum. To anyone who kept an eye on pop culture, the Sex Pistols had quickly become something more than mere music: either a warning signal of a nation's desire for something *hard,* something *real,* something beyond the soft sophistries of political stalemate—curiously, the same yearnings that would soon be appealed to by the new Tory leader, the helmet-haired Margaret Thatcher—or a harmless freak show, a mindless distraction: the latest nutty pop band.

Nobody knew which of these things the Sex Pistols really were. Even in their own camp, there was considerable disagreement as to whether the boys were Britain's answer to the glittering tumult of the New York Dolls or the leaders of some weird new revolution—not a band but a new subculture joining punks to Mods, Rockers, and Teds. To McLaren, the Sex Pistols were still mostly fun, not a career, and although he was beginning to wonder how long he would be able to keep them all afloat without a record deal, he hadn't yet started to take the group seriously as either business or as tools of cultural manipulation. He boasted that he was a manager in name only.

Chris Spedding may have been an ace guitarist, but he was no match for McLaren's manipulations. Although McLaren gave Spedding the go-ahead to produce a Sex Pistols demo, he was hardly convinced that Spedding—who was after all ex officio Roxy Music—should be given the plum of riding on the Sex Pistols' coattails. After several meetings to pick out their best songs ("Problems," "Pretty Vacant," and "No Feelings") the band visited Spedding at his place in Wimbledon, "with the first Ramones album tucked under their arms," he laughingly recalls, "saying *this* is what we want to sound like.

"I didn't think there was anything I could really do for them musically except to capture their sound on tape. So when we finally got into Majestic Studios in Clapham in the last week in May, all I did was to get them drums and amps without any buzzes or rattles, and then—and this is important—I didn't tell them the red light was on, just had them run through their set. Because as soon as young musicians know the recording light is on, they tense up and can't play. So I just got it down on tape: just one five-hour session. I knew *too much* to get involved musically."

It takes only one listen to Spedding's (unreleased) Sex Pistols session (supposedly available as a 1981 German bootleg) to realize that this master musician knew what he was talking about, for even though the band had had only the briefest of studio experiences until this moment, they sound tight as a studio rockabilly band, clear, focused, and strongly controlled. Spedding's tape makes much of the Sex Pistols' later work sound sloppy by comparison.

From the other end of the spectrum, however, McLaren was also coming under the gun from his old anarchist schoolchum from the Croydon days, Jamie MacGregor-Reid. Earlier that March, McLaren had sent a telegram inviting Reid and his girlfriend Sophie Richmond to come down to London from their refuge in the Outer Hebrides to see his boys. "Got these guys," he wrote. "Interested in working with you again."

To Reid, who had been designing pamphlets and posters for the radical Suburban Press almost since he'd been thrown out of Croydon, McLaren's message was like a call to arms. Compared with the solicitous trials of designing clever bumperstickers—"SAVE petrol, BURN cars" read one—or producing books such as Christopher Grey's odd compilation of Situationist texts, *Leaving the 20th Century*—the idea of collaborating with McLaren was like a release from political purgatory. Reid was thunderstruck with the idea of using a rock 'n' roll band to score political points, and soon after his arrival, he began coming up with ideas to turn the Sex Pistols into a Situationist-style anarchists' lair. First, he wanted the band to defeat its fans' expectations by deliberately missing gigs, an old Situationist *détournement*. Then he wanted to push Rotten to write some authentically anarchistic songs. It seems unlikely he got very far, but when it came to infiltrating the band with his ideas, Reid held one card over McLaren, for the dour, anarchist Reid was just as much of a boozer as Johnny Rotten, and if you wanted to reach Rotten's "heart," it was said it was best to travel by the pub first. Rumors persist even today that Reid "gave" Rotten the last verse of "Anarchy in the U.K." during a late-nite drinking session at a local pub.

Reid still maintains that *his* idea for the Sex Pistols was that they climb the ladder straight up the Top 10 and then just disappear. Obviously, McLaren ignored that advice, instead confining his friend's services to designing Sex Pistols posters and paraphernalia, which turned out to be no minor thing, since the Sex Pistols' provocative kidnap letter logo, a seemingly spontaneous layout of letters cut from various newspapers, soon became to punk what balloon letterstyle had been to the hippies: a cool graphic code for pulling punters into gigs.

In fact, many dispute Reid's claim to having originated the logo. "Helen did the first kidnap lettering for the handouts," says Vivienne Westwood. "Jamie thinks he did it, but Helen [Wellington-Lloyd] did it. She grabbed the feeling of what this whole punk thing was about." "I was told it had to be something quick and we had no money for Letraset," says Wellington-Lloyd. "I loved finding letters from different newspapers and making copies of little posters."

Reid's radical obsessions made the most ordinary managerial decisions remarkably difficult for McLaren, most typically when it came to settling such issues as what to do with Chris Spedding's crystalline demos. Reid wanted the Sex Pistols to make a stand, not pop music, but Spedding's tape made the Sex Pistols sound like they knew what they were doing, made them sound like pop musicians. It was "dull," "boring," "lifeless": Where was the anarchy in that? When a photo of Spedding with the band at Majestic Studios appeared in *Sounds* the week after the session—"Spedding's finger on Sex Pistols' trigger," read the headline—McLaren made sure to let word slip out through Spedding's friend, journalist Caroline Coon, that Spedding's help was no longer needed: thanks, but no thanks. Still, *something* had to be done—already there were rumors that El Speddo had played Steve Jones's guitar parts. The Sex Pistols would never get a deal if the record companies thought that the Sex Pistols and Chris Spedding were one and the same.

"Part of why they didn't like my demo," says Spedding, "was that because I like R&B, I highlighted their rhythm tracks with a big bass drum and bass sound, particularly because Matlock had some intensely played bass runs. *They* wanted a guitar soup. Well, I think that whenever you've got an interesting rhythm section like that, a band sounds like they can actually play, and since that was the whole point of my demo—to *prove* they could play—that's what I pushed. When you have a guitar soup, which is what the demo they recorded later sounds like, you have to face the fact that *someone's* trying to cover up the fact they can't play. And that's what McLaren wanted people to think: that they *couldn't* play, that it was just an idea, a way of making all this anarchy stuff happen."

Once "Anarchy in the U.K." was written, however, another demo had to be recorded anyway, and since McLaren had no money, the chore of recording the band now fell to Dave Goodman, the sound-man/van driver who first met the band through a sheer coincidence: his P.A. company had been contracted by Albion Sound for the Sex Pistols gig at the Nashville.

"I don't know how they actually got to be going with Spedding," says Goodman, "but obviously they thought he was the guy to give them the sound, and they played it to me and I thought it was quite dead. I had their live performance to go by, so I said *I* could do better than *that* on my four-track."

Where Chris Spedding had needed only five hours to record and mix three songs (including a few guitar overdubs), Dave Goodman and his Australian sidekick Kim Thraibes took a full two weeks in mid-July before deciding they had finally captured the Sex Pistols' "live" sound. "Malcolm just left it up to us really," says Goodman. "We just turned them full up to eleven and did what seemed natural."

"That session was absolutely atrocious," says Matlock. "It took us almost two weeks and the reason was that we was trying to create a live sound every time but they didn't know when it was good. Whenever it was starting to hit the right one, they kept saying faster, faster, and they was feeding us with coke and all that to try and get the vibe, that real live kind of thing. And the longer it went on, the more we was getting pissed off with playing. It was getting faster and faster and not the right approach at all. Almost two weeks we were there: It must have cost a fortune."

Goodman's tape may have been guitar soup, all reverb and echo, but to McLaren, anything was better than having to admit that the Sex Pistols had been tamed by a Roxy Music session guitarist, and as soon as the demo was done, he sent the Sex Pistols packing on a road trip through the North with Nils Stevenson, a Bromley boy he had promised to make comanager once the band was making money, while he began shopping the new tape to the record companies. Many phone calls later, all McLaren had was a spot on Tony Wilson's *So It Goes* on Manchester's Grenada Television, a rather uneventful live taping of the Sex Pistols performing "Anarchy in the U.K." which began with a staggeringly SEX-clad Jordan introducing the band. "Ladies and Gentleman," she proclaimed to the screaming crowd, "the Sex Pistols are, if possible, even better than the lovely Joni Mitchell."

Malcolm McLaren may have been an industry neophyte—in any event, he thought of himself and the Sex Pistols as rock 'n' roll outlaws railing against a complacent industry, high living, and tired gentleman rockers—but when it came to record companies he knew what he wanted and what he wanted was EMI, home of the Beatles and the Rolling Stones, the biggest and best-known record company in England.

By the end of August, the Sex Pistols had already achieved such a reputation as rock 'n' roll nuisances that they were thrown off the First European Punk Rock tour to France by headliners Eddie and the Hot Rods (finally getting their revenge for the Sex Pistols' bad behavior at the Marquee), and banned from playing at Dingwalls and the Rock Garden for some late-night chair-throwing and window-breaking. ("Who do they think they are?" one rock writer asked. "The Rolling Stones of the late '70s?") Faced with a virtual lock-out from London's rock 'n' roll nightspots, McLaren once again repeated the old fib that playing in pubs was no use to the Sex Pistols anyway, and he grabbed at the connections of an old art school friend who helped him obtain an evening at the Screen On The Green, an Islington art cinema.

It was there, with the Sex Pistols headlining a unique midnight-to-dawn extravaganza of punk bands (including the Buzzcocks and Stranglers, and the London debut of the Clash), Kenneth Anger films, and impromptu stripping by a coven of beauties dressed in SEX gear, that McLaren first established official contact with the record industry's point men, the lowly A&R managers—in particular, a thirty-year-old industry hack from EMI called Nick Mobbs, the one record biz honcho usually given credit for discovering the Sex Pistols.

In fact, Mobbs had been dragged to see the Sex Pistols by one of his A&R scouts, a recording engineer named Mike Thorne. "I just went wandering around and simply stumbled into the Summer of '76," says Thorne, who has since gone on to produce records for Wire, Bronski Beat, Soft Cell, and many others. "Because I was younger [twenty-seven] and EMI was my first A&R job, I was one of the very few A&R men to actually connect. Everybody claims they were there but it wasn't true. I was completely alone at many of those gigs."

"There was a buzz about the Sex Pistols that was getting bigger and bigger," says Mobbs, "and Mike Thorne said I really think you should see them. That Screen On The Green gig gave me this incredible feeling in the stomach: I think I'll remember it until I die. It reminded me of when I was a fan, not having anything to do with the business. And yet, at the same time, my head was saying, they're not very good, and although I knew that wasn't the major consideration, I would lie awake all night thinking about it, wondering whether it was something EMI could handle." (Chris Spedding: "I played my tape for Micky Most and Dave Crowe who were respectively the owner and A&R guy of the label I was signed to, RAK Records, and later that day Crowe went over to Manchester House [EMI's headquarters] and told Nick Mobbs about my tape. Mobbs said, 'Them? I wouldn't sign the Sex Pistols with a ten-foot pole!' ")

As soon as the band returned from an exciting road trip to open the new Chalet du Lac disco in Paris, McLaren phoned Nick Mobbs's office to find that Mobbs was out of town. Mike Thorne took the call. "It was simple as that, really," he says. "Malcolm called me out of the blue and said, 'I've got this group the Sex Pistols and I've got some demos. I'd like to talk to you about it.' I promised I would have a word with Nick when he returned, because I couldn't make a move without him, but meanwhile the demos were there and I passed them over. Malcolm got impatient, so he called Leslie Hill, who was the director of EMI Records—he knew how to pull rank pretty well—and of course, Leslie referred him right back to Nick."

McLaren was also in contact with Chris Parry, a twenty-five-year-old A&R manager at Polydor Records who was also at the Screen On The Green gig. "I had hooked up with Jonh Ingham and Caroline Coon and they didn't have a car so we used to go out together and spin around and see all the bands—the Pistols, the Clash, the Stranglers—all the bands," says Parry, who now manages the Cure and is the head of their record label, Fiction Records. "McLaren came into Polydor with a bit of film footage from the *So It Goes* show on Manchester TV. He wanted £20,000 to sign on to me plus £20,000 for costs and everything else. I thought it was a reasonable deal, so we played Dave Goodman's demo and the *So It Goes* tape for Polydor but they had trouble taking it seriously at first."

While Chris Parry tried to convince his superiors at Polydor that the Sex Pistols would be next year's big thing, McLaren kept harping on EMI to sign the band—titillating the A&R boys one week, ignoring them the next—but EMI didn't much like Dave Goodman's muddy demo, and so Mike Thorne (who was now actively campaigning to get the Sex Pistols signed) didn't have any better luck than Parry. For a moment, McLaren considered signing the Sex Pistols to another label altogether. He quickly made some halfhearted visits to Virgin, Chrysalis, and RAK Records, rushing into the record companies without appointments, but none seemed to take him or the band quite seriously, although Terry Slater, then director of EMI Music Publishing, claims he decided to sign the Sex Pistols immediately. Considering that McLaren's hype was a fast-talking stew of revolutionary rhetoric, Stones-style boasting about the Sex Pistols' bad manners, and inflated industry banter—he normally opened negotiations demanding advances up to £40,000 at a time when most young bands' advances were in the £6–12,000 range—his lack of luck doesn't seem surprising.

"I was never interested in being polite like other managers before me," McLaren told Simon Garfield for his excellent book *Money for Nothing*. " 'You can keep the royalties,' I used to say. 'Give me the money now!' I thought royalties were a very abstract phenomenon to do with creative accounting—like something you might never see. I never believed what they promised, and I always thought they were all crooks—and that's a fact: they are."

Ultimately, it took nothing less than a media brouhaha before EMI and Polydor came to their senses. For the A&R men, the two-day 100 Club Punk Rock festival McLaren organized September 20 and 21 was the match that lit the punk fuse. On the first night, the Sex Pistols, Clash, Siouxsie and the Banshees, and Subway Sect played uneventful sets before a crowd of charmed, pogoing punks—the pogo, a dance of spastic jumping up and down in place, had been invented by the ever-exasperated Sid Vicious in a fit of lunatic, amphetamine energy at the 100 Club earlier that year. But McLaren had also arranged a second night of punk festivities starring Chris Spedding with a pick-up band named the Vibrators, a hastily arranged headline act McLaren manufactured when he realized that none of the other second-night bands (the Damned, the French Stinky Toys, or Manchester's Buzzcocks) would probably fill the house. That second night, Sid Vicious chucked a bottle at the stage during Spedding's set, and it shattered against a pillar, blinding a young girl in one eye.

Within minutes, the police swarmed into the 100 Club looking for the culprit, and Sid, who only yesterday had filled in as a last-minute drummer for the freshly formed Siouxsie and the Banshees, was easily identified and arrested. "It was a terrible, awful thing that happened," remembers Vivienne Westwood. "Sid threw that bottle, but we pretended to the police it was someone else. But it *was* him who did it and he was arrested, and put into some kind of young people's remand home . . . We felt bad but Sid actually didn't feel guilty about it. I think he'd managed to convince himself of his own innocence."

The next day, the tabloids blamed the "punk rock tragedy" on the Sex Pistols although they were playing in Cardiff, Wales, the night Sid was arrested, and the record companies finally began a better-late-than-never campaign to see who could sign up the most punk acts. Suddenly, the ultimate sign of music-biz cachet was whether you had been there the night Sid had tossed that bottle at the 100 Club.

But the 100 Club Punk festival is also memorable for another reason: Sometime on that same afternoon of September 20, McLaren met with the band and his new solicitor, Steven Fisher, insisting that while EMI was about to sign the band, it required that a management agreement be signed first. (In fact, EMI and McLaren were nowhere near an agreement yet.) The contract McLaren and Fisher—who now became a one percent codirector of Glitterbest Ltd, the Sex Pistols' management company—presented was typical by industry standards: that is to say, as greedy as they come. McLaren would own the rights to the name "Sex Pistols" and receive twenty-five percent (plus VAT) for his services to the band over the course of the contract—three years with a two-year option; and the band would, from a contractual perspective, be McLaren's "Sex Pistols." If they signed, weekly wages—£25 a week—would begin immediately; without signing, they were told, it was paupers forever. After hemming and hawing that the contract seemed to give McLaren (in Rotten's words) "total control," the Sex Pistols gulped and signed.

"McLaren introduced us to Fisher, the solicitor, who seemed a bit greasy," says Glen Matlock, "and I read through the contract and took up a point about percentages, but John was quite daft about it. John didn't even read it. He said, You read it, then? I said, Yeah, I read it. He said, Well if there's anything wrong with it, it's *your* fault. And he signed it without even reading it, didn't even go to the solicitors or anything."

Meanwhile, Nick Mobbs had finally woken up to the fact that, as McLaren often told him, he was sitting on the biggest signing EMI had had since the Rolling Stones. Sad to say, but it seems to have been the tabloids, not the Sex Pistols, that ultimately pushed Mobbs to approach *his* boss at EMI, a former General Foods marketing executive named Bob Mercer, about cutting a deal with McLaren.

"[Mobbs and Thorne] came to see me about signing the Pistols," remembers Mercer, "and Mike brought Dave Goodman's demo. It was only a couple of tracks, and I really didn't like it at all. It just sounded fucking awful to me, and I said, *no way.* A couple of days later, sometime in the first week of October, I was going to the States so I came into the office quite early in the morning, and quite literally the whole of the A&R department was waiting for me—which was, I must say, a unique experience: For the A&R department to be up and around before midday was pretty unusual. Basically, their message was, 'Listen, the Pistols may be a piece of shit musically, but it's what's happening in the streets of London. These are the forerunners of the whole punk movement. It's a feather in our cap to be able to sign them. Besides which, what do you know: You're over thirty!'

"So I said fine, OK, go ahead, and I gave them a limit on the deal, which was £40,000 for about two or three records in as many years, with options, which we would pay to record."

McLaren now tried to move the deal forward as fast as he could, shuttling between solicitor Steven Fisher's office, EMI's cold concrete-and-steel Manchester House headquarters, and his own cramped new office, Glitterbest Ltd, located at 40 Dryden Chambers on Oxford Street. But he also let Chris Parry believe that Polydor had clinched the Sex Pistols deal. Indeed, Parry was so convinced that the Sex Pistols were his alone that he booked time for the band to test record "Anarchy in the U.K." at the end of that week—McLaren had insisted that the Sex Pistols record their first single within a week of signing and Parry wanted to test Dave Goodman's recording skills. But EMI was quicker on the draw: The Sex Pistols contract was written, checked, and signed all in a day—supposedly the fastest-ever signing in EMI's history. On Friday, October 8, the very day the Sex Pistols were due to record for Polydor at DeLane Lea Studios, McLaren signed the Sex Pistols to EMI for a £40,000 advance (two albums over two years with two one-year options). He never even bothered calling Chris Parry with the news.

"The next day, Saturday, I called Malcolm to see how it was going," says Parry, taking a long drag on his cigarette. "As far as I was concerned, the deal was set, all done and dealt, and ready for signing, and I had heard nothing to the contrary. And then Malcolm said, 'Look, I've got them signed to EMI last night.'

"We were devastated," Parry sighs, when confronted with the story that he sobbed when McLaren told him the news over the phone. "I dunno if I cried, but it was certainly one of my blackest days. I was very, very upset."

"I had a breathtaking phone conversation with Chris Parry that weekend," recalls Mike Thorne. "We had a real shouting match with each other. He was mad at having things 'stolen' by EMI and I was mad at his presumption. But it *wasn't* stealing. It was just Malcolm playing two-pig-bluff—and we were the pigs. It was fair, but I'd say he pushed it a bit too far."

October 16, 1976: "The A&R manager of EMI, Nick Mobbs, told *Sounds* this week: 'Here at last is a group with a bit of guts for younger people to identify with; a group that parents actually won't tolerate. And it's not just parents that need a little shaking up, it's the music business itself.

" 'That's why a lot of A&R men wouldn't sign the group; they took it all too personally. But what other group at a comparable point in their career has created so much excitement both on stage and off.

" 'For me the Sex Pistols are a backlash against the "nice little band" syndrome and the general stagnation of the music industry. They've got to happen for *all* our sakes.' "

Not everyone in the Sex Pistols' camp was overjoyed by the news that McLaren had signed the band to EMI. Mousy Nils Stevenson, still on the road with the band under the impression that he was to become McLaren's comanager, was furious that negotiations had gone on behind his back; he threatened to, and eventually did, quit, becoming manager of Siouxsie and the Banshees. The Sex Pistols themselves were surprised that McLaren had been actively pursuing a deal for them at all. "When it came," says Matlock, "we were getting on with gigging so it was quite surprising to me that he was even *speaking* to people."

Shocked as they were, the Sex Pistols began their revelry as soon as the ink was dry, starting with a photo session of them grinning down the same Manchester House stairwell the Beatles had used for *Meet the Beatles* and then proceeding directly to Louise's, the Marble Arch dyke bar owned by the same Madame Louise McLaren had idolized back in his Soho days. One night after the signing, however, McLaren cracked the whip, and the next day, the boys returned to the studio to record "Anarchy in the U.K." with Dave Goodman, itself a contentious move. Right up to the signing, EMI had wanted "Pretty Vacant" to be the first Sex Pistols single, but McLaren had been unwavering in his support for "Anarchy in the U.K."; now, after some frantic telephone calls, EMI finally acceded to his demand.

This time, the Sex Pistols were booked into Lansdowne Studios in Westbourne Grove, but at the end of the day, Rotten was caught writing graffiti on the studio wall and work had to be curtailed until another studio could be found.

"I went down to the studio that day to see how they were going along," says Mike Thorne, "and Malcolm took a can of shaving cream and wrote on the control room window 'EMI is here.' It was a frantic scene. They were in uncharted territory and there was pressure to get the single out and it just wasn't working. Goodman's demos had had character because he was basically recording live, but he was completely adrift in the studio. Balances were hopeless and the music clearly wasn't coming at you as strongly as it could. There was certainly something captured but when the tape was presented to EMI, it wasn't particularly good, so then there was an attempt to remix this by the band. Eventually, I went down and sat in the studio a bit, and one night at the EMI studio in Manchester House, I brought things into balance a bit more. But by that point, I was sort of just trying to keep things calm because everybody was so worried that this wasn't turning out."

By now, even McLaren had become dissatisfied with Goodman's work—Goodman eventually took his revenge when he later released his session outtakes in numerous bootleg Sex Pistols albums—and he pressured Thorne and Mobbs to let him start from scratch using a new producer. To many, McLaren's first-choice producer was a total surprise: After all, Chris Thomas's production work on Pink Floyd's *Dark Side of the Moon* was probably as close as one could get to an exact opposite of the punk aesthetic. However, only a few hours into the band's sessions with Thomas and engineer Bill Price in late October, it was clear that McLaren's instincts about the Sex Pistols' music had been on target after all: Even EMI was beginning to see through the hype that the Sex Pistols couldn't play.

"When it finally came out," says Nick Mobbs, "it was incredibly commercial, much more so than I would ever have dreamed. A wall of guitars. When Mike's version had been recorded, we were all set to release that and we would have been very happy to do so. It was Malcolm who chickened out and said that he didn't think it was produced enough. He thought it was too raw. Suddenly he seemed to be backtracking to things he had previously denied wanting. Till then, his whole attitude had been unorthodox, to take risks wherever he could. Now, he just wanted it to be commercial, and surprisingly, it was."

Now came the hours of insomnia, the days of tedious labor, the worried hand-wringing before the moment when virgin plastic would be tested in the marketplace and (it was hoped) transformed into the gold and platinum discs that grace the offices of record companies and entertainment lawyers. For good records and heavy hype are no guarantees of success, and Malcolm McLaren knew this best of all, remembered all too well how the New York Dolls' love of rock 'n' roll madness had failed to find a similarly passionate response with the record-buying public. At twenty-nine, McLaren was no longer (as Sylvain had once called him) "a kid doing his baby marketing," but a full-fledged grown-up struggling to come to terms with an industry: This time, he promised, there would be, could be, no mistakes.

Obviously, McLaren couldn't manage every side of the business like the old pros. He had neither the interest, talent, nor capital for that (increasingly, the sharkish Steven Fisher took over Glitterbest's business affairs). With EMI in the picture, McLaren had finally come to the realization that it was no longer enough just to let the press run with the ball. The game had to be played with total knowledge of the industry's traditional marketing and promotion mechanisms. Accordingly, there was now an element of shrewdness and patience to McLaren's dealings where before there had been only defiance and spite. Even his clothes began to change: With EMI's cash in hand, Jermyn Street shirts slowly supplanted his scruffy SEX shop T's.

McLaren supposedly hated the idea of touring the Sex Pistols simply to support "Anarchy in the U.K." 's release—Jamie Reid saw touring as a kind of indentured servitude to EMI—but he now fell captive to meeting after meeting with numerous fast-talking music-biz record pluggers and tour promoters. Like it or not, it was time to take the show on the road.

He called it the "Anarchy Tour," nineteen dates in twenty-three days, a Sex Pistols party with support from the Damned, Johnny Thunders and the Heartbreakers, and the Clash, and he hired a tour promoter to take word of the Sex Pistols' revolution from Land's End to John o' Groats. Whenever he wasn't dealing with EMI, pushing to get "Anarchy" into the stores and up the charts, his every waking moment was spent finessing the details of the tour: hiring the coaches, sound and lighting systems, hotels, and helpers; planning booking strategy with the tour promoters, Endale Associates; renting the old Roxy cinema up in Harlesden so that the bands would at least have their entrances and exits well rehearsed; and, most important, creating a well-oiled publicity machine so that the Sex Pistols wouldn't find themselves playing to empty houses as they had in Dunstable toward the end of October.

Publicity was crucial. Especially television, because it was there more than anywhere else where you would reach the bored and cynical youth of teeming Britain, children of Callaghan and Coca-Cola; as far as EMI's chief record plugger, thirty-five-year-old Eric Hall, was concerned, that was where the action was. Hall came from the old school (any publicity is good publicity) and he was good at his job, some said, the best, although Hall himself says that the Sex Pistols only made life difficult for him and that he never became a fan. "I remember Eric Hall really well," says Nick Mobbs, "with his lovely Jewish manner, really fast-talking, a real sharp boy, and never wanting to miss an opportunity. Everything was always, 'Great, great, it's just right for you, lots of buzz about 'em.' I mean, if you met Eric Hall you'd find it really amusing because he's the last person who would be a Pistols fan in any way but he was the first to see any commercial possibilities in them."

Hall did his job so well that by mid-November the *Nationwide* news show broadcast concert footage of the Sex Pistols performing "Anarchy" in its special on the punk phenomenon ("London's Outrage") and the *London Weekend* show premiered snippets of a gig McLaren had set up at Notre Dame Hall along with interviews by Janet Street-Porter, the one establishment journalist who had proven time and again that she had her eyes trained on the style underground. McLaren still wasn't convinced that the Sex Pistols had hit their stride in the public eye. Where were *Top of the Pops* and the *Old Grey Whistle Test,* the two TV shows that accorded new rock bands truly national followings? By the end of November, "Anarchy" hadn't even started to edge its way up the charts, couldn't even be found in the record stores, and was being ignored by BBC Radio One, the national pop station. With the tour starting in a week, McLaren applied maximum pressure on Eric Hall to get that final burst of national publicity before going on the road.

Thus, when Eric Hall finally reached him sometime during the afternoon of December 1, boasting of having secured yet another local television appearance on Thames Television's *Today* show, hosted by Bill Grundy—glitter-metal rockers Queen called in a last-minute cancellation when lead singer Freddie Mercury had to have emergency dental work— McLaren's first reaction was to say that the Sex Pistols were not going to make their third television appearance on another local show. There was simply no time for that. With only one gig booked into London at the very end of the tour, it was surely more important to concentrate publicity on either national or provincial outlets.

But Eric Hall persisted, persevered, clambered up to Harlesden in his tiny Granada and shouted McLaren down. There could be no backing out of this: It had already been booked. Besides, EMI *owned* Thames Television: This was a guaranteed outlet, and an appearance on what was essentially an EMI show would be a sign to the boys upstairs that despite their anarchist posturing, the Sex Pistols could be a cooperative bunch after all.

In the end, it could even have been the EMI limousine that finally convinced McLaren to go on with the show: With the Heartbreakers arriving at Heathrow that evening, a limo was worth its weight in gold, especially since McLaren and Thunders had not exactly parted as the best of friends way back in Tampa, Florida. And so Malcolm McLaren finally gave in to Hall's proposition and the Sex Pistols appeared on Bill Grundy's television show, swearing and cursing and carrying on, setting new standards of televised rock 'n' roll outrageousness in just over one minute and forty seconds: "You dirty sod! You dirty old man! You dirty bastard! You dirty fucker! What a fucking rotter!"

Bill Grundy: "I will be most happy to speak with you, but first I must have a whiskey for whenever the dastardly name of the Sex Pistols crosses my lips, I must have a little whiskey. But I warn you: I am myself indifferent honest. . . .

"Now, on this particular occasion, a Wednesday night, it was my night, and [my partner] Mr. Eamonn Andrews was having his feet up and sleeping a bit. . . . When I came back from my *Punch* lunch, I suppose three or three fifteen, I used then to wander into the production office, where I was given a running order. I don't have to tell you what a running order was, or is, do I, Mr. Bromberg?"

Craig Bromberg: *No, Mr. Grundy.*

"Good. And so there was the various people I was going to interview and so on, and who my number two interviewers were going to interview as well, but at the bottom, the last item on the show was 'Bill and the Sex Pistols.' "

Weren't the pop band Queen originally supposed to appear on your show that evening?

"Well, may I just tell you that whomever told you that is either a liar or misinformed because I had . . . well, first of all, I know nothing about pop music. If you ask me about Mozart or Beethoven or Haydn, I think you might get quite an intelligent answer. I didn't know anything about pop music and I saw 'Bill and the Sex Pistols,' that was the first: I didn't know what the Sex Pistols was, is, or were."

Well, who chose the Sex Pistols to appear on your show? Didn't you have any control over the choice of whom you were to interview that day? Wouldn't you have had any notice to prepare in advance?

"I did. I thought I had tried to explain this to you, Mr. Bumbeerg. But even though I had some control, I didn't want to exercise that control every bloody day. . . . No, I didn't give any bugger. I thought I'm interviewing X, Y, or Z, and I can't remember who I was interviewing that day, but the last thing I saw on the running order was 'Bill and the Sex Pistols' and I thought that all I was going to do was, as it were, introduce yet another quite ghastly pop group and—end of program. . . .

"I think I interviewed the prime minister that day. I mean, it's that sort of show, it varies a great deal. But there came a moment when I had to put us into VTR [video tape recording], and while we were VTR, in came a group of people whose hair appeared to have been spiked with machine oil, whose faces—in those days I didn't know about the word *drugs,* I really did not know that they might have been on drugs. And with them were four girls who looked like—well, I am rather fond of women, but they were the sort of girls I wouldn't under any circumstances have, um, slept with. . . .

"But there were eight of them. Four men, four women. It was the last item in the show and I thought, oh, *Jeeeeesus.* I realized that because of my negligence, I hadn't got this one spotted. So we sat down and into my earpiece there came the director. He said, 'Oh Bill, we're just going to play a tape of them,' and he did. And there were these four fucking idiots looking at themselves on the box, the monitor in front of me saying, now, 'Aha-ha-ha: hey, that's oos on telayvision. Loook: that's me, that's me, that's them.' And obviously, I thought—'ello!—we have a right lot here! But I didn't bother in the slightest, I coped with everybody, and we started talking.

115

"And after a bit, one of them, I really do not know whether it was Johnny Vicious or Sam Rotten or whatever their bloody names were, said, 'Don't fooking give me that fooking stuff.' And I thought, well, it's a live show, it's going out at six thirty in the evening, hang on a minute Grundy. . . .

"And I thought, well, I'm not going to be outraged by that. That's an absolute certainty. And one of the others, I can't remember who was the second one, said, 'Hey, don't you fooking talk to us fooking people like fooking. . . .' And then there was a moment when I said, 'Look, if you're trying to offend me you're failing. I was in the Navy during the war before you buggers were born and you don't offend me.' I can't really remember what happened after that, except that their command of the English language appeared to consist only of four-letter words or six-letter words. . . .

"So you can imagine the fuck-up that was when these disgusting creatures said—I mean totally untalented, not a single bloody talent about their bloody brains—you can imagine the fuck-up there was when they said 'fuck' and 'cunt' and 'shit' and so on on the air at six thirty, and when I went down to *Punch* the next week for the *Punch* lunch, the general manager asked me to come into his office. I went in and he said, 'Bill, d'you know what's happened?' And I said, 'No, of course I don't know what's happened.' He said, 'Thames Television rang me up to find out how much you had to drink at lunch.' Now, at lunch, I had what I always had: a glass of whiskey before, a glass or two of wine during the meal. Well, well, well, I thought: What a load of bloody shit. . . ."

Although the first furious call from EMI came spluttering down the line almost immediately after the Sex Pistols left Thames Television's studios, it wasn't until the next morning, long after the obligatory revelry greeting Johnny Thunders's arrival, that McLaren first began to realize that last night's swearing scene on the telly had grown into a scandal of national proportions. Despite all odds—the prime minister was tied up all week secretly negotiating one last loan from the International Monetary Fund—the Sex Pistols now truly were the main event of the evening news and their name covered the banners of every newspaper in Britain for the rest of the week. "THE FILTH AND THE FURY!" screamed the *Daily Mirror*, reporting that a lorry driver was so outraged that his eight-year-old son had heard the swearing that he had kicked in the screen of his new color

TV. "FURY AT FILTHY TV CHAT," ranted the *Daily Express*. "AS THE MONEY ROLLS IN, ROCK GROUP FACE TOUR BAND AND TV CHIEFS SUSPEND GRUNDY," yelled another. "PUNK? CALL IT FILTHY LUCRE!"

In less than twenty-four hours, Malcolm McLaren's world was turned inside out. Before Grundy, McLaren had bumbled his way toward success by making the right mistakes, through the haphazard trial and error of ruses and convulsions; after Grundy, the rumors that McLaren had tutored his boys in televisual provocation would so dog his every move that even he began to see that the accident of the Sex Pistols' success—which he would never admit was an accident in the first place—could no longer be distinguished from his own clumsy scheming. McLaren was like a lucky billiards player whose incompetent bluffing had led to a sudden, incredibly lucky scattering of pool balls into their appropriate holes; from now on, he would have to play the rest of the game as if he had been an expert from the start. "Boys will be boys," he is reported to have told the director of EMI Records, the hard-hitting Leslie Hill, but Hill doesn't quite remember McLaren's notorious *bons mots*.

"He came up to the office," Hill recalls smilelessly, "and I remember that he was cagey, strange, he didn't react. He didn't look anything special to create such a sensation, but then people never do. He spoke quietly and slowly and listened to what I said. I couldn't pin him down on anything. I couldn't get him into line because obviously he didn't want to anyway. He claimed that the band had been goaded and I was inclined to accept that, but my direct boss, who was Len Wood, who himself had run EMI Records at the time of the Beatles, was horrified by the use of the word *fuck,* and I told McLaren that although *I* didn't like it personally, that's not what I'm paid for and that I would try to help him—*if* he could keep the group in line."

But as far as McLaren was concerned, the trouble had started with Grundy and there it would remain. "They were set up for all this by Grundy," he told one reporter. "But there are no regrets. These lads were expressing the mood of most kids these days: They want a change of scene. What they did was quite genuine. Being working-class kids and boys being boys, they said what they felt was OK. They don't regret it."

And once he had met with Hill, neither did McLaren. All the fear and anxiety of being dropped from EMI faded away as the hard slog of arranging the tour (or what was left of it) reasserted its importance over the Sex Pistols' daily activities. By lunch on December 2, tour cancellations started pouring into Glitterbest: First Southend, then Norwich (the debut gig and the site of a small student sit-in after the cancellation was announced), then Glasgow, Newcastle, Cardiff. By the end of the tour, the Sex Pistols would end up playing only three of their nineteen advertised bookings. McLaren's only consolations were that Grundy himself was reprimanded and finally suspended for what Thames Television's programming director, Jeremy Isaacs, scathingly called "inexcusably sloppy journalism," and that "Anarchy in the U.K." was estimated to be selling upwards of eighteen hundred copies a day.

There wasn't much left of the Anarchy Tour by the time the Sex Pistols left London for their first gig in Leeds, but that didn't stop the press from hounding the Sex Pistols as if they were the new Beatles. "It was great," says Steve Jones. "I loved it, seeing our pictures on the front of the daily papers. I thought, this is it, it's *all* happening now. But once we was on the road, it was all these cock-suckers from the press following us everywhere."

For the reporters who followed them, the Sex Pistols were easy prey, a humorous diversion from "real" news, and they seemed determined to follow them until the band was either censored or exploded in the flash-bulb glare of the evening news. No longer would these tabloid news-hounds sit waiting for Sex Pistols shenanigans; each day was now to have its new Sex Pistols scandal, even if it had to be invented.

On December 4, EMI's record-packers—"little old ladies who make sure there's no snap, crackle, or pop on the records," says Bob Mercer—refused to package the "Anarchy" single, and EMI was forced into public negotiations to ensure that their Christmas records would arrive in the stores on time. That made a page-four story.

On December 5, the Sex Pistols pulled into the Dragonara Hotel in Leeds only to be taunted by reporters to throw a flowerpot; the Sex Pistols obliged, saying it would be on the media's head, but the next day the papers reported that the group had trashed their hotel. That story made page two.

On December 7, at EMI's Annual General Meeting for shareholders, EMI's chairman, Sir John Read, issued a statement about permissiveness, censorship, and the Sex Pistols—"If they continue to behave so deplorably they become a liability to this company both morally and commercially"— while EMI directors Sir Geoffrey Howe (Tory Shadow Minister for Defense) and Lord Shawcross (a former attorney general, the head of the British legal system) looked on approvingly: a page-six story.

"Tell him to go —— himself," quoth Johnny Rotten on page four of the *Daily Mirror* when Read's remarks reached him in Leeds. Replied Lord Shawcross the next day: "I think we are being taken for a ride."

To anyone reading the headlines, it seemed clear that the end was approaching rapidly.

"Whatever pressure there was [to drop the Sex Pistols from EMI] wasn't coming from me," says Bob Mercer, the man who oversaw their signing. "The pressure was all coming from EMI's *corporate* side. The feeling was that the last thing we needed at the end-of-November / start-of-December period, which is the biggest sales period in the record business, was a dispute in the factory, because that's when all the Christmas singles are being pressed, LP sales are highest, and so on. But Leslie Hill was really the person who had to deal with that pressure, much more than I."

"I had some personal reservations about this thing," says Hill, a prim Bristolian and churchgoing Methodist who was himself subjected to a twenty-four-hour media stake-out in the days following the Grundy show. "But as managing director of a record company, I felt here we were again with something big. It *was* like another Beatles—fifty thousand sold in just a few weeks—and we'd been talking *for years* about finding a new Beatles. It wasn't just the Sex Pistols that were the problem. It was the damage I knew would be done to us in the recording industry at large, because if we let *them* go, people on the outside would see us again as a fuddy-duddy record company.

"And I remember sitting with John Read and Len Wood on Christmas Eve, at about 7:00 in the evening, just the three of us left in the building continuing to debate this issue because I was resisting letting them go. I was saying things like, 'Do you realize you can go into W. H. Smith's and you can probably buy a hundred books with the word *arse* in it?' And they didn't. Len Wood was furious about the use of the word *fuck,* and I tried to explain that obviously in this world, the world of corporate boardrooms, the word isn't in common use like it is out there. But John Read was concerned that the adverse publicity in America would impact on our ability to sell the EMI-Scan, this wonderful machine which lets you x-ray inside peoples' heads instead of cutting them open. We had the American market sewn up and he was concerned because there were reports of the Sex Pistols on the front page of the *Los Angeles Times.* And that was scary."

EMI and Glitterbest were now clinched in head-to-head talks about the Sex Pistols' future with the label. EMI's message, conveyed from John Read via Hill, Mercer, and Mobbs, was that if McLaren really wanted EMI's support, he would have to moderate the group's behavior. McLaren returned the corporation's fire by explaining that the *press* were more responsible for keeping the band's bad boy reputation in the news than the Sex Pistols themselves, that EMI was making trouble for the Sex Pistols because of internal protests from the company's massive Weapons Systems group (partly true), and that EMI would soon be considered in breach of contract due to its failure to properly promote and distribute "Anarchy in the U.K."

Besides, McLaren told Hill, "I don't run their lives. They are their own agents. I'm not *going* to control them, I don't *want to* control them, and I *can't* control them. They must do what they must do. And they are where they are because of the way they've approached this thing so far."

In the meantime, McLaren encouraged his boys to press on with their outrageous antics.

"You could see that all that swearing and saying this that and the other had created all this excitement," mumbles Steve Jones, "and Malcolm was trying to think of more ways to do that. New schemes. Stunts to pull. Like those gigs what we was getting banned from: I got the feeling he'd called up the gigs and said it's going to be fucking hell there, and then the guys would get scared and not put us on."

For example, in Derby, on what would have been the second night of the Anarchy Tour, local councillors challenged the Sex Pistols to audition for them before allowing them permission to play in their town. Oddly, the Sex Pistols first agreed to the audition and then backed out at the last moment—claiming censorship. And in Caerphilly, South Wales, the Sex Pistols (and their fans) found themselves outnumbered by some two hundred angry Christmas carolers hoping to drown out the punk rock menace, and ended up playing for an audience of eighty.

Even if McLaren didn't instigate these provocations, EMI's corporate heads had already tired of playing the game of assigning responsibility for the furor over the band's behavior to the Sex Pistols *or* their opponents in the media and in the country at large. It was too late for that: The game had already been lost. While McLaren and the Sex Pistols stayed on the road, rollicking through the remains of their tour, running up £10,000 in hotel bills despite further gig cancellations, EMI's corporate board was carefully debating how to drop the group from EMI Records, a tricky maneuver. The decision to terminate would have been finalized by Christmas were it not for Leslie Hill's concern about losing Nick Mobbs, the A&R man who signed the Sex Pistols in the first place.

"I was extremely angry that they were forcing us to drop them," says Mobbs. "But all I could do was to say, 'If you get rid of this band, I'm going to resign.' There was nothing else left for me to do but threaten them."

Mobbs did resign, as did several other younger A&R staffers—"I thought, how could I permit myself to work for a company like that," he angrily recalls, "a signing like this comes once in a lifetime"—but EMI held fast to its decision. For a few days, the company waffled, refraining from announcing the news to the press. But then reports came in that the boys had vomited at K.L.M.'s check-in counter at Heathrow Airport on the eve of a quickly arranged jaunt to Rotterdam and Amsterdam.

"The day after they went to Holland," recalls Bob Mercer, "the *Evening Standard* had a headline that the Sex Pistols had thrown up at the airport and offended one of the K.L.M. check-in girls, so once again, there were early-morning phone calls to Holland and to Graham Fletcher (an EMI minder), and Fletcher said he couldn't understand what all that was about. They hadn't even stopped at the airport: Fletch had had the tickets, so he checked them straight through, and they went from the car to the ramp to the airplane, never stopping at the terminal. So where the press got that stuff from, God only knows. But then I had the chairman back on the line saying, 'All right, that's *it.*' He actually called the head of K.L.M., who confirmed that nothing actually happened, but the chairman now felt it was completely out of control. The press had gotten their teeth into it and there was no longer anything we could do."

Indeed, the only thing left to do was to issue the formal announcement retiring the Sex Pistols from EMI, and on January 6, the EMI Group public relations office finally did just that—without first informing either Glitterbest *or* EMI Records, a move that helped McLaren create yet another wave of turmoil. "EMI and the Sex Pistols group have mutually agreed to terminate their recording contract," the statement declared with thudding finality. "EMI feels it is unable to promote this group's records internationally in view of the adverse publicity which has been generated over the last two months, although recent press reports of the behaviour of the Sex Pistols appear to have been exaggerated. The termination of this contract with the Sex Pistols does not in any way affect EMI's intention to remain active in all areas of the music business."

Legally, however, EMI couldn't just let the Sex Pistols go swiftly into the night, and so as soon as McLaren and the Sex Pistols arrived in Amsterdam, Leslie Hill and Laurie Hall (EMI Records' business affairs manager and solicitor) followed after them. For the next few days, some heated meetings were held over the phone and at the local Hilton, where Hill and Hall were staying.

McLaren may only have been stalling for time or money, but in any event, he rejected the EMI Group's declaration of a "mutual termination" and played up his feelings of rejection to the press. "How can they 'mutually' end it when we haven't signed to end it?" he asked Robin Denselow of the *Guardian* while still in Amsterdam. "Legally, we are still on EMI Records." According to Denselow, McLaren was "surprisingly gloomy" about the Sex Pistols' odds of signing to another label. "I've told them to find us an equivalent contract, but we've had word that most of the major companies won't touch us with a barge-pole. There's nobody after us. If we walk into another record company, what are they going to say? 'You can't play anywhere and we can't hear your records on the radio.' "

In fact, contrary to McLaren's assertions, the Sex Pistols were not merely shoved off EMI without first receiving help acquiring a new contract or a golden handshake. Almost immediately after the Grundy incident, Richard Branson, head of the then fledgling Virgin Records, had phoned Hill offering to take the Sex Pistols off EMI's hands. To his credit, Hill first refused, but then, as the Sex Pistols' naughtiness increased in visibility (the Heathrow "vomiting," McLaren's outrageous public distortions, Rotten's arrest for amphetamine possession), he arranged for McLaren and Branson to meet at EMI. Branson was eager to please and tried hard to charm McLaren over; McLaren pretended to be happy meeting with the man he scornfully called "Mr. Pickle": He would phone him with an answer the next day. However, no sooner did McLaren leave Hill's office, than he rejected out of hand the idea of going to Virgin: Going to a young hippie company was embarrassing when you had previously been signed to the largest record company in Great Britain.

Really, what McLaren wanted was to stay with EMI; what he got instead (which turned out to be just as good) was the cash: whatever was left of the band's original £40,000 advance (approximately £30,000) plus another £10,000 from EMI Publishing.

Once he returned to London, McLaren vehemently continued denying that the Sex Pistols' contract with EMI had been canceled; all of this, he claimed, had been the dirty work of EMI's corporate chiefs. "It's the people at the top—the shareholders—who want to get rid of us," he said. "The vast majority of the people at EMI Records division want us to stay with the label. There is absolutely no reason for breaking the contract that would hold up in court. We have been prepared to tour Outer Mongolia if necessary to promote records."

Meanwhile, EMI prepared to melt down whatever Sex Pistols records remained in their warehouses as copies of "Anarchy in the U.K." changed hands in the street for twice their original list price.

Now McLaren had good reason to be gloomy. At each record company he visited—Chrysalis, Island, and the British subsidiaries of CBS, RCA, and Warner Brothers, just to start—he found much the same responses he had seen earlier at EMI. The more junior A&R people seemed to believe that the Sex Pistols were rock 'n' roll salvation—even they had tired of the amorphous gigantism of stadium rock and had come to recognize that the Sex Pistols weren't just any old punk band, but the chief antagonists of a profound struggle to breathe some life into the industry. But to those on top, the corporate executives and their managers, the post-Grundy-era Pistols looked like a threateningly expensive proposition. Who needed such hassles when record sales were actually *continuing* the industry's historical upward trend over the previous five years? Here was a group that had had a good first single and some wonderful hype, but little chance of playing live locally, a virtual radio boycott of its records, and a very dear price tag—McLaren's new bargaining position often started at £100,000. Surely, went the corporate argument, this was too high a price to pay for the emperor's new punk clothes.

At Polydor Records, for example, Chris Parry, still hungry for a punk signing despite his humiliation at having failed to sign the Sex Pistols the first time around, and then the Clash, had no problem re-presenting the Sex Pistols to his immediate superiors. Once Polydor's executives found out about the purported deal, however, it stopped dead in its tracks. "After they got kicked off EMI Malcolm came back to me and said, 'Look, I do want to sign with you,'" says Parry. "I said I was still up for it despite all that had happened, and we had a meeting with Freddie Haayen, the label manager. He said we'd sign as per the original agreement we've already negotiated—stands good—and Malcolm said he'd be happy to sign it, but then Polydor's board, which is the international board of a Dutch multinational, Philips, refused him permission."

Dealless again, McLaren sulked around the Glitterbest office hoping to escape the rejections that were now coming on all fronts, even from Westwood, ever furious about Malcolm's lack of attention to her, to Joseph, and to the shop. A&M Records director Derek Green remembers calling McLaren at home only to have his phone answered by Vivienne Westwood with a curt, "No, he's not here," followed by a quick click. Another story goes that after staying out at an all-night party, Malcolm returned home to find Vivienne refusing to let him into their house. "She was hiding and pretending she weren't there, so he climbed up a drainpipe and started going 'Vivienne, Vivienne, it's *me, Malcolm,* let me in!'" reports Glen Matlock. "So next time I saw her I said, 'Heard you had a bit o' trouble with Malcolm last night and she said, 'What do you know?' I told her about him climbing up the drainpipe and she said, 'Stupid idiot: I knew it was him all along, that's why I weren't letting him in.' "

Such tales of fumbling intrigue only indicate how far McLaren had come from his pseudo-Situationist posturing, leaving Vivienne Westwood, Jamie Reid, and the cantankerous Rotten with the roles of schoolboy anarchists, while he went out searching for record executives whose ears were not yet shut to the Sex Pistols sound. All was misery until mid-January; then, just after a short hop to Cannes for the annual MIDEM convention—his first music-biz trade show—McLaren made a sudden, strong connection with Derek Green, the managing director of A&M Records, the small, highly profitable American record company owned by trumpeter Herb Alpert and his associate, Jerry Moss, and the Sex Pistols saga rolled onto its next chapter.

"Believe it or not," says the burly, bearded Derek Green, "at the time, I had never heard of either Malcolm McLaren or the Sex Pistols until the very day I talked with McLaren. Because that's the kind of person I am: To this day, I don't read the music papers or watch TV and I barely listen to the radio. It's my determination to protect my career by not being influenced by other professionals. I want to be an audience, and the best way for me to do that is to get into my own thinking.

"So I hadn't a clue, and when McLaren called, I took the call person-ally, because I always have taken calls off the street just as a matter of habit. I said, 'Yes, what do you want?' and he told me he had a group called the Sex Pistols and that they were on EMI, and he made an appointment to come 'round and play me the tape. Having got to know him through this, I think he must have been a bit thrilled that he found a bit of a mug who knew nothing about him."

What Green heard that day—six tracks the Sex Pistols had finished with either Dave Goodman or Chris Thomas at the controls—still sends him into rock 'n' roll orbit. "I was terribly, terribly excited," he says. "Having signed Rick Wakeman, Peter Frampton, Supertramp, Humble Pie, a big list of good, interesting artists on my early seventies roster—I was right eight times out of nine or something like that—I was doing my job but my heart had left it. The rock 'n' roll part of me had left my career. And then I played this little cassette and it just blew me away. Suddenly, I knew what was wrong with me. They weren't another American rock band that was churning out the same thing, and I was thrilled. *Thrilled.*

I couldn't believe what I was hearing. I was terribly excited. So I probably handled it with the I'll-get-back-to-you tactic, but I knew *at that very moment* that I wanted the act badly, and in this business, you rarely do."

What followed was nearly a month of intensive negotiation.

"Malcolm's very good at negotiating on the basis of personality," says Green. "He'd probably assess that I'm a guy who doesn't mind a smile or a four-letter word so he would give me whatever he thought would amuse me. Very funny, terribly amusing, so outrageous in his very styled choice of language. He would purposely crush over our establishment rock acts saying things like 'Super-Duper-Fucking-Tramp' or 'Peter-Fucking-Frampton,' and I was just terribly amused. I mean, you could say he's a guy who just knows how to trick a deal. One minute he'd be charming the pants off me, the next he'd be telling me how Warner Brothers had offered them X money and that I had to beat that to get them. Of course, I had no way of knowing what was the truth."

Nor did anyone else, and McLaren made sure to make each label think he was about to close the deal with its competitors. When Green finally left London in the middle of negotiations to consult with Jerry Moss at A&M's home office in Los Angeles, McLaren followed close behind, desperately rushing over the heads of the other British subsidiaries that had already indicated to their still-curious American label chiefs that they would reject the band if left to their own devices. As it turned out, while both American CBS and Warner Bros. Records found the Sex Pistols interesting, neither of their British affiliates would go forward with the deal; McLaren was stuck with A&M whether he liked it or not.

"Malcolm arrived at the A&M lot on a sunny ninety-degree Los Angeles day, dressed in an all black-leather outfit with a chain tying his knees together," recalls Green. "It had to be one of the funniest things I've ever seen. I mean, here were all these cool L.A. record executives, smoothing out with their new BMW's, and here was Malcolm McLaren. I'm withstanding it, introducing him to the head of marketing, head of sales, everyone else, but without a deal, because through this all there were two or three minor points that we just couldn't hammer out.

"Every one of the A&M staff said they felt, 'Green, you've done it to us before, but this time, you've really done it.' They said this group was going to be horrible, awful, and one by one they were coming off the fence and telling me that I'd really fucked up this time. There were a lot of political points to be taken off me, and I was getting tired of it, so I finally went to Jerry Moss and I said, 'Jerry, I put months into this, love the act. The manager's driving me nuts, the lawyer's an asshole, they're unreasonable in dealing with me. It's like nothing I've ever experienced before, but you're a wise old man: tell me what to do because I'll have to break some company rules to win them.' And Jerry told me that if I really liked the music, I should just sign the deal."

In the end, Green decided that no matter how much he wanted the Sex Pistols, there was only so much abuse he was willing to take, either from McLaren or from A&M's American staff. It was time to get tough. The two or three outstanding points in the Sex Pistols' deal simply weren't going to be resolved unless McLaren was given some sort of ultimatum. "I said, 'Malcolm, you can take it or leave it, but it's over,' and he said, 'It can't be.' I said, 'It is,' left my office, walked off the lot in L.A., and started to go to my plane back to London, and that's when he finally said, 'Hang on a minute, maybe we can still talk about it.' "

From the very moment the Sex Pistols first came together, anyone with two eyes could see that Glen Matlock was somehow different from the other Sex Pistols: not only better-educated and more middle class than the other boys in the band but also more clean-cut and gung-ho about being in a band. Matlock was like a Beatle in a band of Rolling Stones, and as a result, he was ripe for being picked on: In a word, he was a drag, far too wrapped up in his music to be any fun.

Nothing, for example, could have been more incongruous than the sight or sound of Matlock attempting to harmonize with Rotten on "Pretty Vacant" or "Substitute," and yet harmony was something Matlock had insisted on from the very start of the Sex Pistols: Harmony (both musical and personal) and hard work. Matlock loved being a musician. It was his way out of the middle class just as McLaren had used his art school career to get out of the middle class. Being a punk rocker was something Matlock just happened to fall into: Callous aggression could never be his stock-in-trade. While this was not as reprehensible as it later came to be, by the time the Sex Pistols reached the apogee of their fame, Matlock's desire for musicianship had become totally inappropriate to the rest of the band's goals. There was no place in this band for nice boys with good chops and earnest ideas.

The irony, of course, was that Glen Matlock truly was the glue that held the Sex Pistols together musically. Steve Jones may have liked to think he could write the band's hits all by himself, but McLaren and (surprisingly) Rotten knew that the Sex Pistols would never have developed as far as they already had without Matlock's steady musicianship. McLaren was grateful to and protective of Matlock for just this reason, and they even roomed together on the Anarchy Tour, but as the group's infamy catapulted them into the newspapers and up the charts, as Rotten's ego swelled and McLaren grew increasingly confident that the Sex Pistols could survive and even prosper without a musical ringleader, Glen Matlock found himself on the outside looking in, his every word a source of constant irritation to Rotten. The final bust-up with Rotten had come in Amsterdam in early January. "Rotten told me to drop dead," remembers the dozy bass player, "and when I was still there, he looked amazed to see I was still alive."

Whether Matlock finally jumped or was pushed out of the Sex Pistols is a matter of dispute. Matlock says he made the decision to leave the group of his own accord because he had simply become more interested in having his own group, the ironically named Rich Kids, with Steve New, Rusty Egan, and Midge Ure; others say that Rotten told McLaren to get rid of Matlock or risk losing his lead singer. In any event, several weeks before Matlock left the band in early February, Rotten pitched his best mate, Sid Vicious, to be the group's new bassist, and although none of this was announced to the press, by the time McLaren returned from Los Angeles—the deal with A&M still incomplete—it was already a fait accompli.

"As soon as McLaren came back from L.A.," says Matlock, "he called me and arranged for a meeting in a pub and he said, 'Look, *they're* rehearsing with Sid but I want you to go back in there and kick the door down. You've gotta show them who's boss. Just tell them *you're* the bass player and tell them to fuck off.' I said, 'But I'm not interested anymore. I've got me own thing going.' And he went, 'All right, then. Are you sure?' I said, 'Yep.' 'No hard feelings?' I told him 'No, no, none whatsoever.'

"And then the next thing was that telegram in the *NME.*"

On March 9, nearly two months to the day after the Sex Pistols left EMI, A&M Records finally agreed with Glitterbest to the signing of the Sex Pistols for a two-year contract with a £75,000 advance for each year. Needless to say, both sides considered the deal highly unusual. For Glitterbest's side, McLaren and Fisher won the key concession that the Sex Pistols would record eighteen "sides" or single tracks within the allotted two-year contract period instead of two albums in two years, the usual deal. While this allowed McLaren to force A&M to accept the tracks the Sex Pistols had already recorded for EMI, it also allowed A&M the crucial leverage of keeping the Sex Pistols working steadily throughout the term of the contract—or, as one reporter from the *Guardian* noticed with a sigh, it meant the release of one Sex Pistols single approximately every five weeks for the next two years.

But the contractual agreement that was drawn up between the two parties wasn't all that made the deal so unusual for Derek Green.

"On reflection," says Green, "I made a very interesting, personal decision which was that I did not want to meet the group until the actual signing. I felt if I met them, they would put me off and I wouldn't sign them. An intuition. And I wanted it so much that I didn't want to be put off. The other decision I made was not to have them come to the A&M office in London but to our publishing office, which was in a different location, because I felt that if they came to my building in New King's Road and I saw them in juxtaposition to my staff and my company, I'd immediately go off them. So I chose this tacky, drug-orientated building where my publishing company, Rondor Music, was, although Malcolm also wanted a public signing outside Buckingham Palace, which was a totally great publicity idea because their first single for us was to be 'God Save the Queen.' "

On the date of the actual signing, however, Green was given another bit of unusual news that once again gave him pause to consider his haste in signing McLaren's boys: Glen Matlock was no longer a Sex Pistol. " 'Sid Vicious?' I said. 'Are you joking?' And Malcolm said, 'No, he's great.' And I asked him how he played because I thought Matlock was one of the real players and he said, 'Well, he's never played before and that's why he's perfect for the job.' You would have thought that a regular guy trying to sign a deal would have tried to soften it, but Malcolm made it part of the excitement, which really made *me* behave oddly because I ended up saying that it made no difference to me at all."

POST OFFICE TELEGRAM:

Derek Johnson, New Musical Express.
28 February 1977

YES DEREK GLEN MATLOCK WAS THROWN OUT OF THE SEX PIS-
TOLS SO IM TOLD BECAUSE HE WENT ON TOO LONG ABOUT PAUL
MCCARTNEY STOP EMI WAS ENOUGH STOP THE BEATLES WAS TOO
MUCH STOP SID VICIOUS THEIR BEST FRIEND AND ALWAYS A MEM-
BER OF THE GROUP BUT UNHEARD AS YET WAS ENLISTED STOP HIS
BEST CREDENTIAL WAS HE GAVE NICK KENT WHAT HE DESERVED
MANY MONTHS AGO AT THE HUNDRED CLUB LOVE AND PEACE
MALCOLM MCLAREN

"The long and the short of that telegram," remembers Glen Matlock, "is that that was Malcolm's attempt to come up with some idea to show that he was still in control of the group. He couldn't be seen in anybody's eyes to have lost control over the fact that I didn't want to do it anymore, so he had to come up with some story to show that he was still the captain of the ship—namely, saying that *I* was sacked instead of the other way around."

Steve Jones fucked a secretary in the loo; Sid Vicious cracked open a porcelain toilet with his foot; Johnny Rotten drunkenly insulted everyone in sight: As far as Derek Green was concerned, the Sex Pistols signing with A&M Records at Rondor Music on March 9 was all in a day's work. "I've been through a lot of mad scenes," Green later told the *NME* in support of his unshockable nature. "I've witnessed a few with Joe Cocker, thrown buns at waitresses, flown across the Atlantic with George Harrison, and dropped dry ice into swimming pools with Harry Nilsson. . . . Humble Pie behaved every bit as bad in our office. . . . None of this scares me: I knew it was just a lot of media manipulation."

Even the public signing in front of Buckingham Palace early the next morning didn't get Green's goat. Green had insisted (over McLaren's objections) on not being present at any of McLaren's publicity stunts until the postsigning press conference that afternoon at the Regent Palace Hotel, and once again, the Sex Pistols behaved like drunken louts, arriving at Buckingham Palace at 7 A.M. blasted on vodka after a playful fistfight in their limousine. That didn't bother Green either.

"For once, I thought I was sort of enjoying it," he says, "but they were really aggressive, spraying the reporters with whiskey and beer. Vicious was fielding most of the questions because this was the first time the press had actually been allowed to get hold of him since he signed on, and he would answer them with some pretty funny things. One of the first questions came from the *Daily Express* reporter, a girl, and he said to her, 'Come on, why are you asking me that dull, fucking question? Didn't I see you at a party last week stuck on so and so's cock?'

"But some of the questions were rather precise about details of their tour or about the contract and that's the first time I saw McLaren lean into Johnny Rotten's ear and instruct him, and then we'd get a serious response. I mean, I got asked a question at one point—a question about whether I had any contractual obligations over their behavior—and at the very moment I started to answer that there was none whatsoever, Sid Vicious farted."

Green thought that was funny too, but then on the 12th of March, just as A&M Records prepared to press "God Save the Queen," he was called at home by Philip Roberge, the American manager of *Old Grey Whistle Test* presenter Bob Harris, and told that Harris and a friend, record engineer George Nicholson, had been beaten up by Johnny Rotten and company the night before at the Speakeasy, a popular record industry nightspot. A friend of Rotten's had demanded to know when the Sex Pistols would be invited to appear on *OGWT,* and when Harris refused to reply, a fight broke out. Harris was only bruised and frightened—although at one point he told friends he had received a death threat regarding the incident and was going up to the country to hide—but Nicholson required no less than 14 stitches to the head. On Monday morning, Green was told, a full statement—and quite possibly word of criminal charges—would be delivered to the press.

"For the first time I was shocked," says Green. "I was more than shocked, because until then my reaction to the Sex Pistols' bad behavior was that I had said *I'm* not responsible, *I'm* just the head of the record company, what's it got to do with *me?* But after I put down the phone my conscience started to trigger. Hang on Derek, you *are* involved. For the first time, my thinking turned. I'm thinking, this is awful. I don't like the position I'm in. I'm not going to be able to defend them to people because they're basically a pain in the arse and they're serious. This Malcolm McLaren looks very satanic and his manipulation of everyone looks like no fun at all. When these instances occur, he's looking to exploit it. Someone's going to get hurt."

By the time Green arrived at his office the next day, he had decided that *something* had to be done. Having signed the Sex Pistols against the advice of his staff, Green now felt that this latest incident was no longer only a corporate issue but one that demanded a personal response. After a long, silent drive down to Brighton's pebbled beach with a confidant, Green finally decided there was only one solution to his Sex Pistols problem. "I rang Jerry Moss in L.A. and I said, 'Jerry, you know I've been a disciple of this band for months now. The record's going to be a smash, a number one, and we're going to make a lot of money from it, but you know what? I don't want to work with them anymore.' I told him that A&M should stick with the Sex Pistols because A&M is supposed to be there to make money and to try and feed the people who work there and that if we got rid of the Sex Pistols I was afraid people would think we'd look old-fashioned: We're supposed to do contemporary music and contemporary music is punk.

" 'So that's what I think you should do,' I said, 'but I ain't working it. I'll have to leave.'

"And Jerry said, 'Hold off. Are you telling me I've got a choice between the Sex Pistols or you? Don't you think that's a bit unfair?' I told him I was afraid he was right but that that was it. I honestly wanted him to take them over me. 'OK,' he said. *'I'll* make a decision. There's not even a question here for me. You stay. Pay them off whatever it takes. Just do it and they'll go away.' I was shocked but half an hour later Herb Alpert called me, and it had been years since I'd heard from Herb, and *he* said, 'Look, if it's a choice between the Pistols and you, you stick. Pistols, I don't care. These things come and go.' "

The very next day, March 16, exactly one week after the Sex Pistols were officially signed to A&M Records, Green had McLaren and Steven Fisher summoned to a surprise meeting at the office of A&M's attorneys to discuss what they were told would be "a most important contractual point."

"Malcolm was sent up here with no idea whatsoever," he says. "I wrote a two-sentence press release that said 'A&M Records wishes to announce that its recording agreement with the Sex Pistols has been terminated with immediate effect. The company therefore will not be releasing any product from the group and has no further association with them,' and I passed it around. I watched Malcolm's face and Fisher's face as they read it, and let me tell you, they couldn't believe it. At first, Malcolm was shocked and tried to talk me out of it—'Hey, can't we talk about what's going on' and this sort of thing. And I said, 'No, there's nothing to talk about. I just don't want to work with you anymore.' He said, 'That's ridiculous. There must be more to it,' and he laughed. But there really was nothing more to talk about other than how much it was going to cost A&M because I was going to pay my way out.

" 'Whether we've agreed or not,' I said, 'this notice is going out on the wires at 3:00, so we've got between now and then to agree on a sum of money.'

"And then I left them to sort out whatever it was."

As the Glitterbest till clanged shut with A&M's £75,000 payoff in its belly, McLaren once again blithely disavowed any responsibility for the Sex Pistols' naughty behavior. Derek Green, he cynically claimed, had been the subject of "industrial blackmail": McLaren had spied a telegram on Green's desk from A&M recording artist Rick Wakeman jokingly urging Green to yank the Sex Pistols off the label or give the rest of A&M's roster complimentary safety pins, and everyone knew (or so McLaren said) that Wakeman's manager was the same Philip Roberge who was also managing Bob Harris. According to Green, however, McLaren was only half right. There *was* a telegram from Wakeman lying on his desk, but in his haste to read it—upside down, of course—McLaren didn't quite catch the context or the date Wakeman's telegram had been sent—a few days before the Harris incident had even occurred.

McLaren could deny responsibility for the Sex Pistols, but this time there would be no denying that he had been caught with his pants down. "I'm shellshocked," he told the *Evening Standard* at a Glitterbest press conference the day after the sacking. "Four weeks ago I flew to Los Angeles to meet Herb Alpert and Jerry Moss who head A&M, and a week ago we signed up.

"They knew what they were getting, and managing director Derek Green said that he wasn't offended by the group's behavior and that he thought they were fresh and exciting.

"Then at 11:30 last night I got a telex from them saying it was all over.

"The Sex Pistols are like some contagious disease—untouchable. I keep walking in and out of offices being given cheques. When I'm older and people ask me what I used to do for a living I shall have to say: 'I went in and out of doors getting paid for it.' It's crazy."

Even crazier was the common perception that the Sex Pistols had piled up the scandalous sum of £110,000 for having made just one hit single. In fact, the Sex Pistols themselves had made scarcely anything from the sackings: A&M's money had been paid to Glitterbest, not to the Sex Pistols, and McLaren controlled the Sex Pistols' money as tightly as if it were his own. (EMI's £40,000 payoff had been spent almost immediately to retire McLaren's early debts.) "I didn't see a fucking penny of it," says Steve Jones, deliberately poking each syllable with anger. "I was so naive. I didn't have me own lawyer, I didn't dream of having an accountant, didn't even have a bank account. I just used to go up the office and get money off Sophie—and sometimes she wouldn't even give me it." (Not that there's any reason to shed any tears for the Sex Pistols. Within six weeks of the A&M sacking, McLaren permitted Rotten, Jones, and Cook to buy themselves new flats and, in Jones's case, even a new BMW.)

If the sacking from A&M didn't exactly make the Sex Pistols rich, it certainly helped, however inadvertently, to shore up McLaren's own feelings of radical credibility, his desire (in Vivienne Westwood's words) "to get people to fuck up, band together, and fight the world." McLaren made a big show of concern for the band's plight, whisking them away for a short holiday (first to Jersey, where they were promptly kicked off the island by the police, and then to Berlin with express instructions to be photographed by the Wall), doubling their salaries, and redoubling his efforts to find them a new record deal—in early April, he returned to the Glitterbest office devastated after having been rejected by five companies in a single day—but the experience of having been unceremoniously kicked off two major record labels because of what he perceived as the music industry's fascistic intolerance of the Sex Pistols' naughty behavior only made the prospect of having to go through the whole experience again seem terrifyingly boring. The business of actually running the band was now left to Sophie and numerous others while McLaren distracted himself with fantasies of making a major motion picture about the Sex Pistols' travails.

Paranoia now ruled the day. McLaren suspected Rotten of wanting to jump ship to sign a solo deal with A&M (according to one theory, this explains the hasty generosity of a holiday in Berlin); Rotten suspected McLaren of lying that there were no record companies that would have them and that they were being blocked from playing in London by the revival of the Greater London Council's infamous "Code of Practice for Pop Concerts," the so-called Pop Code. To Rotten, life as a Sex Pistol increasingly seemed to come down to a choice between being a member of the greatest rock 'n' roll band in the world without gigs and a record deal or groveling at the feet of Malcolm McLaren for help. The only way out was to rebel, and a treacherous and cold-blooded obstinacy now supplanted Rotten's ordinary mean-spiritedness whenever McLaren so much as hovered in the distance.

Stalemate loomed, when into the breach came Sid Vicious, someone both Rotten and McLaren could agree on, albeit for radically different reasons. Rotten had been a close mate of Sid's ever since the two first met at technical college, but when the Sex Pistols took off, Sid ached with jealousy—his drum experience with Siouxsie had proven to be strictly temporary—and he begged Rotten to help get him into the group as soon as it was hinted Matlock was on his way out. For a while, the two lived at the flat of their close friend Linda Ashby, a lesbian prostitute whose elegant Mayfair bordello was the tawdry squat for the Sex Pistols' inner circle, and Rotten simply ignored Sid's pleading. But then Nancy Spungen showed up, shooting smack from the first day she approached the inner circle and looking to score a night in bed with the famous Johnny Rotten (no one close to Rotten ever called him anything but John).

Rejected by the rather puritanical Rotten and passed onto Sid, the star-fucking Nancy soon began putting pressure on her new boyfriend to force an entrée to the band from Rotten. Some say that had it not been for Nancy's black-minded talent for seeing the worst in everything, Sid might have remained merely a jealous suitor to the Sex Pistols, but in reality Rotten needed Sid in the band. To Rotten, Sid was more than just company; he was protection against the dynamic duo of Jones and Cook, someone who was insecure enough to follow him off the edge of a cliff if that was what he happened to be doing. Once Rotten recognized the benefits of having a close friend in the band, he allowed Sid to form an alliance with him, an alliance that, to Sid at least, seemed as strong as the bond that had originally brought them together in college.

Oddly, it was these same qualities—Sid's insecure sycophantism, his uncontrollable wildness, his bizarre willingness to go anywhere and do anything just because it was outlawed—which also appealed to McLaren. Tall and gangly, with a patch of Vaseline-spiked black hair falling over his deathlike skin and a hyperactive imagination put into creative overdrive by giant doses of speed, Sid Vicious looked and acted like he was born to be a Sex Pistol, and he had long ago earned a reputation around SEX as a reliably excessive personality who had more than a dollop of desire for fame: His one desire was to live life on the edge.

Ever since Vivienne Westwood had first pointed Sid out to Malcolm as someone who had the kind of look McLaren was thirsting for in a lead singer, McLaren had tried to think of a way to use this nineteen-year-old goof-off. It took Glen Matlock's departure from the band for McLaren to realize that the best way to use Sid Vicious—the moniker was derived from Sid's resemblance to Rotten's ill-behaved pet hamster—was simply to let him drag the rest of the Sex Pistols toward the dismal fate that surely lay in store for him. If "Sidney" liked to beat himself up when the action got too tough—and he often did literally beat himself up by throwing his body against the nearest brick wall—that was fine by McLaren, just as long as it took its inevitable toll on the band.

"Sid didn't know bad from good," says Westwood. "He didn't know right from wrong most of the time, that boy. He just didn't *have* an ego, especially not about wanting to perform, even though he was a natural performer. He was just a very affectionate, very intelligent, very funny, warm person."

McLaren seemed to harbor similarly warm affections toward Sid, but ultimately, Sid's jealousy and vulnerability were just two more weapons in the arsenal of psychological munitions he knew he would need to keep Rotten's ego under his control. "When Sid joined the band he couldn't play guitar but his craziness fit into the structure of the band," McLaren told reporters. "He was the knight in shining armor with a giant fist."

However, as Sid's tenure with the Sex Pistols pushed on, it seemed more and more likely that the only destination that fist was headed was down Johnny Rotten's ever-widening throat.

By the middle of May, after an aggressive media campaign waged through odd leaks to the music papers and numerous (failed) ruses to compile a batch of deals with various small record companies around the world into one multinational Sex Pistols contract, McLaren finally caved in and signed the Sex Pistols to Richard Branson's Virgin Records in a straightforward deal—no signing ceremony—for a two-year contract for three albums with an option for additional years and a £45,000 advance. (Almost simultaneously with the consummation of the Virgin pact, McLaren also managed to sign a deal with the French Barclay Records for another three-album, £26,000 deal to distribute the Sex Pistols' records in France and Switzerland, a shrewd move that later payed off handsomely when it came time to put pressure on Virgin to release the Sex Pistols' album.)

For Richard Branson, signing the Sex Pistols was a victory that had long been coming to his fledgling Virgin label. Branson had wanted to sign McLaren's group immediately after the EMI sacking, but at the time McLaren was less than willing to go with this hippie company whose biggest hit till then had been Mike Oldfield's classic progressive rock LP, *Tubular Bells.* Branson fought back, nagging McLaren by phone almost every day for two months, and suffering greatly through McLaren's waffling cynicism. By signing the Sex Pistols, Virgin hoped to haul itself up to the times and pull in more punk acts while there was still money to be made from this new fad. Richard Branson may not have liked to admit it, but he needed punk rock, and he recognized (in a way his top lieutenant, Simon Draper, didn't) that signing a band as infamous as the Sex Pistols when no other record company would touch them would be counted as a coup for his Virgin Records.

For McLaren, signing with Virgin had to be considered something along the lines of a moral defeat. Virgin was simply too cooperative and unshockable to allow itself to be used as fodder for his skills of manipulation. Branson, ever the patrician daredevil, actually enjoyed dealing with McLaren, and his entire staff seemed perfectly at ease with the Sex Pistols' antics, to the extent that the Sex Pistols were welcome at Virgin's offices at any time, even without appointments. Branson was a hippie, and

McLaren had hated hippies ever since his time at art college when people like Richard Branson—cold, suave, and shrewd—ran the student union.

Faced with Virgin's unconventional and permissive business manners, McLaren finally conceived of a plan he was sure Branson would reject—a Jubilee Day boat party down the Thames to celebrate the release of the Sex Pistols' "God Save the Queen"—and was rather shocked when Virgin not only did not reject the idea but welcomed it with open arms.

"Malcolm didn't exactly expect us to invent outrage so much as to collude with him," responds Al Clark, then Virgin's chief press officer, to a question about Virgin's role in facilitating McLaren's public relations campaign for "God Save the Queen." "Initially, he was shocked by our willingness to go along with him. He was accustomed to the record companies being the enemy and spilled out quite a bit of copy to make sure that they knew it even if it weren't so. But I suppose we didn't feel that intimidated. It felt like a great adventure. If anything went against my instincts, I would have said so. I think that because he had been accustomed to EMI and A&M's horror and disbelief at his suggestions he was pretty surprised that we went along."

However, if any single record in the history of rock 'n' roll deserved the kind of outrageous publicity display of a blaring boat ride down the Thames, the Sex Pistols' "God Save the Queen"—originally titled "No Future," but universally known as "God Save the Queen" because of its anthemic chorus—was surely it. Released just prior to the massive celebrations commemorating the queen's Silver Jubilee, "God Save the Queen" was precisely the kind of record that could be counted on to set the nation on its head, and this it did, more successfully than anyone—including McLaren—had ever imagined.

God save the Queen
The fascist regime
That made you a moron
A potential H-bomb

God Save the Queen
We mean it man
There is no future
In England's dreaming

—God Save the Queen

From its crunching power-chord guitar riffs to Johnny Rotten's yelpingly sarcastic vocalizing, "God Save the Queen" still attacks its listeners with unbridled ferocity, and yet the record is much more than just another blast of adolescent anger at the exalted symbols of British royalty. Indeed, while most other anti-Monarchist rants have been forgotten—for example, Angry Young Man John Osborne's 1956 essay in *Declaration* railing against "royalty religion, the national swill"—ten years after its release, "God Save the Queen" still sets off the musical and political alarm systems of its listeners, if only because its chillingly apocalyptic portents of a wasted teenage underclass somehow seem more appropriate to Thatcherite Britain than to the relatively benign years of frustration and compromise under Labour socialism.

However, in the last weeks of May 1977, with the Jubilee Day festivities rapidly approaching, "God Save the Queen" was taken as a defiant and ungentlemanly display of anti-Royalist sentiment—it was said that only a Communist or an Irish republican would have voiced such a dastardly attack on the queen—and the record was greeted with a torrent of outraged newspaper editorials, parliamentary denunciations, retail boycotts (some W. H. Smith's outlets simply left a blank space where the Sex Pistols' name should have appeared on their in-store Top 10 charts), and airplay and advertising bans on both the BBC and Britain's independent radio and television stations—all of which only helped the record (now selling upward of a hundred thousand) to *enter* the charts at number eleven. By the time the Sex Pistols took their famous boat ride down the Thames some two weeks later, with "God Save the Queen" storming into the Top 5 and the Jubilee celebrations in full swing, even Virgin had come to accept the irresistible logic of McLaren's timing.

It was expected that the boat ride would cause even more ruffled feathers and angry leaders in the newspapers, and according to Al Clark, Virgin was prepared for the worst. "To put out a record as contentious as 'God Save the Queen' in Jubilee Week," he says, "knowing that your group already elicits a disproportionate amount of loathing from quite a considerable part of the British public, and then do a boat trip up the Thames with the boat hung with obnoxious banners, knowing it's going to be noisy, emphatic, and anti-Jubilee, is the difference between having the propensity for saying 'Fuck you' and saying 'Fuck you' very noisily and in public.

137

"But Malcolm was persuasive, garrulous, quite eloquent, and very emphatic. And most of all, he made everything sound like fun, even if what was being suggested was time-consuming, useless, or even harmful. He made something like the boat trip feel like something you would really enjoy organizing, that would make you feel terrific, and would occasion something so chaotic and extraordinary that it was really important that you should join in, so that when it was done you would realize how wonderful it really was to do."

Still, no amount of preparation could have readied the two hundred or so assorted guests of the Sex Pistols and Virgin Records for the events of June 8. Floating down the river with a tape of the real "God Save the Queen"—the national anthem—thundering out as the boat passed under the river's many bridges, all was fine until someone threw a punch—most people say it was Rotten's friend Wobble, if only because Sid and Nancy were too busy doing drugs belowdecks to do much fighting—and the ship's captain radioed into the Metropolitan police to quell the fight, which had, ironically, already died down. By the time the boat reached the Houses of Parliament—just as the band broke into "Anarchy in the U.K."—two police patrol boats had become its unofficial escorts and the landing dock was crowded with bobbies and Black Marias. As the passengers disembarked, a sea of police officers clambered aboard to break up the party, and when McLaren refused to come ashore, the men in blue dragged the recalcitrant partygoers off the boat in a flurry of sixties-style truncheon-swinging. Ten people, including McLaren—screaming "Fascist Pigs!"—Westwood, Jamie Reid, and Sophie Richmond, were hauled off to jail.

"I wasn't that scared of the police," recalls Westwood, "because when I saw them I was very drunk. But when I saw Malcolm being dragged off, I couldn't bear the thought, so I yelled 'Oh, God, they've got Malcolm!' All I wanted to do was to get in the van with him and when I did, they charged me with assaulting the police. I didn't assault anyone.

"As soon as I got to the police station I did a cartwheel and we just pissed about, laughing at the police. We were having a very good time, and the police were very stupid, very funny. They were typing the descriptions down and they were actually saying what they were typing—like one policeman said something like 'four sensuous lips' because I had my lips painted in four colors. I wasn't worried one bit about Malcolm once we were there, because all the blokes were put together in a different place, but I did worry about my boys at home not knowing where I was, because I couldn't get any kind of message to them until about lunchtime the next day."

Even with the radio, television, and retail bans on "God Save the Queen" (and the GLC ban on the Sex Pistols' live performances), by the end of June, the disc still managed to make it to the number-two position in the official charts compiled by the British Market Research Bureau (BMRB) and the top position in the independent charts compiled by *NME* and *Melody Maker.* Despite this seeming victory, however, McLaren and Branson cried wolf, claiming that the record had been denied the official number-one position by a conservative clique in the British Phonographic Industry. The newspapers once again delightedly filled their columns with the salacious details of McLaren's latest conspiracy theory—specifically that the Sex Pistols had been kept out of the top slot to make way for the new Rod Stewart single, "First Cut Is the Deepest." Without the bans, said McLaren, "God Save the Queen" would have been "the fastest-selling record in history. . . . It just goes to show, that whatever the industry has thought of the disc, and even if they think of the Pistols as a bunch of troublemakers who can't play, some 200,000 kids disagree."

In just under a week, though, someone did choose to agree with the industry's obstinately conservative consensus on the Sex Pistols, and violently too. One by one, the Sex Pistols and their friends were set upon by angry thugs who had somehow come to the common (and mistaken) perception that "God Save the Queen" described the queen herself as a moron. (Some also speculated that the beatings were due to McLaren's vacuous public denial via a letter to the editor of the *Guardian* that the Sex Pistols were hidden supporters of the far-right racist movement, the National Front.) First was Jamie Reid, viciously attacked by four people near his home in south London and left lying in the street with a broken nose and cracked leg. Next was Rotten, who together with producer Chris Thomas and studio engineer Bill Price was the target of an unprovoked assault by a knife-wielding gang that deliberately slashed at Rotten's face with a razor, stabbed Price in the arm, and cut Thomas's face to ribbons. The next day it was Paul Cook's turn: Banged over the head with an iron bar outside Shepherd's Bush tube.

Suddenly, all the implosive rage and paranoia brewing between McLaren and the band hurtled out at the world: A terrified Johnny Rotten refused to leave his flat; Steve Jones and Paul Cook begged McLaren to make plans for getting the band out of the country; Sid and his American girlfriend Nancy Spungen stayed at home sedating themselves with heroin. McLaren pressed the Sex Pistols' case to the opportunistic media-mongers he had so recently denounced for having provoked the attacks in the first place—knives and iron bars were more than he had bargained for and he somehow believed that a dollop of good press would make a soothing balm of Sex Pistols sympathy—but the reporters wondered whether the attacks weren't yet another example of McLaren's cleverly manufactured publicity stunts, especially when Rotten came in for a second round.

Such utterly circular cycles of paranoia and publicity only infuriated the Sex Pistols more, pitting one half of the band (Jones and Cook) against the other (Rotten and Vicious) in violent, and occasionally even pugilistic disagreement, but by now, McLaren no longer cared very much what happened to the Sex Pistols. Like the sixteen-year-old Malcolm Edwards who had left his old friends behind when he discovered the virtues of art school, McLaren had again decided he was "beyond all that now": Now he was a member of a newer and better club with a better class of people—now, he was *Richard Branson's* equal, and compared with the lovely thrill of sharing in Virgin's corporate power, Rotten's paranoid prima donna number seemed merely precious. More and more, McLaren began taking Jones's side in the daily battles against Rotten's preachy rants about what it meant to be a Sex Pistol. "Who cares about the bloody Sex Pistols!" replied a bitter McLaren. As far as he was concerned, Rotten was ruining whatever it really did mean to be a Sex Pistol anyway. *Steve Jones* had had the right idea from the start: He was only in it for the "piss-up and the birds"—chaos at any cost—and everything else was just icing on the cake.

Punk may have started fat with ideological significance, but by the summer of 1977, the punks' contempt for class politics, traditional sex roles, and rock 'n' roll largesse was becoming just another fashion spread in the glossy magazines, another pop song on the radio. The punks had tried to appropriate the cultural life of commodities for their own radical purposes; instead, they became a new marketing segment for the advertising boys. Even Vivienne Westwood now felt compelled to change the name and decor of her shop. That summer, McLaren and Westwood closed 430 for three weeks and when they reopened their doors, most of McLaren's fifties knickknacks had been replaced by a grainy upside-down photograph of Piccadilly Circus and SEX's heavily grafittoed windows had been swapped for thick opaque glass and iron gates with an elegant, easy-to-miss gold plaque reading SEDITIONARIES: CLOTHES FOR HEROES.

The writing was on the wall, and like any good marketer with his eyes on the street, Malcolm McLaren had long ago read its message and now busied himself with the fantasy film project he had been contemplating ever since he first suspected that the group's stage career was as good as over. Who needed the Sex Pistols live when you could market a film and make just as much money without the day-to-day hassles of being a manager?

In the beginning, McLaren had condoned and encouraged the Sex Pistols' orgy of chaos and naughtiness simply because there seemed to be no hope for success any other way: "Cash from chaos" was a marvelous slogan for launching four untalented yobs into the pop stratosphere. But when it sank into Johnny Rotten's head that *he* was the artist and that McLaren had been put on this world to serve him and *not* vice versa, the tables were turned. Suddenly, Malcolm McLaren, the Jackson Pollock of punk rock—a postmodern artist painting with rock 'n' roll bands, record companies, politics, and clothes—was put in the position of bodyguard, baby-sitter, and businessman—a tiresome old rock 'n' roll manager with cleverly Macchiavellian ways—while Johnny Rotten, his loudmouthed alter ego, was being crowned as the prince of punk rock.

It was a situation that was bound not to last for long.

6
A STAR IS DRAWN

*Fame is a game that attracts the unbalanced on both sides. The Holly-
wood Sign is the alternative Statue of Liberty, hungry for losers, lon-
ers, introverts and misfits to grind down and recycle as brand new
born-again giant-sized loved ones—fame is Nature's way of saying
sorry. The reason why so many entertainers end up stiff after last rites
of Seconal probably has less to do with entertainment* making *people
crazy than with neurotics being attracted to it in the first place, eager
to obliterate the hated self in a white hot other. What makes a star a
star is not that "indefinable something extra" the low-browed girls and
high-heeled boys talk about in reverent, quiet-in-the-library mur-
murs—what makes a star a star is that indefinable something* missing.
—*Julie Burchill,* Damaged Gods

Now Johnny Rotten was undoubtedly a star. Every aspect of his personality was honed and polished, from his very name and scaggy clothes
to the way he rolled his *rrrr*'s or changed diction in midsong, the way, for
example, he would twist the words *Anarchist* and *Christ* in the line "I am
an Anti-Christ/ I am an Anarchist" in "Anarchy in the U.K." And Sid
Vicious was slowly coming *to be* a star, even if it was mostly at Rotten's
expense. But Malcolm McLaren? *His* vehicle—the star's most crucial
asset—was missing.

In some ways, McLaren's first idea for a Sex Pistols movie, which was
to find a producer, writer, and director and to stay far away from the
production himself, was his best. Starting at the top of his wish list, he
gathered up his nerve and called writer Peter Cook, one half of Derek &
Clive, his famous comic duo with Dudley Moore, to ask him if he would
write the screenplay. Whether from lack of money or from genuine lack

of interest, after a long meeting, Cook turned McLaren down. McLaren next phoned up Don Boyd, a jovial, talented twenty-six-year-old producer/director who had parlayed his considerable early successes in filmmaking and advertising into the creation of a complex of film, recording, and book publishing companies, housed in one building in Soho's Berwick Street.

"Through my recording studio and my book company, which was run by a rather crazy man called Michael Dempsey who knew Jamie Reid, I already had an awareness of the punk movement," says the poshly accented Boyd, producer of the 1987 movie *Aria.* "But also because of my youth, the status of being a kind of mover and shaker in the British movie business—after my film *East of Elephant Rock* (with John Hurt) opened, *Variety* called me the 'Whiz Kid in Brit Pix Biz'—I had this aura of being somebody you could come to, and sure enough, who should come into my office one day but Malcolm McLaren.

"He came in with Rotten and he said, 'How would you like to direct a Sex Pistols film?' I said, 'I've just made a movie which cost me under £100,000 so I think we could probably get this together for you at the very least from a financial point of view,' but I also made it quite clear I was interested in directing it."

From the very beginning, McLaren claimed to be interested in making only the most commercial of movies. What he wanted, he said, was something like a cross between Frank Tachlin's *The Girl Can't Help It* and the broad English comedies in the *Carry On* series. Boyd thought that sounded like fun and suggested they talk to the solidly working-class writer Johnny Speight, best known for his classic proletarian sitcom *Till Death Us Do Part,* sometimes considered the spark for the American television series *All in the Family.* McLaren loved this idea, and Boyd immediately made plans for them to meet Speight at his Rolls-studded Wimbledon mansion.

In the intervening weeks, Boyd met with McLaren and the Sex Pistols at his home, and to Boyd's surprise, the Sex Pistols seemed like amiable chaps—all please-and-thank-you and happy to be offered ginger snaps with their tea. "Rotten looked at me and said, 'Don't call me Johnny, call me John,' and he was very careful to explain to me that he wasn't Malcolm McLaren," Boyd recalls. "He made sure to let me know he had his own identity: He said he was an Irish gypsy. Finally, he asked whether he could use my bathroom and he spent an *inordinate* amount of time there. Twenty minutes later he came downstairs positively *reeking* of something that smelled rather . . . sweet. I went up there later, and the bathroom was literally covered with talcum powder. I couldn't decide if this was because he didn't want to smell in front of me or because he just needed a shower.

"That same night, I went to a pub with Malcolm, and before, he had been asking *me* all the questions—he's *always* asking questions—but now *I* got to ask the questions, and he told me he had been to art school, how he'd done various paintings, and how he'd wanted to be an artist but that he had a girlfriend/wife who designed clothes. And I realized he must have been a bit of an operator, an image-conscious person behind all the answers, because he was very keen for me to know that he'd manufactured the band and he described in detail how he had designed them in terms of shock value. And we laughed about it in the way you laugh with somebody who's realized you've rumbled their trip. I said, 'I know what you're up to,' and he laughed and said, 'I'm sure you do.'

"That night cemented us," continues Boyd, "but it also made me wary, because even then I said to him, I'm going to want control, Malcolm. If I'm going to be the director or even the producer, anything I do I'm going to want to control because I know about movies but also I think I know what I can do with this material. And he was very, very easygoing about it. 'Yeah, yeah, no problem at all, Don.' "

After the meeting with Speight, in which the writer demanded the very unproletarian minimum fee of £25,000—"a fee which seemed perfectly reasonable to me," says Boyd—McLaren called Boyd to ask if he could arrange a screening of *East of Elephant Rock* for him and the boys. One day later, McLaren phoned Boyd to tell him how much the Sex Pistols had loved the picture and to express his amazement at how spectacular the film looked considering its little price tag, but the conversation came to a dead end when Boyd once again mentioned the issue of creative control. In the flash of an instant, Don Boyd saw a portent of the entire mess that was about to take place around the making of the Sex Pistols movie.

" 'Malcolm,' I said, 'you'll have to make up your mind whether you're prepared to give me a lot of control because I am insisting on that.' I wanted it clear and I wanted it on paper.

"That was goodbye-time," chuckles Boyd. "The next day, he rang me up and said, 'Don, I've thought about it, and I can't do it, I don't want to be in a position where I'm servant to you, let's just part as friends.' I was amazed it was over that quickly, but I wished him luck and mentioned some other producers to him—Michael White, Jeremy Thomas, and Sandy Lieberson—and I warned him about Sandy because he was the sort of man who saw people and gave them hopes and then didn't always end up delivering, a very high-class post-office boy for 20th Century–Fox. The next thing I heard, he and Sandy were working together."

In fact, McLaren had already made contact with Lieberson through Gerry Goldstein, an acquaintance of Lieberson's from the days when the latter began his career as a producer with the Mick Jagger vehicle *Performance,* one of whose most major characters was inspired by David Litvinoff, an old North London pal of Goldstein's. Now, Lieberson, an expatriated American, was head of 20th Century-Fox's London-based international production and marketing team, and to McLaren's good fortune, the producer was dazzled by McLaren's ideas for making a Sex Pistols movie. "I'd known what the Sex Pistols were doing and I liked what they had to say," says this slight, bearded producer who later became head of production at both Fox and Goldcrest. "I thought that if we were going to make films in England, this was the kind of thing we should do. It was fun, stimulating, exciting, and I found Malcolm very engaging, clever, and ambitious."

With Lieberson's help McLaren now tried to find a bankable British director who could help him turn the trick with the Fox money men. Lieberson set up several hurried meetings between McLaren and directors Ken Loach and Stephen Frears, but after two brief dinner rendezvous with the team of Speight and Loach—the Sex Pistols didn't like Frears's more documentary-styled films—Loach came to the conclusion that "there were, quite simply, more differences than similarities between us" and that McLaren was "probably better off on his own," and McLaren began making public noises about Speight's Rolls-Royce proletarianism.

But by then McLaren had already arrived at the much more clever idea of hiring the American director Russ Meyer, helmsman of such brilliant cult skinflicks as *Beyond the Valley of the Dolls, Faster Pussycat, Kill! Kill!, Vixen,* and *Supervixens.*

"As soon as I heard Malcolm mention Russ Meyer," says Lieberson, "I knew it smelled of the perfect combination. Meyer was a guy who was not going to make something pretentious or add some unnecessary artistic element to the story. I thought it was perfect for the Sex Pistols. A match made in heaven." With Lieberson's aid—Fox had produced Meyer's 1970 camp classic *Beyond the Valley of the Dolls*—McLaren was constantly on the phone to Rory Johnston, a London friend looking after the Sex Pistols' American interests from Los Angeles, to firm up whatever loose connections he had in Hollywood to reach Russ Meyer.

In many ways, Meyer was a brilliant choice to direct a film about the Sex Pistols. For nearly twenty years, the eccentric director had challenged Hollywood with darkly humorous grotesques of America's sexual follies and won a surprisingly large and articulate cult following. Despite his rebellious reputation, Meyer had still made it to the boulevard of star auteurists, and in 1970, Fox gave him the chance to make *Beyond the Valley of the Dolls,* a curiously kinetic combination of experimental camera work, sexploitation antics, and rock 'n' roll chaos—and an instant cult classic, which only made Meyer's reputation that much more appealing to McLaren. Indeed, McLaren considered this tubby, mustachioed sexpot his equal in rebelling against the entertainment industry, and he hoped that Meyer would now be able to use the Sex Pistols against the British film industry in much the same way he had once used *Beyond the Valley of the Dolls's* fictitious all-girl rock band, "the Carrie Nations," to lance Hollywood's puritanism.

Perhaps Ken Loach's advice to McLaren that he attempt to make his own picture from the start was right after all, for by the time the Sex Pistols left for their Swedish tour, McLaren had already removed himself from much of the planning surrounding it. After working at the Portobello Hotel with Virgin radio ad-man John Varnom preparing a treatment for the film he hoped Meyer would make (now titled *Sex Pistols Official*), he was on a plane to Hollywood, to the Land of the Free and the Home of the Brave, to meet his destiny as the producer of his very own major motion picture.

On the day that Malcolm McLaren landed at Russ Meyer's home in the Hollywood Hills, Rene Daalder, a thirty-one-year-old screenwriter, director, and Russ Meyer protegé, was at home with his wife Bianca, waiting for Meyer to call with news about their new friend from London. Meyer had already prepared Daalder to expect McLaren's arrival—a good thing, since (in Daalder's words) McLaren then "rather spontaneously" moved into Daalder's house for most of the next month. To Meyer, who had served in the Army Signal Corps during World War II, any European about the same age as McLaren was more likely than he to have something in common with his ginger-haired guest. If McLaren was anything like Meyer pictured him, Rene Daalder would be a perfect counterpart to him, if only because of their similar ages, European backgrounds, and mutual love for rock 'n' roll.

Meyer may have been wary of McLaren, but he was eagerly anticipating his arrival for reasons that had little to do with any great love for the Sex Pistols or punk rock.

By 1977, Meyer's biggest success to date, *Beyond the Valley of the Dolls,* which was written by the Pulitzer Prize–winning *Chicago Sun-Times* film critic Roger Ebert (now better known as the pudgier half of television's consumer film guide *Siskel & Ebert*), was beginning to look like a fluke. Meyer didn't care that his fame as King of the Nudies had spread to such splendid sleaze-auteurs as John Waters or that his career as an indie producer-director had prospered after so many years of outright flops. Ever since Richard Zanuck, Sr. fired Richard Zanuck, Jr. during Fox's famous 1971 studio coup and the new studio heads denounced *Beyond the Valley of the Dolls* (released just after the disastrous *Myra Breckinridge* and often paired with it on double bills) as an industry embarrassment, Meyer had been looking for a way to prove wrong the Hollywood naysayers who snickered that he was incapable of making a successful mainstream (that is, non-X-rated) picture.

Meyer was just about to start editing down *Beyond the Valley of the Ultravixens,* written by his old pal Ebert, when McLaren called, but when it struck him that the Sex Pistols might be just what he needed to get off the retread trail, he immediately stopped what he was doing. Meyer may have been an oversexed curmudgeon, but even he could see that making a picture about this young, hot, Brit sensation was a smart way of changing tack without going drastically off course; even the name *Sex Pistols* was appealing.

Fortunately for Meyer, his intuitions about McLaren and Daalder had been essentially correct up to now: McLaren and the lanky, blond-haired Dutchman were well suited to each other and became fast friends. "We hit if off much better than anybody would have imagined," says Daalder, "and we went right away to work, knocking out a treatment which became a sixty-page affair, actually quite inspired."

One might have thought Meyer would have appreciated Daalder's efforts, but to Daalder's surprise Meyer threw the treatment he had written with McLaren into the wastebin after a single read. Instead of the "great Jewish comedy" McLaren had said he originally set out to make, McLaren and Daalder had turned out the black saga of a guileless, angry, and incorruptible rock 'n' roll band—the Sex Pistols—who are set upon by a swift-talking manager promising to lead them out of their depressing milieu of endless dole queues and hopelessly overstyled rock stars. "Will success spoil Johnny Rotten?" asked McLaren and Daalder in their expanded treatment. Meyer said he didn't care. As far as he was concerned, this wasn't the script for a Russ Meyer-meets-the-Sex Pistols picture, but an invitation to depression and misery, a tormented tale of gloom and doom on the British isles. A Russ Meyer picture, said Russ Meyer, had to have sex and violence and melodrama, lesbians, cripples, and guns, at any cost.

McLaren did not agree, and things quickly grew heated between these two titans of ridicule with Daalder left to negotiate the picture between their competing views. After a short while, even this situation became unworkable—"it was more dramatic for me than for anybody else," says Daalder—and Meyer called back his old friend Roger Ebert (then enjoying a reputation as the "fastest typewriter in the West") to doctor McLaren and Daalder's script.

"As far as Malcolm was concerned," says Daalder, "this movie was going to be the Sex Pistols movie and since, as it happened, the Sex Pistols liked Russ Meyer's movies, Malcolm hoped that Russ would respect them. He didn't want the movie to become *Beyond the Valley of the Dolls* with the Strawberry Alarm Clock. But of course, when you ask Russ to do a movie, it's going to be a Russ Meyer film. What amazes me when I see the script now, is that the movie didn't somehow violate either sensibility."

Working in Ebert's room at the Sunset Marquis Hotel, McLaren now dictated a new storyline that Ebert whipped into a script at first titled *Anarchy in the U.K.* and then *Who Killed Bambi?*

Who Killed Bambi? solved most of the problems McLaren had been having with Meyer defining the film's relationship to the 'real' events of the Sex Pistols' story. Instead of a dreary, defensive quasi-documentary about the Sex Pistols being victimized by their own success, Ebert intensified each band member's character, tossing in a few subplots to give the film a more entertaining (read: Russ Meyer–like) veneer. While most of the incidental Dickensian ambience McLaren and Daalder initially desired still remained, the script now took on the roller-coaster feel of a Russ Meyer picture with the Sex Pistols engaging in mortal combat against their devious, self-promoting manager, P. T. Proby—based in no small part on Malcolm McLaren himself. "That," says Rene Daalder, "was a conscious decision to intensify Malcolm's personality to the level of parody."

"Well preserved and youthful-looking, filled with limitless if often inane enthusiasm," Proby, writes Ebert, "fancies himself as the nation's leading and most uncanny Trend Spotter. Although he's always totally positive in a socko manner, none of his clients is indispensable. They're here today and gone tomorrow and there are a hundred more to take their places. Implicitly, he stands for all the corporate bullshitters who have crossed the Sex Pistols' path in the past: EMI, A&M, etc. Nevertheless, we somehow tend to like him. Being the ultimate opportunist, he is in fact as anarchistic as the Pistols themselves: A mutant cross between the 1950's entertainer and the 1960's mind-fucker."

Proby is undoubtedly one of *WKB*'s most charming antagonists, but as written, he is certainly not the picture's main meanie. For that role, Ebert invented a character with the unmistakable moniker of M.J.—the world's leading rock star—and devised a convoluted plotline in which Proby dangles fame and fortune before the Sex Pistols as they climb the ladder to infamy, while M.J. (Proby's most famous client) tries to co-opt their act in a desperate effort to salvage his own career.

But Ebert also put his own twisted stamp on the script to satisfy Meyer's penchant for depicting sexual taboos and domestic violence. Chief among these are a scene in which Sid Vicious rapes his mother while she is shooting up and numerous sexual adventures for Steve Jones— always caught by the camera at the "Cambridge Rapist Hotel" in flagrante delicto and simultaneously munching a cold Wimpyburger—as well as the title scene in which M.J. cold-bloodedly kills a young fawn with a steel-tipped arrow. Thanks to Ebert, the disparate worlds of McLaren and Meyer had intersected at last.

Whether through outright guile or simply through his typically cheer-ful blathering, while he was in L.A., McLaren was somehow able to dis-guise from his host, his screenwriters, and his director the extent of the antagonism between himself and the subject of their movie. And yet, no sooner had he arrived in Hollywood than his troubles from home followed him there.

As usual, most of the trouble was coming from Rotten. With the Sex Pistols due to leave for their Scandinavian tour in a matter of days and McLaren in hiding in London, Rotten was furious that McLaren had left Sophie and the band to deal with Virgin's pressure tactics to let *Top of the Pops,* the weekly television revue of Top 10 hits, air a promo film of "Pretty Vacant," their second Virgin single. How could the Sex Pistols claim to be the nemesis of the music industry if the very first thing they did after having their first hit single was to appear with all the other teeny-bop chart-toppers on *TOTP?* This is *serious,* Rotten told a giggling McLaren over the phone. It was absurd to be singing "Pretty Vacant" on the one rock 'n' roll show that was chiefly responsible for the virulent commercial stupidity the song was attacking. As far as Rotten was concerned, a Sex Pistols appearance on *Top of the Pops,* whether live or on tape, was out of the question.

McLaren himself didn't actually care whether the promo was aired, but he had grown so tired of Rotten's bitching that he now simply surrendered to his star's demands to get Richard Branson to yank the clip from *TOTP.* However, a day later, just as the band was about to leave for the airport to begin their Scandinavian tour, Branson phoned Sophie Richmond to announce apologetically that even he couldn't pull the plug on the promo at such a late date.

Angry as Rotten was at Branson, the person he really blamed for this fiasco was McLaren: It was McLaren who had talked the band into doing the promo in the first place—even if no one else did, Rotten remembered how badly McLaren had wanted the Sex Pistols to do *TOTP* the night the group wound up on the Grundy show—and it was therefore McLaren's responsibility to make sure the promo was used the right way at the right time. For the first time, Rotten felt that he had been publicly cuckolded by McLaren, and all for the sake of some measly record sales—sales that would undoubtedly make Branson and McLaren (but not Rotten) very rich men.

There had been numerous other betrayals in the past, inconsequential double-crosses about money, music, and promotion, but this time, said Johnny Rotten, was different. This time, there would be no compromises and no forgiveness, and from here on, Rotten made sure that his legal, personal, and business interests sharply diverged from anything and anyone that was involved with Malcolm McLaren or Steven Fisher. At Heathrow Airport, Rotten tried his best to retaliate by kicking up another storm with the press. "I don't talk to fabricated people," he screamed at one reporter. "Have you ever heard the sound of smashing glass," he taunted another. "Like a camera lens?"

Thus, while McLaren was glad-handing minor celebrities in the hot L.A. sun, and "Pretty Vacant" was zooming up the charts to a spot of blank wall next to the shining silver disc of "God Save the Queen" hanging in the Virgin Records reception area, the Sex Pistols were slogging their way through the chilly Scandinavian New Wave. To Rotten, McLaren's priorities never seemed clearer.

Honored and feted by Scandinavia's fledgling punks, benignly ignored by governments that quite sensibly saw no threat in the punk fad, and toasted by the British music writers Virgin had allowed to accompany the band—McLaren always insisted on leaving the domestic music press behind on foreign tours—the Sex Pistols began sounding off in public with their disgust for McLaren's managerial scheming. "Malcolm, I honestly hate," responded Sid when asked how the band was getting on without the constant presence of their Svengali. "I'm going to beat him up when he comes back from America." And why is that? asked the astonished reporter. "There are so many reasons," retorted Johnny Rotten, "I just couldn't begin to explain."

Following the band's return from Sweden, McLaren arrived back from America, and as soon as he did, he hurtfully responded to Rotten's charge that he had allowed "Pretty Vacant" to air on *TOTP* by claiming that Rotten betrayed the group by allowing Virgin to let the domestic press accompany them on tour. In fact, Rotten had made a big show of resisting Virgin, insisting (in a move that was straight out of McLaren's playbook) that the days of record-company-sponsored press trips were over and that the music media would have to pay their own way if they wanted to get in on the action overseas. To McLaren, the fact that Rotten allowed the music press to come along *at all* only proved that Rotten was abetting Virgin's publicity efforts in the hopes of becoming a pop star in his own right.

In retaliation, McLaren pressed for a complete blackout on the Sex Pistols activities until Virgin released the Sex Pistols' album. He wanted the appearance of absolute state censorship of the Sex Pistols' seditious ways, and any time he was challenged, he pulled out the old canard that he couldn't get the band gigs even if he wanted to, thanks to the GLC's "pop code." It was simply more profitable to keep the Sex Pistols out of the public eye, playing up the great scandal of the rock 'n' roll band that had made more money from being kicked out of various record companies than it had from selling hit records. This was a brilliant (and convenient) strategy: Artificially limiting the Sex Pistols supply would only make the final payoff all the greater—*if* the band survived the ordeal.

Of course, with Russ Meyer due to arrive any second, there wouldn't really be any time to do gigs anyway.

"When Malcolm first brought the idea of Russ Meyer up," says Sandy Lieberson, "I thought: fantastic, because *that's* the way to get Fox involved, and for months I'd been trying to figure out how to get my boss in L.A., Alan Ladd, Jr., to approve the deal. I explained the project to Ladd and the other members of the Fox creative team in L.A., mostly, what it was and the kind of money involved, but I absolutely played down the whole controversy over here about the Sex Pistols, just explained the fact that it was a big pop group, and that Warners were going to do the record in the States—I'd been having discussions with Mo Ostin of Warner Bros. Records, telling him that we wanted to produce the film in order to help Malcolm come up with a U.S. record deal. With the U.S. involved, Virgin didn't want to do the film. It was too big for them, and they didn't have a film division yet, so it had to be Fox."

With Ladd's approval, Lieberson called in the solicitors to start preparing the contracts.

"The negotiations were endless," he remembers with a smile. "I found that Malcolm really was rather perverse in the sense that he would do everything possible to encourage you to get involved and then take certain actions which would actually undermine your involvement. The thing with Russ Meyer went on and off, on and off, I can't tell you how many times."

With Meyer scheduled to arrive in London on August 11 and most of the contractual squabbling left in the hands of various agents, solicitors, and studio execs, McLaren finally realized there was no time left for games. Unless he exploited his property quickly, there might not be a property left to exploit. He was increasingly convinced that Sid might not make it to the end of the film's production unless he straightened up. With his domineering and drug-obsessed girlfriend Nancy Spungen constantly by his side, Sid was quickly becoming the kind of rock star whose public renown was built on his private liabilities, whose fame fueled his running rivalry with Rotten even more, in turn feeding his heroin habit and leading to more and more bad behavior—which McLaren encouraged—and still more fame—which only fanned higher the flames of Rotten's jealousy and plunged Sid deeper into the tragic cycle of his celebrity.

McLaren may have claimed to have been concerned about Sid's health and well-being, but as the ticking of this walking time bomb grew ever nearer and louder, the question of Sid's health became less and less important to him. With Russ Meyer on the way to London, he became so obsessed with making *Who Killed Bambi?* that he even considered selling the legal entity known as the Sex Pistols to another manager so he could get on with the business of making movies.

From the moment Russ Meyer stepped off the plane from Los Angeles with his pneumatic girlfriend Ann-Marie in tow, the rush was on to get *Who Killed Bambi?* into production. "Meyer was extraordinary," says Gerry Goldstein, the one person McLaren trusted enough to leave alone with the director. "As soon as he got to the Portobello Hotel he said, [gruff voice] 'I can work right away—I don't get jet lag—get me a secretary,' and this girl came 'round and he turned her down. 'She's a star-fucker,' he said. 'Get me someone else.' " Within forty-eight hours, Meyer had written a third draft of *Who Killed Bambi?* and was on his way to Bray Studios to inspect the facilities where *Bambi* would be shot.

Rushed though he may have been to get the film into production, Meyer refused to be stampeded into working without the same kind of legal protection he normally had back home, and he actually flew back to Los Angeles in a fit until the contracts McLaren had promised were ready along with a furnished flat for the duration of his stay in London. McLaren was too busy playing games with the attorneys to finish the contracts on time for Meyer's return, but with Lieberson mediating transcontinentally he was encouraged to agree to pay Meyer's hefty expenses (if not his entire salary) *in cash* at the end of each working week, and the director promptly flew back to London with Roger Ebert to begin work on *Bambi*'s fourth draft. From then on, it didn't matter that Meyer grumped about his contracts and accommodations: Once he was settled into his chic riverview flat in Chelsea's fashionable Cheyne Walk and given the first installment of his £30,000 salary in cash, he was heard to bellow that *Bambi* might well be his biggest movie ever.

Oddly, a brief peace now broke out over the project. Rotten may have moaned about the way Meyer was twisting the Sex Pistols into a Hollywood burlesque, but when it actually came to meeting the director he spent most of their meeting silently picking through the contents of his handkerchief while Meyer lectured him on why his movies had to have tits 'n' ass in order to be Russ Meyer movies—which was all Steve Jones and Paul Cook needed to hear before giving their enthusiastic assent to Meyer's script. Indeed, according to Meyer, during *their* script meeting, Paul Cook mostly wanted to know what Meyer's "experience [was] in keeping it up in front of a 40-man production crew," while Jones seemed to take a bizarre interest in Meyer's own sex life, inquiring at one point in their discussion whether Meyer considered his last wife "a good fuck."

Even McLaren, rarely satisfied with anything less than perfection itself, now professed to be happy with Meyer's plans.

"I remember at the beginning, Malcolm telling me how great it was to work with Russ," says Gerry Goldstein. "I asked him why and he said that Russ was great because he didn't want any red buses in the movie. That's why Malcolm said he liked him: because in lots of films in London you see those *bloody red double-decker buses* zooming around, and Malcolm hated that. But then a day later, Russ said to me, 'Y'know I don't understand that Malcolm: He doesn't want any buses in this film.'"

As honeymoons go, however, this one was no less fruitful (or brief) than most. If McLaren and Meyer came up with such clever ideas as casting Marianne Faithfull to play Sid's junkie mother—Sid, of course, wanted Nancy to play the part—they also became increasingly exasperated with each other. Never exactly friends from the start—"I could never really put him together," a mystified Meyer later told *Search & Destroy* magazine, "and I'm gregarious, I get along with most everybody, except a wife or so"—they soon began clashing on the most minor production details: *Who Killed Bambi?* went through nearly a dozen rewrites during Meyer's involvement. Without Daalder to translate his radical Euro-chic into Meyer's colorful grotesqueries, McLaren was powerless to stop Meyer and Ebert—"he gets a big steak, a little booze, and two or three big-titted broads and writes like a cock," said Meyer when asked about the rumor that Ebert had been paid in women—from turning *Bambi* into Beyond the Valley of the Sex Pistols. Before long, Meyer had even given himself a creaky cameo narrating the Sex Pistols fable in a direct address to the audience at the picture's beginning and end.

Of course, if McLaren found it necessary to protect the band from the clowning priapism of Meyer and Ebert's script, it was inevitable that Rotten too would eventually come to blows with Meyer over the many new scenes Ebert wrote portraying him as M.J.'s dour punk competition, a sex-starved antistar whose libidinal cravings lead him to various sordid and anonymous sexual encounters in numerous steamed-up London phone booths. Any way Rotten looked at it, *Bambi* was a no-win proposition for him. Either he was McLaren's guinea pig and had to accept whatever concessions he could get McLaren to wring out of Meyer; or he was Meyer's star character actor—for even if he won some changes in his portrayal he would still only be appearing in a Russ Meyer picture of the Sex Pistols.

Julien Temple, then a twenty-one-year-old graduate of Cambridge studying at the National Film Institute and working as McLaren's unofficial film documentarian—he had originally wanted the Kinks to be the subjects of his senior film thesis but eventually settled on making a film about the Sex Pistols—remembers being astonished at the extent of Rotten's fury with both McLaren *and* Meyer.

"By the time Rotten started falling out with Meyer, it was obvious that Malcolm had totally lost control of the band," says Temple. "Meyer was telling McLaren that the least he could do, apart from all the financial things, was to get the band to cooperate, but by then Rotten was actively sabotaging the film, mostly by not turning up for meetings and being aggressive to Meyer.

"But once, I'll never forget, we went around to his house and he showed me a sack full of the most ridiculous clothes—platform shoes and flared floral trousers and bright blonde wigs. He'd obviously gone to all these jumble sales buying up these early seventies clothes and he was determined that he was going to play a hippie in this ultimate punk film. He kept saying, 'This film is not going to happen, not going to happen,' and that was an accurate reflection of his power because by then he hated Malcolm and *he knew* he could make it not happen."

As the dog days of August rolled on, drying up every drop of joie de vivre anyone in the Glitterbest camp had for *Who Killed Bambi?*, the group suddenly found itself being cared for by the simpatico Boogie, the road manager with the dime-store Indian face, while McLaren fiddled around with Meyer and Gerry Goldstein auditioning actors and making tentative overtures toward an American record deal.

Supported by the stalwart roadie, Rodent, Boogie saw no reason why the band shouldn't go out on the road again, and since he was now the boys' daily minder as well as their tour manager, he had an obvious (some say, obviously financial) interest in getting them back on the road.

For once, all were agreed—including Rotten. Like many members of the music press who had become skeptical of McLaren's constant lies that the Sex Pistols had been banned by the GLC, Rotten had discovered that the GLC Pop Code didn't ban *groups* so much as to make it difficult for *venues* to get relicensed without adhering to the code, which was itself mostly focused on controlling the behavior of fans, not bands. "I'd go out to somewhere like the Music Machine," Rotten said later, "and they would say, 'We offered gigs ages back but Malcolm wouldn't take them.' My mouth fell four foot. I'd been treated like a cunt and I didn't like it."

With Rotten and Meyer breathing down his neck from different directions, McLaren found Boogie's idea of sending the group out on the road to outlying provincial towns such as Doncaster and Wolverhampton as "the mystery group who will be known as the SPOTS"—Sex Pistols On Tour Secretly, but on other occasions as the Tax Exiles, the Hampsters, or Acne Rabble—oddly appealing. On the one hand, it kept the Sex Pistols away from Meyer long enough that the director could actually get some work done; on the other, it also got the Sex Pistols out of McLaren's own hair by appearing to give in (within certain limits) to Rotten's complaints that they had been kept off the road too long.

Like most of McLaren's better moments of intrigue, however, the SPOTS tour backfired in equal proportion to the elegance of its construction. Going back on the road without the heavy carpet of hype McLaren had always insisted on laying down before the group's other tours gave Rotten more confidence about his singing than he had ever had before, but with the heat of the crowd and the intrusive eyes of the press homing in on his every move, Rotten was becoming increasingly dogmatic that it was he, not Malcolm McLaren and not Sid Vicious, who was the brute magnetic force that had turned the Sex Pistols into a great rock 'n' roll band.

Buttressed by Boogie and Sophie's attention to his onstage affairs, Jamie Reid's whispered political flatteries, and Sid and Nancy's petty jealousies—always worth a snarl—it occurred to Rotten for the first time that he now had the power to directly challenge McLaren for the Sex Pistols' direction. Rotten didn't need McLaren to tell him what the Sex Pistols were about: You didn't have to be a genius to see that McLaren had gotten most of the credit and the money, while Rotten was doing all the hard work. Where were you when I was slogging it out on the road, keeping Sid away from the junk, even getting gigs? Rotten supposedly demanded. So convinced was he that McLaren had given up on managing the band, that on one occasion he climbed in the back of a cab with McLaren and challenged him to tell the cabbie his home address. McLaren started to give the driver directions, but halfway through the ride, his face covered in sweat and the red "M" glowing on his forehead, he finally had to admit that he had no idea what Rotten's address was, never having been there. You see, said Rotten, you don't even know *where I live*.

Even Russ Meyer could now see that most of his early notions about the Sex Pistols were the result of some odd romantic ideal McLaren had seduced him with way back in L.A. Now Meyer knew that the Sex Pistols had never been the merry band of anarchistic Beatles he had once been told they were. Although he was often astonished by the boys' concerns— "Sid didn't object to fucking his mother, he objected to shooting up on screen," he later remarked—Meyer thought he could probably handle the band members' individual demands for script changes. However, all of this took money, especially given McLaren's increasingly inflated ideas about *Bambi*. Meyer believed he might be able to maneuver the Sex Pistols into place on a film set, but as a motion picture professional who had successfully mastered the wiles of the independent cinema, the one thing he could not countenance was having the financial rug pulled from under his feet at the very last minute. And that is exactly what happened.

With the cast hired, sets built, and shooting schedule supposedly etched in concrete, McLaren now began making noise to Sandy Lieberson about how little artistic control he had over Meyer. For the first time in the whole *Bambi* charade, McLaren even began representing Rotten's views on the film, saying that Meyer was intent on turning Rotten into a sex maniac. Meyer wasn't fooled. He had long accepted that there were some authentic objections to his script. But the more he perceived that

McLaren was attempting to take command of his picture "on behalf of the band" *without even having control of the Sex Pistols,* the more he insisted on getting his contracts signed and his money paid up front. As one might expect, he got neither.

"Reams of contracts were prepared," says Sandy Lieberson, "document upon document for production and financing of the film. They were endless. And Malcolm was continually changing his mind. The lawyers were saying, 'How could you do this? Are you sure Fox should be involved in this kind of film?' But still we went ahead."

In mid-October, Meyer went to the Wye Valley to shoot the movie's title scene of M.J. (now renamed B.J. to prevent stray libel suits) shooting down a fawn in cold blood, causing several members of the production crew to quit in protest. Ironically, that turned out to be the only scene he would actually shoot: Three days into production, the kitty had run dry.

Meyer was furious that McLaren had failed to secure the necessary funds to keep the picture running. McLaren's excuse was that he couldn't get a completion bond from Film Finances Ltd, and he promised to get more money from Fox, from Virgin, or from theatrical producer Michael White and his associate John Goldstone, all of whom had now been approached by Lieberson to help finance the picture, and who had, one by one, backed out. But by then, Sandy Lieberson had been told to change his tune.

"The people in Los Angeles were really beginning to get worried because the publicity was starting to seep into the U.S.," he remembers. "I was continually getting phone calls saying, 'I don't think we should do this.' I said, 'It's too late, we made a deal and we're exchanging documents, we can't back out now.' " But Fox had seen the writing on the wall. The picture was getting out of hand: What had started as a measly £150,000 punksploitation picture was beginning to look like a very expensive (and potentially explosive) bomb, despite the presence of novice producer Jeremy Thomas, now better known as the Oscar-winning producer of Bernardo Bertolucci's *The Last Emperor,* but then just starting his career. Before anyone could ask who did kill Bambi, Fox passed the word down to Lieberson not even to bother posing the question.

"Before any film was made you had to at least tell the board of directors the films you were making," he says, "and that year the board was meeting in Monte Carlo, because Princess Grace was on the board. Alan Ladd called me from there, telling me that this was not the right thing to be doing. Grace Kelly was not alone in this; a couple of my colleagues had also decided that was it. There was no arguing, no discussion, no reasoning. It was, 'Pay them off, get rid of the thing. If you have to give them the money, give them the money, but tell them to go away. We don't want Fox to have anything further to do with them.' "

Banner headlines blazed with word of Grace Kelly's distaste for *Who Killed Bambi?*—"PISTOLS SEXY FILM HAS PRINCESS IN A RAGE" reported the *Evening Standard*—and although Fox denied the princess's involvement, the Glitterbest staff gleefully cackled that the Sex Pistols had finally tickled one monarch's toes. In a matter of days, Russ Meyer stormed out of London, darkly threatening McLaren—whom he had now taken to calling "Hitler"—with lawsuits for every conceivable abuse under the sun. "I'm going to sue Hitler's ass," he is reported to have raved, and for a time, it seemed he really would.

"[McLaren] just spent too much money," Meyer said after his departure. "I can't really tell you for sure [how much] because I don't know. Sounds weird, but when you've always been your own boss, knowing exactly where every dollar is gonna go and where it comes from and then you're put in the position of just being the so-called 'artistic control' and not being aware of what the financial circumstances are, well, if everything goes out from under you, what can you say: You can only conclude that there was some mismanagement. McLaren just got into water way over his head.

"The sad thing is that the film we might have made could have really launched them on an international level."

With Fox's £150,000 payoff jingling in the Glitterbest till, that was the last thing McLaren was thinking of.

As if he didn't already have his hands full with this continuing cinematic catastrophe, throughout the time of Meyer's tenure in London, McLaren also spent a considerable amount of energy cajoling Richard Branson to finally release the Sex Pistols album.

At first, Virgin tried to pacify McLaren by releasing another single, "Holidays in the Sun"—"I don't want a holiday in the sun/ I just wanna go to the new Belsen"—but with Meyer out of the picture, McLaren was desperately in need of more cash to keep his movie running: After all, an entire production was now waiting to go forward.

Through most of October, Branson dragged his feet on getting the album out—it only stood to Virgin's advantage to milk the record single by single—and nothing McLaren said or did seemed to change Branson's mind. (McLaren also contributed to the delay by insisting, over Rotten's objections, that the album contain several hit songs—"God Save the Queen," "Anarchy in the U.K.," and "Pretty Vacant"—already released as singles; Rotten protested that it would be a travesty if working-class kids had to pay a second time for the tracks they'd already bought as 45s.)

Even today, no one knows who manufactured and released the bootleg *Spunk* album—mostly Dave Goodman's sessions with the band, including a few tracks that were later excised from Virgin's album—that finally forced Branson's hand to release the Sex Pistols LP. (It was common knowledge at the time that there were only two copies of the master tapes from those sessions, one owned by Goodman, the other by McLaren; Goodman has repeatedly denied any involvement with the *Spunk* LP.) In any event, on October 28, with 125,000 copies of the album already ordered, Virgin released *Never Mind the Bollocks: Here's the Sex Pistols* to widespread acclaim, instant gold-record status, and the routine legal mischief and retail bans a Sex Pistols record seemed to bring in its wake: No less than three London record shops were charged with offenses under the 1889 Indecent Advertisement Act and the 1824 Vagrancy Act for displaying the album cover with its prominent kidnap letter logo of the terrifying word "Bollocks."

With the *Bollocks* record in the stores, McLaren now returned to the movie. Without a director or a screenplay, *Who Killed Bambi?* itself was sunk. Ebert's script had been so specifically written for Meyer's directorial sensibility that it would have been madness for anyone else to have attempted to capture Meyer's moviemaking style, but McLaren wasn't yet willing to throw in the towel. At first McLaren considered turning to director Richard Lester (*A Hard Day's Night* and *Help!*) but then he decided to consult with Rene Daalder in L.A.

Daalder's first idea was to do it himself. "I would have loved to force myself on the project but at the same time I realized I could never ever do that if I wanted to retain my friendly relationship with Russ," he says. Instead, he suggested McLaren try contacting two friends he had worked with on various projects through the years, screenwriter Danny Opatoshu and director Jonathan Kaplan—a suggestion that proved to be the undoing of Daalder's relationship with Meyer anyway. "Russ accused me of having forced Kaplan on the project," he explains, "which really was nonsensical because somebody else would have done it anyway."

At first glance, Kaplan and Opatoshu—both then thirty-year-olds with well-established Hollywood track records—might have seemed an unlikely team to work with the Sex Pistols. Top students of Martin Scorcese at NYU Film School, the two had followed their teacher out to Hollywood in the early seventies when Scorcese began directing quickie exploitation pictures for Roger Corman's New World Pictures, and were hired as last-minute replacements when Corman's original writer and director for *Night Call Nurses* fell through. Within two short years, Kaplan, a fast-talking bearded film buff, had directed a bevy of exploitation pictures for Corman or his affiliates about the anger of everyday men and women, including *The Student Teachers* and *The Slams,* starring Jim Brown, both in 1973, *Truck Turner,* starring Isaac Hayes, and *White Line Fever* with Jan Michael Vincent the following year. (Later Kaplan pictures include *Over the Edge, Heart Like a Wheel,* and *The Accused.*) For his part, Opatoshu, the son of renowned actor David Opatoshu, had written and/or collaborated on scripts for numerous directors, including Alan Arkush's classic send-up of sixties rock, *Get Crazy,* but in 1975–76 he had returned to rock 'n' roll itself as an advance man for Bob Dylan's Rolling Thunder Revue.

Within a matter of days, McLaren had Rory Johnston ferrying over to Kaplan and Opatoshu various tapes and clippings of the Sex Pistols, and with hardly a word about money, contracts, Russ Meyer, or any schism within the Sex Pistols themselves, the two made plans to leave for London at the beginning of November. If all went well, said McLaren, they could expect to start shooting the picture by the the new year.

"All I was told was that Russ didn't get along with the band," says Kaplan. "I was told that the band had looked at the dailies of the first stuff he'd shot of some deer-slaughtering at the Queen's Game Reserve and that they thought it was 'fuckin' disgustin'.' But the only real communication I had with Malcolm was one phone call where he asked me to set up a screening of *White Line Fever,* which was a little strange since they had already seen *Truck Turner.* I later figured out that although I had assumed I had the job, it turned out he was still auditioning me, which must be the oldest trick in the book."

On the 5th of November, Kaplan and Opatoshu flew to London and were immediately treated to what Opatoshu calls "four or five days of being intensely Malcolmized. From first thing in the morning to the wee hours of the night, going to two clubs a night and being gobbed at by the audience, Malcolm would tell us the history of the Sex Pistols and the punk movement. The way he told it was as an important political/social phenomenon and he would deliver it with that very superficial, winning, pixieesque quality of his. It was all funny, great stories about how John couldn't sing a note and how wonderful that was, and how he made Sid into a big fad even though he couldn't play a note, and he would underline all these stories with this attitude that it was a great hoax on society and

160

on conventional musical norms, a great putdown on the Eric Claptons of the world who take pride in learning their instruments.

"But as we began learning more and more about it, I realized that his favorite stories always seemed to be about how coincidental it had all been, and it began to dawn on me that all this meant was that nobody else had really contributed to this whole thing, nobody else had anything going for them, that it was all coincidence and that therefore it was all, and I mean absolutely *all*, Malcolm."

However, as soon as McLaren finished telling Opatoshu how central he had been to the development of punk, he then asserted that he really didn't want the movie to be about him or to be a potted documentary of the Sex Pistols: P. T. Proby was to be banished from this set. Not only was this story not to be about him, but from the very beginning McLaren promised Kaplan and Opatoshu total creative control over the picture. They were not to worry about him or new producer Jeremy Thomas or any of the financiers, but to create a loosely based *narrative* film, carrying on from the real story of the Sex Pistols.

"I was always saying to Malcolm, 'Are you sure Fox doesn't have to approve this? Are you sure Jeremy Thomas or Michael White don't have to see this?' And it was always 'No, no, no,'" says Kaplan. "It was always, 'If the band is happy, we're happy,' and to be honest, that's why I thought I could do a good job of it before I even went over. I thought I was being brought there because they thought I could relate to the band. But I also figured I would be able to relate to Malcolm because Rene told me I could, so making this movie would just be a question of getting the band on our side."

While Kaplan went to Bray Studios to check out the sets Meyer already had built—a country & western–type bar assembled as the set of the Nashville pub; a nineteenth-century London street scene originally constructed for *Oliver* but now gloriously mossy after ten years of storage; a dilapidated red double-decker bus with a barely functioning engine—Opatoshu set about writing a treatment.

"Our major concern," he says, "was coming up with something that would be feasible to shoot, that would permit us to showcase the group's dramatic power, satiric humor, and strength of personality while remaining cognizant of their limits of professional discipline. In other words, our biggest question was trying to figure out how to deal with these guys who weren't actors but rock 'n' roll musicians. At no time did we ever imagine that we'd be able to actually write dialogue that these guys would sit, memorize, and then do six takes of. They just wouldn't be interested. It went against the grain of everything they were doing and it would be a total distortion and bastardization of these people to have them recite lines written by two old American hippies.

"So we decided we would get other actors to play the scripted parts and then set up situations with the boys to do it as an improv. We'd say something like, 'Here you're faced with this rich son-of-a-bitch and he's gonna know his lines, but you won't.' And then we'd shoot it four times and do coverage based on that. It would have been loose, but that would have been all right because if the film was going to develop a harder edge, we wanted it to come from the group itself and not some bullshit scripted revolutionary romanticism dreamt up by either us, the money men, or Malcolm. If it ended up being truly inflammatory—great. If not, it would still be satiric, have some music and action, and wouldn't impose too much on whatever the group and the 'movement' actually were."

Although the eleven-page bare-bones treatment Opatoshu and Kaplan handed in on November 22 was nothing like what McLaren had expected, in many ways it remained true to the story McLaren, Daalder, Meyer, and Ebert had already written: once again, a tale of the Sex Pistols' triumph over the record industry's efforts to co-opt and control their wild anarchism.

"We saw this co-optation thing in the cards from the very beginning," says Opatoshu. "We saw it happening because we saw that *we* were already in bed with the people who would co-opt it—we would go from the Sex Pistols world to these elegant wine-laden lunches with Michael White's associate John Goldstone—and it seemed just like the early seventies in the States to me. As soon as you sit over meals of fine wine with the movie establishment that's the end of it. It becomes *Hullabaloo* instead of Woodstock."

This time the untitled picture was to begin with a commercial for Swinging England that would dissolve into shots of the Sex Pistols hanging out in "Dead End," a dismal London district of broken-down buildings and raggedly dressed children, incongruously visited by a red double-decker bus full of tourists. Instead of Proby, Opatoshu created Rod Bollocks, a "hippie pop superstar" returning home from tax exile only to find his home being squatted by Sid and burgled by Jones and Cook. When Rod protests to "Derek," chief executive of his record company, Derek resolves to sign rather than chastise the Sex Pistols, but the band tell him to fuck off: They'd rather make their money their own way.

Of course, against all odds, the Sex Pistols become more successful than anyone had ever imagined, and the ruling oligarchs of Britain decide, in the words of the treatment, "that if they can't stamp it out, they can damn well take it over, and thus declaw it." Rotten is kidnapped by Derek and his evil advisers, intent on splitting the band into pieces to multiply its commercial value. "The punk movement has become too big to be left to punks. Trained Experts are now taking control," writes Opatoshu, and in the penultimate scene of the treatment, the kidnapped Rotten hurls himself through Derek's window in a desperate attempt to escape the claws of co-optation. As Rotten falls, "we see a montage of images of what awaits the Pistols and the whole punk movement in Derek's hands": American TV pitchmen selling Pistols Punk Kits; forty-year-old punk character actors singing "Anarchy" in a suburban Holiday Inn; a typical British family still out of work but with mum and dad now dressed in bondage pants, safety pins, and spiked hair; and finally the Sex Pistols themselves, the new rock royalty, even being knighted by Her Majesty The Queen.

Needless to say, Rotten does not fall to his death but is instead shown suspended from a Union Jack hanging outside Derek's office. When he finally plummets to the ground, surreally landing smack in the middle of Dead End, the other Sex Pistols tell Rotten that that was *no dream,* for that night Her Majesty's government is due to unveil a statue honoring the Sex Pistols in the newly dedicated Pistol Park.

At this, the Sex Pistols commandeer the tourists' double-decker bus, and as the end credits roll and "Anarchy in the U.K." blares from the soundtrack, in a scene reminscent of the end of Lindsay Anderson's *If . . .* , the film closes with the Sex Pistols spraying submachine-gun fire, grenades, and explosives into the midst of the Pistol Park ceremony.

Somewhat predictably, this was a treatment that all concerned parties—McLaren, the Sex Pistols, and producer Jeremy Thomas—could agree on, but when Kaplan and Opatoshu met with McLaren to start planning the production, there suddenly occurred a series of omens that Kaplan quickly recognized did not bode well for the project.

"I don't remember exactly how it happened," he says, "but being from the movie business and having been involved in numerous deals that fell apart, I was prepared to just let things work themselves out because I know usually that I'll be able to convince ninety percent of the people who read a screenplay by executing the movie.

"But one night we had drinks with Malcolm and Viv at a pub and an alarm went off in my head when Viv said, 'How is this treatment different from the Beatles' *Magical Mystery Tour?*' And I thought, 'Ohhhh: we were writing it for *her!*' The minute I heard that I thought, 'Here we go . . .' I had figured we were gonna be able to get by without having to go through the kind of little-old-English-school-teacher treatment you're always subjected to. But from that point on, I figured it just wasn't going to happen."

With his suspicions crowding out his excitement for the picture, Kaplan began to feel that he too was now in need of some paper promises to back up what had been until recently a fairly trusting, verbal relationship.

"Before we had even written the treatment we pitched it to everyone in separate meetings because they couldn't be gotten together in one room," says Opatoshu, "and everyone, including Malcolm, said they loved it. But then, since we already had doubts, we went to Malcolm and told him that we had to get something on paper. To sit down and write a treatment 'on spec' when we'd already put in two weeks of research just went against the grain for both me and Jonathan. We finally had to say, Look, for a treatment, that's X amount of dollars—I think it was in the $10,000 range—and that it would be a pay-or-play deal. Malcolm said, 'Absolutely no problem, boys, it's just paperwork and you'll get paid immediately,' but two weeks later, long after we'd handed the treatment in and everyone still said they liked it, we still hadn't seen any of the paperwork, and of course, we never got a dime."

Not a dime, not even a word, for now a curtain of silence fell between McLaren and his new writer and director. For a very long week, during which Kaplan continued working on the preproduction details of the movie, no one called, until finally, a meeting was set at the Glitterbest office.

"Whatever the problem was, it was clear to me now that I wasn't going to be able to solve it," snaps Kaplan. *"No one* from the outside was gonna be able to solve it. And when Malcolm finally met with us, Danny was incredibly articulate about why we made each decision based on what we observed of the band. Even Malcolm couldn't refute it: It was too logical. So then he said, 'Well, maybe a narrative film is the wrong thing to do. Maybe what we should do is go up to Northumberland and shoot a live concert film, a punk Woodstock—call the cops and let them know about it ahead of time so there would be this amazing riot'—of course, with us there to shoot it. And at that point, I knew I just had to leave, because I did not want to be part of a bloodbath. I flew back to Los Angeles and left Danny to deal with the last details: We had decided to tell Malcolm to give Julien Temple a try."

"It's one thing to hear and respect the anarchist-Trotskyite spiel Malcolm gives you," says Danny Opatoshu, "we thought he was interesting and we respected him. But the longer we were there, I began to see there was a different sort of philosophy behind all this and that was the politics of flim-flam, a politics that licenses you to lie and cheat and steal and double-deal and then celebrate it as a great revolutionary act. Unfortunately, it tends ultimately to be self-promotion and not particularly revolutionary." Opatoshu laughs. "Even at the very beginning, I found it questionable that a real political revolution could be born in a fashion boutique, but I guess I put it out of my mind. But it still seems a little ass-backwards to me, even today."

One might have thought that McLaren would have been discouraged by his inability to work things out with Meyer, Kaplan, et al., that he might eventually have concluded that there was some fundamental antipathy between rock 'n' roll rebellion and Hollywood-style filmmaking, but the opposite seems to have been true. With a number-one gold album in the charts and rave reviews but no way of tapping into the vast markets outside Europe—no American record deal, for example—the movie that had started off as an errant fantasy had become an important stategic lever for reaching beyond Britain. To McLaren, it was just a matter of finding the right director, someone who could conjure up and direct a script as bold and anarchic as the Sex Pistols themselves. One way or another, with or without Hollywood's help—for a while McLaren considered using British soft-core porn director Peter Walker—these Sex Pistols were going to be celluloid stars.

In fact, working with these Yank directors really hadn't been so bad after all. For one thing, the very idea of being in the movies had appealed to the Sex Pistols' individual vanities in such a way that the whole experience momentarily took the heat off McLaren and put it back on the Sex Pistols—particularly Sid, who seemed to stumble daily into new trouble. Even if all McLaren's dealings with the band were now colored by a mutual disgust—"You could say we hate each other's guts," he told *The Times*'s Anthony Holden—even if the band members themselves weren't on speaking terms, this was a vast improvement on the days when McLaren had been held responsible for the minuscule details of each Sex Pistol's daily existence.

But the moviemaking experience with Meyer and Kaplan had also profited the Sex Pistols another way, bringing the group closer than ever to a deal with Warner Bros. Records in America. No matter how much they may have denied it—the Clash song "I'm So Bored (with the USA)" and the Sex Pistols' own "New York" provide ample testimony to British punk's rabid anti-Americanism—McLaren knew there was no substitute for America's critical and financial legitimation. Ever since late May when

165

he had finally closed the Sex Pistols' deal with Virgin Records, he had been talking with Rob Dickins, the managing director of Warner Bros. Music Ltd, the publishing division of that giant entertainment conglomerate's British subsidiary, in the hope of convincing Warner's American record company that the Sex Pistols were now about to do to the American music industry what they had already done to its British counterpart.

Ironically, Dickins had already been warned about McLaren by Glen Matlock whose Rich Kids Dickins had signed to a publishing deal with Warner Bros. Music. Considering that Matlock had written nearly half the Sex Pistols' original material, Warner Bros. felt it had something of a vested interest in signing a similar deal with the Sex Pistols, regardless of Warner Bros. *Records'* lack of interest in being the group's record company. "Virgin made Malcolm a record deal," says Dickins, "but he didn't want to put all his eggs in the Virgin basket. He said, 'To be honest, no one else will take the Sex Pistols' publishing but we need £100,000 to make a movie. We can't bargain, so are you in or out?'

"We said Glen Matlock wrote one half of these songs, so he should get one half of the publishing, but Malcolm wouldn't accept that. The argument was going on and on and on but we finally agreed that if Matlock wrote one quarter of everything, we wouldn't pick or choose, but take the whole one quarter for him. And so we tried to make a deal for the worldwide publishing rights for £100,000 at a time when the average publishing deal was anywhere between £10 and 20,000."

Dickins may not have been aware of it, but McLaren was simultaneously negotiating a publishing deal with Arista Music. Arista was so sure the Sex Pistols' songs would do well in movies, they too wanted the group's worldwide catalogue. Ultimately, McLaren spread his risk over both companies, signing the world rights (except the U.S.) to Warner, and the North American rights to Arista for another $100,000.

While the Warner Bros. Music deal didn't help McLaren much with the parent company, it was at least a toe in the door to a U.S. record deal at a time when the American press was starting to portray punks as the real-life counterparts of *A Clockwork Orange.* Fortunately, McLaren already had someone working for him in Los Angeles who was already a Sex Pistols partisan. Rory Johnston, a former art student whom McLaren had met late in 1976 when Johnston was working at the Portobello Hotel, a favorite late-nite Sex Pistols drinking spot, had moved to Los Angeles to live with his American girlfriend the year before, and McLaren soon began using Johnston as his chief L.A. functionary, often telling people that he was in charge of Glitterbest's Hollywood branch. It was Johnston who had made the first contacts with Meyer and Kaplan, and after the Sex Pistols left A&M Records in March 1977, it was Johnston whom McLaren called to start the process of wheeling and dealing with the American record companies.

"Malcolm was depressed because he was desperate to get 'God Save the Queen' out," remembers Johnston, now director of composer Philip Glass's production company. "We were looking over our shoulders at the other punk bands who were getting deals, and thinking that it was crazy that we had started it but didn't have a record company yet. So he asked me to call some companies and I suggested Warner Bros., Epic Records, MCA, and Neil Bogart's Casablanca Records.

"It was very strange for me," says Johnston, "because I had been dealing with publicists and all these low-level record company people and then, very suddenly, I was taking meetings with Mo Ostin, Bob Regehr, and all the top Warners staff. Regehr, who was director of artist development, was over the top about the Sex Pistols. I remember on one of our first meetings, I showed them this video we had compiled, played them the demos, and on my way out, Mo Ostin, the head of the company, said to me, 'Hey, if I sign this band, do I have to wear all their gear?' There was suddenly a great deal of enthusiasm."

As the summer came to an end, a fierce bidding war for the Sex Pistols' American record contract was waged between the giant Warner Bros. and the powerful Casablanca, a specialist in disco bands and teen acts such as Kiss. Every once in a while, McLaren would fly into L.A. to meet with Bogart or Ostin—on one occasion, he threatened to dump a table full of legal documents onto Ostin's lap if Warner Bros. didn't heed his word about the Sex Pistols' plans to strike deep into the heart of the entertainment industry—but for the most part, negotiations were left to Johnston, who had now become particularly adept at translating the Sex Pistols' anarchic stance into a palatable sales rap with one foot still in the danger zone.

McLaren may have been crude in his negotiating tactics—"sometimes he would have me tell Mo Ostin that he was on the toilet and keep him hanging on the phone for twenty minutes," remembers Rene Daalder, who was again McLaren's Hollywood host—but in early October, he finally closed the deal with Warner Bros. Breaking the Sex Pistols deal into two parts—one for recordings and a second for a movie—McLaren proved yet again that even if he was incompetent at the most ordinary tasks of music management, he could still be formidable at the bargaining table, and he bumped the Sex Pistols price up to nearly $750,000.

With the Warner Bros. deal completed, McLaren decided the time was right to get the band back on the road to support their album, the most conventional promotional strategy in the rock 'n' roll business. A three-month-long Sex Pistols Tour of the World was planned to commence in early December, with a quick jaunt to Holland and the British provinces (winding up just before Christmas at a home for one-parent children in Huddersfield) and then going to America; if all went well there, they would soldier onto Finland and Eastern Europe. Capitalizing on McLaren's own idea of limiting the Sex Pistols' public appearances, Bob Regehr, who was renowned as a master of spectacular record company hype—Regehr died in 1984—wanted the group to play one killer gig at the twenty-thousand-seat Madison Square Garden with tickets held to a punk-priced dollar a head, but McLaren had a far odder idea.

Ever since he had toured through Florida with the New York Dolls, he had fantasized about taking the Sex Pistols on a similar tour through the American South, avoiding the big cities where he was sure the few Sex Pistols fans would twist his tour into an exercise in punk chic, and now he was determined to have his holiday in the sun. While Warner did not agree that this was the best way to break the group in America, McLaren was unbending in his determination not to let the Sex Pistols play the major music-biz markets (N.Y. and L.A.), although he eventually agreed to let the band open the tour with a string of dates in Pittsburgh, Cleveland, and Chicago, and finish it off at Bill Graham's Winterland Ballroom in San Francisco. Apart from that, however, he insisted that the Sex Pistols play only small redneck ballrooms in Georgia, Louisiana, Texas, and Oklahoma. (At first, he wanted the band to play only Texas, because he reckoned that the Sex Pistols would get into bigger fights with macho cowboys.) In the end, there was little Warner Bros. could do to prevent a group's manager from embarking on such a suicidal strategy. Given the Sex Pistols' track record for causing trouble for record companies, it was finally decided it would be less painful to let McLaren call the shots before the tour began and then to squeeze out as many compromises as possible once the Sex Pistols had actually arrived in America.

"We had a choice," McLaren told one interviewer a few years later. "Madison Square Garden, one show, dollar a ticket, coming in by helicopter, or we could do what we wanted to do. And I realized that it may be better to play the Southern states, do the places where no one goes and continue the story of this group, because to play Madison Square Garden at that time tended to sum it up and make you end up doing all the things you had said you hated. It would be like being Led Zeppelin instead of the Sex Pistols. I wanted to continue the adventure, and if you couldn't continue the adventure at Madison Square Garden, well then let's get lost in the swamps."

With the plans finally set for the two-week American tour to begin in late December following the trek through Holland and England, McLaren tried to get the Sex Pistols back into the rehearsal studio to sharpen their renditions of the *Bollocks* album, but now there were two new problems preventing the band from moving smoothly onto the road: Sid and Nancy.

Having slowly pillaged Rotten's antichrist antics for his own, Sid had eventually taken to ever more threatening and violent acts of self-destruction: slashing his chest with broken bottles, appearing for interviews doped to the gills, flinging himself into episodes of gratuitous streetfighting—whatever he thought might elevate him to the status of a Rock Dream. To Rotten's horror, McLaren seemed to be encouraging Sid's self-destructiveness, and many remember hearing McLaren praise the latter in wry, Fagin-like tones—"Good, Sid, that's what being a Sex Pistol's all about! That's how you get to be a star!"—but McLaren denied that he was encouraging Sid. As far as McLaren was concerned, it wasn't his problem. If Sid wanted to behave like a lunatic, that was his choice. McLaren was reportedly so sure that Sid was hellbent on wrecking himself in a blaze of rock 'n' roll glory that upon Sid's acquisition of a flat with a seven-year lease, he jokingly remarked to Sophie Richmond that she shouldn't worry that the lease was too short because he was certain Sid would expire long before the lease.

"Sid was a guy who never saw any sense of danger, a real street kid who never saw a red light," McLaren later told interviewer David Thomas. "He was always the ultimate believer in the Sex Pistols' ideas and attitudes, long after some of them had already got kind of bewildered, long after Rotten had become a bit of a joke, very serious, very career-orientated. Meanwhile, Sid was carrying on with this halo of anarchy around him and would constantly say how awful John had become. Sid saw it from both sides: Once he was a fan, you see, the number-one fan at the 100 Club, but later the entire audience would sort of swerve to the left-hand side of the stage because Sid would be standing there. And everybody would be looking at Sid and Rotten knew it and got fearfully jealous."

Before the Tour of the World could begin, life with Sid and Nancy went from bad to worse. On the last day of November, Sid had turned up at rehearsal only to find that he was once again the only member of the band who had bothered coming. Furious with his comrades in chaos, according to *NME*'s Nick Kent, Vicious spent the rest of the evening getting "morosely, hideously drunk before returning to his room at Bayswater's Ambassador Hotel" whereupon he phoned a hail of abuse at Steve Jones and then attempted to throw himself out the hotel's third-story window. (One version of this tale has it that Nancy saved Sid's life by getting a last-minute grasp on his belt buckle.) Just before retiring for the night at 5:00 A.M., Sid finally took his fury out on Nancy, relentlessly throwing her against a wall until she was bloodied and nearly unconscious. Two hours later, the police at last arrived to investigate the disturbance, and upon a search of Sid's room, arrested Nancy Spungen for possession of an illegal substance—in fact, medication she had been prescribed after a recent operation for a pilonidal opening at the base of her spine. Charges were later dropped and Glitterbest gladly paid a £35 fine left over from Nancy's arrest the previous summer for carrying a truncheon in her handbag, but after the newspapers exaggerated the incident to Sex Pistol–sized proportions, according to Kent, McLaren "hit the roof, and Sid's version of events is that Messrs. Jones, Cook, and Rotten declared in adamant unity that Vicious was to be ousted immediately."

However, as soon as McLaren kicked Vicious out of the band, he remembered why Sid was there in the first place and made a deal with him to "rejoin" the Sex Pistols under the condition that he stay away from "Nauseating Nancy" and clean himself up. "Malcolm did come to my defense all of a sudden," Kent quotes Vicious as saying. "He just realized that my side of things had a point. That what I was doing was just living out the original idea of the band as four complete nutters going out and doing anything and everything. Just having fun, which I always reckoned was the whole thing about the Pistols from the very beginning."

While it appeared to Sid that McLaren had brought him back from the dead, it had become increasingly clear to McLaren that if Sid could be sequestered from the "source" of his problems, there was still a chance he could be kept alive long enough to complete the tour. (Sid: "Them using Nancy as a scapegoat for my problems—Ha! I've been doing every-fuckin'-thing they reckon she turned me onto two years before I met 'er.") It seemed the only thing to do was to devise a plan to get rid of Nancy Spungen.

Within days of Nancy's arrest, McLaren arranged for Rodent, Sophie, and Boogie to abduct the girl and put her on a plane to America in order to prevent from her going on tour with the band to drug-filled Amsterdam, where McLaren feared that Sid would take an overdose. (Typically, McLaren realized the folly of booking the Sex Pistols to the drug capital of Europe only *after* the tour had been fixed.) McLaren bought Nancy an air ticket and gave Sophie orders to offer Nancy a ride to meet Sid (who was then at his dentist's) and instead take her to Heathrow, but midway through the abduction Nancy broke free when Sophie stopped her Mini at a red light, and she tore away from the car and ran into the Holiday Inn near Marble Arch. Oddly, two of her captors were clad in the same turquoise Westwood-designed mac as she, and as Rodent recalls, "it must have been really weird seeing these punks, two of us wearing these turquoise macs, chasing after this other girl who was also wearing the same coat, screaming about being kidnapped in the lobby of the Holiday Inn."

Having cleaved the Sex Pistols into factions in order to maintain his own control, McLaren found that he had for once succeeded beyond his own expectations. For just as the band was finally attaining the very peak of its success, piling up the gold records and winning poll after poll in the music press—even appearing on the cover of the New Year's issue of *The Investors Review* as "Young Businessmen of the Year"—their hatred for one another was coming together in a frightening combustion of anarchy and self-destruction. Rotten hated Jones and Cook for their yobbish ways; Jones and Cook hated Rotten for his superstar tendencies, especially his newfound habit of living in posh houses à la Jimmy Page or traveling in massive entourages. Sid too hated Rotten now: "One time, I took him aside and said, 'Listen matey, just take a look at yourself in the mirror! You look awful! And worse than that, you've become a hypocrite. You're acting just like all those pop stars you started off putting down, mate! Just take a good look!'" And of course, Rotten now became increasingly suspicious of his old friend's jealous behavior, his constant leaks to the press about his "brilliance" as a songwriter (he had written one tune just before America, "Belsen Was a Gas"), his uncontrolled addiction to Nancy and to heroin, and his self-appointed position as a paragon of the Sex Pistols' pandemonium.

As the principal antagonist of this cabal of aggression, McLaren was only too happy to see his boys reaching ever higher peaks of public recriminations. "I really like the idea that the band really hate each other," he told Michael Watts, adding sarcastically, "There's a certain compatibility with me and Rotten 'cause we're both extremists—we bounce off each other."

If McLaren had his way, America would prove to be the inevitable consummation of his wily regime of divide and conquer, for according to both Julien Temple and Vivienne Westwood, before the Sex Pistols even left for America, McLaren was already plotting to radically revamp the group by getting rid of one of the Sex Pistols. Not Sid Vicious—for by now,

McLaren was long convinced that Sid's audacious steal of the spotlight was what was keeping the band in the public eye—but Johnny Rotten, the self-appointed conscience of the group, the self-proclaimed punk rock "revolutionary."

"Malcolm just thought that John was no good anymore," Westwood whispers as if McLaren was still standing right behind her. "After John got beat up he got so frightened he couldn't really perform anymore, and I remember Malcolm phoning me up about kicking Rotten out of the band before they went to America. Malcolm knew that would be hot stuff, illegal or what-have-you, but he thought John some kind of a sissy."

With the Sex Pistols' Tour of the World about to begin, it seems Malcolm McLaren had finally found his ultimate Sex Pistol in the persona of none other than Sid Vicious. Now *there* was a real star.

7
THE GREAT
ROCK 'N' ROLL SWINDLE

Even before the Sex Pistols left for America, there were abundant omens that the American tour was going to be the same kind of unmitigated disaster Malcolm McLaren had left in his wake so many times before. Julien Temple remembers that "there were a lot of people warning Malcolm that he was blowing it, that if he didn't get closer to Rotten and have meetings with Rotten, the group might well break up before the tour." Rodent remembers a meeting with his friends just before the group left for America where "everyone was taking bets whether the band would split up before or after the new McDonald's opposite the Glitterbest office on Shaftesbury Avenue was finished. Malcolm was there," he adds wistfully, "but he wasn't putting any money down because he was too worried about the outcome."

To those closest to the band, it seemed the end was truly at hand, and when the United States Embassy refused to issue visas to the Sex Pistols because the band supposedly forgot to list their previous arrest records on their applications, it took a full week of finagling before Warner Bros. could convince the U.S. State Department to allow the band into the country. That was just enough time for McLaren to milk the tabloids with the accusation that he would have sent the group to Russia if Warner Bros. hadn't come up with $50,000 in bribes he claimed it had paid to the Carter administration through the "clean side of the Mafia"—an allegation Warner considers ridiculous. On January 3, 1978, the Sex Pistols left for New York, leaving McLaren behind to continue working on the film and the remainder of the tour bookings to Finland following the U.S. tour, already threatened because of the recent revelations of the band's arrest records.

For its part, Warner was perfectly happy McLaren had stayed in London for the commencement of the tour. They were unconvinced by McLaren's claim that the Americans had been overly strict with the Sex Pistols' visas and they were angry that McLaren's careless and abusive way of dealing with the problem had resulted in the Sex Pistols missing a sterling publicity opportunity to perform on NBC's *Saturday Night Live*, then in its first flush. (Ironically, the Sex Pistols were replaced by Elvis Costello, whose drummer wore a T-shirt on the air that said "Thanx Malc.")

From the moment the Sex Pistols disembarked in New York on January 4, it was made conspicuously clear to the boys that Warner would be taking charge of their destiny from now on. Herded directly from plane to plane—the first gig was scheduled for January 5 at Atlanta's 525-seat Great Southeast Music Hall—the group sheepishly faced a barrage of flashbulbs as they were hustled onto their connecting flight by road manager Noel Monk and two burly Vietnam vets Warner had hired to be the band's minders. As soon as they arrived in Atlanta, the Sex Pistols were read the riot act—one untrue story goes that Sid was to be handcuffed to one of the minders whenever he wasn't onstage—and the grueling tour of seven cities in fifteen days began at last.

The plan was to go from Atlanta to Memphis (the Taliesyn Ballroom), and then to San Antonio (Randy's Rodeo), Baton Rouge (Kingfish Club), Dallas (Longhorn Ballroom), Tulsa (Cain's Ballroom), and then finally to San Francisco—almost all small-to-midrange halls (the largest being San Francisco's Winterland with a capacity of 5,500) in keeping with McLaren's freshly revitalized assertions that the Sex Pistols weren't about to start "following the established pattern of success" now that they had finally made it to America. "We want to decentralize it, much the same as we did in Britain," McLaren explained to *Melody Maker*'s Michael Watts, soon to be his constant chronicler in America. "There are too many bands playing in New York and L.A. and saying they have cracked it and they have not. New York and L.A. are not America." Typically, Rotten had his own gloss on this, declaring, "We want to play for the poor people of America," but a sampling of 122 respondents taken by a team of sociologists after the Atlanta show indicated that three-quarters of the Sex Pistols' audience were males with a mean and modal age of twenty-four, half working full-time, a quarter students, and a third with a family income of over twenty-five thousand dollars a year. So much for the poor of America.

Meanwhile in Atlanta, the tour was beginning with uncharacteristic restraint. Warned by Warner that the Atlanta gig would be taking place under the watchful eyes of vice squad detectives from Memphis, Baton

Rouge, and San Antonio, Rotten abstained from his usual provocations and instead concentrated on making music, showing off his famous snot-filled hankie as a consolation prize to the eighty or so journalists who had been primed to expect the worst. "You can all stop staring now," the spotty-faced singer said after opening the band's set with "God Save the Queen." "We're ugly and we know it."

The minute McLaren arrived in Atlanta—moments *after* the gig was over—all pretense of good manners disappeared and the simmering animosities that had almost wrecked the group in London once again boiled to the surface. Having worked for years to reach this very point with the Sex Pistols, McLaren was by no means prepared to repeat the Southern scenario he had played out three years earlier with the New York Dolls or to capitulate to Warner's grab for power. Now that the Pistols had finally reached America, however, he was suddenly finding himself caught between the band and its record company—ironically, almost exactly the same predicament that had ruined Marty Thau's relationship with the Dolls before McLaren appeared on the scene. "You know," he told Michael Watts in a great revelation, "I think I have to have a hard job, because I stand in between the record company and the group. Both parties have the same idea of becoming a success—a great rock 'n' roll band—and suddenly the record company people are saying to you, 'You're a great guitarist,' and suddenly you think how good you are. I don't want that."

McLaren couldn't help but feel let down that in the short time they had been separated from him, each of the Sex Pistols had already succumbed to the very worst aspects of the American cornucopia, and the events leading up to the Memphis gig (scheduled for the night of Elvis Presley's forty-third birthday) only brought home how totally he had lost control of the group. Jones and Cook went off in search of "birds and booze"—"six girls and a fifth of Jack Daniel's a day, if I could," recalls Jones; Rotten formed a close relationship with Bob Regehr, surrendering to the star treatment Warner laid on at every hotel and venue; and Sid, proudly wearing his "I'm A Mess" badge, went off in search of a fix, somehow eluding his minders and nearly missing the plane that was to take the group to Memphis. (Later that afternoon, he was discovered at a local hospital with a nasty, self-inflicted knife wound in his arm.) To make matters worse, the Memphis fire marshals ruled that in the interests of public safety, the Taliesyn Ballroom would have to replace the seats that had been removed at McLaren's request to make way for pogoing, thus reducing the hall's capacity to seven hundred. The only problem with this was that *nine hundred* tickets had been sold, and by the time the gig began—two hours late due to Sid, who had once again slipped out to score some drugs—a small riot of angry ticketholders charged the glass doors of the ballroom to get their money back.

With reporters from nearly every major news organization in the world clamoring for violence or at the very least their own personalized rendition of the Grundy incident—the Sex Pistols often refused to talk to the press unless they were each personally paid by the reporters themselves for each interview—the vortex of rock 'n' roll paranoia surrounding the group finally began to engulf the American adventure. Nasty rumors abounded: Supposedly members of the FBI, CIA, and British intelligence were on hand to watch the unfolding of this fiasco ("with all their crewcuts and leather jackets and amphetamines, they were afraid the punks would be 180° the opposite of what the hippies had been," one bodyguard says); and Tom Forcade, the psychotically paranoid owner of *High Times* magazine, tried to muscle in on Sid for an "exclusive interview," but was stymied by the group's bodyguards with their ominous, ever-present briefcases. (Forcade was financing a documentary about the Sex Pistols, and shortly after the American tour, he killed himself with a twelve-gauge shotgun.) In any event, the group was advised by their Memphisian friends to leave town immediately after the gig on their new bus, a plush, overstuffed coach formerly owned by motorcycle daredevil Evel Knievel.

By the time they arrived in San Antonio, the bizarre cycle of fear and curiosity the Sex Pistols had created reached fever pitch. Egged on by taunts from both Vicious and Rotten about "cowboy faggots"—"I see we got a lot of real men out there tonight. You're very fuckin' tough out there in the dark, ain't you?" screamed the hunchbacked Rotten—one heckler finally met the backside of Sid's bass when he allegedly brandished a knife, and as Sid broke into demented laughter, his face and body smeared with blood and the words GIMME A FIX scrawled in bright blue magic marker across his chest like a billboard, Rotten caustically cackled, "Oh, dear, Sidney's bass seems to have fallen off," and a barrage of cream pies, broken bottles, and torn aluminum cans hit the stage. (After the show, Vicious's assailant admitted he had come to the show just to confront the Sex Pistols, whom he called a "bunch of sewer rats with guitars.") Backstage, there was grumbling that Sid had totally lost thread of the music, that he was an egomaniac, and that the rest of the band was ready to throw him off the tour if he didn't straighten up, but this time at least, Sid got off easy, whining that he knew he was "a right cunt, but I just want to talk with the people." The Sex Pistols may have captured the next day's headlines— "SEX PISTOLS WIN S.A. 'SHOOTOUT'," blared the local San Antonio paper—

but Rotten was becoming increasingly upset that he was being upstaged by Sid's brazen antics, and the feeling that the tour had gone bottom up grew daily.

Through snow and rain, the graffiti-laden tour bus (SEX PISTOLS, England, spray-painted across its front like a giant punk license plate) crept through the American interior. Baton Rouge, Dallas, Tulsa: Cook and Jones caught colds and Rotten picked up a bad case of flu—McLaren was becoming more and more paranoid that FBI agents were shadowing the band—but still Sid carried on, begging for another pit stop so he could score drugs, phone Nancy, or meet a cowboy. (Sid always wanted to meet cowboys; John insisted on visiting America's ghettos to see how real Yanks lived.) By the time they reached Tulsa, McLaren, Jones, and Cook decided they had had enough, and immediately after the Tulsa gig the three flew off to San Francisco, leaving Rotten and Vicious behind in the bus.

"There were lots of fights and Sid was crazy, very doped up," McLaren said later, "and they went through the Nevada desert, and since it's the desert, everyone thought Sid could go off, right? So they get into this hotel restaurant and they're eating. Sid always liked these big knicker-bocker ice creams, three of 'em and a steak—he always had an appetite—and he sits down next to two big bear guys with their big bear hats—heavy-duty long-distance truckers. Sid sits in the corner and gets his steak dished up and this guy is apparently saying things about him that are not particularly complimentary. So Sid decides to get up and he walks over to them and flicks open his little pocket knife and gashes the underside of his arm, and he let the blood *pour* over this guy's steak. Apparently they lifted Sid with one hand and threw him about twenty-five yards. He hit himself against the side of the bus and later they found him, dumped inside there.

"You see," McLaren told his interviewer, "it was crazy in places like San Antonio and Tulsa and Memphis, but at the same time you never really know. When you're involved, when you're actually in it yourself, you don't realize it's crazy. But when you look back in retrospect, you realize, My God man, *we were heavy.*"

However, according to Sid's bodyguard, Dwayne Warner, "Malcolm wasn't there, it wasn't in Nevada, and actually it was Sid who picked up *their* knife off *their* table. We didn't let Sid have a knife. I walked Sid out to the bus where we fixed Sid's arm up, and that was that. No one *ever* put a hand on Sid while I was there."

With McLaren growing increasingly despondent that the band was playing right into Warner Bros.' hands by performing at Bill Graham's five-thousand-seat Winterland Ballroom, the Sex Pistols finally gathered in San Francisco the day before their last American gig on January 14. Tempers had cooled somewhat after their short respite from one another—Rotten and Vicious had convinced Noel Monk to let them make a stop in L.A. where they jumped onto the stage of the Whiskey for a song or two—but no one was really in the mood to play another gig, least of all Rotten, who was still suffering from a bad flu. To make matters worse, due to complications in the booking arrangements at San Francisco's Miyako Hotel, Rotten and Vicious were put in another, far grubbier, hotel on the far side of town, and although this was not intended as such, Rotten took it as a snub.

With separate hotels and road managers—even separate interviews on local radio stations—the Sex Pistols had now effectively broken into two camps. As far as Rotten was concerned, McLaren's hypocritical encouragement of Sid's starry-eyed grab for fame was the real root of the group's problems. Ever since McLaren arrived in Atlanta, each gig had become more and more of a shambles as Sid tried to live up to the image McLaren had set out for him, frequently stopping in midsong to gob at the audience or throw back the trash that rained on the band while the other Sex Pistols played on. Ted Cohen, Warner's national director of special projects and Bob Regehr's right-hand man, remembers that "whenever Sid tried to explain why he did these stupid things he would say something like, 'Well, that's what Malcolm expects me to do' or 'Malcolm told me to do this if I want to be big.' There was nothing spontaneous or self-motivated about any of it. He was operating on what he was *told* to be."

While the other Sex Pistols were furious with Sid for trying to be what he clearly was not, McLaren blamed Rotten's increasingly cozy relationship with Warner Bros. for the situation, and in the few days he spent alone with Jones and Cook, he worked hard to convince them that Rotten's ego was the force that was destroying the band.

"When we reached San Francisco," said McLaren, "the band not only hated each other, they had also lost faith in Rotten, because Rotten had been so terribly flattered. Warner's considered him their only realistic hope, a normal, possibly poetic type of guy who could make them feel their investment was secure. In fact, in the middle of that tour, I actually had Warner Brothers executives coming up to me and saying, 'We don't want Sid Vicious in this group after this tour. You understand that. We don't want him in this tour and we don't want him in this group.' That was the attitude. And I said to them, 'You might think that Johnny Rotten is the most fabulous guy on earth but I'm going to tell you now, Sid Vicious is the Sex Pistols, and if you don't have him in this group, you're going to sell less records.' They thought, Johnny Rotten is the guy; the group was irrelevant."

But Bob Merlis, Warner's vice president for marketing and promotion, dismisses McLaren's fears that Rotten would be turned into a Warner solo act as sheer ridiculousness. "Regehr was a big, adult man who knew the rules and I can't believe he would knowingly alienate a band from its management," he says. "We would be sued every single day if we did that. In fact, we're scrupulous about *not* doing that because we don't want to invite lawsuits. You can think it, but you can't say it out loud. I know lots of acts where I would wish that their managers would roll over and die but you can't do it, and you're asking for trouble if you do."

The night of January 14, following rousingly antagonistic warm-ups from two local support bands (the Nuns and the Avengers) and a wise-assed intro from veteran rock philosopher Richard Meltzer—himself dragged personally offstage by promoter Bill Graham after a nasty crack about Tony Bennett—the thoroughly soused Sex Pistols prepared to storm the Winterland stage. "Let's really fuck it up tonight," Rotten was heard shrieking in the dressing room before going on. "We'll fuck up these fucking hippies. We'll turn the tables and do something they haven't read about in the music press!"

As soon as a video history of the band's career was shown, the Sex Pistols calmly walked onstage to the loudest ovation they had ever encountered—Winterland was over twice the size of the largest venues they had played thus far—and slowly plugged their instruments into their amps with a jarring squeal: Somehow everything at this gig seemed to take place in the digitalized ponderousness of slow-motion television. To the crowd's delight, Rotten roared "Welcome to London!" as Sid stretched his fingers to the basslines of the Ramones' "Blitzkrieg Bop," and the hotly anticipated set finally began with a steady stream of paper cups, umbrellas, dollar bills, coins, and spittle pelting the stage.

From the first notes of the first song, "Bodies," the Sex Pistols made it clear that this would be no ordinary gig, but a night when anarchy—utter musical disorder—would require the audience to fill in and create the rock 'n' roll they imagined the Sex Pistols to be capable of making. Each song seemed to have its own jerky stop/go momentum: Jones or

Cook would start up, with or without Rotten and/or Vicious, and a crack-ling, careening sound would echo across the vast hall while Sid acted out an entire history of *ancien régime* rock-star poses. The cheering crowd applauded each and every misstep, each half-started song, each time Rotten picked a cup or can off the floor—absolutely *anything* Rotten or Vicious did—and the singer's taunts grew ever more exasperated as the audience fell into the weird symbiosis of sarcasm and sublimated violence Rotten could so cleverly create. "Tell us what it's like to have bad taste," he yelled to applause, and the audience screamed with delight, happy to be part of this mad punk joke.

Three-quarters of the way through their set, the Sex Pistols finally hit their stride, playing four songs straight through, proving they *could* play if they wanted to, and then, a scant fifteen minutes later, it was over, Rotten hunched over the stage, eyes glaring, finger in nostril, and the last chords of their trademark encore, Iggy Pop's "No Fun," splintering into a million shards of distorted echoes, mistimed chords, and off-key rantings in the rainy San Francisco night.

Typically, Rotten had the last word: "AH-HAH-HAH!" he cackled at the audience. "Ever get the feeling you've been cheated?"

What happened during the next twenty-four hours is still bitterly disputed. McLaren claims that while in Baton Rouge, he informed the group that he was making plans through a stringer from the London *Sun* to take the band to Rio de Janeiro to meet the exiled great train robber, Ronnie Biggs, one of his longtime heroes. But Rotten says he was never told about the Brazilian plans until just before the Winterland gig—and Ted Cohen, who was in the Sex Pistols' dressing room before the show, remembers being the one who broke the news.

"I accidentally broke the Pistols up," Cohen says with a laugh. "John had finally gotten kind of bearable during the last day or so, and I was laughing and joking around with him, and I said something like, 'Well, this is great. One more show and then it's on to Brazil,' and he turned around and said, '*What* are you talking about, Brazil?' And one of the other boys, Steve or Paul, said, 'Oh, yeah, while you and Sid were on the bus, we decided we're going to Brazil to do this poetry reading with Ronnie Biggs.' John thought it was a joke at first, but when they said they were really going he got furious. They were screaming at each other: 'Fuck you!' 'Whose band do you think this is anyway?' Stuff like that."

That night, all the omens about the American tour finally came true. As soon as the Sex Pistols were released from their bodyguards—Dwayne Warner was surprised when Noel Monk told him that his duties would end immediately after the Winterland gig—Rotten went off with his own group of friends (most notably, rock photographer Joe Stevens) while Jones, Cook, and McLaren returned to the Miyako Hotel where Warner's elaborate party for the band had already begun. "Fuckin' awful show, wasn't it?" McLaren told one gleeful partygoer. "They were just like any other rock band." (Bob Merlis: "I thought they were incredible, but then you don't go to see the Sex Pistols because of their great guitar playing.")

Some forty-five minutes later, a very drunk Sid Vicious arrived at the party with a crash, walking straight into the Miyako's shiny glass doors. Sid was only scratched—nothing a little more alcohol couldn't cure—but by the time he left, barely standing upright and deliberately disobeying McLaren's orders not to go too far because they would be leaving for Rio early the next morning, many were expecting the worst. Sid did not disappoint. Early that morning, he finally copped the fix he had been thirsting for ever since he got to America, died, and was revived only by the lucky arrival of Boogie and Rory Johnston, who took him to a Marin County acupuncturist recommended by Bill Graham.

With Sid recovering in the hospital, half the group was now either incapable of or unwilling to make the next day's voyage to Brazil. Cook and Jones were fumed with this latest turn of events, and the next afternoon, following a brief visit to Sid's hospital bed, they returned to the Miyako to confront McLaren. For an hour, the three holed up in McLaren's hotel room smoking cigarette after cigarette until the ashtrays overflowed with ends and ashes.

Finally Jones said the words McLaren had wanted to hear for months. "Malcolm, we've decided we don't want to go on anymore. We're not writing any songs: Fucking Rotten's on his high horse and it's just fuck-all boring. America's changed the fuck out of us. Let's call it a day: We've had enough."

"Well," McLaren supposedly responded, happy to be finished with it, "if *you* think it's the right thing to do, then do it. I can't stand the guy anymore, either. We'll get rid of that fucking singer. He's a fucking joker anyway. Get rid of him and call it a day."

Cook and Jones went downstairs to the Miyako lobby, and there was Rotten, now checked into the hotel, looking, says Jones, "all poncey like a rock star.

"I said, 'We've had enough, John. We want out.' 'Why, what's the matter with you?' he said. 'Why are we going to split up? Let's just get rid of McLaren.' He hated it, hated the fact that we wanted to split up."

It was the closest to conversation the two had come in weeks.

"Listen, John," said Jones, "we're not writing any more songs, and you're acting like a complete toss-pot."

But Rotten kept repeating his new mantra: "Just let's get rid of McLaren, let's get rid of McLaren."

Jones was nauseous at the very thought.

"I definitely didn't want to go on without Malcolm being around," he says. "Lydon thought it was all McLaren's doing, what made us come down and say all this—and some of it was, you know. Because if Malcolm didn't tell us to fucking call it a day, we probably wouldn't have."

According to Rotten, however, Jones's version of these events is a pack of lies.

"We were in San Francisco," he later told Caroline Coon, "and I had a cold and all that air conditioning was giving me nosebleeds. I was told about Brazil—by a journalist, I might add—four hours before I was due to get on the plane. I thought it was a farce. I wouldn't dream of doing anything so stupid. . . . So I told Malcolm he could stuff it.

"I didn't leave the band. They left me. They didn't sack me. They walked out. I caught Paul and Steve packing their cases. Sid was in hospital at the time. They did it without telling me. I woke up in the morning to find out they were leaving. I asked why and they said we're leaving for a load of reasons. 'We can't say.'

"We'd gone as far as we could go. Everyone was trying to turn us into a big band group, and I hated that. I was bored stiff by Sid's juvenile behavior. I was very anti–hard drugs from the start and I tried to help Sid for a year. But I've had enough of that social-work rubbish. Malcolm was setting me up as another Rod Stewart and when I kicked back he didn't like it. It was getting too hideous. *I don't want to be a popstar."*

At six o'clock the next morning, McLaren sent Cook and Jones to the airport to catch their flight to Rio (via Los Angeles) while he stayed on with Rotten in San Francisco to make one last-ditch effort to convince his star to come to Brazil. This time, however, Rotten was coldly unyielding to McLaren's scheming; he refused to get out of bed, much less go to Rio de Janeiro.

At long last, it seemed the Sex Pistols had fired their last round of ammunition, but like most of McLaren's best laid plans, this one too went utterly awry, for by the time McLaren arrived with the tickets to fly into the sun, Pan Am flight 515 to Rio de Janeiro had already departed.

With the lies and recriminations surrounding the final split flying at gale force, McLaren and the rump Sex Pistols finally escaped San Francisco for Los Angeles the next day, leaving Rotten stranded with neither a ticket home nor the cash to buy one—McLaren had been giving the boys only a twenty-five dollar per diem each while they were in America, and when that ran out, Rotten was left to the charity of his friends. Sid, too, was left behind. He had concluded that if there was little sense in carrying on as a Sex Pistol without Rotten, there was even less sense in palling around with the great train robber Ronnie Biggs in Brazil. After arriving in Los Angeles a day after McLaren, he gathered his things and departed for New York where he was taken off the plane in a coma after washing down a mountain of Valium with alcohol en route.

With the American tour now at its grim conclusion—a conclusion McLaren himself had planned long ago, although not perhaps quite so bloodily—McLaren flew back to London (through New York where he checked in on the recovered Sid) to ready legal papers to make the fugitive train robber Biggs the Sex Pistols' new lead singer.

McLaren wasn't in London very long, perhaps no more than a week, but it was just enough time for him to fix Biggs's contract, hire Julien Temple and a cameraman to accompany him to Rio, and arrange a meeting with Island Records boss Chris Blackwell about managing the Slits, an all-girl punk band whose total lack of musicianship struck McLaren as the perfect post-Pistols rock 'n' roll. Apparently, McLaren had a film idea for them too: He wanted them to play a rock band with the hideously mistaken idea of jump-starting their career in Mexico, where they would eventually wind up co-opted into disco purgatory, "getting fucked from one end of Mexico to the other."

While the latter idea fortunately never came to fruition—the record deal fell apart when McLaren demanded £100,000 to get the unrecorded Slits into the studio—McLaren and Temple did fly to Brazil in late January. To everyone else it may have been clear that the Sex Pistols were finis, but Malcolm McLaren was determined to rescue whatever was left of his sinking ship before it went down.

Temple tells the story of the Brazil trip as if McLaren and company had at last succumbed to the idea of making the Sex Pistols' version of *A Hard Day's Night.* No script was written and direction was kept to a bare minimum, mostly just McLaren's madcap ideas for arranging such deliberately self-conscious spectacles as press conferences with fugitive Nazis and sexy Brazilian girls. Days were spent stealing bicycles (McLaren was petrified of being caught), frolicking on the beach, and cruising down the Amazon with Henry Rowland, an older American actor who had played a bit part as Nazi Martin Bormann in Russ Meyer's *Beyond the Valley of the Dolls* and was now enlisted to play a similar role as a garish Nazi stand-in for Sid Vicious; nights were passed nursing horrible sunburns, ingesting large amounts of cocaine and marijuana, and writing lyrics with the great exiled train robber.

As for Biggs, he seemed perfectly happy to be the new Johnny Rotten. "Money talks with Biggs," says Temple. Although the lyrics of the one song Biggs concocted with help from Jones and McLaren were as offensive as anything Rotten had ever written—"God save Martin Bormann/ and Nazis on the run/ They wasn't being wicked God/ It was their idea of fun"—it was clear as the brilliant blue waters of the Bay of Brazil that no matter how desperately McLaren wanted to keep the Sex Pistols alive with Biggs and "Bormann" instead of Rotten and Vicious, the Sex Pistols had truly bitten the dust in San Francisco. Biggs's casually anti-Semitic buffoonery may have been perfectly suited to McLaren's stated aims of proving that anyone, even an escaped robber and murderer, could play in a rock 'n' roll band, but under the circumstances, this must have seemed a rather hollow victory considering that the nostalgically patriotic Biggs— the very essence of a Cockney crook—could never return to the British isles.

After a few weeks of fun in the sun, McLaren returned to London with Jones and Cook, leaving Temple behind as what he called "human insurance" for the instruments the band had thrown overboard during an Amazonian riverboat scene McLaren had intended as a silly bit of one-upmanship with Pete Townshend's guitar-bashing heroics. It took nearly a month before McLaren found the funds to send Temple his ticket home, and when Temple finally came back to London he discovered that McLaren had spent almost all his time (and much of his money) obsessing about Johnny Rotten. In early February, Rotten had flown to Kingston, Jamaica, with Richard Branson and Virgin record plugger Rudy Van Egmond to scout new acts for Virgin's Front Line reggae label, and although McLaren was now in the habit of denouncing Rotten as a "constructive sissy rather than a destructive lunatic," he was still looking for a way to get the singer back into the Sex Pistols. Just after Rotten left for Jamaica, he sent Boogie to Kingston with a camera—just in case the opportunity to shoot Rotten relaxing by the pool presented itself—and orders to find out what Rotten's intentions were vis à vis the Sex Pistols.

Boogie returned from Jamaica with only one photo and the most contemptuous greetings from Rotten, but he did have one piece of news that apparently terrified McLaren. According to Michael Watts's *Melody Maker* profile, "When two members of Devo, who were then negotiating a contentious signing to Virgin, went out to JA to speak to Branson, McLaren immediately decided that there was a clandestine attempt afoot to make Rotten the American band's lead singer." McLaren was infuriated by what he perceived as the alliance of Warner Bros. and Virgin to steal Rotten away from him; Branson says that since Rotten already *was* a Virgin artist, the whole point of the trip was to convince him to *rejoin* the Sex Pistols, instead of going solo. In any event, McLaren ultimately saw *all* these events, good and bad, as more grist for his Sex Pistols movie.

Rotten however, found nothing amusing or even interesting about having his privacy violated so cavalierly, and as soon as he returned from Jamaica he hired lawyer Brian Carr to file legal writs against McLaren for having mismanaged the Sex Pistols' financial affairs, specifically enjoining McLaren's two companies, Glitterbest Ltd and Matrixbest Ltd (McLaren's film production company), from any further use of the names Johnny Rotten or the Sex Pistols.

Rotten wasn't the only one displeased with McLaren's recent decisions. Returning from Rio, Temple was taken aback when McLaren told him that he had once again decided to do a documentary—now incorporating the newly lensed Rio footage—and he spent the next few weeks trying to convince McLaren that a feature-length fiction film was still possible given the material they already had. McLaren held firm. He either wanted a name director—although there were also vague rumors that Vivienne Westwood wanted her brother Gordon to direct—or an established documentary filmmaker. He was by no means sure that the twenty-two-year-old Temple was competent to make a feature movie. The battle raged for weeks, but in the end, McLaren grudgingly agreed to let Temple be the director, and the two began scratching out a vague treatment.

"I thought to myself, if I don't lay the biographical details down now in terms of film, it might be lost forever," McLaren later explained, leaving out the crucial detail that at least part of the reason for his rush was caused by Sid and Nancy's late February arrest on drugs charges. "So we went on a real big scrabble and tried to get any bit of film that was ever shot on the Sex Pistols anywhere in the world, but in fact, there wasn't all that much."

With little more than the title and Virgin's cash—producer Jeremy Thomas was now keeping the lowest of profiles—Temple and McLaren set out for Paris around Easter to film Sid Vicious singing on the stage of the Olympia. The idea was McLaren's—he wanted Sid to sing a sobbing, string-laden rendition of Edith Piaf's "Non, Je Ne Regrette Rien" and then cold-bloodedly shoot numerous well-dressed audience members with a giant revolver—but once they arrived in Paris, Sid said he hated the song and refused to sing. At first, the problem seemed to be just the music, but as the days rolled by and the trek between the recording studio and the Hotel Brighton grew longer and longer, it became increasingly clear that Sid was too obsessed with drinking, drugging, and Nancy to be bothered with singing. "I remember a number of times," says Temple, "trying to wake them up, and I found them both crashed out, heads against the toilet bowl in vomit. And Nancy said to me, 'That's what love is—throwing up in the same toilet bowl.' "

Not for the first time in the making of a Sex Pistols movie, an entire crew had been hired and was waiting in vain for something to do, but Sid would not be budged. Finally, in a spirit of compromise, Jean Fernandez, one of McLaren's contacts at Barclay Records, suggested that if Sid wouldn't sing Piaf, perhaps he wouldn't mind trying Sinatra, and Sid was dragged through the paces of the classic Claude Francois *chanson* "Comme d'habitude"—better known by its Paul Anka translation as "My Way."

Recording Sid Vicious singing Sinatra's wistful retrospective of his career had a whiff of genius that anyone who was even remotely acquainted with the Sex Pistols could recognize—who would ever be able to forget the sight and sound of Sid mangling Frank's beautiful bel canto— but again Sid refused to sing, and after several weeks of keeping some sixty extras, an entire crew, numerous musical consultants, a full orchestra, recording engineers, producers, and even the Olympia booking agents on full salary, a chorus of pessimistic voices was heard to say that perhaps it would be better simply to call it a day. In desperation, McLaren flew Steve Jones into Paris to see if he could talk some sense into Sid, but not even that worked, for by now, Steve Jones was snorting junk.

Instead, Sid and his ubiquitous bottle-blond toughie got increasingly stroppy.

"Through Rotten, through America, through Nancy, Sid had basically come to hate Malcolm by then," says Temple. "He kept saying that Malcolm had to go before he would sing. And the thing that actually made Malcolm go back to London was that Sid just beat him up.

"One morning we came up to Malcolm's bedroom to tell him that Sid still hadn't sung the song, and Malcolm got really angry. He was lying in bed and he picked up the phone, rang down to Sid's room, and he screamed at him: 'Sid, you fucking junkie! I'm not going to have anything to do with you anymore unless you sing that goddamned song!' And then what must have happened is that Sid gave the phone to Nancy because Malcolm was still going on when suddenly this paneled door flew open and there was Sid—in his underpants with a swastika on them and his motorcycle boots but nothing else. He grabbed Malcolm out of bed and he said,

'You don't fucking talk to me like that,' and he shook Malcolm and Malcolm turned white and started to run—with no clothes on—down the floor of the hotel, one of these old corridors that dip up and down. The chambermaids were screaming, 'Monsieur! Oh, Monsieur!' and finally Malcolm ran into the elevator and Sid got in with him just before the doors closed.

"We all ran down the stairs and when the door opened, there was Malcolm, kicked all to pieces. That was enough for Malcolm. He split and went back to England. Sid finally extracted a signed note from Malcolm saying he would no longer be his manager, and then, after we rewrote some of the 'My Way' lyrics together—instead of 'I took the blows,' it was 'I ducked the blows/ I shot it up/ and killed a cat'—he finally broke down and sang the damned song."

With McLaren gone and Sid's recording sessions completed at last, it was relatively easy for Temple finally to begin shooting the "My Way" sequence at the Olympia, using the venerable Eddie Barclay himself as the show's MC. In a few weeks, Temple was back in London, and to his surprise, McLaren now wanted him off the film. "I think Malcolm resented me for being articulate and having ideas," he says. "He resented the fact that if I did something, I was proud of it. If it was my idea, I wasn't shy to say it was mine."

Indeed, even while Temple was still shooting in Paris, McLaren had hired a well-respected documentary filmmaker to shoot straight Q&A interview sessions with Sid and Nancy, Steve Jones, and Paul Cook. Typically, when McLaren failed to come up with the money to pay for the film, according to Temple, the film went missing until McLaren came up with the cash, and McLaren once again went back to working with Julien Temple.

At first, McLaren wanted to turn the Sex Pistols into rock 'n' roll's latest sacrificial lambs (à la Hendrix, Joplin, and Morrison) and he planned fiery finales for each one: Paul Cook was to be clobbered by a venomously opportunistic pop band (the Fabulous Blowwaves) to be led by Sting; Steve Jones was to become a eunuch after parachuting from a plane; Sid Vicious would have his comeuppance in a spectacular motorcycle crash; while Rotten was to be written out (by McLaren) from the start. But then he came up with an idea that cut straight to the heart of what he thought the Sex Pistols were about. Why bother attempting to construct a narrative "around" the Sex Pistols when there already was an epic tale of latter-day

Faginism waiting to be told? Whose story was this, anyway? Stealing a page from the book of a former schoolteacher he knew—Vivienne West-wood—McLaren decided *he* would tell the story of the Sex Pistols himself in ten easy lessons, each one explaining how the group's merciless and often gratuitous imbroglios had been planned by none other than Malcolm McLaren in a coolly premeditated attempt to wreak havoc on, and rip off, the record industry. The Sex Pistols story, McLaren now decided, was the story of *The Great Rock 'n' Roll Swindle.*

With the Lessons, all McLaren's attempts over the years to portray himself as the unwitting victim of the music business were turned on its head and history utterly rewritten. Ruses were turned back into raisons d'êtres; fumbling opportunism was replaced by ambition and industrious-ness; and reckless roguery was swapped for chivalrous derring-do. Of all the many ideas McLaren had had for this movie, *his* movie about the Sex Pistols, only the Lessons embodied the full extent of his essential wicked-ness, turning the Sex Pistols into a subplot in their own movie while McLaren himself was lifted at last into the constellation of the stars.

To Julien Temple, the idea of McLaren delivering this potted sum-mary of the Sex Pistols' career reeked of art-world pretense. McLaren couldn't just talk into the camera for an hour! But then Temple thought of a classic film device that would push McLaren's Lessons into the fore-ground: Steve Jones would play a *film noir* detective searching for the elusive manager as the wily McLaren told the story of how he swindled £695,000 from EMI, A&M, Warner Bros., Arista Music, and, last but not least, Virgin Records. McLaren now became "The Embezzler"; Steve Jones, ex–cat burglar, became "The Crook"; and the other Sex Pistols were all given new monikers: Paul Cook was dubbed "The Tea Maker," Sid Vicious, "The Gimmick," and Johnny Rotten, "The Collaborator."

"We finally wrote it so that there were swindles within swindles within swindles," says Temple. "It was like an x ray of a skeleton, except that here, the skeleton was rock 'n' roll, and each layer of skin and bones became a different level of swindling. There's the basic rock 'n' roll swin-dle of the kids going into a record shop and buying a record with their hard earned cash and getting two hit singles and a mountain of crud, buying a worthless piece of plastic because they've been fed this bullshit about some larger-than-life demigod who's going to instill them with a bit of wisdom. There's the second swindle of the Sex Pistols' stealing the money they'd got. There's the swindle of Steve Jones, who plays the ex–Sex Pistol trying to get his share of the swindled money back from McLaren. And then probably the most interesting swindle of all is the way in which the film was designed to swindle an avid fan of his expectations, destroying the fans' illusions about the Sex Pistols. Of course, as time went on, the final swindle for me was whether Malcolm was going to swindle me or whether I was going to swindle the film from Malcolm."

"This wasn't a film, really, in any traditional sense," says Temple, now better known for his many music videos of David Bowie, Mick Jagger, Janet Jackson, and the feature films *Absolute Beginners* and *Earth Girls Are Easy*. "There was no budget. There was no script. We just did it. We ran out of money and then we would get more and wait a few weeks and shoot again. I used to write a lot of it in the car on the way to the location or even once we were there. Basically, we hadn't written things. We just had some good ideas. Malcolm was very catalytic. He's like a lightning conductor. He inspires you to come up with things and give more than you normally would in terms of energy and ideas, and he really pushes you creatively—until he wants something on the set and then he'll say, 'I want to talk to you,' and grab your elbow at the pressure point, leading you away."

By summer's end, Temple and McLaren had entered the editing room to sort out all the tangled skeins of narrative and documentary footage they had acquired, and almost immediately, McLaren began demanding control over what he repeatedly insisted was *his* picture. Temple soon realized that McLaren's real aim was to direct the *Swindle*.

"Everything had been fine throughout most of the summer," he remembers. "There were some problems with Malcolm, but they had mostly to do with his inability to memorize his lines. One day, for example, we were on Tower Bridge, and he had about ten lines which started with the words, 'Never trust a hippie,' and after about half a day of trying the same scene over and over we decided to see if getting him drunk would help. We wasted hours of film, time, and money.

"That was fine, but when we began editing I was aware of the same kind of underlying jealousy he had displayed toward Rotten. Rotten was the singer, but really, Malcolm wanted to be the singer; now he also wanted to be the director. I kept seeing signs of that when he started using that pressure-on-the-elbow thing. He kept interrupting to tell me he wanted lots of close-ups, and at the time, I thought that was just a difference in our ideas about film, because in my opinion unless you're working for TV, close-ups should be used with some discretion. Later I realized he was only waiting until the production was done so that he could get rid of me. And I have to say I find that obscene. You shouldn't let a guy do it and then get rid of him. You should do it yourself."

Of course, since McLaren had no experience directing or editing a 35mm feature, that was impossible, and so for weeks on end, the two fought until the small hours of the morning, sometimes even locking each other out of the cold Berwick Street cutting room where the *Swindle* was being edited.

"One night we arrived at the studio and it was freezing cold," says Temple. "We were locked out of the cutting room because we hadn't paid this bent accountant and we were standing on one of these unlit concrete stairways, and I remember Malcolm screaming a blue streak that I was fired. 'You're fired! From now on, you're to be the slave in the cutting room! I don't want you to open your mouth. I just want you to get the trims when you're asked because you're the only guy who knows where they are.'

"I was amazed to be treated like that, so I said fuck you and left, although I continued working on the film because I was the only one who knew where the cans were."

Two years in the making, *The Great Rock 'n' Roll Swindle* was at last beginning to look like something close to a movie, in part thanks to Vivienne's brother Gordon Swire, who now took over the editing for a brief period. But just as it was, the subtle echo of consequence—history itself and not the phony travesty of facts McLaren had finally managed to twist into cinematic fantasy—was about to reverberate in Malcolm McLaren's life.

Predictably, the complications started with Sid and Nancy. McLaren didn't want Sid to go to New York—Virgin had just put out "My Way" at the end of July and there was certain to be good publicity in that—but Sid now considered Nancy his manager, and, parroting Rotten's line that McLaren was interested only in publicity stunts, on August 24 they departed for New York, where, Nancy convinced Sid, all the *real* punk rockers were 'hangin' out.'

In some ways, Nancy was right. By the summer of 1978, the spectacular sight of the smelly, spiky-haired punk rockers crowding London's streets had come to be taken for granted by many Britons: The furor was over. From Wardour Street to World's End, punks had long ago invaded the public consciousness as the latest rock 'n' roll fad. Secretaries wore safety-pin earrings to work and colored their hair bright green and orange. Schoolboys ripped their T-shirts and looped gold-plated razor blades around their necks. By September, even Derek Green had gotten over his Sex Pistols debacle, signing the Police, Joe Jackson, Elvis Costello, Squeeze, and other ex-punks. Punk music had finally yielded to the New Wave, or worse: Some punk acts such as Jimmy Pursey's Sham '69 now became the darlings of the Paki-bashing skinheads spearheading the neo-fascist National Front.

New York would be different, thought Sid and Nancy: no more of these New Wave wimps, man. In America, the sword that dangled over every real British punk's head—it was punk or the dole queue—was replaced with the more pernicious problem of death by self-inflicted annihilation: New York was home of the heroin band, a punk rock tradition one could trace from Lou Reed to Johnny Thunders, Richard Hell, and even Blondie. That was America's punk: not subculture so much as drop-out culture.

For Sid and Nancy, returning to New York was like entering paradise, and it didn't take long before Nancy guided Sid into the same drug-obsessed life-style she had been leading there long before they had even met. If anything, Sid's addiction to heroin made him belong to New York in a way that no other Sex Pistol ever could have. Sid was a hero in New York, the kind of naive hero who falls prey to easy adulation and quickly becomes bait for the leeches of drug culture, and those who saw how easily they could take advantage of him did so eagerly. In this regard, Nancy Spungen proved to be Malcolm McLaren's equal in encouraging Sid to ever greater heights of excess.

In fact, Sid was smarter than that. He missed London, and when his solo career in New York (several gigs at Max's with Johnny Thunders and Iggy Pop) failed to get him a record contract, sinking him deeper and deeper into addiction and debt, he vowed to return there after one last night of glory on Halloween in Nancy's hometown, Philadelphia.

Of course, Sid never made it. No one will ever know what actually happened the night of October 12, 1978, the night Sid stabbed Nancy Spungen to death in what Sid later claimed was a bungled suicide pact. But for Malcolm McLaren, Nancy's death proved to be as messy and disruptive as her life had been. Within twenty-four hours of being notified that Sid had been arrested for murder, he stopped work on the film and, on Friday the 13th, flew to N.Y., arriving at court ten minutes into Sid's bond hearing.

McLaren urged the court to release Sid on his own recognizance, swearing to make sure that he would keep an eye on his charge and that he would immediately enlist him in a detoxification program, but the judge was not convinced. Instead Sid spent four miserable days cooling his heels at Rikers Island until McLaren finally got Richard Branson to cough up $50,000 in bail money. (McLaren is also said to have approached Mick Jagger for the money, but according to Michael Watts, it was lawyer Steven Fisher who spotted the Stone in the Savoy Hotel lobby and Jagger apparently " 'hummed and hawed' that it might be difficult to help, what with Keith Richards's trial on heroin charges pending in Toronto.)

Sid's incarceration was deeply troubling to McLaren. He was certain Sid would be eaten alive by the hardened criminals at Rikers who would inevitably want the famous Sid Vicious to prove his masculinity, and he desperately wanted to keep Sid out of jail, even going to the extent of attempting to hire radical trial lawyer William Kunstler, and when that turned out to be too expensive, celebrity attorney F. Lee Bailey and his associate James Michael Merberg. McLaren seemed to genuinely care about Sid—he honestly liked him and never really felt he was responsible for encouraging his excessive behavior—and while he had long anticipated that something like this might happen and had done little to prevent it, if it had to be that either Sid or Nancy was going to die, he was glad it had been Sid who was spared.

Still, McLaren seemed to be operating from mixed motives at the very best, for when Sid tried to join Nancy by mutilating his right arm the week after McLaren bailed him out of jail—when the ambulance arrived, sirens wailing, Sid also tried to jump out the window—McLaren dangled the prospect of an eventual Sex Pistols reunion before Sid as a hopeful reason for his staying alive. He even announced plans for a Sex Pistols reunion in Miami to record an album of Christmas songs to raise funds for Sid's legal defense.

"I don't care what people think about the morality of it all," McLaren angrily declared when a reporter from the *Daily Express* asked him about Nancy's murder. "The fact is that Sid is fighting for his life and the girl is six feet underground."

However, by the time McLaren returned to London a week later, even these supposedly ethical motives had come to be viewed as suspect by most of those around him. For by October 27, Seditionaries, the shop McLaren owned with Vivienne Westwood, was selling T-shirts benefiting Sid's legal defense emblazoned with a cartoon of a rose-shrouded Sid in G.I. Joe duds, with the words "I'M ALIVE. SHE'S DEAD. I'M YOURS."

At £6.50 per shirt, this was one controversy McLaren seemed all too willing to exploit at an affordable price.

It didn't take long for McLaren to convince Cook and Jones, then in the midst of playing various one-off gigs in London with Phil Lynott's Greedy Bastards, that a trip to Miami to record such family favorites as "White Christmas" and "Mac the Knife" would be good fun. McLaren was gratified that they agreed despite their differences with him, but by the time the plans were laid they had already become irrelevant. Absorbed with the editing of the *Swindle* and preoccupied by the steady furor over Sid's troubles with the law, McLaren now had to face John Lydon's lawsuit—note the name change—finally risen to the top of the register at the High Court of Justice.

The particulars of Lydon's suit made many allegations, most of which were related to the legality of the joint partnership agreement Lydon had entered into with Glitterbest Ltd, on September 20, 1976—the date of the 100 Club Punk Rock Festival McLaren had organized more than two years before. Over and over, Lydon's lawyers make the case that the original partnership agreement with Glitterbest, which never legally bound Malcolm McLaren to *manage* the band although he *owned* ninety-nine percent of the partnership, was either invalid or unenforceable. McLaren had failed to keep proper accounts, provide for the band members' weekly remittances, or even make attempts to further the band's career. Instead he used the moneys paid by various record companies and investors (calculated to be at least £750,000 not including an additional £200,000 film advance from Warner Bros.) to make a film that Lydon was legally required to participate in even though he found the scripts—which McLaren had collaborated on—"obscene and offensive, . . . [including] scenes of incest, cocaine-taking, necrophilia, group sex, gross violence, and sexual perversion."

Moreover, while the original partnership agreement had stipulated that McLaren was the source of the name *Sex Pistols,* according to Lydon, this was false: The group had been performing under the *Sex Pistols* moniker for many months before they had signed with McLaren. To top it off, once Glen Matlock left the "original" group, McLaren had never bothered to sign a management agreement between Glitterbest and the partners of the "new" group that came into existence with Sid Vicious. The "new group" had never really existed—and yet McLaren had continued to exploit both the name of the group and the name *Johnny Rotten* long after the Sex Pistols broke up in San Francisco, over a year earlier.

Accordingly, John Lydon wanted the following damages charged against Glitterbest: a legal declaration that the partnership had come to an end; a full accounting of the Glitterbest and Matrixbest finances; the appointment of an official receiver and a new manager; numerous injunctions forbidding McLaren or the other so-called Sex Pistols from using the *Sex Pistols* name or from infringing on any copyright belonging to the Sex Pistols; and, of course, monetary damages for legal costs and "such further or other relief as may be just."

Meanwhile, back in New York, Sid was back to his old tricks. Released into the custody of his mother and probation officer following his Bellevue hospitalization, he once again hit the club scene with a vengeance, and on December 6, after a senseless fight at the New Wave nightclub Hurrah in which Vicious slashed Patti Smith's brother Todd with a broken beer bottle, he was once again taken to jail on felonious assault charges.

This time, no bail money was forthcoming from either Virgin or McLaren. McLaren had decided that Sid was better off drying out in jail where he couldn't get into more trouble, so Sid spent his Christmas holidays in the Rikers Island detoxification center. It was better to let Sid sit and seethe than to send him back into his mother's track-laden arms. "I wasn't prepared to be Sid's nurse," McLaren said later.

Indeed, McLaren had become so immersed in his own legal battles that he could no longer afford to be bothered with the constant pleadings of Sid's mother and lawyer that Sid would surely kill himself if he wasn't bailed out of jail by January 16, the date of his parole hearing. With the cheap bail ($10,000) set by the judge, who was somehow impressed that Sid had already been enrolled in a methadone maintenance program before Nancy's death, McLaren was eventually convinced that setting Sid free was a reasonable thing to do, and he promised to come to New York on the day Sid was to be paroled, February 1. However, as the day drew nearer, McLaren realized that his own legal affairs had become so tortuous that it would be foolhardy for him to leave London, and he promised to send someone else from Glitterbest to help Sid's mum keep an eye on her son. Anne Beverley would have to be trusted to make sure Sid stayed clean.

As it turned out, everyone miscalculated.

Malcolm McLaren never left London. Nor did he send a representative from Glitterbest, as promised. McLaren knew better than to allow Anne Beverley to take responsibility for the son she had raised on the back of a motorbike, but with the date of his own trial set for February 7, he became so distracted by the rumors that John Lydon's lawyers were considering bringing criminal as well as civil charges against him, he seemed to lose track of the days.

On the night of February 1, Sid's new girlfriend, Michelle Robison, held a small party to celebrate his parole at her apartment at 63 Bank Street in the West Village. That night, someone—Anne Beverley later admitted it was she—slipped a glassine packet of heroin into Robison's apartment. Sid's attorneys later established he had been drug-free for the entire week before his parole.

That left the final miscalculation to Sid, and sometime between 11 A.M. and noon on February 2 he died of an overdose of heroin.

He was twenty-one years old.

On Wednesday, February 7, just five days after Sid Vicious's death, the case of *Lydon v. Glitterbest* finally began in Court 37 of the Chancery Division of the High Court of Justice in the Strand.

McLaren and Fisher were ill-prepared for the devastating attack made by Lydon's barrister, Mr. John Wilmers, QC, and solicitor, Mr. Brian Carr. Days before the trial began, McLaren and Fisher tried one last time to settle out of court, but once again their offers were refused, and now the trial they hoped would never reach a court finally had.

To John Lydon, McLaren and Fisher's lack of preparation for the trial seemed like one more vindication of the charge that McLaren had fumblingly mismanaged the Sex Pistols. Indeed, Rotten seemed to truly enjoy the legal circus. Smartly dressed in a loud red-and-blue tartan suit and fat mauve brothel creepers (no doubt purchased from SEX), he laughed when Wilmers laid it on, saying that McLaren "regards himself as the Svengali of these people to do whatever he cares without asking anybody else." For his part, McLaren faintly glowed with nervous energy, the red "M" on his forehead fairly bursting into public view. Although his attorneys (barrister, Mr. John Godfrey, QC, and solicitor, Mr. Steven Fisher) had at least two depositions supporting his theory that there was a conspiracy against him by Warner Bros. and Virgin, McLaren and Fisher had prepared precious little independent documentation to support their claims.

Things went from bad to worse on the second to last day of the trial when Jones and Cook, who were no longer friendly with McLaren, defected to Rotten's side of the case, perhaps recognizing that their financial future ultimately rested on the proper accounting of the Glitterbest funds. "I was totally fucking out of me mind on heroin," Jones sheepishly admits, "so I was just going along with Cook. But we were still tied to Virgin individually and Paul and me were getting this band together, the Professionals, and we needed a new record deal, so that's why it turned round.

We didn't even agree with Lydon. We just wanted the money and there was just no reason to be with McLaren. Me, I was a fucking vegetable with the smack. I just wanted to be in a band again."

Just before the final judgment was handed down, McLaren panicked and began speaking out of turn until the judge warned him that if he did not sit down immediately, he would be charged with contempt of court. With such fierce pronouncements from the bench, McLaren feared the worst, but in some ways, the order handed down by Mr. Justice Browne-Wilkinson was not quite so severe as expected.

Indeed, on the most controversial aspects of the case, the issues pertaining to the mismanagement of the Glitterbest moneys, the justice declined to make "any concluded findings of fact" whatsoever. "The Plaintiff [Lydon] says that the money invested in that film was invested entirely without his knowledge or consent," Browne-Wilkinson solemnly intoned. "I am not at this stage quite clear what was the state of knowledge of, or approval by, Mr. Jones and Mr. Cook. However, all those matters are in dispute and it is not for me to decide them. What I have to do is to see to secure the position until a judge can hear all the evidence and decide on the facts."

Until those facts relating to the Sex Pistols' mismanagement could be determined by a judge (or settled out of court), Justice Browne-Wilkinson ordered the immediate termination of the Lydon-Glitterbest partnership and the appointment of "an independent and reliable outsider . . . a receiver and manager of all the assets which have come to the hands of Glitterbest or Matrixbest or may hereafter come into their hands in the course of their acting as manager of the Sex Pistols." These assets were to include all the rights of Glitterbest and Matrixbest in *The Great Rock 'n' Roll Swindle;* in any recording or publishing contracts; in any activities continuing to exploit the names, trademarks, or goodwill of the Sex Pistols, including acting as the group's manager; and, of course, the actual physical assets held in the accounts of Glitterbest and Matrixbest: the money. Until the substantive issues of the case were resolved—another ten years, as it would happen—the assets were to be held in safe custody by the receiver, Mr. Russell Gerald Hawkes of the London accountancy of Spicer & Pegler.

There was one final point Mr. Justice Browne-Wilkinson sought to make clear. What made *Lydon v. Glitterbest* an unusual case, he said, was that the "only realistic hope of any substantial sums being rescued for anybody in this case is dependent upon the exploitation of the film in which so much money has been invested."

"I should like to make it absolutely clear," he declared in summing up, "that Mr. McLaren, or anybody else appointed submanager, is bound to follow the directions of the receiver and manager. There is no question of his being able to disagree and depart from [their] directions. . . . The law is clear, that anybody who interferes with the possession or the right to take possession of a receiver of assets of which he has been appointed receiver by the Court is guilty of a contempt of Court."

That was enough warning for Malcolm McLaren: The very next day, he hopped a plane to Paris, a location inspired by a faint rumor that John Lydon might now try to bring him to trial for fraud.

The Sex Pistols were over.

From time to time, there would be reports in the press that Jones and Cook might reunite with Matlock or even with Rotten—all were signed to Virgin Records—but none of these rumors ever panned out. Jones and Cook made one album as the Professionals and John Lydon continued doing what Johnny Rotten did best—stirring up trouble. In February 1978, as soon as he returned from Jamaica, and almost simultaneously with the filing of his suit, he created his own band, the ironically named Public Image Limited (PIL, for short). PIL's first, eponymously titled album was released by Virgin in early December, at nearly the same time Sid Vicious was spending his Christmas holiday at Rikers Island. For at least part of the trial, John Lydon is rumored to have lived in Richard Branson's plush houseboat cum office on Regents Canal near Maida Vale.

In death, Sid Vicious was no more fortunate than he had been in life. After Nancy Spungen's parents refused to allow Sid to be buried next to their daughter, John Simon Ritchie aka John Beverley aka Sid Vicious was cremated in New York. His mother was named a defendant in the trial and, with Jones and Cook, eventually switched over to Lydon's side of the case.

Malcolm McLaren continued to fight it out with Julien Temple from his self-imposed exile in Paris. Although McLaren had initially been appointed submanager of *The Great Rock 'n' Roll Swindle,* he ruined his relationship with Russell Gerald Hawkes by being as obstreperous as possible toward the film that had been taken away from him by John Lydon. Every meeting with the receiver now became a battle of wills between McLaren's new solicitors (*exeunt* Steven Fisher), and the lawyers for Virgin Films, Julien Temple, Spicer & Pegler, Don Boyd, Russ Meyer, et al. It was a battle McLaren was destined to lose. At one point, he even sent Hawkes a five-page screed threatening that unless he was given control of the *Swindle* within twenty-four hours, he would sue to have himself removed from it. Hawkes never bothered to respond.

"Right before Sid died, things came to a real climax," remembers Temple. "Malcolm was really scared. He thought people were going to kill him because he was the 'man who killed Sid Vicious.' That's why he packed his bags for Paris: He was paranoid, and even though I supported him in the trial, he was still treating me like shit. Finally I just said to myself, fuck this guy—I've worked two and a half years on this, I'm not going to go away.

"So when it finally came time after the trial, I used the receiver to get control of the film. I played my card, which is being a privileged upper-class Englishman: My father is a man who deserted in the war, the black sheep of his family, but he's from a wealthy English background—Palmerston, a prime minister in the nineteenth century was part of his family. So we have codes of behavior that Malcolm wouldn't understand: It takes five hundred years to learn the secrets. In England, being born of one class is like having an American Express card, and I used that. In that position, it's all I had to use. So I let off a kind of pyrotechnical display of my knowledge in front of the receiver or anyone else who was financially interested in finishing the film. And then I plucked a few chords that I knew would hit home, just doing it with the movement of an eyebrow. And they know what the code is, they know who's from where."

Indeed, Russell Gerald Hawkes was fairly astonished by Malcolm McLaren's lack of rectitude in handling *The Great Rock 'n' Roll Swindle*.

"Before I met him," says the distinguished-looking senior accountant, "I had anticipated, because I had heard about the amount of money that was involved, that I would meet somebody with all the trappings of wealth, having misapplied so much money to his own personal benefit. But I was quite surprised to find a chap who didn't spend *any* money on himself, who didn't drive a motorcar, and who showed no outward sign of having got any money.

"You see, when I was appointed, the judge was just trying to give the boys time to work things out: Let's appoint a receiver to gather in the records, he was saying, and then you boys must go away and sort the other issues out on your own. Basically, Glitterbest was entitled to a certain percentage of royalties, but it collected all the royalties before it paid them out to the group, so the money went into Glitterbest's bank account. Malcolm chose to use that money for a film instead of giving it out to the individuals—supposing Malcolm was entitled to twenty-five percent, he used one hundred percent to make a movie—and Lydon objected to that.

"Now, since there weren't any assets other than a small cash balance, my job was to get this film finished and launch it, which I did. All this was done in a hurry, and so it was suggested by the court, that since I, who have never made a film in my life, was supposed to *finish* a film, I needed someone to help me. Malcolm was appointed submanager but since he wasn't prepared to cooperate, I *had* to find other people to help me."

In May 1980, thanks to the strenuous efforts of Don Boyd's Boyds Co. and the newly created Virgin Films, created solely to acquire the rights to the *Swindle,* the movie was finally given its British release. (To this day, Warner Communications Inc. has refused to distribute the picture in the United States.) Malcolm McLaren could cry all he wanted to about what "they" had done to the movie he claimed was "his" in "THEME, SCRIPT, CONSTRUCTION, ATTITUDE, and above all, STYLE," but at the end of the day, there could be no doubting that he had become the unwilling star, as well as the very last victim, of *The Great Rock 'n' Roll Swindle.*

PART THREE

Everything is plundered, betrayed,
    sold,
Death's great black wing scrapes the
    air,
Misery gnaws at the bone.
Why do we not despair?
            —Akhmatova

8
EXILE ON
PLACE PIGALLE

Like a man who has tried to cover his domain with a map as vast and detailed as the territory it has been drawn to, Malcolm McLaren had tried to substitute his own fantasy of popular culture for the real one, the one that exists by a consensus of law, money, ethics, and desire. John Lydon may have brought him briefly back to earth from his narcissistic aerie at the top of the punk rock tornado, but Malcolm McLaren was unbowed at having been exposed publicly in the courts of law.

Of course, in one way, McLaren's disregard of the "real" had provided him with certain benefits: floating above his culture—its economics, its language, its morals, and even its political geography—he was free to interpret the world as it fit his needs, to take what he needed and to construe the rest as false consciousness or, more prosaically, particularly when talking about John Lydon, as sissy careerism. McLaren didn't mind that he had burned his bridges to the entertainment industries; if anything, he was proud of what he had done with (and to) the Sex Pistols— he was the artist and they were his masterpiece. "We went through £600,000!" he bragged. "We had an amazing time and we just didn't care. Perhaps that's what made us so great."

Nor was he affected by the allegations that his exploitation had brought Sid Vicious to the grave. "People say, oh dear, I used Sid Vicious. In fact, Sid led a very, very exciting life that he probably wouldn't have had if somebody hadn't taken him in. The tragedy was that we didn't see it through to the end. He could have sung the 'White Cliffs of Dover' and changed people's whole view of England."

Punk, said McLaren, was great precisely *because* of its potential to create destruction, and he was delighted to have been at the center of this great unleashing of teenage energy.

"All that chaos gave everybody a tremendous lease of confidence, a feeling that they could do anything and shout as hard as they could and be as destructive as they could, probably for the first time. Fifteen years prior to that, they weren't able to do anything other than learn to be, for want of a better word, *respectable;* which means paying homage to the status quo. By getting rid of that, you made people begin to have another critique with anarchy. It may have *looked* violent. But visually, that was the point. . . . It was just kids breaking loose, having a good time."

That may have been true in the summer of '76, when punk was at its creative best, but by 1979 things had changed: England had changed. All through the winter of his trial, McLaren had cheered the crippling strikes that knocked Britain to its foundations—the so-called Winter of Discontent. First it was just the dockworkers who went on strike, but then the hospitals closed, the garbage piled up—morgue workers macabrely stockpiled unburied bodies on the Merseyside—and the BBC was threatening to blank the nation's tellys: You see, said McLaren, it was Anarchy in the U.K. after all. However, by spring, the polls showed that people had had enough of both the unions *and* Labour's pusillanimous politics, and the Callaghan government was dramatically defeated in the Commons by a single vote. Malcolm McLaren began to worry.

He had already seen the right's full fury when "God Save the Queen" had been taken as an attack on Her Majesty, and with a Tory upheaval now signaling dramatic social and political changes—and continuing talk of a potential indictment on fraud charges—he truly feared for his liberty. If, after so many years of stalemate and compromise, Britain had decided that there was no more room for the chaotic and irresponsible wildcat strikes of the Winter of Discontent, how long would it be before the nation clamped down on the symbolic violence McLaren thought he represented?

It was no time to be taking chances. If there was no future for him in Britain and no future for him in America, perhaps he'd be able to find something to do in Paris.

Just as it had been in the past, McLaren found that Paris was a breath of fresh air. He was perplexed, he was broke, he was having trouble with the language, but it was Paris, it was spring, and best of all, no one knew who he was—no one would taunt him about his thrashing at the hands of Johnny Rotten, and he could unembarrassedly go on with being the man who had created the Sex Pistols.

What made Paris best of all, however, was that so many of his old friends were there. After having been asked by McLaren earlier in the year to accompany Julien Temple to Paris to shoot a video for the Slits, his old friend Robin Scott had stayed on to work with his brother Julian at Barclay Records, and McLaren now took up Scott's offer of hospitality.

"I was working with African music then, particularly with heavy drum sounds like Burundi beat, and I was over at Barclay Records, and there he was," says Scott, who was soon to score a massive hit as the mysterious "M" with "Pop Muzik." "He didn't have anywhere to stay so I asked him to stay with my wife, Bridget, and me. I was encouraging him to do something himself. It seemed obvious to me that that would be his direction. I remember asking him why he worked with all those frustrating people: I kept telling him, if you find them all such a pain in the ass, then why not do it yourself? But he was kind of depressed and a little bewildered by it all. Finally we started kicking some ideas around on the piano at our flat, but by then it was time to go."

McLaren soon left the Scotts' to return briefly to London to play out his last moves on the *Swindle,* but by the time he came back to Paris, he too had picked up the ethnic music bug that was then sweeping through French music circles.

Through its former African colonies, France had always had strong ties to Africa. Senegal, Mali, Algeria, the Côte d'Ivoire—all had vibrant musical cultures, and yet for the most part, none had been commercially exploited in the West, partially because of the inherent linguistic barriers of African music (i.e., many of the songs were sung in various African dialects in a global industry dominated by Anglo-Saxons), but also because of the intrinsic racism of the Anglo-American record industry. Indeed, had it not been for the legion of white urban Britons who had grown up surrounded by the Caribbean emigré culture nestled in the Notting Hill section of London, reggae—the closest Anglo counterpart to the French African *soukous*—might never have found such staunch white supporters as Virgin's Front Line label or Island's Mango. Even then, it was mostly left to white ex-punks nostalgic for the sound of such early sixties Ska and Bluebeat bands as Millie Small, Desmond Dekker, the Skatalites, to merge these diverse cultures in the Two-Tone movement (*viz.,* the Selecter, Madness, Specials AKA, the Beat) that swept London in 1979.

While Paris had been used by many English rock stars as a base for recording—the Rolling Stones had been making records there for years—few had ever invested the effort in really exploring this gold mine of new sounds. To most Western musicians, the traditions and instruments of African music—the narrative power of the *griots,* the lyrical sounds of the *kora* (a twenty-one-string harp), the *tama* (talking drums), and the *balafon* (xylophone)—were simply too rooted in African history to be of much use to the commercial ambitions of rock 'n' roll, and there were few rock auteurs at the time who were willing to blend their own musical styles with the mellifluous polyrhythms of African music. (Peter Gabriel and Talking Heads, two of the best-known pop acts to eventually exploit these Franco-African roots, didn't get around to making their pseudo-African records until 1982–83.) Of course, this was precisely the kind of cultural insight McLaren was so brilliant at exploiting, and fortunately he was already well connected at Barclay, one of the chief producers of the African sound.

At Barclay, a maverick label that often signed the quirky, esoteric acts other French majors wouldn't touch, Fabrice Cuitard and Jean Fernandez took pity on their poor, red-haired friend from England. They had already helped McLaren in the past when he had asked them to rush-import Barclay's own pressing of "Anarchy in the U.K."—one of several gambits he had used to force Richard Branson's hand in releasing the *Bollocks* LP—and they were all too happy to help him now. For one thing, they too encouraged him to make his own record, and although they were not forthcoming with an advance from Barclay, they were happy to help him find his way in the French music world. Ironically, for a while there was talk of McLaren singing Piaf's "Non, Je Ne Regrette Rien" and Virgin Records head Simon Draper even sent McLaren a telegram saying he could have a £20,000 advance (a pittance in McLaren's view) if he would only "stop believing and fueling the conspiracy theory," but until he was ready to get his own act together, the Barclay people gave McLaren entrée to their copious library of African music and the chance to score some soft-porn films with another Englishman—bizarrely enough, Robin Scott's brother, Julian.

"I was drawn into, not so much studying, but collating music for sex pictures," McLaren told Krystina Kitsis in an interview for the art magazine, *ZG*. "The idea in those days was that you normally only used classical music for sex pictures that was recorded by East European countries or members of the Communist bloc because you didn't have to pay copyright; it was a cheap way of obtaining a soundtrack."

Meanwhile, McLaren stayed with his old friend Jean-Charles de Castelbajac. Reunited for the first time in nearly a year, McLaren and Castelbajac once again became friends although Castelbajac was a little put off by the on-again, off-again quality of McLaren's friendship. "A few days after he arrive at my house," he recalls, "I say let's go see the dead, *allons voir les morts.* So I take him to Père-Lachaise where he never been. And that was really a big day in our friendship. We saw the graves of Jim

Morrison and Edith Piaf and it was very beautiful, very spiritual, with all the officers of the Empire. And we laughed because someone even photographed us for *Melody Maker* and they thought I was his bodyguard, and I liked this idea very much because he needs to be protected."

Soon, McLaren had put together an entire network of Parisian supporters, meeting for coffee or dinner with French pop celebrities like radical singer Serge Gainsbourg, vocalist France Galle, and groups such as Telephone and Aux Bonheur des Dames, a revival twist band. McLaren's most important support, however, came not through Barclay but under the auspices of his old enemy, Warner Bros. Records, whose French publishing head, Jean Davouste, first met McLaren when the *Swindle* was still being shot.

"I tried to help him find money from our end, from Warner in England, and from various record companies in France in order to help him set up an operation here," says Davouste. "The French were so impressed by him, by his personality and talent and so on, but they wouldn't take the risk."

Even with this base of support, McLaren was still adrift in the City of Light. Castelbajac was pestering him to work with some Hungarian rocker he had taken an interest in—a "genius," he said—but McLaren wasn't ready to commit himself to a new project. He was only starting to come to terms with living in the post-Pistols era. But once he had left Castelbajac's fastidiously bourgeois apartment with its magnificent antique marble-topped tables to move into the apartment of Castelbajac's assistant, a young fashion designer who goes by the name of Spider Fawke, things began to loosen up a bit, and McLaren went off in search of his Parisian adventure, hanging out with the transvestites in the Restaurant Siam in the Rue Tiquetonne, and even having a love affair on the side. On and off for the next year or so, McLaren shared Spider's flat in Pigalle, the picturesque slum that houses so much of Paris's immigrant community.

"People would gravitate to Malcolm like he was a star in orbit," she remembers. "We would have these huge talks about life, about the universe, and he was very obsessed with Roger Vadim. He seemed to know hundreds of things about Brigitte Bardot, and he was already quite involved with the whole myth of being a Svengali figure."

Indeed, among the small circle of punks then inhabiting Paris, Malcolm McLaren was still god. Few knew the story of his defeat in the courts, and those who did found it amusing. They considered themselves lucky that McLaren had chosen Paris as the place to get his post-Pistols life in order and were charmed by his tales of Sid Vicious and Johnny Rotten. Eventually, some even began to work with him.

"Malcolm was just searching for something to do, and he came over here to read our songs," says Stephane Pietrie, a former punk music critic collaborating on writing song lyrics with Pierre Grillet, a writer who had already made a name for himself working on *Metal Hurlant* comics. "One day," says Grillet, "he says, 'I want to do the first soft-core porn rock 'n' roll movie for kids: *The Adventures of Melody, Lyric, and Tune.*'

"The original idea was very simple," explains Grillet. "Melody, Lyric, and Tune were three fifteen-year-old English girls who were picked up in a harbor by a French music manager living in the Moulin Rouge, *in* the actual Moulin. The idea was to use all the historical sites of Paris as locations for the film, as places of *seduction*, so there is a song called 'Sexy Eiffel Tower,' a song for Versailles, a song for Pigalle, all of them. And each one of these sightseeing monuments would be the excuse for another sexual encounter. Sex with adults, but never forced. In fact we talked a lot about this question of force. For me, in the end the only way to do it was to make it done in a very winning way, never adults against the kids. Malcolm quite liked what we came up with, but he also kept asking, 'When do they fuck?' "

Storyboards and lyrics in tow, the team of collaborators now set out to find someone who would interpret their ideas into music. "Malcolm wanted to mix the beginning of a sonata, then add Beethoven for a few measures, then go back to Bach, taking the best of these composers to mix them into a song with the Burundi rhythm behind it," says Grillet. "But we couldn't find anyone to do it. We even went through the phone book to check all the piano teachers in town, calling and saying, very politely, 'Hello, we would like to do this and this, would you accept to play for us and mix Mozart and Beethoven.' " Grillet laughs. "Everybody hung up on us. But then Malcolm meets an American piano student who plays in St. Germain."

McLaren had actually met Eric Watson, a twenty-four-year-old Oberlin jazz pianist and music composition student, several months before, at the dance concert of Watson's girlfriend, one of the founders of Calck Hook Dance Theatre. Typically, at the same time McLaren was working with Grillet and Pietrie, he was also working with Watson (for about $2,500) to see if they could turn the "Eton Boating Song"—"It's jolly boating weather. . . ."—into a rock 'n' roll hit, and when that didn't work, to begin the long process of combining the classics with Burundi drumming *and* rock 'n' roll. "He was in love with the idea of stealing music," remembers Watson, "but in a very sophisticated way, because he knew damned well you can't steal Mozart—that's beyond stealing, it's sacred, it's unsellable. But I don't think he cared. I don't think he cared about anyone's music, including my own."

In July, McLaren began commuting between Paris and London.

Vivienne Westwood says it was she who persuaded McLaren to return to London—"I can't remember what the reason was, but he blamed me for having persuaded him to come back"—but with two collaborations in the offing and others in various states of disarray—and no further speculation of his possible criminal indictment—it must have seemed clear to him that it had already come time to test his ideas in the marketplace. The French music industry, McLaren now knew, was too small to support the kinds of things he wanted to do. In London, he hoped, the money he was after would still be considered relatively little.

At first, he tried to keep a low profile, but he soon found that his name had become tarnished after the Glitterbest trial. For the first time since the Sex Pistols made the headlines, he was having trouble getting appointments with A&R people. After a few leaks to the press about his plans, however, sometime in October, McLaren was finally granted a meeting with Arista Records, where he had previous connections from the Sex Pistols' publishing deal with the company's North American publishing group.

"Arista wanted me to manage a group and I said I wasn't really interested," said McLaren. "They said, 'What do you really want to do?' and I said I had been working in France and making films for £50,000 and I said that's an incredible feat and I'm talking about writing, producing, and editing, just for £50,000 a film. Now the films are soft-core sex pictures, I said, but nevertheless, provided the content may be that much more, provided I put in a load of music, I can offer you the opportunity to make a picture of good music for £50,000, using all the experience I had from these people in France."

Of course, McLaren already had *The Adventures of Melody, Lyric, and Tune* script, but when Arista saw what he meant by "soft-core kiddie pornography" they were aghast. There was no way any entertainment company could ever get behind such an overtly pedophiliac movie; besides, everyone knew you couldn't make a picture on location in Paris with a full musical score for just £50,000. Try it again, said Arista, and we'll give you £10,000 for your next rewrite.

McLaren worked with Westwood on revisions of the script and then returned to Paris to show his latest draft to Pietrie and Grillet. "There was no more sex between kids and adults in his new script," remembers Grillet. "It was sex with kids only now. All the objections I had with the violence in our first work with him now went away because now it was kids fighting—and fucking—kids, and there was no more adults."

The Mile High Club was focused on a group of savage fifteen-year-olds who come upon a small fifty-seat jet tucked away in a wood and decked with pennants reading MILE HIGH CLUB—the name of a legendary society of air-travelers who have made love one mile in the air. Once aboard, the kids go wild, throwing a weird wedding party cum hijack, centered on Lieutenant Lush, the "captain" of the plane, and his sister, Betty. Betty is about to "marry" her friend Louis Quatorze and as her wedding party begins, so does the captain's imaginary plane ride, and he goes wild making announcements as they "fly" over the traditional tourist sights of Paris: "Attention," this counterfeit captain announces. "We're holding at Le Bourget due to congestion of fucking."

The party soon deteriorates into a chaos of teen rituals and rock songs, and before the bride and groom can say "I do," Louis grabs a gun and screams "This is a hijack, take your clothes off!" It's Louis's party now, and he grabs the mike to announce the hijackers' philosophy: "We the Homosexual Apaches condemn the world outside of its filthy way homosexuals are treated and demand that homosexual freedom in schools be given. As well as artists such as Shakespeare, Plato, and Elton John be totally segregated from the rest of heterosexual filth in libraries and museums throughout the world."

As the imaginary flight circles over Paris, waiting for permission to land at Le Bourget, Betty Lush masturbates in the toilet and Louis Quatorze calls the tower with the hijackers' latest demand: The plane must be refueled by a ground crew clad only in swim trunks. In the background, the kids break into the Homosexual Apache theme song—"Give us your vote straight away/ To restore our tribal way/ Ridding us of their company/ Heterosexuality/ U-omo Uomo, U-omo Sex Al Apache/ Bow-wow-wow-wow-wow-wow-wow-wow"—and a long and violent tribunal is held for everyone who won't go along with the Apaches' madness.

Like every project McLaren ever touched—from the Sex Pistols themselves to the screenplays he had collaborated on with Daalder, Meyer, Ebert, Kaplan, Opatoshu, and Temple—*The Mile High Club* had to end on a note of victory over the forces of co-optation. This time, it would be the kids' *real* parents taking over the plane with a real captain and flying off into the sunset. "We want the Mile High Club to be a children's club for sex gang babies to make love," Melody says to her mother, Mary Lush, as the flight takes off for real. "Membership will be based on sex!" demands Tune. "Is it going to be free?" asks another club member. "The best things in life are not free," replies Melody. "It will be sex for fifty p." And as the adult captain announces his name ("Hi! This is Jack!"), Melody, Lyric, and Tune all dance together, bumping radio G-string to radio G-string, buttock to buttock, as the grown-ups reach for their checkbooks.

"Now," McLaren said later, "this was delivered and the record company absolutely loathed it, said it was terrible, just absolutely terrible, and they told me to go away. To tell you the truth, I was really shocked because I thought it was good. It might have needed a rewrite—it was a rough job—but the intention, the core, the idea was good. It was simple and direct. And it was at that time that I met Adam Ant, whose girlfriend was pestering me to work with him. I really wasn't interested but at the end of the day, I was deciding whether to go back to France and carry on and maybe even to make that picture there and raise the money in another way, but I decided to hang on and see Adam. And that's what I did."

From the very beginning, Stuart Leslie Goddard—aka Adam Ant— knew he was going to be a star. Even at Hornsey Art College, back in the days when he was copying the glossy pseudo-sado paintings of Allen Jones and playing bass in the rock revivalist band Bazooka Joe, Adam told his friends he'd be famous. And he worked hard at it.

His career began in 1976 with the same determination and ambition that later helped him make it into the Top 10, and like many punk careers, it began at SEX, soon after Bazooka Joe and the Sex Pistols had their legendary tussle at the latter's first gig.

At first, Adam was afraid of Malcolm McLaren and Vivienne Westwood's shop; shy from the start, he seemed to shiver at the very thought of entering through that graffitoed portal. Only later did it become clear why Adam had such an intense reaction to the place: His crush on Jordan was so extreme that in order not to have to face the object of his affections he would slip love letters through the shop's mailslot before she even got to work. "Adam saw pictures of me in a magazine like *Club International,*" remembers Jordan, who is now more or less Adam's manager. "It was 'Sado-Sex of the 70s' it was, and there was a picture of me dressed up in rubber, and he took Xeroxes off that and used to send them to me with lovely little messages on the bottom. Really cute, really nice."

Before long, Adam and Jordan became best friends, going out for drinks at the local pub and writing songs—one bit of apocrypha goes that Adam once asked Jordan to write the work *fuck* on his back with a razor blade and then passed out cold on the pavement outside the shop—and Jordan soon became a regular part of Adam's band, the Ants.

With Jordan behind him one hundred percent, Adam and the Ants had a following almost from the word go. Adam was SEX-y, clothed his powerful frame in lots of rubber and leather, kohled his eyes till they bled black streaks, and spouted a blue streak about Jean Genet, Lenny Bruce, *The Outsider,* Nietzsche (whom he later admitted to having never read), drug-free living, and the joys of sado-masochism. Articulate and charming offstage, a punk's punk who terrified the music journos with his aggressive orations on fighting the tyranny of the evil adults who ran the record industry, Adam was a terror once he was onstage too, an entertainer's entertainer despite all the punk rhetoric.

While his live act had a frightening headbanging intensity, fusing weird teenage morbidity with high camp horror, in the age of the antistar, Adam's ambitions to conquer the world for what he variously called ANT-MUSIC or SEXMUSIC put off the more radically anticommercial punks. Before long his cult became contained to starry-eyed fourteen-year-old girls and their punk boyfriends who seemed to have daubed the words ANTMUSIC FOR ANTPEOPLE (or sometimes ANTMUSIC FOR SEXPEOPLE) on every wall in London. To the new school of rock critics who were then busy transforming the weekly music papers *(New Musical Express, Melody Maker,* and *Sounds)* into an ideological launch pad for punk politics, this kind of stargazing was more appropriate to the hoary days of rock 'n' roll excess than to punk's purist attack on superstardom, and Adam and the Ants were slagged off as just so much pandering pedophilia. To those who thought he was just an errant careerist, Adam's ironic cameo in Derek Jarman's 1978 punk film *Jubilee*—Adam stared obsessively into a TV set showing his own image while Jordan pranced around him in ballet togs— didn't help.

Adam's ultraloyal teen following was so anxious for a record that there were supposedly some thirty-one bootlegs before the release of his first official LP, but by 1979, after a failed start with Decca Records and one album for Do-It Records—co-managed by the ubiquitous Robin Scott—his career was stalling and he was worried. In true McLarenite fashion, Adam attacked the music press and began looking for new career opportunities, provoking charges that he was a sellout after all. "They don't understand what I'm doing," an infuriated Ant told one writer for *Sounds.* "They haven't got a clue. They don't want punk alive. They want it dead because it scares them too much. They like to get into something else, like mods. Something nice, safe, and pedestrian. As for ANTMUSIC, they haven't got an idea what it's about. This album [his first Do-It release, *Dirk Wears*

White Sox, dedicated to Ant-hero Dirk Bogard] was made for ANTKIDS, people that wanna hear Adam and the Ants. . . . It's the kids that matter, fuck everything else."

Try though he might to convince the music press that he was more than a pose, Adam was still unsuccessful, and in desperation, he turned to McLaren, whom he revered as a master image manipulator. "I was at a party and Malcolm came in and said, 'Hello, Adam, How's the Ants?' I nearly freaked out! The guy's my hero. I've always admired him and he started to talk to me about what I'd been doing. He seemed a great bloke and what he was saying was amazing."

Indeed, McLaren did have some heavy ideas to lay on young Adam: *The Mile High Club,* homosexual Apaches, hilarious tales of his experiences in the world of pornographic film (now embellished to the point that McLaren said he had starred in one as a postman), and of course, tons of talk about the music he had "discovered" in Paris, the heady, heavy sound of Burundi beat. It was stirring stuff and Adam wanted more, dispatching Jordan to send word to McLaren that perhaps they might be able to work together soon. "The man in my opinion is a genius," said Ant, "and he's the only genius I've ever talked to."

McLaren, however, was less convinced of Adam's talent, and for nearly a month, he dithered about how to deal with the handsome punk. "Malcolm felt it wasn't his style to be carrying on with so many things at once," remembers Westwood. "But then he realized that he could give Adam some sort of package that he wouldn't be involved in but would give Adam the ideas he needed."

"I remember talking to Malcolm and trying to convince him to manage Adam," says Jordan. "Finally, they reached an agreement whereby Adam would pay him £1,000 for services, which were just to be advisory, about image, clothes, what he would singing, publicity"—everything but day-to-day managing.

For the first week or two, all seemed to go well. McLaren gave Adam ideas about how to clean up his act, told Adam to leave Do-It Records (he soon did), to shape his songs into tales of teenage sexuality, and Adam obeyed his master's voice, issuing press releases through Do-It about McLaren's masterly direction of the Ants' new video for the song "Car Trouble." Adam's band, however, were at first less adept than their singer at interpreting McLaren's ideas, and McLaren himself was incapable of demonstrating, much less explaining, to them the complex rhythmic structures of African music. But then, McLaren had a flash: Simon Jeffes, string arranger for Sid's version of "My Way" and leader of the acclaimed art band Penguin Cafe Orchestra, was a great fan of ethnic music. Why not have Jeffes teach Adam's band what to play?

"Malcolm came to me with a cassette of quite a few things, a French version of Burundi Black speeded up to 45 rpm's with piano and electric guitar on it; Hank Williams, some quite lateral kinds of things, and asked me to work with Adam's band," says Jeffes. "We sat down in the pub and I dove straight in and told them about the way polyrhythms work in African music. When you're listening to African music, what you're hearing is not *African* music necessarily, but actually a certain kind of rhythm, and I talked to them about the kinds of rhythms there were and how you can approach playing your instruments in a way which breaks away from the usual way you might play a guitar, for instance. They were kids, not professional musicians, but I think they grasped a great deal of what I said."

While Adam's band—Dave Barborossa, Matthew "Maf" Ashman, and Leroy Gorman—not one over the age of twenty—took music lessons from Jeffes, McLaren worked with Adam on his lyrics. "Malcolm decided that if Adam wanted to get anywhere, he was going to have to change his tack when it came to writing and performing," says Lee Gorman. "He said, 'Why don't you let these three musicians write the songs and you just do the lyrics and the singing?' So us cowboys, who had never really written a song in our lives, were given a tape of about fifteen different songs—from Gary Glitter to Hare Krishna, Turkish music, Hank Williams, Burundi drums, everything—and we had to do our own versions of them. He told us just to pick what we wanted and try and come up with whatever we could.

"Well, we did it, and we did it really badly. We just did it like punk rock and it turned out shit. He wanted to sack us. He said, 'You're shit, get out of my sight.' He was terrible. And we just said, sorry, let's have another go at it. So we had another go with that Burundi Black song and we figured out something. He said, 'Hmmm, you do that one best,' so we concentrated on that and built up on it. And suddenly, me and Dave, we found we had this kind of thing: this rhythm thing."

For the Ants, "this rhythm thing" was nothing short of remarkable. Dave "Barbe," the Ants' drummer since June 1977, had a good sense of what this band was supposed to sound like, but Lee Gorman, a funky bass player from the East End, had only just joined the Ants a few weeks before McLaren came on the scene: He hadn't the slightest idea of what playing with Adam and the Ants would be like, and he was frankly baffled by all the talk of polyrhythms and such, even though his funk experience would later prove crucial to establishing the band's sound. With Jeffes's help, the boys discovered an entire range of musical styles they had never known existed until now. Suddenly, Gorman and Barbe looked up and realized they didn't *have* to play at maniac 4/4 time. As long as someone else was looking out for the melody, the backbeat and a steady filler guitar (chikka-chikka) was all they needed. The new sound had arrived, and everyone seemed to hear it. Everyone, that is, except Adam Ant.

"Adam would come in about 3:00 and we'd have to have like two bits of music prepared for him," says the lanky Gorman. "And Adam would work for a while and then Malcolm would come at 4:00 and that would be the real bastard deadline because he'd sit there in judgment, just waiting for us to fuck up."

"You could see there was something snide going on with Adam, but we never realized what Malcolm was like," says Dave Barbe. "He kept saying to Adam, 'Why don't you go off to Earl's Court where you live, boy. 'Ere's some books from the library, go and do some lyrics and let me work with these lads here, and it'll all be hunky-dory when we get together next time,' and Adam would go 'Yeah, whoopee, that's what I'll do.' "

But by now, McLaren had already realized that he had the core of something unique. The Sex Pistols had barely been able to play their instruments in the early days, but these guys were picking it up after only a few sessions, creating a dense stew of Burundi drumming and rock 'n' roll, a monstrous bottom-heavy, beat-heavy sound that was nothing like any other rock 'n' roll band in the world, and certainly nothing like the Sex Pistols—a most important marketing distinction.

Just to confirm his impressions, McLaren invited Dave Fisher, a friend of his who specialized in arranging and engineering pop bands, and Fisher told McLaren exactly what he wanted to know: This was indeed a unique rhythm section—the guitarist was a bit weak—but that singer, Adam Ant, well, he just didn't cut it.

But what could McLaren do with these polyrhythmic pioneers? After all, you couldn't just *take* Adam away from his Ants: The very thought of all the lawyers that might be involved were he to steal the Ants away from Adam was enough to frighten McLaren. On the other hand, it was easy to see that these boys were awestruck with him; even Adam looked to McLaren as a musical guru. Odds were, if the Ants were given just half a chance to break out of Adam's reach, they might go off with their new mentor with nary a word, leaving Adam Antless.

With Adam tethered to McLaren's lyrical leash and the Ants given carte blanche to write their own material, the schism McLaren hoped would open up finally did. With each rehearsal, Adam moved farther and farther from the band, quite literally standing in the corner, while the Ants pushed ever closer to the uncharted musical territory McLaren had laid out for them.

McLaren finally made his move just after the New Year.

"One day Adam went off and Malcolm got me and Dave in the pub," recalls Lee Gorman. " 'Look,' he says, 'we all know Adam is shit. You're gonna throw him out. I'm taking you guys and we're gonna make a new band, and by this time next year, you'll be the biggest thing in England.' We just went 'Fuckin' great, Malcolm! Fuckin' great! Brilliant! Oh, God, we'll be fucking great!' "

"I was Adam's right-hand man till then," says Dave Barbe, "really his henchman, and we used to talk all the time. He used to stay 'round my house and bring all these girls around. But it just seemed to disintegrate when Malcolm gave me the license to do what I wanted. So when he said that Adam's gotta go, I thought, hmmm, shitty job, but I gotta do it. I was so under the euphoria of his personality, I would have gone out and fucking shot someone if he told me."

While McLaren wasn't willing to do the dirty work himself, there was no way he was going to miss the sight of the Ants' firing their leader. Come the day, McLaren sat on a stool at the Ants' Camden Town rehearsal studio, with a screwed-up smile on his face and a cigarette dangling from lips, while the boys gave Adam the bad news. So there would be no mistakes, the whole thing was rehearsed before Adam even arrived.

"Adam, I got something to tell you," said Dave Barbe with a slight grin on his face as the head Ant walked through the door. "I don't want to be in the group anymore."

"Come on?!" Adam said. "You must be joking."

"No, Adam," said Barbe, "really, it's over. We're going with Malcolm."

Adam Ant turned to Lee Gorman. "You too, Lee?"

"Yeah, Adam," mumbled Gorman, "I'm going too."

"So it's just you and me, huh Maf? Just you and me?"

"No, Adam," said the rail-thin Matthew Ashman, glancing at the floor. "I'm with them."

"Adam sort of smiled and sniffed and stopped a bit and then he started crying," remembers Barbe, "and then he goes, 'That's fucking good: sacked by me own band! Well, you can do whatever you like, but no matter what you do I'm keeping the name Adam and the Ants. I'm off.' And he just split, he sulked off. Malcolm went after him and bought him a cup of soup or something, and when he came back he told us he said to Adam that maybe he could be our hairdresser! That was how cruel he could be, and it was undeserved because Adam went on to be a fucking star and made it on his own, and we became Bow Wow Wow"—Barbe giggles—"and look at us."

9
HIS MASTER'S VOICE

The search for meaningful distinction is a central part of the market-
ing effort. If marketing is seminally about anything, it is about achiev-
ing customer-getting distinction by differentiating what you do and
how you operate. All else is derivative of that and only that.
—Theodore Levitt, The Marketing Imagination

Intention, resolution, accident, result: Where does one end and the others begin? With Malcolm McLaren, the thin line distinguishing cause from effect—and confidence games from artistic process—is not easily discovered. Did McLaren *intend* to steal the Ants from Adam? Or was this simply a happy accident, the fortuity of like-minded individuals who happened to come together at a unique moment? Or should we say—as McLaren does—that he merely answered the door when opportunity knocked, that it was the conditions of the moment (rather than the individuals involved) that made the split possible?

McLaren's version of events, of course, conforms to no one else's but his own: not Adam's story and not the story of the band that became Bow Wow Wow. According to McLaren, the problems with Adam began only *at the end* of the four-week period for which he had been hired as Adam's image-meister. "It was at that point the band and Adam had a bit of a to-do," he later said, "and *I* think because the band themselves had never been given the opportunity to write anything. I put them all on an equal level and I didn't realize the politics of how that band was administered."

In fact, had it not been for Granada Television, says McLaren, he might have ended his work with Adam after the allotted working period and that would have been that: In a word, Granada is McLaren's excuse for why he continued working with the Ants after their famous "to-do" with Adam. For in the middle of his Antwork, Granada approached McLaren through documentarian Andy Harries to host a special television program it was preparing titled *An Insider's Guide to the Music Business.* McLaren was at the bottom of Granada's list of potential hosts, but it was curious about what Malcolm McLaren—the man who claimed he had been out to destroy the record business right from the start—might have in mind.

Like most of his more recent schemes for making films, the idea McLaren now cooked up for Granada was brilliant and byzantine, chock-full of the radical mischief of total teen autonomy he had put forward ever since his early days at Let It Rock. Just as he had looked out his window in 1976 and had convinced himself that the average British teenager was champing at the bit for rock 'n' roll that didn't pander to its fans with precious theatrics and rock royalty—and had been lucky that the culture at large happened to be moving in a similar direction as the Sex Pistols—so he now looked out the window of his new Whitechapel flat (he had finally moved out from Vivienne Westwood) and convinced himself that the teenagers of the eighties would soon be champing at the bit for control over their *technology,* specifically the new technology of miniaturized cassette recorders known as the Walkman, introduced by Sony that year.

Typically, McLaren said he got his evidence for this historical change from the kids. He wasn't particularly interested in the trendies who visited Seditionaries, just as he had never really been interested in the Teds who came to Let It Rock, the Bikers who shopped at Too Fast To Live, Too Young To Die, or even the Punks who pushed their way into SEX. If you looked at the kids, the real kids, he said, you couldn't help but see how the new technology was giving them intense pride and power over their lives.

"I was in Wood Green, near to Adam Ant's drummer's house," he later recalled, "and I was in a hamburger bar and I witnessed a guy with one of those huge bazookas, one of those big ghetto blasters, totally unknown to anyone, completely absorbed in putting his cassette into this machine and switching around the dials, and suddenly a guy came over and told him to stop playing music: no music allowed in this particular burger bar, you know? And the guy got up, music still blaring out, and poised this huge machine on his shoulder and just walked out. He was a tall, elegant black man, and he just seemed to me to be oblivious to everybody else. Suddenly, it all came to me for the *Insider's Guide:* Well, that's it, people *are* buying music—actually, records in record shops—but they're not *listening* to music in that way anymore. They don't buy *rec-*

ords and take them home, they *tape* things—from their friends, off the radio, wherever—and they go *out* with it."

If you put together the new and ever-cheaper *hardware* of miniaturized cassette recording with the sharp fiscal scalpel of Mrs. Thatcher's monetarist revolution—Thatcher had been elected prime minister while McLaren was still in Paris the previous May—you had a recipe for kids eventually leading the industry to support a historical change in the way the *software* of cassette technology was being used: Cassettes, thought McLaren, would slowly take the place of records and home taping would ultimately subvert the copyright and royalty process by which record companies make their money. It was (as McLaren intended to say in the Granada program) "Music for LIFE, for FREE!"

"When I got back from France," he said, "the whole ambience of the country looked miserable and everybody looked very insecure, felt insecure. There was an incredible tightening of the screws and Thatcher was making everybody feel bad that they didn't have a job, but this kid was out on roller skates, and he was so bright, and he had this big bazooka, and I thought, my God! This is where the music industry should be—with this guy."

Suddenly, McLaren saw that his work was already cut out for him. If home taping was *piracy*—from the perspective of the British Phonographic Industry (BPI) every blank tape sold meant another record unsold—then the kids were the buccaneers of this new technological revolution: *Kids were the new pirates!* Kings of the Wild Frontier!

Now he just had to convince the kids.

"That weekend," McLaren continued, "I went home and wrote this song, 'C-30, C-60, C-90, Go!' "—the numbers represent the recording playback times of cassettes available in 1981—"and I told the musicians that this was going to be the theme song of this documentary. I gave Granada a rough script, said it's going to be about the ascendancy of the cassette in the world of the record industry, told them I'd rather have a Spike Milligan or a couple of comedians than myself, and that we'd do a whole thing about record stores and home taping, with information about records and cassette players, and a debate between the two, asking a lot of rock stars what they think of their records being taped off the radio. We'll make it controversial, but we'll give you an insider's view, my personal insight into the music business. They went for it, and two weeks later, they didn't go for it anymore," he giggled. "I've had a lot of situations like that, OK?"

In fact, according to Andy Harries, at least one reason the Granada project never got any farther than the "C-30" song was McLaren's notorious inability to get the job done without great controversy. "Granada had done the Sex Pistols on Tony Wilson's *So It Goes* show in 1976," he says, "at a time when the music industry was just crossing over into punk, and Tony Wilson just became infatuated with the Pistols. But the next day after that show, there was a row between the technicians and the producers, and the technicians were fantastically appalled by the show, and had the *So It Goes* sets destroyed the next day." Granada never forgot that incident, and some four years later, it still wasn't ready for another fiasco on that order.

McLaren now had a band without a singer, a script without a producer, and a song without music. And yet through it all, the one thing he did have was a strong *idea,* the idea of rock stars as pirates, thieves, and buccaneers, and he told Westwood to start looking through her history books at the Victoria & Albert Museum costume library to see what she could find on the period of *"les Incroyables et les Merveilleuses"*—a three-year period of post-Revolutionary decadence in France ushered in by Napoleon's wife Josephine in 1795—one of the ideas Grillet and Pietrie had wanted to use in their script.

"Malcolm had the idea that we should be doing something romantic because that seemed to be the feeling around London at the time," says Westwood, "and we took a long time to do it. I did a whole collection of things from around the time of the French Revolution—the 'Incroyables and Merveilleuses' thing he called it—and I gave it a sort of frock coat feeling, but then Malcolm said he wanted it to be more like pirates. He wanted me to go back a couple of hundred years and make it more Three Musketeers. But there was already this feeling on the streets, anyway. We were just picking up on it a little late because Malcolm was in Paris."

Indeed, down at the Blitz, a tacky nightclub/restaurant just off High Holborn, a Tuesday-night-only club had developed among the children of punk who were now fashioning themselves as the style police of the eighties. Over the past year, at Billy's (the predecessor to the Blitz), and at the Blitz itself, Steve Strange, Steve Dagger, Robert Elms, Rusty Egan, Chris Sullivan, and a host of other so-called Blitz-kids had developed an entire range of fashion retreads, substituting studied fashion bricolage for the punks' torn and shredded antifashion style statement. Lots of it was stolen straight from the official David Bowie handbook—on any night, one might find the Pierrot, the Thin White Duke, the Action Man, Ziggy, and scads of post-Jordan makeup jobs—but the kids were all right: They had broken the tyranny of punk stylization and rhetoric and come up with something new, a style revolution that would soon come to be called the "New Romantics." Instead of punk's class-based rants of anarchy in the streets, artifice and the arrogant realpolitik of fame for fame's sake—in a word, *fashion*—now became the order of the day.

Once more, the wheels of style co-optation churned in the McLaren-Westwood camp, and Westwood now began to design the oversized pirate shirts and pants, Napoleonic hats and sashes that would soon be known as the Pirate Look. The timing was impeccable: With the gold foil of a Benson & Hedges cigarette pack wrapped around her front tooth, Westwood's piratic gleam became a fittingly cynical response to the ten-month-long, Hollywood-style romance of Prince Charles and Lady Diana Spencer. Unfortunately for McLaren, he had already given Adam Ant the same lessons he was now giving to Westwood: McLaren and the ex-Ants had accidentally left their rehearsal tapes behind with Adam, and the grapevine now had it that the Ant would soon be performing dressed as a pirate, replete with white geronimo stripe across the face.

"For Adam, what came out of it was, in my mind, the best thing that could have happened for him," says Jordan. "Because whenever Adam's faced a drastic problem like that, he gets going in a big way. And that same night he got sacked, I went 'round to his flat in Earl's Court and we worked up a game plan. 'You've been working on Burundi, right?' I told him. 'Well, get there first!' 'Shall I just let them do it?' he said. 'Or shall I do my version, of how I think it should be done?' And I said, 'You're going to do *your* version the way *you* think it should be done and you're going to start right *now.*' So he called up Marco Pirroni that very night, and they went on to write a brilliant album, *Kings of the Wild Frontier.*

"Adam Ant went through a lot of shit before Malcolm McLaren ever got involved with him," continues Jordan. "He learned about the business and about the hard knocks and about being rejected and playing to just a few people and he *never* gave up. You don't knock someone down like that very easily. You learn to ignore the headlines, no matter how embarrassing they are. Malcolm likes to have a little roster of stuff so he can say 'I invented this, did this, invented that,' but this is one time he didn't get away with it."

With Adam Ant at his back and the potential of a great band staring him in the face, McLaren now set out to get his new group going as quickly as he could.

"Malcolm really started being a heavy then," says Lee Gorman. "Really got under the thumbnail. Every morning we would get wake-up calls at 8:30, 9:00, every half hour, until we were out. After a while we'd be waiting for the call, it was so bad. He'd be going, 'You're shit Gorman! You're *shit* if you can't get your act together. You're wasting my time! I'm a fucking genius and you're wasting my time!' "

Once they were dressed and out of bed, McLaren would meet them at the Centrale, a greasy Italian caff in Soho. "He'd say he'd meet us at 10:00 on the button," remembers Dave Barbe, "and he wouldn't be there till 12:00 and we'd wait, we'd be there like ragamuffins, holes in our shoes, to turn up the guru, the man that was going to save us.

"He'd come in, and first off, he'd tell us about his sex life with Vivienne, which was nil. He'd say what a fucking 'orrible bird she was and how he hated being in bed with her, and we found it very offensive: I blew up sometimes, told him to shut up, 'cause he was so nasty. To us, Vivienne Westwood was a person who designed bondage trousers. We didn't wanna know.

"Then he'd sit there and hold audience with us—and this is for about three months, remember—and we'd be his freewilling listeners. It was like fuckin' recitals, it was. Always the same thing: 'Sex, Style, and Subversion.' 'They're all whores, they all have their price.' 'Never wash your Dirty Linen in public.' 'Don't be precious, Don't compete, and Don't be a grocer—a grocer's a money grabber and he don't spend his money when he have it': Malcolm always believed you should spend money if you've got it.

"And then, there was the big hook. Because what really made us so subservient, so pliable, would be that he'd tell us fucking glorious stories about Jones and Cook and the life they used to lead, all the sexploits and champagne. And he got us in such a way that he'd always compare me and Lee to Jones and Cook, who were sort of like idols to us. He'd say 'You're just like Jones and Cook, you and Gorman.' And that would be the greatest fillip for us, to carry on doing these dirty things."

Indeed, it was only after their rehearsals that McLaren really began to educate the boys in his wicked ways, taking them around Soho and quite literally coercing them into having sex with prostitutes.

"He'd be walking ten paces in front of us," says Dave Barbe, "hands in his lapels with a cigarette hanging from his lips, and we'd be hobbling along behind, trying to keep up with him until he finally got us to these clubs."

"Homosexual Apaches is what he wanted us to be," says Gorman. "He took us to Heaven when it first opened because he wanted us to be gay for a little while—he thought gay bands would be in vogue—and he'd say, 'Come on, boys, I want you to try it, you'd be great as a gay band.' But when he realized that wouldn't work, he said, 'OK: I'm going to make you into a bunch of sexual perverts.' He just took us around and showed us all these little doorways with their models and that, and then he'd say, 'All right, then, here's eight quid, get up there and do the business.'

"So you'd go up there, because he'd have this thing," Gorman says angrily. "You'd have to do what he said or you'd be totally terrified. The power he had over us really was that all three of us really wanted to make this work and we were all terrified of getting thrown out. Because every day he'd say, 'Everyone's expendable, boys—*everyone.*' It's hard to describe his method of, well, not exactly brainwashing, but somehow getting us naughty and in this kind of fighting, spirited mood. He just wanted us all to be real rock 'n' rollers. I was a quiet guy from the East End and he wanted to totally subvert me and make me into some sort of sexual thing, make us all sex-mad. He didn't even like us having girlfriends, mothers, anything like that. He hated 'em. And Dave was married at the time, had a baby too."

Night after night, McLaren took his boys to the Soho sex clubs, threatening them with expulsion if they didn't do his bidding, and nearly every night, the boys complied with their master's demands.

"One of the first times he gave me the eight quid," says Gorman, "I went up there and the whore said, 'Well, have you done this before?' and I took my clothes off, did the business, and I thought, *What* am I doing! I'm fucking this whore just to please Malcolm McLaren! But then again, I got into it, and I enjoyed it, and then we all got into it. One time we found this particular one, a beautiful Italian girl about eighteen, and we all went through her, one after the other, including Malcolm.

"And even after that he still didn't think I was experienced enough, so he took me to meet this art dealer, Robert Fraser, at the Regency Club." (Fraser, who died of AIDS in 1987, was one of Mick Jagger's oldest friends, dating back even before the time he and Jagger were arrested on possession-of-cannabis charges some twenty years earlier.) "He left me with a rather well-known rock star's ex-wife, and says in front of everyone, 'Lee's a nice boy, I want you to take him home and fuck him.' I went, 'Ah, Malcolm, *shut up!*' but Malcolm insisted, and I went home with her. Then he took me to Ronnie Scott's jazz place, and he'd whisper, 'I want you to fuck that woman: You don't fuck her and you're out!' And if you didn't, the next day he'd slag you off and give you a terrible time. He'd make me feel really bad: 'You're no good, you're a wanker, you can't lay that fucking pussy, you're no good.' Over and over, until finally he didn't have to do it no more, 'cause we just became complete slags."

Even with the boys firmly under his thumb, McLaren still had to find a singer who could front his merry band of sex fiends. But now he wanted a girl singer: not another Johnny Rotten or a David Johansen, but a young girl with all the soulfulness of Brenda Lee, the innocence of Little Frankie Lymon, the charisma of the baby Michael Jackson. It was a tall order.

At first, McLaren went direct to the local music community. Among those he considered were Kate Garner, Lizzie Tear, and Kirsty MacColl, and while all three were professional, sexy, and musical, none was soulful or young enough for what he was after. Tiny ads were placed in the back of the music papers, and the boys were sent around to the discos to find the new Miss McLaren, but none of these auditioners seemed to work out either.

Finally, McLaren asked Dave Fisher to help him find a singer, and while Fisher turned up a few faces McLaren thought interesting, no one seemed to interest McLaren as much as a young half-Burmese girl named Myant-Myant Aye Dunn-Lwin whom Fisher met at his local Shamrock dry cleaners on a desolate stretch of West End Lane, just down from the West Hampstead tube and only blocks away from the young girl's house.

Myant—or as she now wanted variously to be called, "Bess Man," "Bess Arabia," "Skid Marks" (in honor of her dry cleaning days), and finally, "Annabella"—in English, her Burmese name means "cool, cool, high"—had just turned fourteen and, according to her mother, she was only working at the cleaner's because her brother Simon, who usually filled in at Shamrock's during holiday season, had gone to university. In fact, Annabella had wanted to work in a local pâtisserie, but her mother refused to let her "because I thought she had such nice skin and a nice little figure and if you eat too many cakes you get fat."

For £8.50 a day, however, Annabella's mother, a registered nurse who had left her husband, an officer of the Burmese Navy, when Annabella was two and a half years old, was willing to let her daughter work at the dry cleaner. The Lwin family—three boys and Annabella—could use every penny of that £8.50 and the bright and cheery Annabella was happy to get out of the house. So happy, in fact, that the day Dave Fisher happened to pass by, the radio was on and she was singing Stevie Wonder's "I Wish," a song she often played on her brother's creaky old music center. Fisher asked Annabella whether she liked singing, and when Annabella shyly nodded that she did, he asked whether she'd be interested in auditioning for a new group. Early the next week, Fisher picked up Annabella (and her friend Alberta) and took them to Tower Bridge Studios to meet the band.

Annabella was amazed by the band's equipment. She'd never even seen a microphone up close before, but when the band played her the only songs they had at the time, "C-30" and two rockabilly numbers, "Wedding Day" and "Cast Iron Arm," she grabbed the mike and belted out the songs. "All these other people had been very inhibited," says Lee Gorman, "but when she got the mike and went 'Where were you on my wedding day?' you could tell she had so much confidence. We were blown away. She was a bit dumpy, just a typical fourteen-year-old schoolgirl, but we thought, Jesus, she's got something. We didn't quite know what: She had this little face and we thought, well, maybe we *can* do something with this. So we told Malcolm about her and Malcolm came down and saw her."

Of course, this is not even close to the story McLaren tells. "I found Annabella in a laundromat," he jabbered to the papers. "I couldn't help noticing what a great voice she had. I asked her what she wanted to do for a living and she told me she wanted to be an airline stewardess or a singer. So I offered her an audition . . . but she wasn't keen. I didn't want her to get away because we had spent months looking for the right girl. We had hung around outside every comprehensive school in North London like dirty old men looking for likely girls and asking them to audition.

"When she turned up at the audition in one of her mother's old blouses which was ten sizes too big, the band thought I was crazy. She was a total closet case. She had never been to a rock concert and only seen *Top of the Pops* twice. She didn't know anything about music but she liked to sing. One look and I knew she was the girl of the eighties. So I went to meet her mother."

And almost immediately the trouble began.

At first, all was cordial. Annabella sang to an Earth, Wind & Fire record on her brother's music center and everyone laughed. But then McLaren brought up the issue of a contract and the discussion froze. "He set up the terms right there," Annabella's mother, Amy Dunn-Lwin, remembers. "A contract for three years and she would be working with this group he kept calling ex-Ants. To me, it was all new and fresh because I didn't know who the Ants even were."

Indeed, at the start, Annabella's mother was more concerned with her daughter's education than the details of her contract. She didn't want her fourteen-year-old daughter to be coming home at all hours of the morning. How would she ever get through school like that?

As Annabella started rehearsing with the new band, however, the answer to that question became quite clear. "If you want to be in a rock 'n' roll band," said McLaren, "then school is out: School is for kids, not for stars." But Annabella wanted to go to school—she said she wanted to be an airline stewardess—and as the band became more and more of a real entity, with rehearsals taking place every day, the pressure grew for her to leave school, to leave home, to leave her friends behind. And when Annabella refused, the band just kicked her out.

And called her back. And kicked her out again.

"After a while," says Dave Barbe, "we realized it weren't working with Annabella. She was just too young. And then Malcolm came up with the magic reason why it wasn't working. The Sixty-Four Thousand Dollar Fucking Judgment: 'She's a fucking virgin ain't she?'"

"Well, what happened was that 'cause Matthew lived 'round the corner in West Hampstead, Malcolm got us all together and then he had us all draw straws in the Wimpy Bar, and Matthew got the short straw. . . . So Maf got the job, poor sod, and we said, 'All right, Maf, off you go,' and we gave him twenty quid."

"The girl was driving us all crazy," McLaren later explained to the *Sun*. "She couldn't decide if she wanted to stick with the band and become a star. I wanted to find some way to make her commit herself to the group. I thought it might help if the guys in the band flattered her and tried to fancy her. So I gave one of them some money and ordered him to seduce her. I made him get up early and wait outside her school gates and get her to play truant. He tried everything. He got himself drunk. He got her drunk. He took her to the movies. Annabella was having a lovely time but still she couldn't decide whether she really wanted to be a singer with the band or become an air stewardess and see the world that way."

Dave Barbe: "Eventually he got her back to his place, this shitty room full of stacked sodden newspapers in the corner, a rancid old bed in a squat. He really loved his bird Gabby, Maf did, but he had to do the job. He started kissing her, but she wouldn't do nothing: she was fourteen years old. But finally she decided to have a go at it. . . ."

McLaren: "Then suddenly, she began whistling . . ."
Barbe: "The fucking 'Marseillaise' . . ."
McLaren: "And at that the poor guy just lost his sex drive."

"Malcolm enjoyed being perverse," says Lee Gorman. "We used to sit up with him in this pokey hole he had in Whitechapel at four or five in the morning, and he used to say there was nothing wrong with being perverted. 'Evil is better than good,' he'd say. 'More exciting than good.' I'd say, 'What? Is it exciting people getting murdered and children having their heads ripped off?' And he'd always come back to the same point: 'Evil is not evil. Evil is only evil by definition, and that doesn't mean you can't make it good; and if it's good, that doesn't necessarily make it unexciting.' "

In some ways, the so-called seduction of Annabella did just the job McLaren expected it to. Annabella was so embarrassed by the snickering, jibing, and poking of her band mates, she simply had to stick with the boys. Besides, McLaren now arranged for Annabella to take her lessons from a tutor and Annabella's mother was slowly coming around, finally giving the girl more freedom to come and go as she pleased. At the ripe young age of fourteen, Annabella was already being considered an adult: Whether she liked it or not, she was now committed to the band, body and soul.

And yet in other ways, the most obvious ways, Annabella's seduction was a failure. "In her subconscious grew this festering hatred for me, Lee, Maf, and Malcolm McLaren," says Dave Barbe. "There was a spark, and from that point on it was all uphill. We couldn't get her to do *nothing*. We knew she was right [for the group]. It was just hard to get it out."

Indeed, nothing came easy to the new band: It was a hard slog twenty-four hours a day. Despite Amy Dunn-Lwin's promises that she wouldn't intervene in her daughter's career, the girl's mother never trusted McLaren or the band members and she now determined that the screws had to be tightened even further on Annabella's work with the band, insisting that Annabella have chaperons wherever she went and that her tutor file weekly reports to the Inner London Education Authority. McLaren was furious with this interference and he and Amy Dunn-Lwin fought like cat and dog. But Annabella's mother refused to back down. If McLaren wanted Annabella in the band, this was the price he was required to pay.

To add to this misery, the first recording sessions with Dave Fisher in late April—still supported only by McLaren's own money—were a disaster, not dissimilar to Dave Goodman's early sessions with the Sex Pistols. And it was no better when the band went back into the studio one month later to record with Simon Jeffes—their repertoire now expanded to "C-30," "Giant Sized Baby Thing," "Homo Sex Al Apache," "Sun, Sea & Piracy," and a few rockabilly numbers. McLaren raised hell in the studio, lambasting Matthew Ashman in front of the other boys. "He'd get Matthew up," says Gorman, "and say, 'Lee, show him how to play the bleeding guitar,' and I'd *have* to play it even though I knew I'd be humiliating Maf."

Nor did McLaren let up when the sessions were over. Annabella's brassy belting, he now decided, was fine for recording the occasional demo, but he was convinced her voice wasn't strong enough for the real thing—on one song, Annabella spent six days trying to sing one line the way he wanted her to—and after a cruel tongue-lashing, he threw the girl out of the group, sending the boys onto the streets to search for a replacement while Annabella was still at the studio. "We literally stood on the corner outside Morgan's Studio in Willesden, this real heavy black area, waiting as people were passing, getting on buses, asking 'em to come in and sing the song," says Lee Gorman. "But by the end of the week we decided that we couldn't find anyone that could even match Annabella, so Malcolm decided to try to sell the tapes around the companies just as they were."

This time, McLaren had a new sales strategy. No more double-dealing and cheating: This time, he planned simply to march into the A&R offices, acetate in hand, and force the head A&R man to make an on-the-spot decision. Here's the new group: Love 'em or leave 'em.

"I went round to every record company and I couldn't even get in the door," he said. "It was paranoia everywhere. I went to Warner Brothers, they said, 'We don't care if you've got the Beatles, don't come here!' That was it *everywhere*. Of course, it was all from the Sex Pistols, but I was amazed it still existed in 1980.

"Finally, I went to a little record company called United Artists and they said, 'Sorry, we can't sign you.' But a friend of mine there from the days when EMI still had the Sex Pistols said, 'You know we're being taken over by EMI, why don't you go and talk to Terry Slater.' Terry Slater? 'Yeah, you remember Terry Slater, he was in charge of the Sex Pistols' publishing at EMI, the guy who defended you to the last.' I said, 'Oh, really,' and I walked up to Manchester Square. And as I was walking in, I thought to myself, only play this tape *once* because it's your last shot. Because if they discover what's in the lyric, there's no way they're going to bring this record out: One thing I've noticed with A&R people—they don't listen to lyrics, they just listen to the beat and if the beat and the sound is good, that's as far as it goes.

"So I came into Terry's office, and he had just got this job and was moving furniture and getting all his bits together, and I said, 'Look, drop everything you're doing because I've got a hot record here and you're going to love it. Now, listen to this: You've got *one* shot at it. A lot of people are interested, but I'm coming to you because *you're my man*—I just heard you got this job, and I think this'll be terrific for starting your new career.' So he drops everything and we play the record. And he said, 'Well, I think it's good, but of course we've got to bring everybody else in to make a decision on this. Can you leave this with me for a few days?' And I said, 'I'll leave it with you for *half an hour* and then I'm coming back, and you've got to make a decision then because otherwise I go around the corner to Chrysalis, because I want to sign this record *today.*' So I went around the corner for a cup of tea, and in half an hour I was back, and he said, 'Malcolm, as long as it's not a lot of money, you've got a deal.' So I said OK, rang up my lawyer, and we signed that deal in three or four hours."

Those who knew McLaren only as a rock 'n' roll manager were astonished by his next move. With EMI's £50,000 advance (for one single!) jingling in his pocket, McLaren now had the gall—and the capital—to send the unknown ex-Ants to harden themselves on a three-week road trip—supposedly to southern France, Spain, Italy, and Greece but actually to the north of England—while he and Westwood refitted 430 King's Road for the new buccaneer gear he hoped this piratical rock 'n' roll would bring to the fore.

Compared to the postapocalyptic minimalism of Seditionaries, the new shop design by McLaren and David Connor was a radical departure. Battered pine floors slanted awkwardly like a galleon's deck down to a gray-shingled Georgian window and crooked steps on the street forced a fun-house sense of scale, while a large gilt-edged clock with its hands whirling furiously counterclockwise further exaggerated the funky surrealism of the place. When the aptly named Worlds End [*sic*] opened that fall, it gave a surprising boost to the career of McLaren's new band, which were now struggling in the boonies of northern England—the real world's end as far as McLaren was concerned.

But what did the band know? McLaren had barked, and they had heeded his call. And indeed, from now on the band was to be named Bow Wow Wow, in honor, said McLaren, of the famous trademark of Nipper, the dog whose mournful face, gazing into the horn of an ancient gramophone player, is known world over—with one exception—as the trademark of the RCA Corporation. That one exception, of course, is the United Kingdom, where Nipper's carefully controlled trademark is owned by HMV (His Master's Voice) Ltd, a giant retail record chain owned, as nearly everyone in the U.K. knows, by none other than EMI.

In his masterful pamphlet *The Eighteenth Brumaire of Napoleon Bonaparte,* Karl Marx writes that all "great, world-historical facts and personages occur, as it were, twice . . . the first time as tragedy, the second as farce": and so it would seem with Malcolm McLaren and EMI.

Signing Bow Wow Wow was a calculated risk for EMI. Once the market leader in popular music in Britain—a position held since 1954 when it sold its radio and phonograph manufacturing plants to Thorn and then made millions through the success of the Beatles and the Rolling Stones—by 1979, EMI had gotten into trouble and was ironically acquired by that very same Thorn. As Simon Frith notes in his seminal book of rock sociology, *Sound Effects,* "Thorn-EMI is a leisure company for the 1980s, a combination for the video age: Thorn makes and distributes the hardware, EMI will make and distribute the software."

McLaren liked to claim that the reason EMI had failed to stay independent in the late seventies was because it had let the Sex Pistols go and that the company had signed Bow Wow Wow to restore its rock 'n' roll credibility by hiring back the very man who had first taken them to the edge of success with punk rock. But the truth seems to have been much more mundane than that: With its new corporate overlords in place, EMI desperately needed fresh product to prove it was out of its slump, and McLaren's charming sales talk of Bow Wow Wow's gold-dusted sartorial splendor seemed well suited to the new Thorn-EMI marriage. For once, McLaren had pegged the A&R boys right: All those images of pirates and buccaneers spelled Video Gold, and whatever misgivings there may have been about dealing again with McLaren were dispelled by the glimmer of Bow Wow Wow's potential bounty.

Still, in the interests of both parties, it was decided that Bow Wow Wow would be committed only to a one-year contract (with options for additional songs) with EMI. Everyone benefited from the way this deal was constructed: EMI got some leverage against the (likely) prospect McLaren would attempt to make fools of them this second time around, and McLaren got some much needed maneuvering room to protect himself in case the band did get into trouble with the label. (For McLaren, there was also the additional advantage of a heavily frontloaded deal: £50,000 for one single, and additional, less-expensive options to be taken up if EMI felt continued interest in his product.)

Needless to say, the shit hit the fan as soon as the ink was dry. To start, while the A&R, promotions, and marketing departments loved the rap McLaren was giving them about home taping, kiddie piracy, and the buccaneers of the future, the executives upstairs were, as McLaren said, "shaking by the knees." They had signed Bow Wow Wow because McLaren's gibes about the record industry seemed rather cute, especially when mouthed by a fourteen-year-old Burmese girl: "Everyday I get a brand-new show/ off the TV, records, and radio/ I breeze with the sleaze on my new cassette/ I don't buy records in your shop/ I tape 'em all/ I'm *Top of the Pops*/ C-30 C-60 C-90 GO!" But when EMI released "C-30" in early July as a 45 (b/w "Sun, Sea & Piracy"), and then announced it would be releasing the two tracks as a ten-minute cassette in August—the first so-called cassingle—the BPI did not find it quite so amusing, and an official complaint was registered with EMI.

In fact, EMI had simply not realized what "C-30" 's lyrics were about: The execs had misread one lyric—"Policeman stopped me in my tracks/ said hey you can't tape that/ you're under arrest/ 'cos it's illegal"—as an *anti*piracy message. Fortunately for McLaren, EMI stuck to its guns even after it realized its mistake, and the company's new managing director, Cliff Busby, wrote the BPI that as the "band's signing took place before my appointment, any action I could take would only create more publicity than has already taken place and would not serve any useful purpose."

McLaren had a field day with the press over this one. "BPI says home taping costs the industry £228 million a year in lost revenue," he told the *Daily Star,* "so they're not happy that Bow Wow Wow have already reached No. 25 in the singles chart. . . . In fact, it's the classic story of the 80's. It's about a girl who finds it cheaper and easier to tape her favorite discs off the radio. The tape cassette is a liberating force, which is why the record companies are so petrified. Not only does it allow you to spend your money freely—going to clubs, having drinks or whatever—it also allows you to listen to music *anywhere:* a cassette recorder can be carried around. Taping has produced a new lifestyle. Look around: Kids are finding punk, ska or heavy metal clothes irrelevant. Soon they'll want their clothes to match their cassette machines. . . . Kids want their imaginations ignited and I think Bow Wow Wow's record is doing just that."

Or so McLaren thought, for in reality, "C-30" barely even made it into the Top 50, much less the Top 10.

"We were sure it was going to go up to about twenty or twenty-five," says Lee Gorman, "and it stayed at forty-seven for two weeks. We realized something was up—and this is without Malcolm's intervention. So we tried to find out what was going on, because we found out it had sold more than another record that had gone up. Then this guy from EMI told us that it had been pulled from the charts because it was subversive, antiestablishment, promoting home taping, and the BPI protested. It turns out all these Freemasons got together and put pressure on the BPI to send a letter to the managing director of EMI. It was a fuckin' conspiracy. Malcolm found out and got a copy of the letter the BPI had sent, but he lost it, so we had no bloody proof."

There was no conspiracy, as McLaren knew all too well. "C-30" was simply too sophisticated for the young record buyers McLaren wanted to reach and too obviously hyped for those consumers old enough to remember who the Sex Pistols were. Nor was the single's advance up the charts helped any by the nearly simultaneous release of Adam Ant's first post-McLaren single, "Kings of the Wild Frontiers," featuring the pirate-clad Adam Ant. As far as the Bow Wow Wows could see, their record had been squashed without a chance in hell of making it, and they were angry. What can we do about it? they asked McLaren, and their leader told them that the only thing they really could do was to go up to EMI themselves and complain, to make right nuisances of themselves until EMI gave in. That's the way the Sex Pistols would have done it, he said.

"We went to see Cliff Busby," says Gorman, "and all four of us, even Annabella, confronted him and gave him a real hard time for about an hour. We smashed up his office, scared him real bad. Especially Maf: He picked up all the gold records off the wall and flung 'em around. Even Annabella picked up a clock and threw it out the window. Even Annabella! It seemed like Busby had a mild heart attack. Busby had to get out. He was shaking and holding his chest and we were screaming, 'You bastard, that was our first ever record we'd made and you fucked it up just because of your stupid business ideas.'

"Malcolm was outside waiting, watching with a cigarette falling from his lips. And then just as we were about to go outside, Malcolm said to us, 'Throw that ashtray through the window'—it was one of them tall round ones—and Dave threw it in front of all these security guards and they did nothing."

"I did do it," says Barbe. "Malcolm would never do nothing like that. But he *was* waiting there with a photographer from the *Evening Standard.*"

Even if Bow Wow Wow wasn't yet a hit with the kids—a major disappointment even by their manager's standards—McLaren was delighted he had hit a nerve in the industry. To the BPI, home taping represented not only an economic, but also an *ideological* threat: If kids were encouraged to reproduce their favorite records on tape without paying royalties to artists and record companies for the original compositions and performances on those records, there would be fewer and fewer reasons for artists to make records. Take away copyright controls, went the BPI's argument, and you take away the fundamental legal protections that make creativity and originality profitable enterprises in capitalist society. There was no telling where things would go once the kids went down *that* slippery slope.

EMI, on the other hand, wasn't really all that upset by the cassingle brouhaha. After all, "C-30" was only a single, and since Thorn-EMI was in the business of selling (and manufacturing) both records and prerecorded *and* blank tapes as well as the equipment for them to be played and recorded on, McLaren's home taping hype really couldn't hurt it. Far from having been scared off by the attack on Busby, EMI even threatened to pull out of the BPI in support of its new group. Perhaps the company figured that Bow Wow Wow might even help spur new sales in prerecorded cassettes. Let McLaren hype his band's lyrics all he wanted, said the EMI bosses; in the end, EMI would only profit from the massive publicity he had given to cassettes, which were still a relatively novel format in 1980.

While the sales figures on "C-30" were disappointingly low, the cassingle rumpus proved at the very least that Bow Wow Wow would be useful for promoting cassettes, and to McLaren's surprise, EMI now exercised its first option on the band, paying his management company, Moulin Rouge Ltd, an additional £20,000 for which the band was to come up with some twelve new songs—songs that McLaren said Bow Wow Wow already had. In fact, only four songs had been written by the time the band entered Abbey Road studios in early September, and McLaren put tremendous pressure on the boys to write new material and record at the same time. That might have been no big deal for an experienced rock 'n' roll group, but with their manager constantly lashing out and scapegoating them— McLaren often banished Matthew Ashman to a tiny Abbey Road practice room to work on his guitar parts "until you can play the fucking thing right"—Bow Wow Wow found it virtually impossible to concentrate on making music. Inevitably, the recording sessions took longer than expected, only adding to the jangled nerves of the EMI executives who were anxiously awaiting the new Bow Wow Wow album.

What album? barked McLaren, pressing EMI to release the band's first long-play project in cassette format *only*. But EMI were loath to spend so much money promoting a new band without a vinyl product, regardless of their interest in advancing the progress of prerecorded tapes. How many kids actually owned cassette recorders, anyway? McLaren didn't care. After his rout at John Lydon's hands, his credibility as a politically minded rock 'n' roll manager had taken a beating, and he refused to be budged on this issue.

McLaren actually had his own doubts about the cassette-only format. Considering that Bow Wow Wow's first product was to be released at nearly the same moment as Julien Temple's *Great Rock 'n' Roll Swindle*—with McLaren now the star of the show, but hardly to be seen in the movie's credits—this born marketeer was concerned that audiences would fail to perceive the substantive contrasts between Bow Wow Wow's uplifting, multinational message of teenage liberation and the Sex Pistols' nihilistic abandon. At first, McLaren thought that he would clear the air by writing his own biography and he even began dictating his memoirs, tentatively titled *The Great Jewish Bastard,* to journalist Barry Cain. But then he came up with the idea of producing *Chicken* magazine, a small staple-bound kiddie-porn rag on top of which he hoped to glue Bow Wow Wow's new album-length cassette. If you put the cassette in a little corner of a record shop, said McLaren, it would simply disappear, but pasted on top of *Chicken* there was no telling who the new band would reach.

"Malcolm wanted us to be the reporters for this magazine he wanted to do," says Lee Gorman. "The idea was to take this £1.99 cassette and glue it to the cover. We would be the reporters and we each had different jobs. Mine was to go 'round all the whores and to write a story about going to a whore: what you do, what you pay, what the best streets are for whoring. All that. And I did it, fucking wrote it, and handed it in. And he got some other guy to write about technology, all the video games that were coming out, all the new hi-fi's and Walkmen. He wanted young kids of fourteen or fifteen to go to whores, lose their virginity, and play with video games. Be on roller skates. Be cool and don't work. 'Demolition of the work ethic,' he said, 'that's what it's all about.' "

To handle the production of this new magazine, McLaren hired his old friend Fred Vermorel to be the editor and asked Brian Clarke, a British artist better known for his massive stained-glass projects, to design. "I saw the opportunity to launch an antidote to *Smash Hits* and committed myself and my publishing company to the venture," Vermorel later wrote in a scathing article for *Sounds*. "But here for the first time, I saw a new Malcolm McLaren. Someone who seemed concerned to hurt people and quite unconcerned with their feelings and integrity. Who was a greedy person: greedy for power, acclaim and success. Who was casual about people getting injured or even dying."

With Vermorel generating copy and sorting out a dummy layout with Clarke, McLaren and Westwood began to work with photographer Andy Earle (also Clarke's assistant) on the new mag's pictorials.

"First one," says Dave Barbe, "[Malcolm] got me down in rehearsal room, took all me clothes off, and covered me in this oil. Then they made me play soccer—kick the ball, jump, get high kicks, all that."

"I had to be a 'Homosexual Apache,' " says Gorman. "I was in the library of EMI Records with all the famous Beatles tapes locked in this cage, with a load of dogs. I had to pose with me bum in the air and me shirt off and a white line across me face and all this brown stuff all over me. Supposedly, that was an Indian.

"It was sick, really sick, but then it got a lot worse. 'Cause we didn't mind that: That seemed like fun. But then he said he thought *kids* should be having sex, and he started doing these photo sessions with a seven-year-old Indian boy and this little nine-year-old girl with makeup on."

What happened next is anyone's guess, but news stories later reported that the parents of the little girl were apparently shocked when McLaren started having the kids photographed with the band members in overtly sexual poses in Robert Fraser's flat (ironically, on Cecil Beaton's old bed). Details were sketchy—one report said that "the nine-year-old girl was reduced to tears as she lay in bed, partly undressed"—but one photo that was later released showed a dour looking Lee Gorman wearing a "radio G-string"—two chains with a radio over his genitals—while a little Indian boy wearing bikini underwear sat atop his shoulders. While the photos themselves may have been more provocative than pornographic—until the ensuing brouhaha, noted BBC producer Alan Yentob (now director of BBC 2) and director Robin Denselow were filming the progress of McLaren's latest project for the BBC-TV show, *Arena*—Fred Vermorel was outraged at what he considered the harassment of the little girl, and he threatened to take McLaren to the police if he didn't stop this nonsense immediately. Eventually, Vermorel leaked word of the sessions to one of the tabloids (and called Amy Dunn-Lwin to explain what kind of filth her daughter was involved with), and before one could even say the word *chicken,* the Special Branch of the Metropolitan Police were swarming all over Bow Wow Wow.

"Fred came to a point where he said, 'You've gone too far, Malcolm,' and we did as well," says Gorman. "Malcolm went completely crazy. He wanted me to chat Fred up, try to get him to come 'round again, and once Malcolm came with me to Fred's place and they had a fight on the doorstep. Vermorel was saying, 'You're just a dirty old pervert, McLaren! Get away from me!' He used to force the issue with us too by saying, 'Look, if two fourteen-year-old girls want to have it off, why shouldn't they?' That seemed logical, but what he was really trying to say was that older men should be able to get seven-year-old girls into bed if they want to."

"He really hated us for blowing that out, but we had to, because we knew it was intrinsically wrong," says Dave Barbe. "I mean, I had a kid and a wife, I knew what it was about. We weren't intellectual about it, but we knew our gut feelings. The man's a fucking voyeur."

Remarkably, McLaren got away unscathed. He may have lost one of his oldest friends, lost a great chance to be the subject of a BBC documentary, lost the respect of many at EMI, but he was unbothered by the whole experience except insofar as it may have affected his plans to distribute the Bow Wow Wow cassette through newsstands. Indeed, even a year after *Chicken,* McLaren still didn't see what all the fuss was about. "Pornography is just a summary of society as it is" he told *ZG*'s Krystina Kitsis. "That's the bathroom of its brain, and from a perverted point of view, it can be the laughter of a great brain. You can use it so well because it typifies so much and is something that aggravates so many. It's something that is such a taboo and yet it can be so amusing."

If his *Chicken* did not hatch, McLaren still had his way with EMI, and in November 1980, the first Bow Wow Wow longplayer, *Your Cassette Pet,* was released in cassette format, and cassette format *alone.* Sold for £1.99 in a specially designed flip-top paper box replete with piratical design—clever promos were issued sealed in a tin can marked "DOG FOOD: A Bow Wow Wow Can: Hot Tropical Sounds From Madagascar"—*Your Cassette Pet* stalled in the charts at number fifty-eight and then died, despite the presence of several songs with obvious pizzazz, all clearly snatched from McLaren's *Mile High Club* porn-movie plans: "Sexy Eiffel Towers," "Louis Quatorze," and a neat rendition of the Johnny Mercer classic, "Fools Rush In."

McLaren had finally got his sound, and for the first time since Bow Wow Wow was formed, he let the group celebrate by arranging for EMI to finance their U.K. performance debut, to be held later that week at the

Starlight Roller Disco, home of the new cassette mobility. Like most of McLaren's more inventive plans, however, this gig proved impossible to execute, for when Bow Wow Wow set up to play, the roller disco's stage became a veritable electrical Fourth of July and the resulting show was canceled. Annabella's mother, dressed to kill in a fur coat and Dolly Parton cowboy boots, was sure McLaren had planned the colorful firework's display on purpose.

For both McLaren and Bow Wow Wow, the aborted Starlight gig only added to the disappointment caused by the failure of *Your Cassette Pet* in the charts. Explanations abounded for the cassette's failure—no dance floor action since most clubs weren't equipped to play cassettes and no airplay since the audio quality of cassette tape fell far below the minimum standards for broadcast-quality sound—but McLaren typically shifted the blame to other parties and held fast to his latest conspiracy theories. According to McLaren, the BPI had sent a new protest letter to EMI saying that *Your Cassette Pet* didn't qualify for the album charts because it wasn't vinyl; as a result EMI had stopped production of the cassette. EMI, of course, told a different story: Since *Your Cassette Pet* was too cheap for the album charts and too dear for the singles charts, many of the record shops that sold the cassette didn't know where to list its sales: Was it an album or a single? Quite possibly, *Your Cassette Pet* had done better than EMI had heard, but that was no reason to step up production.

McLaren was incensed that EMI had fed him what he considered such an obvious cock-and-bull story and he now began shopping the *Cassette Pet* material to other labels, hoping that someone would buy the material off EMI, if only for a more traditional record release. For its part, EMI wasn't yet willing to part with Bow Wow Wow although Arista Records seemed interested in making a deal. If Bow Wow Wow wanted to leave EMI, McLaren was told, they first had to complete their contractual obligations: twelve songs and nothing less. (To date, the group had recorded only ten songs.) As to McLaren's claim that EMI was worried about the BPI, EMI responded that it no longer cared whether anyone construed *Your Cassette Pet* as being propiracy. Indeed, if Malcolm McLaren could have taken off his rose-tinted spectacles for only a moment, he might have seen that the tape was a significant *blow* to the dreams of home tapers. How many kids actually owned the *two* tape recorders that would be needed to copy *Your Cassette Pet* from one tape to another? As far as EMI was concerned, Malcolm McLaren's subversive rhetoric had just chased itself up the ass.

McLaren took no notice; piratically speaking, he was bound to get Bow Wow Wow off EMI Records by hook or by crook. This time, he played it by the book, sending the Bow Wow Wows back to the studio to fulfill the terms of their agreement by recording "W.O.R.K.," a clever contrivance of Burundi disco cheerleading he hoped kids would take as a new rallying cry against the tyranny of labor: "T.E.K. Technology/ is de-molition of Daddy/ is A.U.T. Autonomy/ 'cos work/ is not the golden rule." However, not even this morsel of tasty hook-filled pop made it out of the cellar, despite a glistening, echo-laden production job by former Cliff Richard sound man Alan Tarney. Released in seven-inch, twelve-inch and cassette formats, "W.O.R.K." started at number sixty-two in the charts and sank from there.

Nor were matters helped any by the sudden reappearance of Stephane Pietrie and Pierre Grillet, the two French writers McLaren had worked with in Paris. They had heard about the release of Bow Wow Wow's first major effort and now they wanted their royalties from the eight songs they wrote with McLaren, registered at SACEM, the French Performing Rights Society. "At the beginning we spoke to a lawyer about it," says Pietrie, "but it just got too ridiculous. We told the papers, we saw Malcolm, we took another agreement with Malcolm on 'Cowboy' [not released until late in 1982], and at the end of the day, it was a tough period. For myself, I don't trust him anymore on copyrights. All the time an idea is the property of an author, but legally the author is defined as the person who was able to formulate the idea *completely,* to take the idea to completion and sell it. Now I know: With Malcolm, incomplete information—an idea—has no *valeur,* no price, it's nothing."

With nearly six months still to go on Bow Wow Wow's EMI contract, and nearly all his gambits used up—the last part of the swindle always was a mess—McLaren was stumped by the lackluster response to Bow Wow Wow's records. Some said the problem lay precisely in McLaren's overly obvious manipulation of the band. How could anyone believe this weird pantomime of a fourteen-year-old girl singing about having an orgasm on the Eiffel Tower: "I feel sexy up so high/ feel my treasure chest/ Let's have sex before I die/ be my special guest" ("Sexy Eiffel Tower"). Teenage autonomy? Not around Malcolm McLaren. "I know everyone thinks it was Malcolm's idea to get a sexual kind of turn on," Annabella told *The Face,* "because I was breathing like having orgasms or something, but the actual thing is that I was supposed to be falling off the Eiffel Tower. . . . It makes me happy when I sing it. I get a real happy feeling 'cos I imagine how I'm falling. The words express things, but they're just words to songs. You don't have to take it dead serious. I don't think, 'Oh, God, it's disgusting!' It's not like that—it's meant to be fun."

All too typically, McLaren failed (or simply refused) to hear the growing chorus of critical music media and industry voices sniggering that Bow Wow Wow's failure was no one's fault but his own. Indeed, the more McLaren thought about it—if ever he truly thought about it at all—the more he came to believe that the reason for Bow Wow Wow's lack of success was not him, but Annabella, and he now contrived to push her out of the band once and for all.

Of course, getting rid of Annabella was not exactly a new idea: The young girl had already been tossed out of the band and retrieved so many times that she had become used to the cruel cycle of McLaren's reign of management by terror. What made this time different, however, was that McLaren had finally decided to allow Bow Wow Wow to go on its first U.K. tour starting in late February 1981, and to buttress Annabella's weak voice, he began looking for new backup singers.

For once, one came readily to mind. His name was George O'Dowd, and McLaren had met him one night while George was working as a DJ at the Planets disco where George's friend Philip Sallon had his own club on Thursday nights. At the time, McLaren dismissed George as just another one of those queer futurists from Blitz-land who aimed for nothing more than their requisite fifteen minutes of fame: his competitors. But when it came to dress, George O'Dowd *did* have a certain odd panache. With his face covered in weird greasepaints, his long, black, plaited wigs reaching down to his knees, and his costume changing nightly from Carmen Miranda to Mary Magdalen, George was hard to miss—his photo often appeared in the tabloids—but McLaren took little notice when the stilleto-heeled boy (he was only twenty) with the bird-covered straw hat waltzed over and drunkenly inquired whether (as he had heard) Bow Wow Wow needed a new singer.

"Whenever Malcolm ever does anything," says the singer who was soon to become known as Boy George, "there's always a rumor for months and one wonders whether he will get it off the ground. So that night, I was incredibly drunk and I was walking up the stairs, and I went up to him and said, 'Hi, I'd like to be in your band. Have you found your singer yet?' And he laughed. 'Not yet, no.' I said, 'Can I audition?' He laughed again and said, 'Yeah, yeah, yeah. We'll be doing this big gig in a few months at the Rainbow and we'll have all these jazz bands and a fairground set in the hall and we'll have all these jazz singers. You can sing with one of them as support.' You see," says George, "I was into jazz in those days—I dressed like Pearl Bailey. Anyway, he told me he would get back to me in a few months' time, and then he disappeared, and in the meantime, I forgot about the whole idea."

Over the next few months, George slowly moved closer to the inner circle surrounding Bow Wow Wow through several different networks of friends that came to travel together. George already knew Matthew Ashman through his girlfriend Gabby who worked at Peter Benison's modeling agency where George made extra money modeling as a "youth type," and by the time George next came in direct contact with the Bow Wow Wow crowd, he had moved into the Goodge Street squat of his friend Mad Jean, a costume designer who had occasionally worked as seamstress for Vivienne Westwood. (Later, her boyfriend, playwright Jonathan Gems, would have a relationship with Jordan and write screenplays for McLaren.)

Another connection to McLaren that was mostly unknown at the time was through McLaren's new girlfriend, Andrea Linz, an eighteen-year-old mulatto German model who had become acquainted with George's fashion friends. McLaren had started dating Andrea just before the Abbey Road sessions, and as Lee Gorman remembers, for a while, he was utterly infatuated with her. "When we were in Abbey Road, he'd go on and on about his bloody sex life," recalls Gorman. "Everyday he'd tell us about this half-caste bird he was fucking, and he'd say, 'She's a German *shvartze*, a German *shvartze,* can you believe it!' We'd be in the studio working all day and he'd say, 'But she wants to go to the clubs every night! I've got to fuck her and then I've got to come here. I'm worn out I tell you, I can't take it!' "

One night there was a party at Mad Jean's Goodge Street squat, and as it wound down, about 4:00 in the morning, Matthew Ashman grabbed an acoustic guitar and started to sing. George joined in, and while the heavens did not exactly open up before them, Ashman told George he had a lovely voice and invited him to audition, warning him that, as George tells it, "the two other guys were Young Men of Heterosexuality and that I should be wary of them when I did come to the studio. 'Too far gone straight,' he said. 'Popeye complex.'

"About four days later," George says, spilling out his story as fast as his tongue can travel, "I took a bus from my little squat and I went to this studio down in Kennington. I had plaited all my hair and put little bells in it and had done the whole works. I was one of these people for any occasion: I could work bar mitzvahs, weddings, you name it. I'd gone along all dressed up in chains and skirts, and the two heteros were just standing there, really hostile, although Matthew was fine. He was great.

"They were playing and they were brilliant musicians. I couldn't believe how brilliant they were, especially the drummer. So they gave me the words to 'W.O.R.K.' and said I had twenty minutes to learn the song. I was so freaked out, but then we did some other ones. We did 'Cast Iron Arm' and one or two others. But the two guys hated me. They were totally intimidated by my personality. British bulldogs. *I* snapped out of it and got my personality back and was myself but *they* couldn't cope with it because they didn't have much personality between the two of them. So I left around 7:00 and walked home because I didn't have any money for the bus and I remember thinking they hated me and: *no way.* "

And yet a few weeks later in October, who should turn up at Mad Jean's but Malcolm McLaren.

"It was about three in the morning," says George, "and my bell went off, and I saw these two figures through the door, a curly red-haired figure and this other skinny thing, and it was Malcolm and Matthew. I said, 'Hi,' and Malcolm goes, [in *Dragnet*-like tones] 'All right, George, come with us.' They took me in this taxi to Queensway where Malcolm had this little apartment and it was quite exciting." (Soon after Bow Wow Wow had started up, McLaren moved from his tiny Whitechapel flat to a slightly posher, and ever so slightly bigger, flat in the more centrally located Craven Terrace, a few blocks from the Queensway tube. He and Andrea set up house at this flat for most of the next year.)

"All the way there, they were bombarding me with this big spiel: 'We're going to sign you and get rid of Annabella. You're going to be massive.' He was saying we would do a big massive tour and I could take over from Annabella—kick her offstage, if I wanted. I think he wanted me to be really sadistic to her.

"So he took me 'round his apartment in Queensway and when we arrived—it was a real small flat, one room with a bathroom, above an Italian restaurant—there was holes in all the windows and a cassette player busted on the floor. I asked him who did that, and he told me Vivienne had. 'What happened?' I said. And he told me he had just played 'W.O.R.K.' for Vivienne. 'She just came 'round,' he said, 'and had a fit about Annabella's singing and smashed the cassette player. Smashed it on the floor and had a fit. Said it's rubbish, poppycock, boring. She was going mental,' he said, 'and then she ran out on the street and picked up these house bricks and threw them through the window.' You can imagine what she looked like dressed in all this pirate gear. All the people watching from the restaurant were going, 'Crazy woman, there she goes, crazy.'

"From that moment," says George, "I realized Malcolm was not a material girl living in a material world. I found out *his* attitude. He reminded me a bit of Mick Jagger: the fake Cockney accent. He puts that on when he's trying to impress little boys 'n' girls. Like he's trying to come down to my level, right? Laying on the old Cockney charm.

"I listened to what he had to say, and right then and there, at 3:00 in the morning, he starts telling me to write songs with Matthew. *Right then.* I was supposed to be Lieutenant Lush, and Matthew was playing the guitar and singing with this cassette machine. We did about three songs that night with Malcolm reading out these lyrics from a notebook. It was amazing. The thing that really had me about him is that I've never met anybody who would write a song about absolutely *anything* at all. Just anything. He would write a song about pissing in a corn flake packet! I was just looking at him going, Blimey! because it was *soooo* funny."

George came back to McLaren's Queensway flat to rehearse a few more times with Matthew Ashman, but for almost a month, McLaren kept him in limbo. One minute, he would be the next great star, a real Homosexual Apache, the next, he was no one. In the interim, George rejoined his friend Kirk Brandon's postpunk gloom-doom band, Theater of Hate. And if, as occasionally happened, George's rehearsals conflicted with Bow Wow Wow's, McLaren gave George a spot of cash—"£40! which was like gold to me then," says George—to persuade him to not to leave.

Three days before the big Rainbow gig, McLaren finally gave George O'Dowd the green light. "He told me that Annabella was back in the picture—she was the best one they could find—but he said that I was going to do one song, 'Cast Iron Arm,' and that they were going to break me in slowly. It was better than a kick in the head, so I did it."

True to his word, McLaren had turned the Rainbow into an amazing one-night spectacle. Pink cards admitting each person to the Mile High Club were issued to the punters and numerous brightly lit carnival rides—cotton-candy stands, carousels, even a giant helter-skelter—had been trucked into the hall. For once, McLaren had thought of everything—he had even hired the jazz band George was originally to sing with—and George was just the icing on the cake.

"When I turned up at the Rainbow," he says, "I had this big flowered picnic basket full of makeup and I was wearing this black dress with a big bow 'round it, a lace-tiered skirt and a huge baggy blouse made out of furniture chair material with pictures of pink roses on it and tights to match, hundreds of plaits and ribbons in my hair, which was a long black wig, and Vivienne just stared at me as I walked in the theater for rehearsals. Two hours later she turns up with all this pirate gear and says to put it on. I wouldn't. 'Why not?' 'I'm not part of the band,' I said. 'I'm making a guest appearance. This is how I dress.' She got really stroppy and told me to put it on, but Malcolm didn't care. He told me to wear what I wanted.

"I was so petrified when it was time for me to go onstage, they had to push me on. I was psyched but I was terrified: It was the first time I had ever been on any stage in my life. But I was really cocky. Once I got out there I thought, 'I have waited *years* for this,' and I went totally mental, dancing like mad. But then Malcolm said, 'He's too arrogant, no vulnerability.' So that was that."

Indeed it was. McLaren had found that Bow Wow Wow's fans were by no means prepared to accept an overtly gay singer onstage with Annabella, who had increasingly come to be accepted as the Lolita of the new rock 'n' roll. The night of the Rainbow gig, George's debut performance was met by a hail of spit—ye olde punke gobbing—and when George next showed up at McLaren's Queensway flat, according to Leroy Gorman, "Malcolm just hid behind his curtains until George stopped ringing the bell. We never had much say in it. Malcolm just said, 'Look, he's just a fucking raging queer and I don't think we can handle him.' We didn't care. We'd normally bash someone like that."

George joined Bow Wow Wow for the first three dates of their first U.K. tour, but according to George, when the band got to Manchester, a photograph of him and Annabella appeared in *NME* with the headline "George is no longer in Bow Wow Wow." "I couldn't believe it," says George. "I thought, 'Thanks a lot for telling me, Malcolm.'"

Some two weeks later, while Bow Wow Wow were still pressing the flesh on tour, George received a phone call from Ashley Goodall of EMI, offering him a solo singing deal. George was desperate to begin his own career, but after the experience of having been Malcolm McLaren's Lieutenant Lush, he decided he'd had all the molding he could take for now.

Never one to enjoy the excessive delights of rock 'n' roll touring, McLaren stayed back in London while Bow Wow Wow went on the road through most of the spring.

Like most of McLaren's decisions about the timing, scheduling, and style of his tours, this decision to stay home while the group whooped it up on the road was disastrous. "The very first U.K. tour was when the break with Malcolm started to become apparent," says Gorman. "We had a great time on the road—Annabella was mostly ambivalent about it 'cause she had to have a tutor come along—but we were finally doing what he'd told us the Pistols had done, and it hurt him to know that we were having a great time without him. For a year solid, every single day, we saw each other, and then we were gone."

But McLaren had enough on his mind without having to go on tour. For one thing, his relationship with Vivienne Westwood was, confusingly, both booming and falling apart at the same time. On the one hand, McLaren was in love with Andrea, and Westwood was fuming with jealousy, even though her own relationship with McLaren had been deteriorating ever since McLaren had gone to America with the Sex Pistols. Indeed, the fight George O'Dowd had just missed the night McLaren and Ashman picked him up from Goodge Street, was over *Andrea*, not Annabella.

In terms of the fashion business, however, the McLaren-Westwood partnership was more successful than ever. That April, Worlds End was due to give its first real fashion show—with Bow Wow Wow as the runway soundtrack—and despite all the rough times between them personally, McLaren and Westwood had continued to work together to establish the pirate look as a complete fashion collection. Of course, most of the ideas were still derived from McLaren.

"Malcolm's analysis of the pirates," says Westwood, "was that the whole of the English empire was based on pirates and their seafaring, and just like those pirates, we'd plundered the world's culture. Ever since we'd done punk rock we'd created a culture of our own, so now we'd start looking at England and the world and plunder that. We realized you could place anything from one period of history and geography together with any other thing, and it would work. It would be eclectic just like a punk rocker's dress was to some extent eclectic in terms of London."

With tasseled sashes and plastic jerkins that swayed over shirts with masses of gold buttons and broderie anglaise, regal muslin gowns, and floppy suede square-toed boots, the first Worlds End collection—dedicated to "a new age of glamorous heroes standing tall and slim and proud"—was a hit and made it into the fall sportswear lines of Macy's, Bloomingdale's, and later the Victoria & Albert Museum's history of dress collection.

Concurrent to his work with Westwood, however, McLaren was also still trying to sell Bow Wow Wow to another record label. EMI, he had realized, would never go along with his ideas. They just didn't understand that the central idea of Bow Wow Wow was to *reach the kids.* If only they weren't so worried about the *message* of the music, and took good care with their end of the job—promotion and distribution—the product would sell itself. EMI were just too provincial to understand.

Once again, McLaren had a difficult time finding a new label. "When things got bad," says Gorman, "Malcolm would really get nervous and start ringing us up, complaining, crying, tearful, desperate. We'd lose our respect for him. He'd say, 'I'm going back to bloody Paris, I've had enough.' Suddenly, *we* were being the troopers, going out on the road, writing new songs, taking care of Annabella, and *he* was crying about how hard it was."

But then McLaren had a new idea: Maybe the Americans would understand what he was talking about. After all, who knew better about reaching the kids than big American record companies like WEA and RCA?

Fortunately for McLaren, Rory Johnston happened to be in London once again, now as comanager of Michael Des Barres's band, the Chequered Past. Johnston flew back to New York for negotiations with WEA and RCA, and while WEA wasn't sure it could guarantee Bow Wow Wow an American release, RCA's chief A&R person, Nancy Jeffries, seemed to understand what McLaren's new band was up to. After another lengthy negotiation, McLaren signed Bow Wow Wow to RCA worldwide in yet another heavily frontloaded deal, reputedly a $750,000 advance to be spread over three albums. (Ironically, singing with RCA also brought the Bow Wow Wow name back to Nipper's real home.) McLaren wasn't happy signing a long-term deal where he would be held responsible for coming up with such vast amounts of new product in such a short period, but Bow Wow Wow now seemed to be going along well on their own steam, and he reckoned (correctly) that as they got older and more experienced and got better and better producers, he would become less needed. They would crank out the product and he would be free to do what he wanted. And in fact, with the exception of one or two controversies surrounding the production of Bow Wow Wow's second album, that is more or less what happened.

By the spring of 1981, Bow Wow Wow had become an extraordinarily talented and musical new band. The songs written over the next few months for their first RCA longplayer—from the start RCA told McLaren not to expect any cassette-only releases—were tuneful and elegant. McLaren still provided most of the words—mostly outtakes cribbed from his work with Pietrie and Grillet—and the inspiration for most of the music: For weeks he worked with Matthew Ashman stealing riffs from old swing hits, rockabilly songs, and various bits of Africana. But now Bow Wow Wow had added their own twist to the material, replacing McLaren's mania for Burundi drumming with Dave Barbe's discoed world beat, a rhythmic groove made even stronger by Annabella's steadily improving vocal abilities, Lee Gorman's funky bass playing, and Matthew Ashman's spaghetti twang-bar guitar.

With RCA behind them, Bow Wow Wow now got top-notch producers (Colin Thurston, Alan Tarney, and Brian Tench), and, as usual, whenever musical talent was involved, McLaren got nervous. He simply couldn't see any new hook for promoting these tuneful melodies and he worried that Bow Wow Wow were now going to become *musicians,* exactly the same route that had turned Johnny Rotten into a good-for-nothing *artiste.* A new scandal had to be concocted, and McLaren now turned for help to Nick Egan, a gangly twenty-eight-year-old ex–art student who had gotten involved with punk graphic design through Bernie Rhodes of the Clash, for help.

"We spent days and days working together in the National Gallery library, looking through piles of pictures because Malcolm had the idea of re-creating a photo from art history for the next album cover," says Egan. "Then, one day, almost simultaneously, we both had the idea of doing a photo shoot of Manet's *Dejeuner sur l'herbe,"* the notorious impressionist painting (c. 1863) in which a nude girl stares directly at the portraitist while her completely clad male companions sit by, idly chatting through the afternoon.

Lifting Manet's *Dejeuner* seemed the perfect gimmick for McLaren to push his idea of kiddie-piracy one step further, from the world of sound into the world of images. It was a steal, and like stealing music from unsuspecting African tribesman, he wouldn't have to pay anyone permissions or licenses or royalties; in fact, *he* would get royalties for stealing from someone else.

But even Manet could use some spicing up. What was considered pornographic (or at least, a monumental put-on) in Manet's time—the flagrant juxtaposition of a classically naked Venus against the banal modernity of the lunching picnickers—would hardly be considered shocking in the early 1980s. And so with photographer Andy Earle and Vivienne Westwood, Egan and McLaren set up a photo shoot in Box Hill, Surrey. It was to be an innocent little scene, a faithful re-creation of the original painting—a naked girl seated at a picnic, staring straight at the portraitist, while her companions chatted by her side over a lunch basket—but McLaren wanted Annabella to be nude: just like the girl in the picture. "Don't worry," he told her, "it's just going to be a bit o' flesh—very tasteful." But Annabella knew her mother would object if she caught wind of it. "I actually wanted to do it," she says, "but I was scared. It was made into a choice of being in the band or not being in the band, but I'd already made the choice by leaving school." McLaren would not be budged. Instead he doubled his attack, telling Annabella not to think of the Manet pic as some dirty old man's idea of fun "but an artistic thing to do." Amy Dunn-Lwin wondered what was wrong with her daughter, but Annabella, fifteen going on thirty, knew that if she told her mum, it would be all over.

"On the day Annabella went out," Amy tearfully remembers, "we were waiting for the tour manager, Andy Corrigan, to take Annabella away, and she was looking very worried: She didn't say a thing to me. I saw she had taken with her a Burmese sarong, a *longyi,* and she'd put it in her bag, and I was wondering what she was doing with it, but I thought, better not. If only I had asked her that question before she had left she would have told me—and I would have stopped it."

Typically, McLaren got his way again. Annabella's mother claims her daughter was gulled into doing the shoot with a few vodka and oranges after a five-hour debate over the photograph at a local restaurant, but Annabella says it was actually the soothing ice cream cone McLaren bought her before the shoot, rather than the little vodka she drank with the boys, that eventually convinced her. "When we finally started shooting," she says, "Malcolm was much more interested in the placement of the cherries in the fruitbowl than he was in my being naked."

The next day, Annabella finally broke down and told her mother what she had done. True to form, Amy Dunn-Lwin was furious. Annabella was still legally underage, and Amy was determined to make McLaren pay for what she called his "child pornography." Now, Amy climbed up each rung of the scandal ladder, first phoning the lawyers, then the papers, then the managing director of RCA in London, and finally, the chief executive officer of RCA in New York. McLaren tried to calm Amy down, sending Gorman and Barbe, with a twinkle in his eye, over to Amy's with the last undressed photos from the shoot. "She took one look," says Dave Barbe, "went 'AAAAH!' and come flyin' at me with a knife." In the end, this round went to Annabella's mum, and another photograph of Annabella, fully clothed in her mum's translucent *longyi,* was finally substituted in place of the re-created Manet for the album cover. Until Annabella reached sixteen—in any event, just over half a year away—that would have to do.

Once again, another of McLaren's attempts to deliberately create a scandal had gone awry, and yet he was typically unbothered by the consequences. As long as the net effect of his actions still achieved what he wanted, McLaren was positively happy—for the moment. For as a result of Amy Dunn-Lwin's protective actions—forcing Annabella to swear out a statement against Bow Wow Wow, then pushing her to quit the group—Annabella finally broke with her mum, and that gave the other Bow Wows something to cheer about: Now Annabella was one of the boys. Best of all was the effect the scandal had on Annabella's image, for the papers now proclaimed Annabella the new rock 'n' roll sex kitten—or as one tabloid called her, "THE CHEAP NYMPHET"—and that was what McLaren had really wanted all along.

And still the records failed to score. Neither "Prince of Darkness" (released in July 1981) nor "Chihuahua" (released in October) ever made it into the Top 50, even though "Chihuahua" was arguably the band's best work to date, a hypnotic, rockabilly number with lyrics that cut to the core of the Bow Wow Wow paradox: "I can't dance I can't sing/ I can't do anything/ I can't even find my way 'round town/ I'm 15 and a fool can't you see/ so don't fall in love with me."

With their first RCA album, *See Jungle! See Jungle! Go Join Your Gang Yeah! City All Over, Go Ape Crazy,* scheduled for release in November, a new plan of battle was in order. Rory Johnston: "It seemed clear the scandal strategy wasn't working, so we finally decided that the only way people would be convinced [of Bow Wow Wow's quality] was if we put the band on the road and toured them extensively through Britain and America. We were sure the American market would open up to us if we kept them out touring solidly through the Midwest."

Long tours were now set up for Britain and America, and if all went well, the band would be on the road continuously from October 1981 to late August 1982. But just as the band was about to leave for the first leg of their British tour, Annabella's tutor wisely decided she couldn't go on the road with the band for such a long time. "No problem," said Amy Dunn-Lwin: "I'll go myself." "Like hell you will," said the Bow Wow boys.

"We were just about to leave for the tour and Annabella's mum was insisting on going with us," remembers Lee Gorman. "We couldn't get a tutor so her mum said she had to come along, and she was totally mad, nonrational. So there we were with Amy Dunn-Lwin and she was driving us crazy, and then we had a two-day stay in London before we went up to Nottingham. We were just about to leave from the RCA building, and we said, 'Right, this is the time: Let's get rid of her.' It was totally spontaneous. We were all waiting on the bus and Dave pretended he had to take a piss, but instead he run up to the fifth floor and phoned down to reception that Bill Kimber [managing director of RCA] wanted to see Amy Dunn-Lwin right away in his office. We all started going 'Whoo, Amy! Bill Kimber wants to see you: Wonder what he wants?' So Amy goes up on the lift to see Kimber and Dave run down the stairs; I got her bags, threw 'em in the hallway, and we drove off! And Annabella loved it most of all! She laughed, thought it was fun. She knew her mother was crazy."

With Amy-Dunn Lwin gone and no tutor or chaperon on the bus, Bow Wow Wow had no interference from *any* adults—call it *Mile High Club II*—and the band grew closer and closer, finally culminating one night in Matthew Ashman giving Annabella a Mohawk haircut on the bus. While the assiduous touring schedule set up by Rory Johnston undoubtedly accounts for most of the turnaround in the band's fortunes, many credit Annabella's new haircut as the "event" that finally got Bow Wow Wow barking in chartland.

"The turning point actually came when Annabella could be promoted on her own," says Richard Routledge, the RCA press officer in charge of promoting Bow Wow Wow's records, "when she showed up at one of the gigs with her hair in a Mohican. Visually, she transformed herself into an absolutely beautiful woman. She looked absolutely stunning: fashion editors, Fleet Street, they all went crazy after that, and everyone wanted to know what it was like to be, as she sang, 'a rock 'n' roll puppet in a band called Bow Wow Wow.'

"But no matter what she says or feels now, we didn't exploit her. I never used her in any of the photo sessions as a piece of meat. She had star potential, but the only way to get her off the ground at the time was to take the shots that were risqué. One shot in particular shows what I mean. *Record Mirror* took a picture of her wearing a string vest, her Mohican haircut all nice 'n' new, gold braids in her hair, and a big metal belt buckle—waist deep in a pool. She looked great but you could obviously see her tits hanging through the string vest. *Record Mirror* gave it a great caption: ' "I'm no sex puppet," says Annabella.' And that worked. Men melted when they saw that."

With the completion of their second U.K. tour in late October, *See Jungle!* was released with a barrage of publicity. Slowly, it crept up the charts: to number thirty-one. Bow Wow Wow prepared for their marathon road trip through the United States—two separate tours broken up by a three-week rest period back home—and again, Amy Dunn-Lwin, who had now taken to wearing her name in rhinestones on the back of her denim jacket, attempted to block the band from leaving the country. This time she alleged that there was rampant drug use among the male members of the group, and while the allegations were partly true—mostly the usual cannabis consumption—Amy Dunn-Lwin had cried wolf so many times in the past (once even having Bow Wow Wow's tour bus pulled over to the side of the road for a drugs inspection) that Scotland Yard refused to investigate any further. Amy then had McLaren hauled into court to control Annabella on tour, and he was pressed to accept numerous stipulations on Annabella's conduct in America, including three hours of study a day with a tutor/chaperon, the constant presence of her brother, and a midnight curfew, none of which were ever kept to.

If this indefatigable mother did not exactly ruin the American tour, she still achieved a partial victory by wearing down the equally indefatigable McLaren with a constant hail of vitriol. From this time on, most of the day-to-day responsibility for dealing with Bow Wow Wow was left to Rory Johnston, Nick Egan, and road manager Andy Corrigan. The American tour, opened in New York by Zulu Nation rapster Afrika Bambaata, was a surprising hit.

McLaren accompanied the Bow Wow Wows across the ocean, but he soon returned to London to work on a couple of other projects that had cropped up over the past few months—a country & western concept band called She Sheriff; a half-hearted production job for Castelbajac's mad Hungarian synth-wizard, Peter O.G.I.; and a potential rhythm and blues act for George O'Dowd. However, none of these projects seemed to engage his interest either: Somewhere, a corner had been turned.

Over the next few months it seemed obvious to those who worked with him that McLaren was suffocating under the Bow Wow Wow banner. Increasingly, he couldn't be bothered with the details of the group. Strategy, images, schemes: all this he had, it was true—for the Bow Wow Wow's U.S. tour he had even come up with the idea for a giant plastic cassette stage backdrop for the group—but the details were almost always left to Johnston, Egan, and Corrigan while McLaren busied himself with She Sheriff, George O'Dowd, and tempting conversations about a musical—starring himself. He was desperate to escape back into his own ether before it was too late.

"You see, with the Sex Pistols," he told journalist David Thomas, "I was a manager but also I wasn't a manager, if you see what I mean. But with Bow Wow Wow I was becoming too *much* a manager, and I began to feel I really didn't like my job. I remember sitting in Foyles bookshop with my girlfriend one day, going through shelf after shelf and knowing all the time we'd been in there, maybe about three hours, that I was supposed to be at a marketing meeting at RCA discussing how to flog the next Bow Wow Wow single, and I just couldn't make that meeting. I began realizing, I *have* to get out of this job."

On those few occasions when McLaren *did* get involved with Bow

Wow Wow again—those few occasions when the band was back in the U.K.—he found himself being battled by the band members, Amy Dunn-Lwin, or RCA. Despite his best efforts, he often wound up on the losing side.

One time in particular stands out. Bill Kimber, RCA's U.K. managing director, was sure that "Go Wild in the Country" was hit material, and he suggested to McLaren that the song be remixed as a twelve-inch single. McLaren refused to allow Kimber to remix the record, and in the heat of the battle, he sent Lee Gorman over to Kimber to relay the message that he would prefer that Kimber keep his mitts off the band's material.

"Malcolm really did a number on me," remembers Gorman. "Said, 'You've got to do the job, it's a *job*,' and he'd worked so hard to instill soldierly spirit in me, I couldn't refuse. So I went up to Kimber's office with him and then all on me own, I had to tell him, 'Look, this will never be a hit,' and I knew in my heart that it *would* be a hit. I was really torn between these things. Then, Malcolm left, and Kimber did *his* number on me. 'If you say yes to this,' he said, 'we're going to do some wonderful trips for you—send you to Holland, put you up in this hotel, and get you a good time.' He sat me in his car, had me listen to his remix, and I thought, What's he gonna do if I don't give in? And then he told me: 'OK, then, if you won't agree to it, I'll just do it without your permission.' And he did, and it was hit, our first big hit, it went to number seven, as was our next one, 'I Want Candy.' McLaren hated that one too and it went to number nine."

Dave Barbe: "I only wished he'd fucked off earlier. It would have been a great help, because once he started leaving, we started getting on, selling records and making money. Before that it was just the same old Sex Pistols thing: 'Cash from Chaos.' He'd never do *anything* by the front door. It always had to have some weird angle, and he'd always look good and we'd just suffer. It's just like he says in his record 'Buffalo Gals': He's always the man who's 'Round the outside, round the outside.' "

For Bow Wow Wow, the last bridge was crossed when McLaren booked them as a support band for the European tour of Queen, ironically, the same pop group the Sex Pistols had replaced as guests on Bill Grundy's *Today* show over six years ago. It suddenly occurred to them that McLaren might be sabotaging them now that they had become successful on their own.

"Malcolm had already set up the European tour when he called me from London to ask me what I thought," says Rory Johnston. "I told him I didn't really know: I'd never advise you to put them on with Queen in the States but I didn't know what the Continent would be like. I asked him whether he would go on the tour with them, and he said, 'No, I'll send some other guys, I'm too busy.' " That was a dreadful mistake, and midway through the tour, after hostile reactions from their European fans, Queen asked Bow Wow Wow to bow out.

"Immediately following that tour we went to Japan to support Madness," says Johnston, "and he didn't come with us there either, which was very surprising to me because he knew we would be big there. We came back from Japan through Hawaii and while we were there, Matthew and Lee began to moan a lot that they weren't seeing Malcolm at all and that it was really becoming difficult to work with him, and they started making intimations about having me manage them. I felt some loyalty to Malcolm since I had been brought into this primarily to handle the group's affairs in America, and since I didn't want to move to England—I was also working with a couple of other groups as well at the time—I told them to hold off. I could understand that they were upset but I thought they should go back to England and that Malcolm would be forced eventually either to shit or get off the pot. But then when we got back to New York, Malcolm called to ask me whether I would spend three months in London managing the band so that he could go off and do other things. He wanted to be an artist. He didn't feel he had enough room to breathe with all of his other projects taking up so much of his time."

In fact, that spring, McLaren had already signed himself to Charisma Records as a solo act and was starting to look for a producer for his first record. Although he still clung to his management association with the band—Bow Wow Wow would continue paying him royalties for his quarter share of their lyrics as well as management commissions from the years that still remained on their contract with him—by August 1982, he had become so involved with preparations for his own work as a recording artist, that it was only a matter of time before a legal split was effected and Rory Johnston could be made the group's official manager. Nearly a year later, Matthew Ashman—now heavily involved with heroin—broke his arm falling off an American stage and the rest of the band was forced to stand by while Ashman was in the hospital for a diabetes condition discovered while he was having his arm fixed: And Bow Wow Wow finally came to a parting of the ways. Annabella Lwin made her own solo record for RCA in 1985; Dave Barbarossa and Leroy Gorman still play together; and Matthew Ashman joined forces with Paul Cook to form the neo-punk band, Chiefs of Relief. None has been successful—yet.

Once again, Malcolm McLaren had got away unscathed.

10
THIEVES LIKE US

He that is nourished by the Acorns he pickt up under an Oak, or the Apples he gathered from the Trees in the Wood, has certainly appropriated them to himself. No Body can deny but the nourishment is his. I ask then, When did they begin to be his? When he digested? Or when he eat? Or when he boiled? Or when he brought them home? Or when he pickt them up? And 'tis plain, if the first gathering made them not his, nothing else could. That labour *put a distinction between them and common. That added something to them more than Nature, the common Mother of all, had done; and so they became his private right.*
      —*John Locke,* Second Treatise of Government

By its very nature, the business of music management is a syncretic affair, more dependent on the sum of its parts than on any single aspect of the manager's diverse array of business interests. Negotiation of music publishing and recording contracts, the hiring and firing of lawyers, accountants, publicists, and tour promoters, the merchandising of an artist's ancillary products, the steady maintenance of an artist's growth—all these are essential components of the managerial trade. Of course, many managers—not only Malcolm McLaren—get far more involved with their clients than this, and their advice often extends to consulting on artists' clothes, lyrics, musical styles, concert arrangements, and even "personal" affairs. While there can be no final estimation of the degree to which a manager can become involved with an artist's "artistic" decisions—especially in popular music, where whatever sells best is often the best artistic strategy—the tried-and-true route to success has usually been found when managers attend to artists' business and artists stick to their art.

Malcolm McLaren on the other hand always claimed that *he* was the artist and that managing rock 'n' roll bands was just one aspect of his peculiar form of artistry, one medium among many that he wanted to use to make his art. Fashion was another. "Instead of using the canvas, I have to use human beings," he said with a straight face, early in 1982. "It's just the work I've chosen to do—not through any personal choice originally, but what I decided was my best path to follow when I left art school. What I could automatically get a response from quickly seemed to be fashion because of my knowledge and background. It was just a subject I harnessed myself to and used."

For McLaren, the syncretic aspect of being a manager had nothing to do with business and everything to do with the way rock 'n' roll, fashion, marketing, and public relations all fit together to confront the spectacle of commodity culture—which was what everyone *thought* he had been trying to do with the Sex Pistols. That success, of course, had been mostly accidental, and when McLaren attempted to turn his accidents into plans with Bow Wow Wow, the failure of that group during his tenure (and their quick rise once he had left them), proved just how lucky he had been. McLaren's long charade of artistry-by-management was over: It had finally come time to get down to the nitty-gritty of being an artist.

This wasn't, however, nearly as dramatic a change of careers as it may have seemed; for McLaren, it was mostly a matter of changing his *legal* status from that of "manager" to that of "artist." In fact, since he was unable to read, write, or play music—he couldn't even find the right knobs to twirl in the studio—he would still be dependent on the talents of others to create his product. But that didn't bother him. As McLaren knew all too well from his time in Paris, uncopyrighted musical material was plentiful and studio musicians were cheap, especially when record companies were willing to foot the bill for so-called recording costs. What he couldn't write (or hire others to write), he would steal.

It began in New York, in August 1981. McLaren was there for the opening of Bow Wow Wow's first American tour, scheduled to coincide with the giant New Music Seminar where he was to give a lecture on the seduction of rock 'n' roll by the star-making machinery, but due to Matthew Ashman's arrest for tossing a brick through a window in Great Yarmouth Street, the band had been unable to get visas, the gigs were canceled, and McLaren had time on his hands. (Ironically, John Lydon's

Public Image Limited played on two of those nights in a hastily arranged gig in which PIL stood behind a giant opaque scrim while a video camera projected images of the band playing behind.) On one of the nights Bow Wow Wow had been scheduled to play, he and Rory Johnston were taken up to the South Bronx by a black video artist named Michael Holman to meet DJ Afrikaa Bambaata (aka "Bam"), chieftain of the Zulu Nation, a loose conglomeration of ex-gangs, now supposedly coexisting peacefully under Bam's inspired leadership. It was a harrowing experience—"a big fight broke out," remembers Johnston, "and we ran over to a wall and stayed put until someone told us it was OK since it was only someone with a knife: no guns that night"—but to McLaren, the new scene that was developing around rapping and scratching was amazing. He'd never seen or heard anything like this before, and while he was still in New York, he made plans with Bam for him to open Bow Wow Wow's next U.S. tour.

The next day McLaren went to RCA Records to take care of some last-minute business before returning to London, and to his surprise, he bumped into Steve Weltman, a rather bluff working-class Brit who was then head of RCA's international division. Weltman was glad to see McLaren: Some Japanese associates of his were about to return home and they were looking for a new wave act to do some backup bits on a commercial for Shiseido perfumes back home. All the Bow Wow Wows had to do was to learn a few bits of phonetic Japanese. Why don't you come to dinner with us, asked Weltman, and we'll talk about it then. McLaren and Johnston accepted, and by the time they came to their coffees, McLaren had begun telling Steve Weltman how bored he was managing Bow Wow Wow and how much fun he'd had on his trip to meet the Zulu Nation. Weltman thought McLaren was brilliant that night—"when two Jewish boys meet," he says, "there's always a great spirit between them"—and he suggested to McLaren that if this Zulu stuff was as brilliant as he said it was, perhaps he'd like to make his own record with them. McLaren said he was interested, but because he was still tied down with Bow Wow Wow he told Weltman that he'd have to get back to him in a few weeks.

Several *months* later, back in London, working with Nick Egan on the neo-country band She Sheriff and exhausted from his battles with Amy Dunn-Lwin, McLaren called Steve Weltman to see if the offer still stood. He still didn't have any firm ideas about how he would use this new rap music but he was definitely interested in making his own record. By this time, however, the tough, fast-talking Weltman had already left RCA Records to become managing director of Tony Stratton-Smith's Charisma label, one of the first independent British record companies, and the home of Genesis, Lindisfarne, and Monty Python, among many others. Weltman was not new to Charisma. He had worked for "Strat" (who died of cancer in 1987) when the label first started in 1969, leaving Charisma in 1974 to go into management and then to RCA. But by the early eighties, with the international record industry in an alarming slump—an overall drop of twenty percent in U.K. sales in 1979—Strat needed Weltman back again. Meanwhile, says Weltman, he had gotten so excited by the idea of making a record with McLaren, that when Strat first asked him to return to Charisma, Weltman says he told his boss he'd do it, but only on the condition "that I would get to make this record with Malcolm. Strat said, 'What? That Sex Pistols man? He can't sing, can he?' And I told him that *I* thought it was very important.

"Malcolm and I met about two days later," Weltman continues, "and he asked me whether I thought RCA would still be interested and I told him I was going back to Charisma. His reaction was extreme: 'Charisma! That's that hippie label with that big fat bloke, Tony.' I told him it's not who's there that counts, it's what you go in with. It's the commitment, the belief in good product. You can go out and spend ten thousand on an act worldwide in promotion and have a hit but you can also spend two million building a band up and sell nothing. The *public* is still the final arbiter."

McLaren was convinced by Weltman's argument, but when it came time to discuss exactly what kind of record he could make, all he could say was that he still wanted (somehow) to work with the hip-hop scene, which he sensed was the closest thing America had to London's subcultures of resistance.

From the way they tied the laces on their Adidas, customized their beat boxes, or "bombed" New York City subway cars with graffiti, the B-boys had built up a subculture that was blacker than black. The B-boys were the real American punks and they were into being *fresh*—not merely vivid, new, visible, but bold and spicy too—impudent and rude: real homeboys were self-styled black outlaws who had no time for white boys or their racist record companies. Fresh was the beat too: with a scratch DJ and a fast-rhyming rap, inherited from doo-wop, funk, gospel, disco, and soul, hip-hoppers could concoct an insistent, itchy sound full of the sirens, ghetto-blasters, and unexpected explosions that turn New York City streets into blazing canyons of noise.

Suddenly, Malcolm McLaren was styling himself as a hip-hop expert, and as he soon found out, hip-hop, originally a music supported by black and latino kids in the parks of the South Bronx, was already starting to percolate outside the slums: After nearly four years of obscurity to everyone but the law, scratchers, rappers, breakdancers, and graffiti-writers were just beginning to break into the mainstream—particularly in the art world where so-called graffiti-artists like Dondi White, Keith Haring, and Fab Five Freddy were finding acceptance in the new East Village gallery scene. There was no time to waste if this new black punk scene was to be exploited, so when Steve Weltman asked McLaren what he wanted to do, he blurted out that the more he thought about it, the more he had realized that the key to it all wasn't the music—in six months every kid would be rapping, he said—but the dancing. And not the contorted twisting of the breakdance crews, not the vernacular get-down-and-boogie dancing of everyday parties, but *folk dancing.* All the world knows how to dance, said McLaren, but only in folk dancing is everyone united in the *same* purpose. Folk dance was the perfect beat for the eighties.

As McLaren told Krystina Kitsis in March 1981, "The audience was what was exciting about punk rock, the attitudes. The music was only a vehicle. Today the music has become the most important thing. They all talk about what great production, about the mechanics and the mechanics are selling the record. The content is irrelevant. That shows you where we're at. That's why the records are depreciating. That's why I believe people will be more interested in dancing, getting involved in communication with the guy across the floor. The whole idea of having to ask someone 'Will you please dance with me?' makes you feel a bit of a jerk right? But if you've got a song telling everybody to get up and dance, you're going to get together in that group with that girl. . . .

"I'm going back to roots and finding that, at the end of the day, people will gain inspiration from it. Putting something back in, rather than constantly taking out. . . . That's your consumer society and the cynicism that was brought about with the advent of punk rock becoming unfashionable and less interesting. Everybody just decided to make a quick buck. Now I want to put something back in. What I want to do is make the audience stars—get involved with dancing. I want to do a record that can really inject a lot of ideas in music, in people's cultures—and the way to do that is to get them to dance. . . . You know what folk dances are like—I'm taking from Latin America, from Peru, Bolivia, from the Dutch and French Caribbean, North America. I think it's going to be very big."

Even though McLaren's sole musical performance to date was singing the old vaudeville classic "You Need Hands" in *The Great Rock 'n' Roll Swindle* and even though he had no musical talent or studio expertise to speak of—as one musician who worked with McLaren later on put it, "he couldn't record his way out of a paper bag much less program a 4/4 beat on a baby drum machine"—Steve Weltman gobbled up his black-punk-folk dance spiel without another thought. Weltman was utterly entranced by McLaren, felt he would be a shot in the arm for Charisma's "old hippie" reputation, and by April 1982, McLaren made a deal with Charisma to provide one album for an advance of £45,000 (plus recording costs) with an option for a second record. (By the time McLaren signed with Charisma, he had already signed a publishing deal with April Music, Ltd., the U.K. subsidiary of CBS Songs, for an additional £60,000; later, Weltman also helped McLaren get a U.S. recording deal with Island Records.)

With the deal finished, McLaren and Weltman began to talk producers, and one of the first names Weltman came up with was Trevor Horn's, the exact opposite of what Weltman calls McLaren's "grown-up punk act."

Horn would have been anyone's first choice at the time. Something of a childhood prodigy—he played the double bass in the Durham Youth Orchestra when he was twelve—by the time he was nineteen, Horn had given up his day job as an accountant to start a studio in Leicester, and he soon moved down to London to make his way in the world of pop music. In 1979, Horn and his partner, keyboardist Geoff Downes, scored a worldwide number-one hit as the Buggles with "Video Killed the Radio Star," and when the lead singer and keyboardist of Yes, Rick Wakeman and Jon Anderson, respectively, quit that veteran progressive rock group the following year, Horn and Downes signed on. For nearly a year, the new Yes toured and recorded, and when the group disbanded yet again in 1981, Horn and Downes went their separate ways, Downes to the supergroup Asia and Horn to the studio (and a second Buggles album), always his first love. In a matter of months, Trevor Horn had come up with a very impressive (and *very* satisfied) client list: the Abba-styled pop duo Dollar, for whom Horn did everything but sing; Sheffield synth-poppers ABC, who scored a number-one platinum album with their Horn-produced album, *Lexicon of Love;* new romantics Spandau Ballet; and several other odd jobs. Only six months into his first year as a full-time producer, Trevor Horn was boasting of a ninety-five percent success rate and was suddenly being talked about as the Studio King of British rock.

Horn was utterly baffled by McLaren's black-punk-folk dance rap. The audience as star? Of course. But the 1980s as the age of folk dance? You have to be joking. "Here, I had been doing all these very focused things like ABC," says Horn, "but then Malcolm showed up with an idea that was so totally vague and enormous, I couldn't really make it out. We were to make an album that encompassed all, literally all of music. He kept calling it a trip around the world, and I didn't know *what* he meant. But then he played me 'Buffalo Gals' by Peyote Pete, a video of Jimmy Stewart singing 'Buffalo Gals,' some stuff from Peru, a lot of different, surprising things, and I realized he was making me listen in a different way."

Indeed, according to Gary Langan, the slender, well-organized re-cording engineer who had worked with Horn ever since his early Buggles days and later went on to work with the group Art of Noise, originally a loose group of synth and keyboard wizards founded by Horn and rock critic Paul Morley, Horn found himself immediately and almost indis-criminately influenced by McLaren. Horn doesn't deny it. Over the next six weeks in the spring of 1982, at nearly the same time Horn was mixing the new Spandau Ballet record and McLaren was ostensibly managing Bow Wow Wow, Horn and McLaren met often to figure out some way to make McLaren's trip around the world a feasible musical proposition.

"The reason I went along with Malcolm was because I thought I could learn something from him," says Horn. "He made me laugh so hard and he didn't take himself seriously as so many people do. But the more we talked about it, the more I realized he didn't really know what he was doing, and that actually made it even more promising because it would then be a more open process of working with him. I knew we had two options. Either we could take a Fairlight"—a digital sampling keyboard that can clone any sound from any source and convert it into the notes of a musical scale—"copy the rhythms from all the different sources Malcolm had and then go out and make songs from that, or we could actually go out and get the sounds from the actual people, capture the real thing on a Nagra." Finally in mid-June 1982, it was decided that instead of traipsing around the world with a two-track Nagra recorder, McLaren, Horn, and Langan would go to New York. "It's a cesspool of nations there," McLaren told a wary Trevor Horn. "You'll love it."

For the next week or so, McLaren left Langan and Horn to languish in their room at the Mayflower Hotel while he went off in search of the great ethnic experience with Nick Egan and Terry Doktor, a New York fashion pioneer McLaren had met through his old friend Gene Krell, former manager of Granny Takes a Trip. One day McLaren returned to the hotel gasping for breath: He had found a Cuban connection at Folk-ways Records who would put him in touch with all the varieties of Latin music New York had to offer. The next day, McLaren, Doktor, Horn, and Langan went down to Folkways where McLaren proceeded to interrogate his Cuban discovery. "Malcolm just leapt right into him," remembers Langan. " 'You got to organize these bands. I want to hear your music!' Demands, demands, and more demands. And of course, this poor little gay red-haired Cuban was led to believe that Malcolm was going to make fame and fortune for him."

Unfortunately, Kuango, as the gentleman was called, turned out to be a rather mainstream Latin musician, and after a few days of rehearsals, Horn decided he was awful. ("Malcolm was yelling away about how great it was," remembers Langan. " 'All you have to do is jazz it up a little,' he said.") Typically, when it came time to tell Kuango that his services were no longer required, McLaren asked Horn to do the dirty work, but Kuango wasn't pleased when he got the word. "He got real upset because he thought he was going to be on the record," remembers Horn. "But then he went to the toilet and the conga player said, 'I know just what you want,' and gave me his phone number. He turned out to be right. He got four guys and we went to Media Sound. They charged us $4,000 and at first they were totally inaudible. They were doing more drugs in one session than I'd ever seen in my whole life. But then Terry got them a crate of Stolichnaya, and set the microphones up and let them play, and they were great."

Almost as soon as the sessions were over, however, McLaren suddenly flew back to London. "One morning," says Langan, "he called me up and said, 'I'm not happy with Charisma, so I'm going back to get a new deal.' But then Charisma got word of this and they stopped paying our hotel bills. After about three days Malcolm returned and he was real dodgy about what was happening, and I was sure everything was going to come to a grinding halt. But it didn't. Malcolm sorted it out and we started going around to all these housing projects in Harlem. We'd have to find this African guy, or that Dominican guy, or this Peruvian guy. Always someone new."

Now Horn balked at the project. There seemed to be no point to all this errant running around for weird ethnic musicians. What was it all *for?* McLaren had to decide who the *central* artist of this record was going to be or else Horn would be on the next plane home. "Trevor was very despondent with all this hypnotic music," said McLaren. "He didn't un-derstand how he was going to sell it or turn it into a commercial record, and I had this huge argument with him. 'Does it matter?' I said. Finally the thing that convinced him was one of these guys said, 'Look, they're singing this and the reason they're singing this is because it works in and around the beat,' and he played it on the keyboard and removed the voices and it just sounded like fuckin' Debussy! And that was what finally got Trevor to stay." (Others say, however, that the only reason Horn stayed is because McLaren spent the entire night after their fight writing lyrics.)

Horn and Langan now began the long task of recording each group. On one occasion, they hired a Dominican band leader, Louis Calaph and His Happy Dominicans, and although Horn was quite happy with Calaph's band (who was paid about $2,000), the next night the Happy Dominican came back with a different group of musicians who were even better. Next, two Peruvians dug up from a tiny art gallery in Queens came to the studio with pan pipes and twelve-stringed acoustic guitars made from armadillo shells. Then it was back to the studio with Cubans. Horn and Langan were amazed at all the intricate varieties of world music. McLaren went off in search of the latest scratch DJs, convinced that a scratch version of *E.T.* would make a massive hit.

But just when Horn was about to go into the studio to record the DJs McLaren said he had found for his scratch *E.T.*, McLaren sprang a new idea on him: "hilltopper music," he called it, and the next morning, he left for Knoxville, Tennessee, telling Horn and Langan he would call them soon with full details.

When Horn and Langan met him a week later at Tri-State Studios in Knoxville, McLaren had already set up sessions with a well-known old-timey band he had "found" in the hills of East Tennessee. "They were actually called the Mountain Hilltoppers," says Gary Langan, "and they were a whole family: grandmother, grandfather, aunt of the grandmother, two daughters, a son, and two of their children, and they all came down in this battered old pickup with two shotguns on the back. They had a violin—they called it a fiddle—a semblance of an acoustic guitar, a tub bass, a washboard, and a squeeze box, and they were terrible." Finally, Horn asked the studio technicians if they knew any musicians, and the next day a crew of ace "utility pickers" (traditional session men) showed up. For a while the two parties just stared at each other across the room: No one had ever seen anything like this before.

Horn and Langan were becoming increasingly concerned with the quality of the sound they were recording. At Tri-State, in particular, they were working on a sixteen-track machine in a studio that was so antiquated the control board was located in the recording studio with a record pressing machine nearby. "Malcolm didn't understand what the big deal was," Langan sighs. "He said he'd recorded in all sorts of places with Bow Wow Wow and everything had been fine. He could hear the beat just fine. 'Hey, I can sing along with that,' he said, and Trevor and I just stared. All along Trevor had been asking Malcolm what we were going to do for a singer, and Malcolm kept saying we didn't need one because it would be all-instrumental. But then he just announced that he'd sing, and we were shocked. For ages he had put it off and then in Tennessee he decided he could quite get into this country & western stuff. So he tried it on two numbers and it threw all these great utility pickers into total disarray. He had no sense of rhythm whatsoever, so he quickly abandoned that idea. We recorded the tracks and went back to New York, and there we found these two guys, Just Allah the Superstar and C. Divine the Mastermind."

The World's Famous Supreme Team, as they were called, were just one of many scratch crews who rented late-night airtime (mostly with income from selling their own commercials and holding on-the-air lotteries) on a small uptown radio station called WHBI, and although McLaren claims to have discovered the Supreme Team on his own, both Terry Doktor (who was then taking him to see *Blade Runner* and *Tron* and introducing him to the East Village graffiti scene and double-dutch skipping) and Gary Langan seem to have given him cassettes of these boasting black nationalist scratchers. To McLaren, the Supreme Team spelled sonic gold and he negotiated with them to come to London as soon as Horn and Langan could put some sense into their tapes. But as with all things McLaren touched, that would take more time and money than could immediately be had.

For most of July, Trevor Horn locked himself in the studio while McLaren scurried around London planning the next leg of what he persisted in telling the media was his "trip around the world." ("We lied like mad to anyone who asked," giggles Horn.)

In fact, whenever he wasn't with Horn and Langan—in other words, most of the time—McLaren was busy with Vivienne Westwood and stylist Roger Burton readying the design of a second shop to supplement the increasingly successful Worlds End. For as usual whenever McLaren turned over a new leaf in his career, a change in the clothes he and Westwood sold had to accompany it. It was almost as if he was naked without a new shop to show that his outrageous ideas had some practical value. This time was no different, and in early spring, at around the same time McLaren was slowly separating from Bow Wow Wow and negotiating with Charisma, he showed Westwood a record cover of a Bolivian dancer, giving her instructions to design a collection based on the idea of a "disco on Hadrian's Wall where all the kids would be folk dancing." It was time, McLaren told Westwood, "to listen to the caller and stop all this water-treading and voyeurism."

The Buffalo collection, as the new line came to be called, was a radical departure for Westwood. Working mostly on her own, she now came up with an array of muddy-colored, rough-hewn garments that were a far cry from her previous designs. Slouchy and oddly shaped, with flaps and skirts that took their line from the action of the body beneath the cloth, the new collection represented an entirely different way of thinking about clothes for Westwood or anyone else.

Clever enough to recognize the newsworthiness of her new clothes, Westwood was still insecure enough to believe that her new line would not be properly received unless it was presented in the official Paris collections. In Paris, however, Westwood's application to join in the twice-yearly *prêt-à-porter defilés* in the Jardin des Tuileries was suddenly rejected and it fell to McLaren's friend Pierre Benain to find Worlds End a new location. That March, Westwood presented her first ever couturelike runway show at Angelina's Tea Room—across the street from the main shows in the Tuileries. There, Buffalo was something less than a smash. As Jane Mulvagh writes in the *Vogue 20th Century History of Fashion*, "the Parisian press and industry found her clothes irrelevant, rooted as they were in the culture of British urban youth, while some in Britain found her self-imposed exile unpatriotic."

Westwood was not deterred by the poor reception, and by the time McLaren returned from his late-summer forays in the fields of ethnic music, she was anxious to move on to her new shop, in chic St. Christopher's Place, just behind Oxford Street.

Based on McLaren's idea that young people were searching for the roots of their culture in primitive societies, the new store was to be called Nostalgia of Mud *(nostalgie de la boue)*, a moniker McLaren stole from another of his heroes, the French *poète maudit* Charles Baudelaire. To illustrate just how deep into the muck and mire McLaren wanted the new line of clothes to go, he and Burton planned to remove the floor of the shop down to the basement and to erect a scaffolding platform that would lead patrons to a deep muck-covered pit, in the middle of which would be a pillar surrounded by a primeval pool of bubbling mud mixed with motor oil for a viscous postindustrial look.

To McLaren's chagrin, the plans to open the new store were held up by the complicated design he and Burton had started, and while the construction dragged on, he decided to take the next part of his trip around the world: to Africa, the very source of all his primitivist fantasies.

That August, McLaren flew to Johannesburg, South Africa, to record the next part of "Folk Dances of the World," telling Trevor Horn and Gary Langan that he would call them as soon as he had found the right group of musicians and studios. And this time, he told them, they would actually do complete sessions, not just musical anthropology.

"The budget was really going up ridiculous," said McLaren, "but I didn't give a shit, really. I just thought I've got to get to Africa. I was very concerned and very aware of South Africa politically, and you know, if you've seen the Michael Caine film *Zulu*, you've got this fabulous image of the Zulu tribe as the one people who beat the English. I thought, well, *that's* a tribe that's worth meeting, and I left.

"At first, I traveled around only in the context of trying to get a feeling for the whole place because it was just so new to me. And what I discovered is how proud all these people were and how much hatred they have for the white man. It was very heavy at times, but I just got on a bus and went 'round to Soweto, where no white man goes, and I just experienced it like they experienced it. I was going into the unknown, going in there and finding out for myself. And because there's a curfew and you've got to have fucking good papers, just to keep things fairly cool they kept me locked up in this garage after 8:00 and I ended up staying overnight in their garret, sleeping with about ten of these enormous black guys, head to head."

In fact, McLaren (and Weltman) had already set up most of his South African trip through Phil Hollis, the head of Dephon Promotions, the record-pluggers for Polygram's local subsidiary, Trutone Records. According to Hollis, McLaren had done his homework quite thoroughly before he arrived in Johannesburg, and in the three weeks before McLaren summoned Horn and Langan to South Africa, Hollis and an ex-boxer/musician named Lulu Maseelela started working with the surviving members of Maseelela's old band, the Boyoyo Boys, a hot *mbaqanga* dance band from the early seventies who had come together under the auspices of a wide group of producers, arrangers, songwriters, and vocalists known as the Mavuthela team. "We tried to do this in a rehearsal room in Johannesburg," says Hollis, "but there were problems getting the musicians in and out of Soweto, so we finally decided to set up another room in a Soweto garage, and every day Malcolm and Lulu would go out there, until they were finally happy with the sound they were getting."

Once this setup was complete, Horn and Langan flew in, and before they even set foot in South Africa, McLaren's shenanigans began. First, they weren't allowed into the country because McLaren had only bought them one-way tickets and the South African authorities will not allow anyone into the country without return airfare, purchased in advance. (They were eventually helped by a stewardess who kindly bought them tickets home.) Second, although McLaren had booked Horn and Langan into the same hotel he was staying at, he was not to be found anywhere in Jo'burg. "After two, three, days just waiting for Malcolm to turn up," remembers Langan, "we phoned back to London: Yeah, Malcolm's in South Africa, haven't you found him yet? Apparently, Malcolm was at the hotel, but he'd been living this existence of going out to Soweto on all these workers' buses to visit these *shabeens* [illegal workers' bars]. He would go all night long and consequently he would sleep during the day so we kept missing him. Then on the third or fourth day, Trevor bumped into Malcolm in the hotel foyer. Malcolm said, 'Oh, you're finally here! Why didn't you tell me you'd arrived?' "

Once again, McLaren thought he had found the perfect studio location, and once again, as soon as Horn and Langan saw the place, they wondered how they would ever be able to record there. No problem, said Hollis, and the assorted crew was now taken to a modern twenty-four-track studio, apparently the only other studio in Jo'burg that would risk renting out to foreigners. For the next three weeks, the three Londoners worked late at night with Lulu's band, men with names like Archie and Big Voice Jack (a singer), and a troupe of girl singers, one of whom McLaren later claimed he had an affair with: "I slept with a few Zulu girls and that's very dangerous indeed. But the girls were hard to resist and I also thought that by sleeping with them I'd get to know the country quicker."

Lyrics were written on the spot, on a giant roll of paper McLaren carried wherever he went, and they ran the full gamut of his momentary preoccupations, with each song ostensibly based on either traditional Zulu folk dances, double-dutch skipping, or some other incantation ordered on the level of traditional square dance calling. As for music, as far as Trevor Horn could see, McLaren seemed to be relying on Lulu Maseelela's band to come up with tunes for which Horn would then be asked to add a few new arrangements. McLaren would then add his vocal track, and: *voilà*, a song! As far as Hollis and Lulu Maseelela knew, McLaren fully intended to purchase the copyrights for these songs, several of which had been written around 1974 by the renowned *mbaqanga* guitarist Marks Mankwene; as it transpired, McLaren planned no such thing. (For his part, Horn says he was working on the assumption that these were "traditional" songs.)

The sessions were undoubtedly a gas. Marijuana flowed freely and McLaren told the Zulus great stories about the Sex Pistols, which they couldn't believe had really happened. Soon a happy rapport was struck up, and McLaren took his first real stabs at singing the songs he had just "written."

"I just pissed myself with laughter," says Langan. "I couldn't believe it. I was trying to get a level, but I was laughing so hysterically, I just left the recording machine on and left the room. When I walked back in, Malcolm was taking off his headphones, and he said, 'All right then, I've done it, I've sung it,' and of course, he'd only done one take and thought it was really fab, and it was atrocious. I said, 'You have to sing it again, Malcolm, because you're shouting.' He said, *'Shouting?* I've just done the song. Didn't you record it boy?' I said, 'Malcolm, you can't just do it *once,* you've got to do it a few times before we get a good take,' and he said, 'What do you mean? I'm a one-take-wonder!' " At this point, Horn walked in and explained to McLaren that he needed to sing his part again, this time with "timing, tuning, and feeling." McLaren was incensed. "Hold on a minute," he said. "You mean you want me to sing in time, sing in tune, and sing with some kind of emotion too? *That's* asking a lot!"

Twelve songs were finally recorded—among them the songs that would later appear on McLaren's album as "Double Dutch," "Punk It Up," "Jive My Baby Jive," and "(Living on the Road in) Soweto"—and McLaren paid off the musicians. "I had to troop down to this rather awful record company," said McLaren, "to get the money, which was at least twice what you pay a session musician here for such a short period— something like £2,000 for nearly three weeks work—and they were loath to pay these Zulus so much and were trying all sorts of ways to convince me not to pay them. But the greatest thing really was paying them, because these guys were all so knocked out that one guy bought himself a wife, another guy brought his wife back from Swaziland, and another guy bought two cows. We brought them all back to Trevor who was doing some final mixing and back-up vocals with some of the Zulu girls, and Trevor just couldn't believe it. He was absolutely amazed, and *that* was one of the most heartfelt moments of the whole thing. It was just incredible because you realized what you had just done for them, that you paid them what they actually deserved, for their brilliant talent, and they just felt really good. And I didn't patronize them, but I told them as soon as I could I'd get them to London and get them on the stage and onto that TV set."

Of course, what McLaren really meant was that he wanted them to be in his video, and he now stayed in Jo'burg for another week to travel some eight hundred miles into the bush with a South African film crew Steve Weltman had managed to hire after a long argument about how expensive this entire project was getting to be. Horn and Langan knew a good thing when they saw it, and returned to London to start sorting out the masses of material they had now acquired.

Several weeks later, McLaren was back in London and arranged with Steve Weltman to pay for the World's Famous Supreme Team to be sent over from New York.

C. Divine the Mastermind and Just Allah the Superstar were not exactly the easiest people to work with. Daytime pickpockets in Times Square, by night, these two were hardened players in the rough-and-tumble of the scratch scene. Once they arrived in London, they quickly cottoned onto who this Malcolm McLaren character was, and made numerous demands for special record decks and stylus arms, over increasingly loud protests from Charisma that this had to be the longest and most expensive album ever recorded in the company's entire fifteen-year history. For McLaren, however, there were no such words as *can't* or *don't*, and Justice and Divine, as they were called, soon got everything they needed even though McLaren still hadn't the foggiest idea of what he was going to do with them once he actually got them into the studio.

"Whenever Trevor asked Malcolm what he was going to do," says Gary Langan, "he always had the stock answer that 'You're the producer, I'm just the artist, how should I know?' and we didn't even think about how weird that really was. I mean, he would say, 'That's why I've got you here boy: You're going to make the record—I'm just the bleeding artiste!' and that always seemed to settle it."

Then McLaren came up with the idea that would turn "Folk Dances of the World" into a real album. Instead of actually traveling around the world himself, *the Supreme Team would go around the world for him,* in the studio. *They* were to be the link between all these different varieties of music. The only problem now was deciding how those connections were to be made: Would the Supreme Team sing on each track? Or would McLaren sing and use the Supreme Team as the narrative seams *between* the tracks? Or perhaps the Supreme Team would scratch all the different bits of tape together, just as they might scratch several different records together in New York?

It seemed obvious that scratching was the centerpiece of McLaren's idea, and indeed, scratching, made by dropping the stylus head over discrete bits of a record a DJ might want to mix together with different bits of a totally different record on a second turntable, had all sorts of connections to both the history of art—as a sonic form of collage—and the history of rock 'n' roll. The scratching sound itself is nothing but the momentary backcuing of a record while the DJ is manually sliding the disc under the stylus head, but the effect is radical, a whooshing, sliding sound that can only be the result of a deliberate elision of modern turntable technology.

Without coming to any definite decision about how or what the album was to be—the first sessions mostly consisted of the Supreme Team unsuccessfully attempting to duplicate their radio show in the studio—the obvious first step in order even to allow the possibility of the Supreme Team scratching the album was to make records from all the different bits of recorded materials that had been acquired since mid-June. Since making a single copy of each tape as a record would be prohibitively expensive, it was decided that acetates—the recording equivalent of rushes from a film—would be produced so that the boys would have something to play with. Acetates, however, are very soft pieces of plastic—the grooves will usually just wear out after half a dozen plays—so multiple copies of each acetate had to be made. Expensive again, but obviously necessary if McLaren was to push forward the rather avant-garde concept of making a record from scratching other records.

Progress was slow at first. Horn would give the Supreme Team a beat he would tap out on the Linn drum machine and Justice and Divine would scratch the records under his rhythm. To the Supreme Team, it was strange to be scratching the gentle melodies of Peyote Pete's "Buffalo Gals" against the rapid-fire hip-hop beat, but as Horn and keyboardist Anne Dudley began to fill out the sound with some lush synthesizer parts and Fairlight fills, these Manhattan homeboys slowly got to enjoy ripping apart what they called "this KKK music," rapping their own lyrics over the strange sound.

Once this part of the song had been finished, it was time to add McLaren's vocal over the complex figure of scratching, synth parts, beat box rhythms, and odd Supreme Team word raps. Such a tangled network of rhythms would present a challenge for any singer, but McLaren had tremendous difficulty even singing his part of the song, the square dance calls from the original Peyote Pete version of "Buffalo Gals," on his own.

"This track was obviously really rhythmically orientated," says Langan, "so any singing that was going to be done on it had to be good and we'd already got this rap that Justice and Divine had done which ended up being the middle eight of the song. We set Malcolm up in the studio and played him the rhythm track and needless to say he was just all over the place as if he was singing to another record in his headphones. Timewise, what he was singing bore no relationship at all to what he was being given.

"Finally, Trevor said, 'How are we *ever* going to do this?' and I told him that I didn't know but that he had better figure it out soon because you couldn't put a record out like this. It was awful. So Trevor went out in the studio and stood in front of Malcolm, thumping out the beat on his chest, literally hitting him and shaking him on the chest, four on the bar to keep him in time. To any other musician *that* would have been the most embarrassing thing in the world, but Malcolm was so different than any other artists Trevor and I had worked with, that anything could quite easily become the norm. In fact, after a while, the fact that he couldn't sing but was going to be the singer on this record seemed perfectly feasible. He never got embarrassed about anything."

To nearly everyone who worked on it, "Buffalo Gals," completed in early October, had hit written all over it. Everyone was happy. McLaren felt vindicated; Charisma was pleased that it would have at least one single to sell; and Horn now had a formula to continue working on the rest of the album. There was tons of material to go through—so much that for a while Charisma considered making the record a double-album—but still no means of linking it all together. McLaren was no help either: The only time he was to be found in the studio was when he was needed to cut his vocals. But then, Trevor Horn had an idea: Why not use the little cassette tapes of the Supreme Team that Langan had recorded as the links between the songs, turning the entire record into a single, seamless whole, as if the Supreme Team were narrating the "trip around the world" McLaren still claimed he had taken.

By early November, "Buffalo Gals" had become a solid hit in the U.K., shooting up the charts to number nine in a matter of weeks, and Malcolm McLaren was suddenly being proclaimed a hot new recording artist in his own right. ("I am an artist," he solemnly declared in one *NME* interview. *"I am.* I always was and I always will be.") McLaren had a great time with the press, playing up Trevor Horn's role as the archetypal hippie superstar in much the same way he had previously accused John Lydon, Adam Ant, and Bow Wow Wow of being errant careerists caught up in the rock 'n' roll racket; castigating those who would accuse him of stealing the sounds of those he had simply paid off ("Did Chuck Berry get copyright from the Beatles?" he asked; in fact, Berry did); and steaming ahead with what seemed an unlimited number of schemes for new projects.

Indeed, McLaren now seemed to be engaged in no less than three projects at the same time, all in various stages of crisis. Most immediate was Nostalgia of Mud, finally launched with Westwood's latest spring line in the Grand Tent at the official *prêt-à-porter defilés* in the Jardin des Tuileries. Titled "Hobo/Punkature" (punk couture) and consisting mostly of lighter versions of the previous season's unsuccessful Buffalo collection—an odd combination of floppy, oversized jackets with low-slung lapels and tiny preshrunk shirts, often with bright satin brassieres worn African-style *over* the shirts—the show was the smash hit of the Paris collections. Her critics confuted, Westwood was suddenly being acclaimed as a very special artist in her own right whose vision happened to be revealed in clothes rather than paintings.

McLaren too, shined brightly in the reflected glory of Westwood's success, and he made sure to let the fashion press know that he had been deeply involved in the collection, although Westwood had deliberately kept him out of her workroom until the last minute before her clothes were taken to Paris. (McLaren and Nick Egan also did the music for the show, giving Worlds End some of the outtakes from the very first sessions with Trevor Horn.)

Concurrent with the debut of the Hobo collection, McLaren was also beginning to think of ways of turning his new album into either a musical or a film utilizing the Zulu backup singers (whom McLaren called "the McLarenettes"), Louis Calaph's Happy Dominicans, the Cuban and Peruvian musicians he had found in New York, and of course, the World's Famous Supreme Team, now safely back at WHBI after having attempted to blackmail Horn and Langan by not appearing at sessions unless McLaren made them the stars of the album. Batting around ideas one day, McLaren called the Royal Court Theatre and was referred to Jonathan Gems, whom he already knew from his Bow Wow Wow days.

"Malcolm and I were walking through Soho, and he was on one of his adrenalin kicks," says Gems, "going back and forth between doing the album as either a musical or a film. Finally, he said it had all been fixed with Charisma and that he'd talked to the Royal Court, talked to Andrew Lloyd Webber, and talked to Michael White, and that he was going to put it on as a musical at the Astoria Theatre. 'It's no problem, it's all fixed. We're gonna get thirty Zulus,' he said, 'get them all over from South Africa, bring them over to London, and get them to make their music and do their dances, get the Double Dutch girls from the States, get the Cubans, and the Peruvians, and the Dominicans'—and I stopped him and I said, 'Wait a minute! That's a cast of fifty! Think of how much money that will cost!' 'Not to worry,' he said. 'You just think of a way of linking all these little bits of music and dance. Make it like a Marx Brothers routine. And don't worry about the money, you'll get paid.'

"So I got busy," says Gems, a playwright and screenwriter whose best-known films include Michael Radford's *1984* and *White Mischief.* "I phoned him up and asked him whether he wanted to be in the musical himself, sort of like a Pan figure, flitting here and there, introducing these little bits of music and dance. I'd just been reading about Greek mythology, and there's this one god, Pan, who pops in and out, making messes everywhere. 'Yeah,' he said, 'I do want to be in it myself and I've already worked out this opening sequence.' He was going to be called Mr. McTavish.

"But then I had to ask him again, how he was ever going to finance this. I knew that the only way a musical of that expense—at least £1 million—could work was if everybody was committed to a nine-month contract at the very minimum. I asked him if he was ready to do that, to go to the theater *every day and night* for nine months? He said, 'What? I'm only going to do it for a few weeks. And if you don't tell anyone, I'll tell you how. Tony Stratton-Smith—he's an old theater man, and he loves the idea—he's going to put £500,000 into it. And this other guy, the producer, he's going to put £200,000 into it. I'll get Michael White to throw in some more, Chris Blackwell to throw in some more, we'll have this big opening night at the Astoria, I'll go on, I'll do my bit for a week, and then the second week, I'll be off to America. I'll disappear! So I finally asked him why, and he said, 'Ahhhhh! Situationism: *Destroy the spectacle!*' 'Malcolm,' I said, 'but *you're* creating the spectacle!' He said, 'Yeah, but I'm creating the spectacle so that I can *destroy* it!' "

Although it does seem several meetings with some of the above parties were held, none of the financing McLaren claimed he had received had actually been committed. Indeed, at this stage, most of McLaren's time was spent locking horns with Charisma over which song was to be released as the next single from his forthcoming album, now called *Duck Rock.*

" 'Buffalo Gals' had sold half a million copies," says Steve Weltman, "which is a lot of records. There were a lot of kids who suddenly knew who Malcolm McLaren was. Phonogram was pressing me for an answer, so I told them the next single would be 'Double Dutch,' but when Malcolm heard, he was adamant about doing 'Soweto' as the second single. It's true, we had a brilliant film for what I knew was a very good song, but I thought it was a bit out of touch with the rapping thing which by now had started to catch on in London."

As usual, McLaren got his way, and he now left for Soweto and New

York (stopping in London to promote "Buffalo Gals" with a square-dance party at Philip Sallon's new Mud Club) to shoot additional footage for the new promotional videos he was secretly intending to use as the basic footage for a movie.

Now began the great and nasty struggle between Charisma and Malcolm McLaren, which was to last for the next two years. The problems began with the release of "Soweto" in early February 1983. "At first," says Weltman, " 'Soweto' got a tremendous amount of airplay. For about two weeks, it was the number-one record on Radio 1. But then it didn't happen. It dropped to thirty-one, *fast.* Every single kid had heard 'Buffalo Gals' and was trying to breakdance to it, and then suddenly we were taking the kids from New York and the Supreme Team to Soweto and Zulu rock 'n' roll. Nobody bought it. And at the very end of the day, Malcolm couldn't live with that fact. The seeds of animosity had been sown.

"But as soon as Malcolm got to New York, his plans changed. We had decided on a budget of $70,000 for Malcolm to finish ten 16mm films by May, but when I came to see Malcolm in New York, all of a sudden he wanted to spend $350,000. I was speaking to our office and our lawyers and his office and his lawyers, and in the end, a lot of heavy shit went down. There was a pattern of him going over budget: One night Malcolm had a party in his hotel room at the Parker Meridien, and all his friends were invited to order whatever they wanted from room service: We got a $14,000 bill! We decided we just weren't going to let Malcolm have his way again and spend another $350,000 to make another six or seven promos. We already had all the footage we needed for four or five films, so we couldn't see why he should then go on and do another ten, especially with such an enormous budget.

"Anyway, the next thing we know we get this letter from Island saying McLaren told them he wanted his name off the album. He said he'd sue if they put his name on it, and that touched off another confrontation about the credits on the record. Because Malcolm had already had a fight with Trevor about where Trevor's name appeared on the record. Nick Egan did the artwork and on the back of the cover, in tiny print in the lower right-hand corner, it says 'produced by Trevor Horn,' and I found that so insulting. At my insistence he finally put in some credits for the Zulu Nation, and I said, 'Make sure you thank Trevor and Gary and Terry Doktor.' His response was nil: 'No way, what for?' Then, after we sent the artwork to the printers, he finally had an attack of conscience and out of the blue added a note that said "Thanks to my producer Trevor Horn who through all the madness, soldiered on to rediscover the origins of Rock 'n' Roll.' "

Nor was the acrimony limited to Charisma. For soon after *Duck Rock* was released, McLaren engaged in all-out warfare with Trevor Horn (conducted mostly via tabloid tittle-tattle) and Phil Hollis back in Johannesburg.

For his part, Hollis was annoyed that McLaren had listed the song credits on *Duck Rock* as having been written by "McLaren/Horn." "I started the legal ball rolling," says Hollis. "These songs were normal, registered songs. They were not 'traditional' songs, but songs like any other song that's already been registered with ASCAP or BMI or any other performing rights society, and to use them you would have to do a split, usually at least 50/50. Malcolm said he'd give me a small percentage and I objected. I said, 'You're treating me like you're throwing peanuts to a monkey, and I'm not a monkey.' And if you look at these songs you see that they are real. "Jive My Baby Jive" is actually "Thina Siyakhanyisa" by N. Bopape/M. Mankwene of 1394 Khiawelo, Maraco, Soweta. "Double Dutch" is "Jive Mabone" by R. Bopape/E. Peliso. "Soweto" is "He Mdjadji" by Mijaji Shirinda. The others that appeared on the album were "Tsotsi" (also by P. Mareli) and "Fikhuelekile," but I can't remember what tracks those were."

In the end, Hollis sued everyone—McLaren, Horn, April Music, Malcolm McLaren Songs, and Unforgettable Songs (Horn's publishing company)—and although judgment was eventually offered in his favor, the case was settled out of court for legal fees. "It's true that Malcolm paid the musicians three or four times what the normal studio fee is for musicians in South Africa," says Hollis, "but he was greedy over the publishing and he shouldn't have done that. He should have done a deal and then everybody would have been happy, just as we were very happy with Paul Simon. At the end of the day, I'm not angry, because Malcolm only helped to turn the world onto the unique qualities of South African music, which is different than anywhere else in the world, including Zimbabwe. If I had to say anything to him now, in fact, I would just tell him to use the other seven songs he *didn't* use. Put the damned things out, but make sure you credit the songwriters."

In 1986, Earthworks International, a British indie distributed by Virgin, released *Duck Food,* a reissue of the record *Umculo Kawupheli (There's No End to the Music),* originally released on the Motella label (LPBS 20) on February 2, 1974, and performed by The Mahotella Queens, The Mgababa Queens, The Dark City Sisters, and Irene and the Sweet Melodians, all of whom are renowned for the *Mgoashiyo* (Indestructible Beat) sound they created in the early seventies. Among its tracks are not only the above named "Jive Mabone," "Thina Siyakhanyisa," and "Isisi

Somhambi" by E. Mkize/M. Mankwene (appearing as "Punk It Up" on *Duck Rock*), but also two other songs that were obvious sources *for Bow Wow Wow's material* as well: "Umculo Kawupheli" (also by N. F. Bopape/M. Mankwene) is note for note the Bow Wow Wow song "See Jungle! See Jungle!" and the chorus of "Akulaiwa Esoweto" bears a close resemblance to Bow Wow Wow's "Mickey, Put It Down!"

Needless to say, Trevor Horn has a different version of these events. "What we did," he says, "is to take these traditional riffs and then change them around, but just slightly, because normally, the publishing on a traditional song goes to the arranger. The publishing credit on the album was supposed to read 'Trad. arranged by,' but somehow it was credited to McLaren/Horn, and the guy who owned the studio said he found the person who had supposedly written the material the week after we left. It was a setup, because really we all wrote it together."

In a funny way, McLaren's fight with Horn was a mirror image of his legal tiff with Phil Hollis. For upon the completion of "Duck Rock," Gary Langan began working in the studio with Horn and Jonathan (J.J.) Jeczalik and Anne Dudley, who together became the Art of Noise. "Trevor would not admit it," says Langan, "but Art of Noise really began because of the work we did on Malcolm's album, and Malcolm claimed that since he had been responsible for Trevor's success, he was also responsible for Art of Noise. He even offered to manage us. You see, Malcolm never gave Trevor any credit, and Trevor, therefore, never gave Malcolm any credit, so the two of them just started slagging each other off in the press. And when 'Beat Box,' our first single came out here, it did nothing in England, but then Chris Blackwell took it to America and made it a cult hit in New York. Which made us even worse as far as Malcolm was concerned because he wanted 'Buffalo Gals' to be number one and it never went very high over there. He thought we stole the number-one slot away from him."

Trevor Horn: "Let's put it this way. On *Duck Rock* there were quite a few moments where I became the artist and Malcolm became the producer. And it's stupid because whenever anyone claims the credit for an idea, you have to stand up and say it's a team that did it. It's a pointless thing. But when it comes to publishing, when someone treats you as if you were stupid, you have to have some hard words for them. So when I had heard he'd been offered around $100,000 dollars and a substantial royalty for the publishing, I decided I wanted half, because it wasn't worth doing unless I got that much.

"Look," Horn says with exasperation, "I like to work with people who are stars, and Malcolm is definitely a star, but it's awfully funny to be called a technician after you've done all that work."

For years, London's most fashion conscious people had followed the twists and turns of the Worlds End story with morbid fascination. Worlds End was a house divided, and everyone had his favorite partner. Many, hearing McLaren claim fashion expertise, nearly choked; others wondered why McLaren needed Westwood at all. People wondered if there would one day be a fight to the finish between Worlds End's constantly bickering partners.

At a party following the Hobo/Punkature show in Paris in November 1982, McLaren and Westwood were introduced by Lucia Raffaelli, senior fashion editor of Italian *Vogue,* to two Italian fashion publicists, Carlo Dimario and Giannino Malossi, both of whom were then working for Elio Fiorucci. Dimario and Malossi were quite enamored of Worlds End's clothes, and soon after the Hobo line was unveiled, they set up a second showing of the collection in Milan, enabling Westwood and McLaren to sign an agreement with powerful Milanese fashion agent Alberto Raffaelli, Lucia's husband.

Over the next six months, while McLaren was scurrying between Soweto, London, and New York, Westwood began working on her next collection. For the first time, Westwood's new line, called "Witches" because McLaren said it reminded him of a book he had been "reading" on Haitian voodoo, pushed beyond her partner's ideas into a realm uncontaminated by his obsession for cultural thievery. Where McLaren had quite literally ripped off the customizing idea from hip-hop kids who tagged every article of clothing with their names—McLaren's idea of customizing was to commission graffiti-artist Dondi White to decorate his ghetto-blaster with horns and antennae—Westwood incorporated the idea of customizing *into the fabric of her clothes* in such a way that the wearer of the garment defined the way it looked just because of the way it fit his or her body. Constructed of soft, woolen jersey that took its inspiration from athletic wear and colored in bright shades of fuchsia, mustard, and gray with Keith Haring's weird urban hieroglyphs carefully scrawled on say, a single shoulder, Witches had a radical result, helping to reconceptualize fashion anarchically in terms of its effects on individual wearers. Designers as different from each other as Jean-Paul Gaultier and Rei Kawakubo and Comme des Garcons freely admit the powerful influence of this collection on their fashions.

"To me, customizing was a question of technique," Westwood explains. "I'm not exactly sure when it occurred to me to put a hole that you stick your head through on a T-shirt in a different place, because a T-shirt is a T-shirt, after all. But if you change the place of the hole the fabric plays and touches around the body, it bunches up in different places. It touches one hip higher than the other and gives you a feeling of curvaceousness, a little like Marilyn Monroe when she's undulating in the movies. Clothes that are too small or too big set the figure in circulation, in motion. They give it style and that gives someone a feeling of heroism—and that's where we began with punk because the straps that connected the legs in the bondage trousers really made you feel heroic."

Suddenly, it seemed all of Italian fashion had fallen in love with Vivienne Westwood and her winning tube skirts, skintight woolen jersey skirts inspired when McLaren happened to catch Westwood wearing what she considered a cleaning schmatte. Elio Fiorucci wanted Westwood to design a collection for her; Lucia Raffaelli made sure to feature Westwood's clothes in *Vogue;* Alberto Raffaelli was anxious to get Westwood to produce her clothes in Italy where they could be mass-produced in new high-tech facilities; Dimario wanted to become Westwood's manager, and in any event, soon became her boyfriend.

McLaren was incensed when he heard that Westwood had signed a 50–75 million lira contract with Fiorucci to design a jeans-oriented "World School" collection. He and Westwood were legally co-owners of Worlds End, he claimed, and Westwood had no right to engage in contracts on her own with the Italians. He had taken a special dislike to Carlo Dimario.

" 'You're a Judas!' he told me," says Westwood. " 'A Judas!' I said, 'Malcolm, you went away with another woman three years ago. What are you talking about? How can you say such things?'

"To be honest, I had stopped thinking it was his business ever since the Pirate collection," she says. "Because when the Sex Pistols were finished, Malcolm told me—and I believed it to be so—that I really did have the potential to break out of this shop and go to Paris and really influence the fashion world with our ideas. I was very clear with him all along. Our lease came up for renewal and I said, 'Malcolm, I will do this, but I need some sort of financial help, I can't do it all on my own, and *you've* got to help me find somebody to help organize it, because I don't want to renew the lease if you won't help. I'll support you in the music business if that's what you want me to do, but I can't do this on my own.' And Malcolm said, yes, he would help, and then very soon he was off with Adam and Bow Wow Wow and he never found me a backer or any help. For years, he hadn't even signed a check, and I had to do all the struggling on my own.

"So finally I thought, well, all right, I've got to find people to help me finance this thing on my own, and that's when Carlo came into the picture."

By the time Witches was shown in Paris in late March 1983, Westwood's trust in McLaren had been so bruised that she decided to keep him out of her workroom until the week before the clothes were shipped to Paris. And then to no one's surprise but Malcolm McLaren's, Witches was a smash hit. The night after the show, a giant party was held in Westwood's honor at a luxurious Parisian gymnasium filled with palm trees and swimming pools, attended by the best and the brightest of Italian fashion—Madonna gave her first European performance there that night—and McLaren flipped out. "He never understood the situation in Italy," says Giannino Malossi, then Dimario's partner in their Casanova public relations firm. "It's an old story: The English don't trust the Italian businessmen in fashion. Malcolm just didn't like the project. He felt his designs were getting out of control."

The next day, Westwood flew back to Milan to continue work on her collection and McLaren flew back to London in a rage. Within days he sent a telex through his attorney to Brescia, to the Kronos factory producing the Witches collection, claiming that Westwood had stolen the patterns for the new line from Worlds End's London workroom. The immediate effect of this message was to throw what Westwood calls "a big scare" into the Kronos company, and production on the Witches collection ground to a halt.

Now McLaren had betrayed the one person who had made possible the very transformation he had already undergone from manager to artist—a twenty-year "collaboration" in which Westwood did most of the work while McLaren provided the ideas—but he was by no means content to stop there.

"Malcolm tried to get everybody in London to band together against me," says Westwood, gulping down the words as if she never wanted to speak them again. "He tried to convince everyone, all my employees who had worked so long for me, that they were now working for him. They didn't even sell within the shop anymore. They could do whatever they wanted. He gave them a pep talk and told them they were important and they'd been supporters of him for ages, and all this kind of thing, and a lot of people bought it.

"Had it not been for Gene Krell," she continues, "I would have lost both of my shops. As it is I only lost Nostalgia of Mud because Malcolm didn't give any money to the wholesale company—which is me—and therefore I wouldn't give them any wholesale merchandise, so the store had no stock. Then he changed the numbers of the bank accounts and the locks on my workroom while I was away, and put any money belonging to me in those accounts."

On April 12, McLaren and Westwood had a showdown in London, but not before McLaren leaked his side of the story to the *Evening Standard.* "I will fight tooth and nail," he declared. "Worlds End may continue with or without Vivienne Westwood. The Worlds End mark is more significant than the likes of Fiorucci. For the past four years I have personally financed and developed our concerns. I haven't struggled for ten years to see them go off to Italy. Worlds End was born out of *English* fashion, in particular our street culture. . . . What we create on the streets out of the dustbins of England is an extremely exportable commodity. If Vivienne wants to go down a more bourgeois road, fair enough. But she owes some consideration to the partnership here."

But what are you so afraid of, asked the reporter? "I'm afraid that she'll end up making a verbal agreement with the Italians," McLaren shrilly replied. "She does tend to get embroiled in spaghetti dinners and fall for Italian charm."

Within three weeks, McLaren told the newspapers he had given in. With Nostalgia of Mud reporting debts of nearly £10,000, he had to surrender. "I am pulling out and handing it all over to her," he told the *Standard.* "She wanted it more than I did."

But now Westwood wanted nothing more to do with McLaren or the renegades who had taken his side in the entire imbroglio. Throughout the rest of the summer, the Worlds End soap opera continued—"It's all a bit like *Dallas,*" McLaren said in one of his kinder moods—but Westwood, encouraged by Dimario, would not back down on her demands for creative control over Worlds End. McLaren tried everything he could to change her mind, at one point even flying to Brescia to see whether he could repair the damage caused by the utterly fallacious telegram he had sent to the Kronos factory, but when Westwood failed to heed his charms, he continued his war of attrition through the newspapers, repeating the story that "We've locked Vivienne out of her studios and have seized all the patterns. I'm trying to protect Worlds End from going to the Italians. If we can't reach agreement, *I'll* just have to design the clothes."

Later that summer, Nostalgia of Mud finally ran out of stock, and with debts mounting daily, the turncoat shopkeepers closed the boutique's doors amid a welter of complaints from local councillors that the shopfront, with its mud-colored bunting and wooden maps of the African continent, was an eyesore and fire hazard. Westwood continued to work on her next collection under the auspices of Alberto Raffaelli, who refused to let McLaren get out of the mess he had made by selling out his fifty percent share in Worlds End, but with all the brouhaha and accusations, Hipgnosis, as the new line was called, was barely produced in enough quantity to supply the Worlds End shop, much less any other stores still clamoring for Westwood's athletic style. Inevitably, those who have seen the Hipgnosis collection, the culmination of Westwood's *gymnasium* look, with springy rubber-fringed Greek motifs and bright fluorescent appliqués, say it was some of her best work.

"The whole thing was like a movie," remembers Giannino Malossi, whose partnership with Dimario ended in the middle of the whole mess. "It was like Fellini, with the English against the English, the Italians against the Italians. People were crying and fighting like cat and dog. I have seen nothing like it ever since."

For several years after the debacle that was Nostalgia of Mud, Vivienne Westwood's career seemed to lie in ruins. While her clothes remained popular among fashion editors—the powerful *Women's Wear Daily* defended her collections regardless of their diminished range—the public never quite followed her work as closely as it had when the bands Malcolm McLaren managed had worn her clothes. Try though she might to resurrect the Italian connections that had taken her from King's Road to the Jardin des Tuileries, Westwood and her boyfriend/manager, Carlo DeMario, seemed prone to running into new obstacles every way they turned. In 1984, for example, Westwood made a seven-year licensing deal with designer Giorgio Armani and his partner Sergio Galeotti to produce and distribute Westwood's intricately cut and eccentrically textured clothes in return for a $3 million fee. But when Galeotti died of AIDS a year later, the deal fell through, and Westwood was once again left to dance without a partner.

After a year as fashion's invisible woman, Westwood finally made a return to form late in 1985. First she designed the puffy, bell-shaped mini-crinolines which became an international fashion success story but never got produced—although they were copied worldwide the next season. Then, in 1987, she followed up with a collection of odd Harris Tweeds, clothes for a wiggy Sherlock Holmes. Some criticized the new clothes as being too conservative, a virtual "paean to tradition and royalty." But Westwood has stuck to her guns, dressing her models as mock royalty, and even making a guest appearance on the cover of *Tatler*, convincingly disguised as Margaret Thatcher. By November 1988, her relentless perseverance had paid off, and she finally opened her very own boutique, deep in the heart of fashionable Mayfair.

11
MY
WICKED, WICKED
WAYS

I enter a whorehouse with the same interest as I do the British Museum or the Metropolitan—in the same spirit of curiosity. Here are the works of man, here is an art of man, here is his eternal pursuit of gold and pleasure. I couldn't be more sincere. This doesn't mean that if I go to La Scala in Milan to hear Carmen *I want to get up on the stage and participate. I do not. Neither do I always participate in a fine representative national whorehouse—but I must see it as a spectacle, an offering, a symptom of a nation.*

—*Errol Flynn,* My Wicked, Wicked Ways

With the release of *Duck Rock* in May 1983, the transformation of Malcolm McLaren from manager to artist was finally complete. Particularly in Britain, where he was now seen as a colorful and eccentric figure, the elder statesman of punk rock, McLaren had come to stand for a bizarrely futuristic vision of a Britain positively glowing with style. When television needed a soundbite to explain the profusion of the so-called New Pop cropping up across England—Duran Duran, Wham!, Frankie Goes to Hollywood—it was McLaren they turned to for explanations. If someone needed gossip, McLaren was there with a juicy tabloid tidbit. Malcolm McLaren was now an A-list celebrity: his lifelong gambit to invest himself with the aura of the star was successful at last.

That this metamorphosis should have taken place at the same time that that greengrocer's daughter turned prime minister, Mrs. Margaret Thatcher, was so forcefully propounding a return to the Victorian values of hard work, thriftiness, and the virtues of meritocracy, can only be the greatest irony. As Malcolm McLaren himself loved to point out, his career was built upon precisely the polar qualities: McLaren loved to tell people he was a thief, a profligate, and a betrayer.

Indeed, push aside the sleekly self-conscious ideological trappings of these two alteregos, and Thatcher's penny-pinching monetarism and McLaren's fumbling marketing of subcultures will be seen to share a strikingly similar root: the typical middle-class preference for money over ideology. Thatcher, the born monetarist, could hardly care less *how* money is distributed in Great Britain, as long as ever-increasing amounts of cash circulate throughout her economy with ever-increasing velocity; Malcolm McLaren, the born huckster, could hardly care less what subculture he is at present exploiting (Teds, Bikers, Punks, Zulus, and so forth) as long as his latest trend is showing a profit. No matter the rhetoric, for both, politics has finally become the pretext for making or controlling money.

Oddly, while Thatcherism would seem to be the supreme environment for McLaren's idea of style as the cutting edge of postindustrial society, McLaren's high-handed dismissal of the most basic rules of business had left him with hardly a friend in the British music industry. Increasingly, his lifelong hustle to invest himself with the anarchist's aura was coming to be seen for exactly what it had been all along: a hustle. The veneer of political street credibility McLaren had used to forward his career ever since he was sixteen had finally been stripped away. It was suddenly clear that the only transformation McLaren had ever desired was personal, not social and not political. It would not be long before he was off to America, where the moral distance between crime and pretense are not so clear and the words "change me!" are as common as apple pie.

In the autumn of 1983, Malcolm McLaren made up his mind that he was going to get out of his deal with Charisma Records. He was particularly disturbed that *Duck Rock* had failed to be a worldwide smash, and he blamed its failure on Steve Weltman, whom he claimed was "more interested in money than music." McLaren wanted Weltman fired: "You fire Steve Weltman, I'll stay!" he told Tony Stratton-Smith. But to McLaren's chagrin, Strat was unwilling to let McLaren leave the label without fulfilling his contract: one more album. Strat, customarily loquacious, told McLaren to "get stuffed."

McLaren now set lawyer Howard Jones on Charisma, but when Jones got no farther with Stratton-Smith than McLaren had on his own, McLaren fired him and hired lawyer Irving David, from the firm of Elton

Weinman. David now came up with numerous proposals, offering Charisma *Duck Rock*'s outtakes if it would only let McLaren go, but again the answer was no. "Charisma had all the rights to the tracks recorded so far," recalls Weltman, "so it wouldn't exactly have been a fair trade to accept those tracks as fulfilling his contract." With continual rumors that McLaren was quietly peddling his wares around town, Weltman had the sudden realization that the reason McLaren wanted to get off Charisma actually had little to do with the way *Duck Rock* had been handled: "It came over me that Malcolm was really stuck for money," Weltman says with a grin that would do a Cheshire cat proud, "but he was also legally stuck—no one was coming up to save the day for him. So we finally came up with the idea that if he would make a *third* album for Charisma, for which we would give him an additional advance, one of these albums could be composed of the tracks that had been recorded from *Duck Rock*."

McLaren was stuck. That week he signed a new Charisma contract and left London as quickly as he could, setting up shop in New York at Greene Street and Blank Tapes studios, carting in nearly a score of boxes containing the *Duck Rock* outtakes. Now McLaren moved as if he had only one goal in mind: Fulfill the obligations to Charisma starting with *Duck Rock 2* and then move on.

For an artist with a big ego and a tiny budget, there was no musical genre better suited to that aim than the craze for "dance music," then in its first flush thanks to Michael Jackson's *Thriller* and Madonna's Top 20 hits "Holiday" and "Everybody." Produced specifically for extended action on the dance floor, dance music relied more on digital sampling and painstaking remixing, taking one beat and multiplying it over a number of measures with added percussion effects, than on traditional musical artistry or even the artistic ingenuity of a studio whiz like Trevor Horn. The last thing McLaren needed was *new* music: Ever since his return from Soweto, McLaren had had all the "music" he needed. What he did need, however, was new *songs:* more product to fulfill his contract. It would all be so simple, he thought, simple to get a hot DJ who was edging his way into the remix game—Johnny Dynell, then having his first success with the song "Jam Hot," fit the bill perfectly—and cut some new songs from Trevor Horn's old cloth. Anybody could do it, right?

As McLaren found after nearly a month playing around as a producer-songwriter, writing rap lyrics with Dynell and rap singers Angie B. and Sharock, and adding vocal tracks from a championship cheerleading squad from Harrison, New Jersey, this dance music thing was harder than it seemed. In late fall, after months of desperation in the studio, coming up with such obvious retreads as "Duck Rock Cheer" and "Eiffel Tower"—

both of which were later to appear on his third LP, the embarrassing *Swamp Thing*—McLaren phoned Steve Weltman back in London to help him find a new producer to rescue his latest project.

Among the producers Weltman was then in contact with were two Bostonians who had made a good reputation for themselves at Synchro Sound, the recording studio owned by the Boston-based rock group the Cars. Stephen Hague and his engineer Walter Turbitt had had a big hit that year with the Rock Steady Crew—"Hey DJ"—and Weltman thought they'd be perfect for McLaren too. "One night Malcolm phoned me from New York out of the blue," says Weltman. "It was as if nothing had ever happened. But he said he wasn't going anywhere with Johnny Dynell and he needed help. Rock Steady Crew were the best breakdancers in New York and in a way, they were like Malcolm: They couldn't sing or play, but they could dance. I figured if Hague could get a Top Ten hit with them, he could probably do the same thing with Malcolm. Of course, Malcolm being Malcolm said, 'Who's this Hague and Turbitt? Get me Quincy Jones!'"

For nearly a month, McLaren's new coproducers, Hague and Turbitt, regurgitated Trevor Horn's old *Duck Rock* tracks into *Duck Rock 2*. "Really it was just Stephen and me, sitting at a piano or playing with a synthesizer and a beat box, and then Malcolm coming in and adding his vocals," says Walter Turbitt. "Most of the time Malcolm would be at his hotel or having lunch, and then he would come in and add his lyrics. That was fun, because Stephen would set Malcolm up in the studio and just let him talk with an occasional prompt or two. It might have sounded like he was giving a serious rap when the record came out, but he was laughing his balls off. It was great, great fun."

Five or six tracks later, however, the spirit of this enterprise seemed to lead to a dead end. No one was happy with the results, and after all the work that had been done, there still wasn't enough material for an album. But then McLaren came up with an idea Hague and Turbitt thought was "kind of goofy": "He wanted to set up a beat box with an opera melody," remembers Turbitt. "He kept saying he wanted to 'expose the beauty of opera to the public.' I thought he was off the wall."

McLaren's idea may have seemed like spontaneous jiving to Hague and Turbitt, but McLaren had been wondering how to mix the classics with rock 'n' roll ever since he worked with Eric Watson back in Paris. Of course, no one else knew that apart from McLaren, but the number of people who claim credit for having been present at the creation of this idea certainly attests to McLaren's genius for cultural trend spotting.

For example, Nick Egan says that McLaren first began to think seriously about opera when Vivienne Westwood heard She Sheriff's first demo tape. "Vivienne told Malcolm that he'd be better off having Pip sing the aria from *Madama Butterfly,* and Malcolm cracked up when he heard this idea, but it must have stuck in his head because one day we actually did have her do it, but the demo didn't quite measure up."

Jonathan Gems, the young writer who had turned out several treatments for *Duck Rock,* has a different story. Gems remembers that McLaren went to see Chris Blackwell about producing a movie with him, and when Blackwell responded negatively to McLaren's idea of making a street movie, McLaren blathered and came up with the idea of doing a movie about a mob of average Australian teenagers who kidnap their favorite rock star. It was called, obviously, *Fans.* Blackwell liked that idea much better.

"Malcolm got out of his meetings with Blackwell and his financial director, and then rang me from a phone box, because I was the only writer he knew then," says Gems. "He says, 'Johnny, you've got to get right to work. I'll be over in ten minutes.' And then he told me about this idea he had just tossed out to Blackwell. And we both hated it. We hated Australia and we hated fans, and it had to be set in Australia and it had to be titled *Fans.* So for the next three months we worked together, and we were so desperate to get away from the idea that we set about making the film about the kind of fans people use to keep themselves cool."

Yet another source remembers being stunned when he heard that McLaren was attempting to mix rock and opera. "Just after Malcolm came back from promoting *Duck Rock* in Australia he came to see me about doing a film," remembers Don Boyd, the very same producer-director McLaren had first approached when he wanted to make a Sex Pistols movie. "He told me that he wanted to make a film about fans, by which he meant a film about enthusiasms, and he told me it was about these two young girls who write excessive letters to this Australian rock star. He even told me about his opening shot, which would be the backside of the Beatles looking out onto the audience and seeing these kids screaming and crying at the camera. And at the very end of that meeting, he asked me what I was doing and I casually told him about *Manon,* my project on *Manon Lescaut* by Puccini, and I also told him about my film *Aria,* which at that stage was called variously, *Imagine Aria* or 'RCA Opera Project.' We discussed the whole question of opera and popular culture, and I actually said to him, 'You know something I've considered doing for *Manon* is taking opera music and getting rock 'n' roll people to adjust it.' Now he said he had been interested in doing the *Madama Butterfly* song, so I'll grant him that, but at that time *Fans* was absolutely a project that had to do with something quite different. And because it was so different, at the end of that meeting, I told him I'd be very interested in producing it, and we arranged to meet the following day. And you know, I called three or four times, and he never called me back. I could just see him snickering, 'Y'know, this one is *a better idea than the one I've got.*'"

Regardless of the sources of McLaren's opera idea—one can even include the Who's *Tommy* and Andrew Lloyd Webber—it had now fallen to Hague and Turbitt to turn what seemed a rather outlandish idea into something approaching a pop song.

McLaren's first operatic target was the aria "Un bel dì" ("One fine day") from *Madama Butterfly*. After listening to a record of *Puccini's Greatest Hits* over and over, the two producers began the process of building the song from scratch, enlisting the help of Tim McFarland, a teacher at the New England Conservatory of Music to bring them some local conservatory students to sing "Un bel dì."

According to Turbitt, McLaren wasn't even around when the song that later became known as "Madam [*sic*] Butterfly" was finally written.

"Hague had a rhythm machine going," he remembers, "and I just sat down at the piano with the tape of the aria going to a click track [a metronome] and hammered out a line that seemed to fit the singer's voice. That became the basis of the song, and we then had Malcolm start to write some lyrics. And if you look at the back of the jacket, I think you'll find a remarkable similarity between Malcolm's words and the opera libretto." (Indeed, so similar were the words of McLaren's "Madam Butterfly" to those of Puccini's aria, that when the record finally came out, the attorneys for the Puccini estate wanted to sue McLaren for copyright infringement; to their chagrin, they found that the opera had entered the public domain shortly before the record was released.)

With "Madam Butterfly" completed, nearly everyone seemed to feel they had yet again reached a cul-de-sac. Where did you go after Puccini? "Butterfly" seemed too different to be included on the same record with *Duck Rock 2*'s outlandish disco cheerleading but all had mixed feelings about going on to make another album composed solely of opera/R&B remixes. Then McLaren came up with another fresh idea: *Carmen.* "In all of popular culture," he declared, "there is no one sexier than Carmen." Hague and Turbitt wrote more music and McLaren jotted down some lyrics, but, says Weltman, "they didn't seem to be getting anywhere. Malcolm was on the phone whining away about money and how the budget was going, but after what we'd been through we weren't going to come up with any more big budgets, so everything that came out of the budget at that point was coming out of his own personal advances. Our position was once bitten, twice shy."

With the "Butterfly" template in hand and some additional backing vocal tracks for the famous "L'oiseau rebelle" aria from *Carmen,* McLaren and his two producers flew to London to do additional recording at Advision Studios. After another month of slogging it out, however, Hague and Turbitt were exhausted. "A creative funk was hanging over everyone," says Weltman. " 'Butterfly' had come totally out of the blue, but now they had spent so much time trying to get 'Carmen' right, and they were all tired."

"Malcolm was beginning to think Stephen was getting to be a little too precious, too serious about all the opera stuff," says Turbitt. "And I just couldn't see how we were going to get a whole album out of it, so I suggested to Stephen that we pull out. By then, it was more or less a mutual thing and Malcolm was fifty-fifty himself."

With a little over half of one album finished and the bare bones of another waiting to be realized, McLaren and Weltman decided to look for another producer who wouldn't add too much to their recording costs. Robby Kilgore, a twenty-seven-year-old synthesizer session player who had worked with Hall & Oates and had also produced "Let the Music Play" by Shannon, one of the highest charting dance records ever, was the perfect candidate. Kilgore had been one of the session men McLaren had used during the first New York sessions to record *Duck Rock 2,* so he already had some idea of McLaren's working style, and he was delighted to be asked. It was the first time he'd ever been hired to produce a full album.

McLaren and Kilgore now worked daily at New York's Unique Recording, first listening to the material that had already been recorded, then trying to figure out "pads" (harmonic riffs) to be recorded over the operatic material—the very opposite of standard studio composing practice.

"The arias were recorded to a click track with a piano accompaniment that wasn't recorded," explains Kilgore. "When they sang, everyone wore headphones while the accompanist would play. So then you'd have to make up a [musical] track at the same tempo as the click track and it was very difficult. I kept thinking that no one had ever done this before. Usually records are made once the music is composed, and then the vocals are added later, but here we were starting with the vocals and adding the accompaniment, so I knew I just had to bear with it. I had been a composition major in school; if I could do that, I thought I could definitely do this."

Recording continued for nearly two and half months at Unique, by which time the studio began demanding to be paid for the extraordinary amount of time McLaren had used, apparently in excess of $100,000. "Malcolm said he was going to get it extended," remembers Kilgore, "but

I was getting nervous because we didn't know where the money was going to come from, and we were hearing stories that Charisma was going bust. Finally Malcolm moved us from Unique to the Hit Factory, which is nearly twice the price. Luckily, just as we were finishing up the last details, we heard Charisma was folding and was going to be taken over by Virgin."

Charisma had not, in fact, gone bust. What *had* happened was that Virgin Records, already Charisma's distributor and marketing arm, was now planning to go public, and wished to expand its artist roster by snapping up Charisma Records, whose artists then included Peter Gabriel, Julian Lennon, and . . . Malcolm McLaren. However, so great was McLaren's dread of once again coming under the aegis of Richard Branson's now powerful Virgin organization that he rushed to fulfill the remainder of his recording obligations on *Fans* and then swiftly hopped across the corridor to a cheaper Hit Factory studio to mix down the remainder of the songs from *Duck Rock 2*—now called *Swamp Thing*. As far as Malcolm McLaren was concerned, it was to be his last experience in the record business for a long, long time.

McLaren has proclaimed that his decision to use "Un bel dì" as the signature of his attempt to cross-pollinate opera with rock 'n' roll was born of his realization that both are musics of great passion. Passion, he said, is what distinguishes great opera and great rock 'n' roll from the pap of popular culture: "Opera is the most dangerous artform of all, because it can leave you totally drained of emotion."

Coming from one who only a few short years ago had proclaimed his indifference to all music and his hatred of the status quo—the self-proclaimed father of punk rock—many were initially surprised by McLaren's sudden interest in opera. As one *Time Out* journalist wondered, "Has the man once described by Johnny Rotten as the most devious fellow he'd ever come across, gone soft?"

Of course not. McLaren's use of opera was as insidiously historicist as any of his other dilettantish dabblings in marginalized cultures: It had nothing to do with opera for its *own* sake. Mixing opera with pop was just McLaren's latest scheme for exploiting the latest trends and technologies of postindustrial culture. As McLaren has Cho-Cho-San sing, "Gotta have something to believe in": Without a subversive program of some sort attached to the music, the absolute historical beauty of opera would be lost on him.

And so it was with *Fans,* a record riddled with contradictions and conundrums about McLaren and his use of opera.

Based on a one-act play by David Belasco after a short story by John Luther Long, Puccini's *Butterfly* is about a true-hearted geisha married to an American naval officer who callously deserts her and returns to Japan with an American wife. Upon seeing Lt. Benjamin Franklin Pinkerton with his American bride, the fifteen-year-old "Butterfly" (Cho-Cho-San) takes her life with the sword her father had committed hara-kiri with when she was a child. *Madama Butterfly* is not only the story of this tragic betrayal, but also the story of an irresponsible American naval officer's exploits, for in the opera, Pinkerton never has any intention of staying married to Cho-Cho-San: "I'm marrying in the Japanese fashion," he tells his friend the Consul Sharpless, "for nine hundred and ninety-nine years— with the right to be freed every month!" Sharpless warns Pinkerton that this is grossly irresponsible conduct: "It's an easygoing creed," he sings. "It would be a great sin to strip off those delicate wings and perhaps plunge a trusting heart into despair." But of course, Pinkerton does not heed his friend's words and the tragedy unfolds.

Now there are at least two sides to every story, and in *his* "Madam Butterfly," Malcolm McLaren turns the opera's scenario on its head: Indeed, it is McLaren who sings Pinkerton's side of the story. From McLaren's perspective, the "problem" of the opera is Cho-Cho-San's "little Butterfly" and the way she has used her son to maintain her grip on the rich American sailor: "she got a problem," he warbles at the start of the song, "she got a little Cho-Cho."

If McLaren's inversion of the traditional operatic tale is just one more self-justification in his own "easygoing creed" of irresponsible behavior in the name of some higher ideal (that is, anarchism), it is not the only inversion he attempts on this oddly appealing record, for on the liner notes of *Fans,* he also turns around the definition of what it means to be a fan. "The real business of fans," he writes, "is to attract attention." While most real fans would dismiss this as patently untrue—it is the *star's* business to attract the attention of the fans—for McLaren, both the fan's fetishistic love for the star and Cho-Cho-San's unrequited love for Pinkerton represent the burdens of unwanted responsibilities. Cho-Cho-San is the millstone around Pinkerton's neck, and as a result of his irresponsible behavior, he will end up caring for the son he had by her; similarly, the star is contractually committed to keep coming up with new product to keep the cycle of adulation spinning at the same speed as the wheels of commerce: for McLaren, the industry is the millstone around the artist's neck. "All work/ No joy/ Makes Mac/ A dull boy," he sings on another track inspired by Puccini's *Turandot.*

It had been only a year and a half since McLaren first made his fantastic transformation into a star, but already he was beginning to chafe at his new obligations as a recording artist. For the first time in his life, he now had exactly what he wanted—the most expensive suits from Yohji Yamamato and a handsome flat off Russell Square where he could while away the hours with his exotic mulatto girlfriend—but the myth he had worked so hard to create was already beginning to unravel. It was time to bail out once again, and with at least one lawsuit threatened and another pending—from Stephen Hague and Walter Turbitt claiming that they were entitled to a fifty percent share of the royalties on "Madam Butterfly" since they had written the music—in late October, he was off again to safe haven in New York.

Typically, McLaren was as disappointed with what he considered Island Records' lackadaisical approach to promoting his latest record as he had been with Charisma's. *Duck Rock* had become a hit in spite of Island's publicity machine, McLaren thought, and, as he told a reporter from *Billboard* to Blackwell's great irritation, he was convinced that if U2 had been on CBS Records instead of on Island, they would have sold "ten times as many records." *Fans,* he reckoned, was just as important a record as *Duck Rock,* and *that* had been plugged with a McDonald's advertising campaign focused on double-dutch skipping. If Island only promoted *Fans* the same way, McLaren earnestly believed it would be the record that would break him in America. He just couldn't seem to accept the fact that *Fans* had a much more limited audience than the previous album. Rock opera may have been well suited to making headlines, but the Top 100 seemed to be immune to McLaren's operatic charms.

Indeed, the greatest interest in *Fans* seemed to come from the rather esoteric worlds of fashion and art. The fashion connection is easy enough to understand, not only because of McLaren's own connection to the rag trade, but also because of the scantily clad models draped on the album cover and posing in the video made by Terence Donovan, inspired by the recent vogue for photographer Deborah Turbeville's sepia-toned fashion shoots. Upon his arrival in New York that fall, *Details,* the hot fashion magazine Gene Krell now worked for, gave over its cover to a full-sized mug shot of McLaren hiding behind a fan.

However, the art world seemed to connect to McLaren in a way that suggested a confluence of aims rarely found between the visual arts and popular music. Postmodern artists (like Kathy Acker in fiction or Sherrie Levine in the visual arts) liked to trumpet their opposition to modernism by "appropriating" images and texts from art history they claimed were historical carriers for sexism, racism, and capitalism, and some said, *Fans* seemed like a similar appropriation of classical music. To McLaren's great satisfaction, he now found himself lionized by the New York art world with the same degree of seriousness and respect he had been accorded by the British music weeklies back in the early days of 1976. One young art critic, Australian expatriate Paul Taylor, even initiated plans to bring McLaren back into the art world, arranging for him to attend the 1986 Sydney Biennale and working on a show of various McLarenalia he had long wanted to do, and now found an interested party with the New York's New Museum of Contemporary Art.

Naturally, McLaren was excited by this first flush of acceptance by the downtown art world and for a month or two, he played the burgeoning East Village gallery scene for all it was worth while he and Rory Johnston tried talking up his idea for a musical based on *Fans* with various theatrical producers around town, including Francine LeFrak, representatives of the Nederlander and Shubert theater organizations, and, most important, Joseph Papp, director of the acclaimed Public Theater.

Although McLaren asserts that the original idea of *Fans* as a musical was generated by him, Jonathan Gems claims that the structure of the musical McLaren laid out for these producers was taken directly from a play Gems had written for the Royal Court Theatre (and produced there in 1982) called *Doom Doom Doom.* A comedy about the end of the world, *Doom*'s central theatrical device was a stage split in two with a downstairs level where the characters are "living in hell" and an upstairs where, says Gems, "all the people who represent the rest of the world up in heaven are persuaded to come down into hell."

Apart from its operatic setting, this was almost word for word what McLaren also told Papp's organization. Tom Ross, now director of musical plays for the Public Theater, then Papp's executive assistant, remembers McLaren telling him that "the idea was simply to take these three opera characters, Madame Butterfly, Tosca, and Carmen, and put them on the upper level of the stage and then to put their real, eighties' equivalents downstairs: three New York City schoolgirls with extremely passionate love affairs. The idea was that the opera singers would be 'pulling the strings' of these three girls down below, that the real girls weren't in complete control of their passions and so they would get into all sorts of trouble."

Papp thought McLaren's idea exciting. Find the right writer and director, McLaren was told, and workshopping could begin immediately. But before the plans could get any farther, McLaren dropped from sight.

Indeed, unbeknownst to the Papp people, even before their early talks, McLaren had also been mulling over an idea to make a movie.

"At one point we were really sick of working on *Fans*," says screenwriter Johnny Gems, "and we were both very depressed. And I remember thinking, 'Please, God, what's a good idea for a movie? Give me one now, God.' I just wanted to cheer Malcolm up because he was so depressed with *Fans*, and then I suddenly thought of the *Beauty and the Beast* story, which was perfect, because what Malcolm needed was a good sexy story. And I told him the story—the Beauty who gets captured by a Beast who falls in love with her, is about to rape her, and instead falls for her; how he wants her approval so badly and she begins to pity him until finally she falls in love with him and then he's not a beast anymore—I just made it up from what I remembered. So Malcolm says, 'Great! What we'll do is update it and turn it into the story of a famous fashion designer.' He had just finished reading this picture book about Dior and we thought we'd make the Beast a very successful fashion designer, like a cross between Christian Dior and Calvin Klein, and we decided to call it *Fashion Beast*."

Gems may have given McLaren his best ideas, but when it came time to look for collaborators, McLaren never seemed to get farther than whoever happened to be in front of his face at the time; in New York, it was screenwriter Kit Carson, introduced to McLaren by Johnny Dynell, then working as a DJ for LaRocka, a nightclub owned by Carson's older brother. McLaren was excited by meeting Carson, the first writer with any Hollywood clout McLaren had met since he had tried to make *The Great Rock 'n' Roll Swindle*. Cowriter of Jim McBride's remake of Jean-Luc Godard's *Breathless*, Carson had also coscripted Wim Wenders's *Paris, Texas* with Sam Shepard, the surprise hit of 1984, and according to his friends, he was getting desperate that he hadn't yet found a new project to follow up on his *Paris* success.

As soon as McLaren found Carson, all his previous plans—to make an independent film of *Fashion Beast* with clubowner and producer Robert Boykin or to work with the Public Theater on *Fans*—went out the window. Hollywood, where McLaren was now scheduled to do a *Fans* radio tour, beckoned. And fortunately for him, Kit Carson's string of classy credits had the powerful backing of Erica Spellman, a smart and aggressive agent then at the William Morris Agency. Late that November, McLaren, Carson, and Rory Johnston met with Spellman to arrange a trip to the coast, and after just one meeting, Spellman set up nearly a dozen

powwows for McLaren and Carson with various studio execs and producers. No one knew it then, but it was to be the last time this particular group
of people would ever set foot in the same room together.

Planned in as little as a week, the trip Erica Spellman arranged for
McLaren, Carson, and Johnston was nonetheless orchestrated with all the
flair of a major publicity campaign. Spellman prepared a little media kit
about McLaren—the *Fans* video, an hour-long documentary about
McLaren that had recently been aired on London's *South Bank Show,* the
Details cover story, and a collection of his records—Carson booked them
into the Chateau Marmont, and with Rory Johnston acting as McLaren's
de facto manager, the three took off for L.A. with a rough sketch of
Fashion Beast under their seat belts.

For Kit Carson, as for Erica Spellman, meeting McLaren was like
being put under a strange spell: Indeed, those are the words one hears
over and over again from many who had dealings with McLaren in Hollywood. All knew vaguely McLaren's reputation for strewing chaos in his
wake, but none seemed to believe that this clownish redhead could ever
bring harm to their little corner of the film industry. "We *were* entranced," says Kit Carson, "but judiciously so. I mean you take Malcolm
out to dinner and then at the end of the evening, he staggers out to a cab,
and whether he's really drunk or only pretending to be drunk, it's in the
middle of a rainstorm and you're left picking up the check. I thought I
could handle him. I mean there are lots of pirates in Hollywood. In Wim
Wenders's film *An American Friend* he had all these director friends play
swindlers, and when someone asked Wim why he did that he explained
that 'All directors are swindlers.' So I'd met Malcolm's kind of personality
before, and I thought he would be no problem."

Of course, that's exactly the kind of talk a confidence man loves to
hear, for the moment someone has finally come to believe they are as hip
and conniving as the con man himself is the moment a sucker has been
born. And indeed, as soon as McLaren began to see that *Fashion Beast* and
Fans had pricked the interest of a few producers, he tried to ditch both
Spellman and Carson, turning client against agent in a round-robin of
betrayals.

Spellman was first to go. Immediately following his first meetings with
executives at Motown, Geffen, Warner Bros., Columbia, Fox, and with
several independent producers, McLaren began telling his various inter-

locutors that they were not to report back to William Morris: From now on, he was handling his own affairs through Rory Johnston. "Malcolm decided there was enough heat on the situation that he could outmaneuver Erica," explains Kit Carson. "He said that it was obvious that people were more interested in him than they were in Erica and that he didn't need Erica, and that's when he began to tell people that Erica was not directly involved—even though she had set up this whole chain of meetings."

Spellman was furious when she heard what McLaren was saying. In Hollywood, where agents are often more important to the making of a deal than the writers they represent, business is just not done with such cavalier contempt for an agent's services. "Before they left for L.A.," says Spellman, "we agreed that if there was a deal to be made with anybody I had sent them to, *I* would make the deal. Malcolm said that was fine, except for one person he knew at Columbia, and we agreed that if the deal came out of that situation, I was not to be involved.

"The next thing I knew, it was as though I had not done anything and was not to be involved. I would call whoever it was at the studio, the producer or the executive, to find out how the meeting went, and be told that they were told not to speak to me. Malcolm had decided to do everything on his own. And I said to Kit, who had been a close friend and a client for many years, 'Hey, wait a second, we're not running a dating service here. I'm not fixing you guys up just out of the goodness of my heart.' And then Kit tried to hedge around and keep his connections to Malcolm without me knowing it. It was the single most distasteful thing that has ever happened to me as an agent."

However, if Carson felt he was getting away on McLaren's magic, he was sadly mistaken, for as soon as McLaren got a nibble from Lynda Obst, then creative head of Geffen Films, he too found himself being cut out of the deal.

"Malcolm came to my office at Geffen," remembers Obst, a former editor at *The New York Times Magazine* who later produced the smash hit *Flashdance* for Paramount, "and it was the most memorable pitch of my career. It was a performance of stellar quality that I have since discovered was entirely rehearsed, because later on he did the same pitch for David Geffen word for word, beat for beat, step for step. He had this inchoate idea that was worked out historically through the life of Christian Dior and also through *The Beauty and the Beast,* and there was a teeny idea of a movie in it. But for two hours, my room was his stage. He tripped the light fantastic. He walked around, he picked up things, he performed, he posed, and he was wearing the most amazing clothes I'd ever seen in my life, maybe even a kilt. He would weave his stories with incredible historical detail that was entirely made up, that didn't matter, lots of stuff that was only remotely true, and name-dropping like there was no tomorrow. Incredible, exquisite stylistic images. It felt like a movie even though there was no story and there were no characters, or only the most mythic characters."

"During the first meetings we had," says Carson, "we had nothing on paper. We would drive around in the car, and learn more of the story from each meeting. That's why the meeting with Lynda Obst was so exciting: It was the first time we told the story from beginning to end. We got halfway through the story together, and then Malcolm went to the restroom, and by the time he'd returned he'd come up with a few more details to complete the story, picking up the ball where I was at. But after that meeting, which turned out to be my last meeting with Lynda Obst, we started to write a treatment, because everyone said they wanted to see something on paper.

"Around Christmas we finally had this thirty-six-page treatment and we started turning it around. I registered it with the Writer's Guild, Malcolm went to France for Christmas to visit his friend Jean-Charles, and I drove down to Prescott, Arizona. And when I came back about ten days later, he had moved to another hotel, to Le Mondrian down the street, and I began to find it hard to get in touch with him."

Indeed, while Carson had been vacationing in Arizona, McLaren had returned to L.A. to meet with Lynda Obst, and although Obst had taken an interest in *Fashion Beast* on the basis of the story she had been told by the team of Carson and McLaren, she was dissatisfied with Carson's treatment. "I immediately told Erica that if I was going to work on it, Kit had to go. It was very aboveboard," she says. "I simply didn't like his treatment, and I decided I would attach Malcolm to another writer. I had the seams cut loose on Kit in a minute and then we worked on a new idea."

Kit Carson: "When I came back from Arizona, we met for dinner at Spago, and we walked back to the hotel on Sunset Boulevard. Malcolm said that he was getting feedback that people didn't care about the story. He said that the first thing Lynda Obst said upon reading the treatment was, 'Now that we have the treatment why do we need Carson?' 'You see,' he told me, 'nothing matters to these people but flash.' It was an important lesson. 'When people want to co-opt you,' he said, 'you co-opt yourself quickly, and first. If people say "we don't need that, we want this after all"—just a tiny item of it—you don't fight and say "We want substance," you say "All I want is Cyndie Lauper's belly button too." 'People just didn't care about this story.' I said that I didn't understand why he had jumped to that conclusion. I had spent nearly a month working with him, wrung myself out on the experience. And then he disappeared. Malcolm disappeared on me. This was his farewell, and for the next month or two, I didn't know where to find him."

With Kit Carson out of the picture—"Malcolm sold *him* down the river in a minute without so much as blinking an eye," remembers Spellman—Obst began looking for a new writer, and within a few weeks she had found what she thought the perfect match for Malcolm McLaren: Menno Meyjes, a young Dutchman who had had his first success with the sleeper *The Children's Crusade* and had just finished adapting Alice Walker's novel *The Color Purple* for Steven Spielberg.

"Menno is an extremely avant-garde, classically trained Hipster," says Obst. "He's himself about style, but he's profound. He's the hippest of the hip and at the same time, he knows that three acts are required and he's written enough to know which rules he can break, and I knew that with Malcolm you'd need to break rules. I just knew they'd fall in love. That's what I do. When I get a great idea I try to put the right person together with it.

"So I put them together and they did fall in love and they started working together. For about a week or two, Malcolm was my greatest fan. It was like I was his manager or agent and he was my client, even though we had no deal. He would call me on the phone four or five times a day at the least, and it was very hard to convince him that I had other things to do. I had to get him a lawyer and get him in touch with our lawyer and he was convinced he would be undone by them. It was like dealing with a rock star. Everything was a special case. The rules that apply to ordinary people during the pitch process don't apply to Malcolm for Malcolm. Trying to turn him into a regular person pitching a treatment was one of the hardest packaging jobs I ever attempted."

Complicating Obst's job, moreover, was the sudden proliferation of ideas that typically accompanies McLaren's first success with anything. Within days McLaren and Meyjes—Obst called them the "Four M's"—not only had a treatment for *Fashion Beast* but also a new treatment for a musical of *Fans.* Now, McLaren wanted Geffen to take on both projects, and over the next six weeks, the fiendishly complicated dealmaking process went back and forth between McLaren's attorney, Peter Dekom—found for him by Obst—and the Geffen Company.

"As soon as we started to talk about making a deal, a hundred projects bloomed," says Obst. "I couldn't keep him on the track of being a person pitching a movie. Malcolm became very, very difficult to deal with and started calling David Geffen in the same way that he was calling me, and then David, because this is unprofessional behavior, special-case behavior, started wondering *what* was going on here. He told me that this is what *I* was supposed to be doing. It was, 'Who is this guy and why is he giving me such a headache?'

"My problem was that I could never get Malcolm to go from *A* to *B*. *A* was this glorious pitch but *B* was work, and he could only do what was easy to him, the winning of the convert. The actual doing of the work was not up his alley and as soon as the deal process started, he became so unrealistic and so grand, he wanted hundreds of thousands of dollars for doing things he'd never done before. He got very cabalistic and conspiratorial. He started taking ideas from me: I put him together with the cream of the crop, with Tom Headly who had written *Flashdance* for me, and he started *sssssucking* them dry. Then it was: 'Why is Lynda doing this? Why is David doing that?' "

To make matters worse, Erica Spellman still considered herself responsible for McLaren's connection to Geffen, and on the morning of a party being held in her honor at Obst's home in L.A., she informed her friend that the William Morris Agency still expected to be paid its commission from the Geffen Company.

"Lynda and I had gone through eight years of friendship at that point without having ever had a fight," sighs Spellman. "We had worked together when she was an editor at *The New York Times Magazine* and we worked together in Hollywood, and we had never had a problem, not professionally and certainly not personally. And on the morning of the party, I called Lynda, and I said, 'Lynda, this is not a conversation between you, Lynda Obst, and me, Erica Spellman, this is a conversation between William Morris and the Geffen Company. I have been told that we are to consider Malcolm McLaren's deal with the Geffen Company to be commissioned by William Morris. And Lynda went crazy. She got very upset and I got very upset. Somewhere she knew that if she brought this up with Malcolm, he would have a fit. She didn't want to offend him because he was now *her* guy.

"So that night, I got to the party early, and the first person who walked in was Malcolm McLaren. And I said, 'Lynda how could you do this to me. I mean, here's this man who has made me look like a fool in my company, and here he is at your party!' I waited about an hour and then I left the party and the next morning I left for New York, which I had planned to do anyway, but certainly not like that. Lynda and I didn't speak for several months after that. Happily, we were eventually able to get over McLaren."

As it happened, McLaren's deal with Geffen fell through in a matter of weeks. Rory Johnston explains McLaren's poor behavior at the negotiating table as a matter of dollars and cents. "Malcolm didn't see himself as a first-time film person, but as a successful person from the music business who had already had a great deal of experience with film, but Geffen didn't see it that way," he says. "They offered us an advance that would have been an insult to anyone. We figured that Malcolm was worth between $500,000 and $1 million, but the numbers they were coming up with were in the $50,000 range. Malcolm was insulted: He thought that Lynda either didn't want to or couldn't come through for him when it counted."

Lynda Obst: "It was a cacophony of neurosis, and I just come from the Life-Is-Too-Short school. Once he started going over my head, I realized I had too many other projects to take care of, so I cut loose, and he couldn't believe it! Couldn't believe it! I said, 'Honey, I'll introduce you to other executives [Obst giggles]. Now, goodnight.' 'But Lynda, I'm with Geffen!' And do you know, he'd already told people he'd had the deal, and the deal numbers he was telling people were outrageous!

"You see, I had finally realized what he was doing: He gets with you, becomes yours, takes what he needs from you, and moves on to the next person. And frankly, at that time, I wanted to do it to him before he did it to me. I didn't want him to cause me any more damage. I had given him very good creative input and introduced him to very good people and he gave me nothing but *tsuris*. So I just said, 'Malcolm, here's other people—go meet Ileen Maisel at CBS'—she was perfect for him—and I said, 'Live and be well! and that was that.'"

Erica Spellman: "Being with Malcolm was like having some weird, strange drug reverberating in my head. I was hearing me say one thing, hearing all these other people in the room agreeing on one thing, and then, it was like *Alice in Wonderland:* We would all leave the room and go do whatever it was we had agreed to do and then it was as though none of the discussions we had had ever taken place. Malcolm was off whirling and twirling and doing whatever the hell he was doing as though we had never talked. He's one of those people who was perfect for his time, because he was like cocaine and that's when everyone was into it. You see, people didn't know the difference between Malcolm and drugs. Because you get very euphoric when Malcolm comes bouncing into your life. I mean there he is—attractive, charming, all the rest—and then before you know it you're down on your hands and knees with your eyes all blood-shot."

McLaren was convinced he could turn Hollywood into his kind of town. "I think I'll change Hollywood," he told one writer. "I believe that. I believe I'm just the tip of the iceberg."

In fact, he was a lonely, unhappy man. England, he now realized, was truly his anchor, its culture and politics mother's milk to him. Suddenly, he found himself missing London's slow pace, bluff, dreary weather (the sun was wreaking havoc on his skin), and close-knit geography: He still hadn't learned to drive and before long he had to hire someone to take him to all his meetings. He even seemed to miss Andrea, whom he had kept at arm's length through most of the previous fall, spending most of his time out and about with Johnny Gems while she pined away for him at home. "Malcolm would spend one day a week with her," remembers Gems. "That was the plan. Very Victorian. And that was always Saturdays. Every other day of the week he was out, but on Saturdays they'd get up early and go out and buy cheese and flowers from Covent Garden. Andrea was very angry about this because they'd come home and Malcolm would spend about two hours arranging the flowers and he wouldn't allow her to get anywhere near. And cheese? Andrea hated cheese.

"So she had her own life and it was mostly centered around modeling and cleaning. Malcolm's flat on Hunter Street was like a hospital! Until finally Malcolm had her kicked out when he came home from Hollywood to collect his things. Andrea got called by Malcolm's secretary in London saying that he had decided he could no longer give her any more money— he had been 'paying' her around £80 a week—and then a bit later she got a call from Malcolm's lawyer saying she had to be out of the flat immediately or else he'd have the bailiff around to throw her out. But then it was as if none of this had happened: Once he really started spending time in L.A. he started going crazy and he phoned Andrea up and asked her to marry him. By then it was too late, and she said no."

But then McLaren had a change in fortunes. He found himself being pursued by actress-model Lauren Hutton, the gap-toothed beauty queen who had once adorned the cover of *Vogue* fourteen times in two years and later appeared as a femme fatale in films such as *American Gigolo* and *Once Bitten.*

They had met at Morton's, one of the ultimate power restaurants in Hollywood. McLaren was there with Rory Johnston and photographer Michael Halsband during the middle of McLaren's negotiations for a job at CBS, and as the three were leaving, Hutton and actress Beverly D'Angelo ran into them. McLaren had never heard of Lauren Hutton, but he was flattered when she told him that she knew of him, and after a short chat in the parking lot outside the restaurant, the assorted crowd left for a once-popular lesbian hangout called Peanuts. "I'll have you know I couldn't even look at her properly," McLaren told *iD*'s Dylan Jones. "I was too shy. I didn't know that much about her but I liked her a lot." According to McLaren, *"she* called me. . . . She had obviously spent a few days in Tower Records finding out about me because she started singing 'Madam Butterfly' down the phone. It cracked me up, man!"

However, others say McLaren was not quite so easy to catch as all that and that Hutton had to show true perseverance to get McLaren even to think of going on a date with her. One story goes that she was so flummoxed by his typically erratic hours that on one occasion she kept guard outside his door at Le Mondrian, surrounding herself in a bed of flowers outside his door, until he finally came home early that morning. The way McLaren tells it, however, it was *he* who pursued Hutton—"When I set my eye on Lauren I said I'm going to get that woman and I did, the very next day." According to McLaren, their first date was spent making love under the bushes of Griffith Park.

"I've never felt this way about a relationship before," he said at the time. "It's a very difficult and different relationship from any one I've ever had before. I don't think I've ever loved anyone before Lauren. For the first time, I'm feeling responsible in a relationship. I really *care.*"

With Hutton under his arm, McLaren gained fresh confidence in his new moviemaking career. Even though every aspect of his work till now would seem to have militated against his accepting the Hollywood gospel of great-art-as-great-commerce, he finally succumbed to the cabal of culture-vultures who waved the magic wand of creative control and big bucks in front of his face. With the conclusion of the CBS deal, he finally decided to commit himself to Hollywood even though he was well aware that he was utterly unsuited to the job, and closed down his London office and home.

"Working at CBS corporate," he said soon after he began working there, "will have to be on my terms. That's the reason it's been so difficult for me so far in Hollywood. You've got to respect people if you want to work for them. I've never worked for anybody my whole life! There's certain things—like compromises—you just have to make. When you're making films, they're just too big for one guy to deal with. You've got to be prepared to work with lots of generals and colonels and soldiers. Easy if you're in fashion. A little easier if you're making records. And easier still if you're a painter, because it's just one to one, you and the canvas. But in films there's a lot more maneuvering and explanations. And that's the one thing that worries me about CBS."

And yet, in many ways, McLaren's job at CBS was the deal of his life, the one he had been looking for ever since 1977 when he first tried to get the Sex Pistols movie off the ground. Signed as an untitled in-house producer to CBS's newly established Theatrical Productions division—his two-year contract was rumored to give him a salary in the high six figures—McLaren's job was simply to develop for CBS at least four new projects over the next two years, including both *Fashion Beast* and *Fans.*

For those who were to be McLaren's bosses at CBS—Allen Levin, president of CBS Theatrical Productions, Bernie Sofronski, senior vice president and creative head, Ileen Maisel and Rob Goralnick, vice presidents for development and production—hiring Malcolm McLaren was considered a rather high-risk proposition, but one that was absolutely necessary given the network's increasing slippage in the rating wars.

Like the other regular broadcast networks, CBS had always had a theatrical productions division, however limited to producing a small number of hours of in-house programming under antitrust regulations dating back to the mid-seventies. But in the wake of the damaging libel suit brought against the network in October 1984 by General William Westmoreland and separate attempts by archconservative senator Jesse Helms and cable network entrepreneur Ted Turner to purchase CBS early in 1985, the theatrical productions division—until then a backwater unit of CBS Productions—was reconstituted under the wing of the CBS Broadcast group and given a new bailiwick to make it more competitive with cable television (particularly with HBO and MTV). CBS Theatrical Productions, as the new division was to be called, was now to be responsible not only for generating movies, telefilms, and the occasional television series, but also for international syndication and sales of these productions to other companies with whom CBS already had distribution arrangements (Warner Bros. for theater and film; CBS/Fox for home video product). Production and marketing were now to work hand in hand to create new product for the youth market.

Within the industry, the creation of CBS Theatrical Productions was greeted with great skepticism. Some speculated that the expansion of CBS's production wing was intended to shore up its relations with the Hollywood community after the embarrassment of the Westmoreland debacle. Others wondered whether this brittle, embattled corporation could afford to take the kinds of creative risks it would need to become successful in Hollywood. With such widespread suspicion, Allen Levin and Bernie Sofronski weren't taking any chances, and after signing a megadollar development deal with singer David Lee Roth, they decided that a truly avant-garde figure like Malcolm McLaren might be just the thing CBS needed to give the new unit the appearance of having taken the trouble to hire a genuine creative wizard. McLaren was to be CBS's diamond-in-the-rough, and he was the only in-house producer the company would hire during its short year of existence.

From the very start of his tenure at CBS, McLaren found working within the company's heady corporate environment an arduous task. Even after all his experiences with record companies, film companies, and dozens of lawyers, he was still not used to the idea of appealing for his needs through a bureaucracy, and at any studio, bureaucracy—in-house politics—is rampant. To the CBS executives, McLaren was something of a weird duck, a clown who dressed in pink cashmere cardigans buttoned up the back, paisley pedal pushers, and hi-top Converse sneakers. He had great difficulty being taken seriously. When he wanted his office—John Wayne's old, mirror-covered dressing room—painted glossy black, it had to be approved by at least two people, and he resented having to politic for what he thought was his due. (In the end, he didn't quite get his way.) Whenever he wanted to take a trip to New York or London, or simply to go off the lot for any extended period of time, he was supposed to inform his immediate supervisors (Maisel and Sofronski) where he was going and what he would be doing there. This he often failed to do, and as Gary McCarthy, CBS's vice president for finance and administration, recalls, McLaren was "a little like a loose cannon. He just wasn't fiscally responsible. He'd take these trips and then we'd have to ask Ileen where he was, and she never knew."

Since McLaren came to CBS with two projects already under way, those were to be dealt with first. As it turned out, neither one was quite as finished as McLaren had led CBS to believe. *Fashion Beast,* in particular, was mired from the word go, for as soon as word got out among the screenwriting community that McLaren was trying to find a new writer to finish off what Kit Carson had started (Menno Meyjes had opted out of working on *Fashion Beast* while McLaren was still negotiating with Geffen), Carson himself turned up to ask for the compensation he thought he was owed for the thirty-six-page treatment he had written with McLaren just before Christmas.

"All along Malcolm was working by trust," says Carson. "He really understands the way trust works: He fosters it, then breaks it, then gets people caught in the middle, and very calculatedly says, 'I trust you and therefore you've got to break the trust someone else has [in you] because *we're* in on this and they're not.' This is the way he was dealing with me and this is the way he dealt with Erica and the way he dealt with Lynda Obst, and that's why everybody got so angry. But I finally understood enough about this process so that I was then able to play on *his* trust. When I first registered the treatment, I showed him this piece of paper that was registered with the Writer's Guild with both of our names on it, and I could see he didn't understand what that meant. He trusted me, trusted that he could get rid of me, but months later I came back to haunt him with that same piece of paper until he finally realized what it meant to register a treatment with the guild.

"It took a while to find him but finally, my lawyer, Henry Holmes, said he'd found him at CBS and would be sending a telegram the next day. Weirdly enough, we both had the same law firm at the time, so his lawyer from Cooper Epstein and my lawyer, and the two of us, had this meeting there. Malcolm gave his version of the story, which was basically that he had sat and dictated this treatment to me. Then Henry turns to me and says, 'Now you tell your side of the story,' and Malcolm started interrupting. Henry said, 'Now, Malcolm, we've let you talk, you have to let Kit talk too.' And at the outcome Malcolm poormouthed: 'I have no money, I'm just an Englishman, England's a Third World country, and even if I wanted to I don't have money to give Kit for his work in this.'

"Malcolm then had his new lawyer, Peter Dekom, throw all sorts of stuff at us, but Henry finally got CBS to see that they didn't really own anything, that they only had half the rights to something I wrote *with* McLaren. And finally they paid me $35,000.

"I don't know why Malcolm didn't get the movie made with Menno or anyone else. I wanted to, and I concluded that he didn't because his business is literally just scamming. He's afraid to actually do something. Earlier in his life it seemed he wanted to scam *and* do things at the same time, but by the time he got to L.A., there must have been a loss of purpose because nothing ever happened."

"Malcolm has a most original mind that is harder and harder to find in L.A., and I hired him because I thought we could make a feature from his ideas," explains Bernie Sofronski, the former television producer who was McLaren's overall boss. "But Malcolm seemed to think that every time he had an idea, it meant it had been green lighted. I was telling him that *I'm* the one who says it's a green light or not. He felt we should do everything that popped into his mind. I'd say to him, 'Malcolm, you wake up in the morning and you have ten ideas. Do me a favor: Why don't you look into your ten ideas and give me the best one rather than asking me to do your homework for you? Don't ask me to break it down for you. Do your own homework. Don't position me to reject you, because I don't want to play that role. That's not why I'm here, that's not why I believe in you.' "

But to McLaren, CBS was all about restrictions, rules, and responsibilities, and Sofronski and Maisel were the enemies of his cool creativity. Every time he wanted to use a screenwriter from outside the small loop of writers who were Maisel's flavor of the month—Claire Noto and Laurie Frank were both put through the wringer—Maisel and Sofronski vetoed his choices, and often did so in ways McLaren felt were embarrassing. McLaren particularly hated Maisel, whom he suspected of wanting to use him as dinner-party bait for attracting rock 'n' roll stars such as Diana Ross and Cyndie Lauper. On one notorious occasion at the Ivy, a popular Hollywood eatery, a drunken McLaren waltzed over to Maisel's table to say hello. Maisel stood up to greet him, and as she was about to sit down, McLaren jokingly pulled her chair out from underneath her and left her sprawled on the floor. McLaren may have apologized the next day, but Ileen Maisel never forgave him.

Such asinine behavior certainly didn't help his cause any, but according to Bernie Sofronski, McLaren's big problem at CBS was not that he had extreme ideas about what he wanted to do (or even that he behaved so poorly or looked so strange), but rather that he could never settle on any one idea or writer to achieve his aims.

Always on the lookout for another subculture to exploit, McLaren fastened on surfing as the one aspect of Hollywood life that had even the slightest resemblance to the style wars of his London days. "Surfing is the only thing in L.A. that really says something to me about how to step out," he said. "It's the only way for kids to step out of everyday life. As I studied it, I realized its essence is really ancient Hawaiian culture and it has a deep mythology around it that takes you right up to the present. Forget Jean-Paul Gaultier! Forget Body Map! It's here, right here, with these kids wearing these funny long shorts, these blonde beach gods."

Heavy Metal Surf Nazis, said McLaren, would be a cross between *The Magnificent Seven* and *Lord of the Flies.* "It's about a group of young kids who exist on an island far away from the mainland and who descend from old surfers who once escaped from the modern world to this distant paradise. These kids beat each other up to keep control of this island, but one day one of them takes off to find these mystical ancestors. This kid is our hero. He was born in the sea and when he drifts out on a magical board to find his magical ancestors, he discovers that they now live in these crummied-up old Chevvies, and together they return to the island to seek their revenge on the gang that took control of it—only to find a much bigger menace there when they arrive."

According to one source, however, McLaren would invite one writer after another to take meetings with him, asking each one to write a treatment for him "on spec," which would then be passed on to the next in line. McLaren supposedly went through nearly a dozen writers—including the writers of *Robocop*—before finally settling on music videomaker and action/adventure writer, Jim Linehan. But even Linehan's script was eventually rejected.

"Malcolm kept firing people," says Sofronski. "Everyone we wanted or even people he wanted would come in and take meetings and then he could never make a decision. There were several times where we hired writers and then he ended the relationship and created a lot of bad feelings with agents. We finally had to say that Malcolm couldn't take meetings unless I or members of my staff were present. Whether he hired them or fired them or seduced them, he finally created a lot of problems for me and for CBS, and our reputation could not stand people being used like that. You have to be here in good faith—'Yes, I like your idea,' or 'No, I don't and I won't use it, but thank you very much'—but you can't say I'll just use you for a few weeks, tell you I love you, take your ideas, and then say fuck you."

Even before McLaren had been hired by CBS in the spring of 1985, the giant corporation had already started selling off various segments of its operations, including CBS/Fender Musical Instruments and CBS Toys, in an attempt to create additional capital to buy back its own stock and insulate itself further from hostile suitors. "The freeze," as it was called, affected each of CBS's four groups, and the Broadcast group, which now contained within it CBS Theatrical Productions, was no different. For McLaren, the freeze bore a double onus: For while CBS now became increasingly obstinate about spending money for movies it knew would never be made, as an in-house producer, his salary was recoupable against his first production—and he would make additional money only from producer's fees as each picture he was working on came to production.

With such heavy incentives for getting his projects going, a panicky McLaren now put aside his petty rivalries with Maisel and Sofronski in order to concentrate on getting at least one project off the ground before the CBS Board of Directors—scheduled to meet with white knight Laurence A. Tisch that November—made a final decision to sell off or close down the Theatrical Productions division. Thanks to the canny advice of his agent, Jeremy Zimmer of ICM, and the diligent and conservative work habits of his development assistant, Paige Simpson, McLaren was finally able to get half a dozen projects into salable position by the time the CBS board finally announced the shutdown of the Theatrical Productions division, to begin at the end of the month.

The first of these was *Fans.* Over the summer, Sofronski and McLaren had taken a meeting with Joseph Papp and Tom Ross, and plans were made for *Fans* (still in the version written by Menno Meyjes) to be workshopped that November, with James Lapine possibly sitting in the director's chair. As the rumors about the demise of CBS Theatricals intensified and eventually became reality, McLaren nervously asked Menno Meyjes to introduce him to Steven Spielberg, for whom Meyjes had just finished writing *The Color Purple;* for a while, it was rumored Spielberg himself might produce the musical. Over most of the spring, phone calls went back and forth between McLaren, Spielberg, Zimmer, and Joe Papp's Public Theater, but in the end, nothing seemed to happen, and for most of the next year *Fans* was to lie dormant.

Fashion Beast didn't fare much better. The script had now been through so many changes that the story no longer resembled its origins with Johnny Gems or Kit Carson. One idea remained intact through each rewriting: In the words of screenwriter Laurie Frank, "Malcolm saw clothes as the ultimate expression of the reality of the world. Clothes represented class structure, power, and wealth, and they were the metaphor through which everything else had to go." Kenneth Robins, a New York screenwriter who had written the avant-garde film-ballet *Swan Lake Minnesota,* was now given a shot at it, but then on a trip to New York after the fall of CBS—Lauren Hutton's NoHo loft now became McLaren's second home—McLaren discovered the comics of the renowned English fantasy book writer Alan Moore, and made plans to hire him. Moore brought *Fashion Beast* back to its origins with Dior and Cocteau, but the breakthrough came too late for McLaren to get the project off the ground before the final freeze at CBS.

Heavy Metal Surf Nazis—Sofronski was so offended by the title he eventually forced McLaren to change it to something like *Surf Explorers*—had an equally exasperating history. After McLaren rejected Jim

Linehan's first script and rewrite, he had Marvel Comics senior editor Larry Hama and producer Gabrielle Kelly (who had already been hired by CBS for another project) try their hands with the *Surf Nazis* concept, but they too fell short of his expectations, and he then went back to Linehan—who told him to get lost. By now, however, McLaren had so thoroughly drenched Hollywood with gossip about *Heavy Metal Surf Nazis* that a group of independent producers and writers affiliated with Troma Pictures picked up the idea and made *Surf Nazis Must Die*. As far as Hollywood was concerned, *Heavy Metal Surf Nazis* was buried in the sand.

Finally, McLaren initiated yet another handful of projects just as CBS Theatricals closed its doors that November.

Art Boy was a screenplay brought to him out of the blue by a twenty-two-year-old punkette named Megan Daniels. Originally titled *Man Falls off the World* and loosely based on the meteorically hyped career of painter James Mathers, a former boyfriend of Daniels's whose career took off with his appearance as a pinup boy in a Rose's Lime Juice ad, Daniels's screenplay was rough but caught McLaren's attention, as well as his bosses'. After a few meetings at which the two seemed to hit it off, McLaren set Daniels up with an office at CBS, helped her get an agent, and sent her off to New York to pick up more color, but as soon as the two began working together, he began demanding that she turn what was originally meant to be a small personal film about the perversion of one boy's solitary artistic process by commerce into a big budget picture about wild L.A. art gangs.

For nearly three months, straight through the closing of CBS, Daniels and McLaren worked together—the day they finally left the CBS lot they covered the walls of McLaren's office with a giant graffito reading FUCK YOU!—until finally Daniels broke away from her new mentor. "I finally realized I had to do it on my own," she says. "I realized that the people I admired the most who had worked with Malcolm weren't like Sid Vicious but people who had stepped out of his shadow to do their own thing, like Boy George or Adam Ant." Within weeks, Paige Simpson had sold Daniels's script to Warner Bros., where it still sits, waiting to be produced.

Also started at CBS was *Rock 'n' Roll Godfather*, a picture that was to be patterned on *Godfather II*, based on McLaren's theory that the British music business had been infiltrated by the Mafia in the heyday of rock 'n' roll's British Invasion. McLaren approached Disney producer Mark Johnson, best known as the producer of Barry Levinson's films *Good Morning Vietnam* and *Diner*, among others, to hire British screenwriter Barry Keeffe *(Long Good Friday)*, but when Keeffe's script finally arrived from London, McLaren was deeply disappointed by it. He and Johnson have apparently been in search of a new writer ever since.

Last of all was an untitled high-concept picture brought to McLaren by former television commercial director and screenwriter Terry Kahn, based on an idea by actor Malcolm Danare *(Lords of Discipline, Heaven Help Us)*. The story of a nineteen-year-old boy who has been brought up by his hippie mother (à la Sid Vicious) and who goes searching with the help of a *Rolling Stone* journalist for his long lost dad—now a faded, zonked-out guitarist for a group like the Grateful Dead—this picture might have neatly conflated McLaren's own childhood myth with that of Sid Vicious's, but it too came undone. McLaren and Kahn obtained the commitment of writer John Patrick Shanley—who would later win an Oscar for *Moonstruck*—but before they could get much farther, CBS Theatrical Productions came crashing down around them.

When CBS Theatrical Productions finally closed its doors in late November 1985, Malcolm McLaren had come to believe that Hollywood was a kind of fool's paradise where fools like him were allowed to make all the scandals they wanted as long as they kept providing ideas for other people to rip off. Although CBS gave him a handsome payoff (the remainder of his contracted two-year salary), allowed him to continue working in its offices, and even provided a cubbyhole for Megan Daniels to continue working on *Art Boy,* McLaren was depressed that nothing he had started there had got made during his short tenure. Maisel and Sofronski, he felt, had solid, reputable careers and their reputations had only been enhanced by his so-called outrageousness. He, on the other hand, had been left high and dry.

According to Sofronski, however, the closing of CBS Theatrical Productions had little to do with McLaren's inability to get anything done there: Indeed, McLaren had been invited to submit his resignation just before the studio shut down.

"Malcolm swings back and forth between the polls of seduction and destruction," he says. "We had chosen to have faith in him and to see where it would go, but we found out rather quickly that it wasn't working. It got to the point where we could see we were playing with ourselves. Finally, I told him he was taking advantage of us. I think it was a mistake that we continued to let it seem we were getting along well on the surface, but that's OK. He's an extremely charming, very likable guy, and there'll always be someone to buy his projects. And maybe that was my fantasy: that if things were handled in a certain way, we might have been able to pull something off—we might even have bought him off. But then, maybe it never could have happened, because what I was finally seeing was that Malcolm would have prevented that from happening if only because he loves to destroy anything he's touched."

With the studio shut, all McLaren's CBS properties—*Surf Nazis, Fans, Fashion Beast,* and *Art Boy*—were now put in "turnaround"—to be held by the studio until sold elsewhere. If any of these projects were ever to be made (not just bought), he would have to set them up with other producers who would then buy the properties from CBS. Essentially, Malcolm McLaren now occupied the same position as any other young Hollywood screenwriter whose projects had been bought by a studio but were languishing on the shelf, waiting to be produced.

It is not clear why McLaren chose not to embark on such a strategy. Perhaps he was too busy learning to drive the black Volkswagen Cabriolet he bought to match Hutton's white one. However, in late spring, he hit on the clever idea of doing a remake of Frank Tachlin's *The Girl Can't Help It* set in the surf world. For the next eight months, McLaren worked with screenwriter Lewis Colick to develop *All She Wants to Do Is Surf,* the story of a down-and-out East Village rock 'n' roll manager who is kidnapped by Murf the Surf to turn his girlfriend ("the girl who can call up waves") into a star.

With a commitment from renowned indie producer Ed Pressman—a "critic's producer" whose credits include Terence Malick's *Badlands,* David Byrne's *True Stories,* and Oliver Stone's *Wall Street*—Colick began churning out a screenplay, giving new pages to McLaren every few days.

"That turned out to be a major mistake," he says. "Instead of knocking this off in three or four weeks like I had originally intended, I would give him pages which he would respond to by saying that he couldn't figure out the writing and which he would demand to be rewritten with the two or three or four ideas he had come up with since we last talked. The large majority of his ideas were worth listening to and I bent over backwards to accommodate him, but it meant I had to change the basic script so many times that we were late getting the script into Pressman, who really wanted the picture to be a summer movie. He had commitments and he needed it then—not for the summer of 1990 but for right then. Malcolm refused to let me finish that goddamned script simply by saying that everything had to be just so. I never worked so hard in my whole life. I was crazy."

For once it seemed one of McLaren's projects was finally going to reach production—on one of his periodic trips back to London, McLaren even tried to get a directing commitment from Rocky Morton and Annabel Jankel *(Max Headroom)*—but just as Colick was about to hand in the first sixty pages of his script, McLaren read an article about surf pools in the Midwest and demanded that Colick do a rewrite to reflect his latest infatuation. Colick refused—"Ed had specifically told us that time was of the essence," he says—and McLaren went to Pressman to back up his latest idea. As Colick tells it, a meeting between him and McLaren was held at Pressman's office with Stuart Cornfield, producer of *The Fly,* in attendance, and Colick was paid additional money to incorporate the changes McLaren now wanted in the script. "I really began to understand that Malcolm had no idea of what a writer does," says Colick. "Malcolm thought that taking a story meeting was the same thing as writing a story. He thought he was doing all the work, but all he was doing was coming up with atrocious ideas and writing them in the margins. Any writer knows that's not writing."

Although Colick eventually finished *All She Wants to Do Is Surf—* setting much of the story around surf pools in the Midwest—by the time Pressman got the script in early January 1987, it was too late to proceed. Malcolm McLaren had finally got his way, but once again, success—even this limited success—had come at his own expense.

Everyone loves the rogue with the golden heart, especially when roguishness is the pretext for a grand, theatrical success, but what happens when the rogue is no longer the fun-loving mischief-maker he was in his younger days and everything the rogue touches crumbles to dust? Malcolm McLaren moved to Hollywood, got a famous girlfriend who helped him stay in the gossip columns, and schemed his way from project to project, but his failures there have done no more to humble him than did his failures with the Sex Pistols or Bow Wow Wow.

In 1988, McLaren's rhetoric seems to have flattened out. On the one hand, he is careful to use the sunny rhetoric of California life—of commitment, artistic responsibility, and caring relationships. He dresses in business suits, speaks with antique etiquette, and gives long-winded speeches about the good old days when being "bad" was clearly better than being good. Those days are long over, he says, but then in a wink of an eye, he is off and running with grand stories of his days with the Dolls, the Sex Pistols, Bow Wow Wow, and even Adam Ant and Boy George. He boasts how he beat Paul *(Graceland)* Simon to the punch in Soweto, how he single-handedly revivified opera for the masses, and how he is now going to do the same for the "Blue Danube Waltz." Seemingly tricoastal, McLaren pretends he is performing in (or on) America only to win the attention of the Brits back home. In fact, he has become well suited to Hollywood's sharkish manners. His skin even has the smarmy gleam of one who has used too much sun block.

For eight long years, McLaren's legal battles with John Lydon in *Lydon v. Glitterbest* dragged on inconclusively in the British courts. No one would give up, so the pennies accumulated daily in the Glitterbest and Matrixbest accounts. In January 1987, John Lydon emerged grinning and victorious from an Old Bailey courtroom. Each Sex Pistol (including McLaren) had won at least £200,000, a far cry from the £1.5 million McLaren might have had to himself had Lydon never sued. At the end of the day, McLaren had seen that Lydon would never give up. Without conceding on the substantive issue of the case, that he had in fact mismanaged the Sex Pistols, McLaren would never get his share of the Glitterbest/Sex Pistols money. He had to concede, and at last, he did.

In a matter of weeks, Malcolm McLaren did what he swore he would never do following his fiascos with *Fans* and the atrocious *Swamp Thing* (aka *Duck Rock 2*): he marched into Muff Winwood's office at CBS and signed no less than a *seven-album deal.*

It took over two years and at least six producers (Andy Matthews, Phil Pickett, Robby Kilgore, Mary Kessler, Bootsy Collins, and Dave Stewart), a seventy-piece orchestra, and several internationally renowned pop stars, but Malcolm McLaren finally finished his new record titled *Waltz Darling.* For much of the time, McLaren had struggled simply to find a producer who could merge the galloping ¾ time of waltz music with rock 'n' roll's solid 4/4 beat. McLaren will undoubtedly have a new spiel to justify the expense of his latest attempts to derive cash from chaos when the record finally appears with its strutting Bootsy-produced rendition of Strauss's "Emperor's March" a song about the startling pains a teenage girl supposedly experiences when her breasts begin to blossom ("Jumping in My Shirt," guaranteed to give the British tabloids a run for their money); its neo-Victorian dance number ("Algernon Is Simply Awfully Good at Algebra," produced by the Eurythmics' Dave Stewart); its ode to the AIDS era fashion/dance craze called vogueing ("Deep in Vogue"); and its oddball version of the "Blue Danube Waltz," starring the wailing sounds of Jeff Beck's guitar and hundreds of humpback whales.

Each song on McLaren's new album has its own story, its own history of betrayals and recriminations. One story goes that in the heat of the battle to twist waltz-time into rock-time, McLaren interfered so often and so totally with one producer that the young musician developed a severe skin condition and came at McLaren with fists flying. Much later, in New York, where he had flown to escape the watchful eye of CBS in the studio, McLaren abruptly dumped his New York producers, Kilgore and Kessler, while they were on a long-planned vacation in France, and ran off to record with Bootsy in Detroit. None of that, of course, will be reported.

What the world *will* hear is that the new album is about romance: "I feel strongly about that whole idea of partners and being swept off your feet," McLaren told Dylan Jones of *iD* long before the record's release. "There's something wonderfully chivalrous and romantic about it all—the first kiss, the big dance, having your breath taken away. I was driving down Santa Monica Boulevard, thinking of my surfing soundtracks and seeing all these gray skies and mile upon mile of surfing beaches and I was pumping Strauss on the cassette deck. I found it a great contrast to that modern world of machines, power stations, Caterpillar pool rigs, fluorescent boards stuck on the beach, and all the enthusiastic surfers running about and being modern. And Strauss seemed to add romance to the whole setup. I thought that it was *so* big, *so* epic, and *so* gallant that it had to work."

And perhaps it will. 1988 was a bumper year for McLaren: one project—Paul Taylor's museum show, *Impresario: Malcolm McLaren and the British New Wave*—actually came to fruition. On opening night at New York's New Museum of Contemporary Art, McLaren stood bathed in the glare of the paparazzi's flashbulbs, while Lauren Hutton hovered nearby. A few weeks later, at a symposium sponsored by the museum and New York's Fashion Institute of Technology, where McLaren was surrounded by adoring fans, critics Jon Savage and Greil Marcus, fashion designer Steven Sprouse, poet Richard Hell, and even a few hecklers, McLaren gave a long speech to explain the method behind the madness." "The best way I can do that," he began, "is to give you a sort of explanation about myself from a very early age. I think it can be summed up, as it often is in the press, as being a very . . . *bad* . . . boy."

Unquestionably, McLaren will get at least one or two more projects off the ground. *Fans,* on again, off again, is, as of this writing, off, after McLaren had apparently yet another dispute with director Tommy Tune and producer Stevie Phillips. *Fashion Beast* is once again on hold, still with Alan Moore's script. Ed Pressman, clever enough not to let McLaren produce an entire film by himself, is continuing to work with McLaren as a coproducer on director Kathryn Bigelow's *New Rose Hotel,* based on cyberpunk writer William Gibson's short story of the same name, with a script by Gibson and John Shirley. Others who have recently been mentioned as participating in McLaren's projects include Steven Spielberg's Amblin' Films, David Henry Hwang, and Harry Kondolean.

Meanwhile, McLaren continues to free-associate on sex, style, and subversion—the legends of his radical past. His friends tell us that he is challenging us to explore the ruses of the new princes who enslave us to the big lies of Western life, manipulating and deceiving us with false riches. No doubt, there will be those who, in buying his records, attending the movies or musicals he has helped produce, or perusing a museum show centered on him, will buy into the sublime illusion of McLaren as a gallant postmodern artist prying open the ideological lid of postindustrial life. Some will even say that McLaren is a *bad* character for *good* liberals, a vehicle for thinking about the significant issues of our time (copyright, originality, ad nauseam).

But all of this is to say that the very principles of lying and self-delusion that have governed Malcolm McLaren's career will probably receive the best reception from those who almost certainly know better. Those who delight in the realm of surfaces will continue to fancy the recombined hand-me-down scraps of Malcolm McLaren's style of amusement. But those who need no reminder of the ordinary vice and violence humans live through daily will not be distracted by one who has so charmingly packaged music as noise and disruption as entertainment. They will not be fooled by his wicked, wicked ways.

LIST OF SOURCES

Josh Baer

Dave Barbe

Simon Barker

Luca Bastagli

Pierre Benain

David Berson

Ruza Blue

Don Boyd

Boy George

Robert Boykin

Fred Braithwaite

Peter Brandle

Richard Branson

John Broderick

Rosetta Brooks

Julie Burchill

Roger Burton

Kit Butler

Kit Carson

Jean-Charles de Castelbajac

Miles Chapman

Al Clark

Brian Clarke

Ted Cohen

Lewis Colick

Michael Collins

Steven Connoly

Caroline Coon

Peter Cresswell

Andy Czezowski

Rene Daalder

Megan Daniels

Jean Davouste

Rob Dickins

Terry Doktor

Simon Draper

Amy Dunn-Lwin

Johnny Dynell

Roger Ebert

Nick Egan

Robert Elms

Spider Fawkes

Duggie Fields

Andrew Forge

Laurie Frank

Robert Fraser

Marty Frommer

Rob Guralnick

Jonathan Gems

Vivienne Goldman

Gerry Goldstein

John Goldstone

Dave Goodman
Valerie Goodman
Leroy Gorman
Burt Gower
Derek Green
Pierre Grillet
Bill Grundy
Eric Hall
Larra Hama
Andy Harries
Russell Gerald Hawkes
Cynthia Heimel
Richard Hell
Leslie Hill
Phil Hollis
Michael Holman
Trevor Horn
The Ismans
David Johansen
Simon Jeffes
Rory Johnston
Steve Jones
Jordan
Terry Kahn
Jonathan Kaplan
Keith of Smile
Ben Kelly
Mary Kessler
Robby Kilgore
Krystina Kitsis
Gene Krell
Gary Langan
Steven Lavers
Steve Leber
Francine LeFrak
Sandy Lieberson
Ken Loach
Andrew Logan
Annabella Lwin
Clive Lwin
Jamie MacGregor-Reid

Giannino Malossi
Lisa Marcus
Luciana Martinez de la Rosa
Glen Matlock
Gary McCarthy
Malcolm McLaren
Bradley Mendelson
Bob Mercer
Bob Merlis
Billy Meschel
Nick Mobbs
Tara Moran/Fiorucci
Trevor Myles
Paul Nelson
New Museum of Contemporary
    Art, N.Y.
Lynda Obst
Peter OGI
Danny Opatoshu
Sara Palmer
Chris Parry
Steve Paul
Carolle Payne
Stephane Pietrie
Malcolm Poynter
Alissa Van Poznak
Ed Pressman
Russell Profitt
Theodore Ramos
Sophie Richmond
Kenneth Robins
Heidi Robinson
Richard Routledge
Johnathan Rudnick
Philip Sallon
Jon Savage
Robin Scott
Wendy Shankin-Metzker
Paige Simpson
Jill Sinclair
Bernie Sofronski

Brian Southall
Chris Spedding
Erica Spellman
Neil Spencer
Debby Spungen
David Staines
Howard Stein
Nils Stevenson
Ray Stevenson
Janet Street-Porter
Gordon Swire
Sylvain Sylvain
Paul Taylor
Julien Temple
Dr. Stephen S. Teich
Brian Tench
Marty Thau
David Thomas

Jeremy Thomas
Mike Thorne
Richard Torry
Walter Turbitt
Roger Trilling
Fred Vermorel
Judy Vermorel
Dwayne Warner
Eric Watson
Michael Watts
Helen Wellington-Lloyd
Steve Weltman
Ben Westwood
Joseph Corrie Westwood
Vivienne Westwood
Michael White
Alan Yentob
Peter York

INDEX